Llewellyn's

2004 Magical Almanac

Featuri

Peg Aloi, Elizabeth Barrette, Shira Bee, Stephanie Rose Bird, Nina Lee Braden, Dallas Jennifer Cobb, Nuala Drago, Ellen Dugan, Denise Dumars, Ember, Emely Flak, Karen Follett, Breid Foxsong, Lily Gardner, Magenta Griffith, Elizabeth Hazel, Eileen Holland, Christine Jette, Raven Kaldera, James Kambos, Jonathan Keyes, Laura LaVoie, Anthony Louis, Kristin Madden, Edain McCoy, Muse, Olivia O'Meir, Sharynne NicMhacha, Gina Pace, Scott Paul, Daniel Pharr, Robert Place, Diana Rajchel, Roslyn Reid, Janina Renée, Steven Repko, Laurel Reufner, Sheri Richerson, Michelle Santos, Tannin Schwartzstein, Sedwin, Cerridwen Iris Shea, Susan Sheppard, Maria Kay Simms, Lynne Sturtevant, Julianna Yau, and S Y Zenith

Llewellyn's 2004 Magical Almanac

ISBN 0-7387-0126-2. Printed in the United States.

Editor/Designer: Michael Fallon

Black & White Cover Illustration: © Merle S. Insinga

Color Application to Cover Artwork: Lynne Menturweck, Llewellyn Worldwide

Calendar Pages Design: Andrea Neff and Michael Fallon

Calendar Pages Illustrations: © Kerigwen

Interior Illustrations © Helen Michaels, pages: 17, 19, 25, 26, 33, 41, 50, 61, 79, 92, 99, 114, 121, 123, 135, 137, 139, 141, 160, 161, 162, 168, 174, 241, 242, 246, 251, 255, 265, 270–272, 283, 289, 299, 311, 312, 323, 332, 337, 339, 341, 344–45, 351–52, 355–56, 363, 365

Clip Art Illustrations: Dover Publications

Special thanks to Amber Wolfe for the use of daily color and incense correspondences. For more detailed information, please see *Personal Alchemy* by Amber Wolfe.

You can order Llewellyn annuals and books from *New Worlds*, Llewellyn's magazine catalog. To request a free copy of the catalog, call toll-free 1-877-NEWWRLD, or visit our website at http://subscriptions.llewellyn.com.

Moon sign and phase data computed by Astro Communications Services (ACS).

Llewellyn Worldwide
Dept. 0-7387-0126-2
P.O. Box 64383
St. Paul, MN 55164-0838

About the Authors

Peg Aloi is a teacher of film studies and a freelance film critic. She is also media coordinator for the Witches' Voice Inc., located on the web at www.witchvox.com.

Elizabeth Barrette is the managing editor of *PanGaia* and assistant editor of *SageWoman*. She has been involved with the Pagan community for more than thirteen years and lives in central Illinois. Visit her website at: http://www.worthlink.net/~ysabet/index.html.

Shira Bee, a California-based writer, is drawn to obsolete artifacts, oddities, insects, and dark themes. She has published general-interest articles, poetry, and book reviews in various small magazines—including *Morbid Curiosity* and http://gothic.net/.

Stephanie Rose Bird is an artist, writer, herbalist, healer, mother, and companion. She studied Australian Aboriginal art and ritual as a Fulbright Senior Scholar, and she is a faculty member in the painting and drawing department at the school of the Art Institute of Chicago. Her column "Ase! from the Crossroads" is featured in *SageWoman.* She has a book on Hoodoo forthcoming from Llewellyn.

Nina Lee Braden is the author of *Tarot for Self Discovery,* published by Llewellyn. Tarot is the basis of Nina's spiritual path, the bedrock upon which she grounds all else, and she enthusiastically teaches tarot whenever she has the opportunity. She also teaches English at a community college near her home in Tennessee.

Dallas Jennifer Cobb is determined to make a living writing about what is close to her heart: mothering, gardening, and alternative economics. Dallas gardens intuitively, and she makes herbal-based natural body and health care products. She tries to squeeze in her writing whenever her daughter, Terra, naps.

Nuala Drago is an author, musician, folklorist, and self-initiate who has practiced her own form of Witta for more than thirty years. She has been a lifelong student of ancient cultures and

extinct languages and speaks Irish Gaelic. She enjoys her life "out in the country" with her various and sundry pets.

Ellen Dugan, also known as the "Garden Witch," is a psychic-clairvoyant and a practicing Witch of more than seventeen years. Ellen is a Master Gardener and teaches classes on gardening and flower folklore at a community college. She is also the author of *Garden Witchery,* published by Llewellyn. She lives in Missouri.

Denise Dumars is the cofounder of the Iseum of Isis Paedusis, an Isian study group chartered by the Fellowship of Isis, Clonegal Castle, Enniscorthy, Eire. In her professional life she is a college instructor and writer, and she is currently researching the practices of the Gaulish Druids. She lives in Los Angeles's beautiful South Bay.

Ember follows a path of nature-centered spirituality and writes poetry and articles about nature and magic. Her work has appeared in various literary journals and in several Llewellyn annuals. She lives in the Midwest with her husband.

Emely Flak is a freelance writer based in Daylesford, Australia, who is also employed as a learning and development professional. She writes on a range of Pagan issues for such publications as *Witchcraft* magazine in Australia. Much of her work is dedicated to embracing the ancient wisdom of Wicca for the personal empowerment of women in the competitive work environment.

Karen Follett has been a practicing Witch for over thirty years. She was first taught by her great-grandmother, a midwife and healer, and is now a member of a local coven of the Georgian tradition. In her mundane life, Karen is a registered nurse specializing in maternal and child health. She is also an empath, psychic channel, medical intuitive, and reiki practitioner.

Breid Foxsong is a British traditional Witch who lives in western New York. She has been living the craft for more than twenty-five years, and has focused on laughter, song, and sweat as equal tools in ritual. She is the former editor of *The Sacred Hart.*

Lily Gardner is a lifelong student of folklore and mythology. She is a priestess in the daughters of Gaia coven and a member of the Fat Thursday Writers. Lily lives with her husband in Portland, Oregon. She is currently working on a novel about family.

Magenta Griffith has been a Witch more than twenty-five years, a high priestess for thirteen years, and a founding member of the coven Prodea. She leads rituals and workshops in the Midwest and is currently librarian for the New Alexandria Library, a Pagan magical resource center (http://www.magusbooks.com/newalexandria).

Elizabeth Hazel is a mystic astrologer and tarotist interested in the ancient history of divination. She is a member of the International Tarot Society and the American Tarot Association, and she enjoys attending tarot conferences.

Eileen Holland is a Wiccan priestess and a solitary eclectic Witch. She is the author of *The Wicca Handbook* (Weiser, 2000) and coauthor of *A Witch's Book of Answers* (RedWheel/Weiser, 2003). She is also the webmaster of Open, Sesame, a popular witchcraft site found at www.open-sesame.com.

Christine Jette is a registered nurse and holds a bachelor's degree in psychology. She is a therapeutic touch practitioner and professional tarot consultant, and she teaches adult enrichment writing part-time at the University of Cincinnati. Her Llewellyn books include *Tarot Shadow Work, Tarot for the Healing Heart, Tarot for All Seasons,* and *Professional Tarot.*

Raven Kaldera is a Neopagan shaman, homesteader, activist, musician, astrologer, and wordsmith who did time in many cities before finally escaping. If you want to know more, do a web search on his name.

James Kambos has had a lifelong interest in herbs and all forms of folk magic. He has authored many articles on these subjects and holds a degree in history. He passes time at home in the Appalachian hills of southern Ohio writing, painting, and gardening.

Jonathan Keyes lives in Portland, Oregon, where he works as an astrologer and herbalist and has written books on astrological health and on herbs. He is currently working on a book titled *Healers,* a series of interviews of various herbalists, curanderos and medicine people from around the United States.

Laura LaVoie is a professional recruiter with a degree in anthropology. She has been practicing Paganism for ten years and was vice president of a Pagan student organization called Ancient Altars during her senior year of college. She is also a contributing columnist for *PanGaia* magazine. She lives in Michigan.

Anthony Louis is a psychiatrist with an abiding interest in symbolism and mythology. He has lectured internationally and has published numerous articles on astrology and tarot. He is also the author of the books *Tarot Plain and Simple* and *Horary Astrology,* both published by Llewellyn.

Kristin Madden is a homeschooling mom who was raised in a shamanic home. She is director of Ardantane's School of Shamanic Arts and is a Druid and tutor in the Order of Bards, Ovates, and Druids. In her spare time, she writes books, works as an environmental chemist, and rehabilitates wild birds.

Edain McCoy has practiced witchcraft for more than twenty years, during which time has studied many magical traditions—including Wicca, Jewitchery, Celtic and Appalachian traditions, and Curanderismo. She is listed in the reference books *Who's Who in America* and *Contemporary Authors.* She is also the author of seventeen books.

Muse is a twenty-something woman who has loved fairly tales and fantasy stories since she was a child. After discovering magic and Wicca ten years ago, she has been making her fantastical dreams come true. An aspiring writer, college graduate with a degree in European history, and a professional in the e-commerce field, she is happy as a clam and living proof that magic exists.

Olivia O'Meir is a writer and public relations specialist. She began studying the occult about nine years ago. In 1997, she discovered Wicca, and now she is a member of a Celtic traditional coven. Her interests include tarot, crystals, mythology, Celtic studies, and Druidry.

Sharynne NicMhacha is a teacher, writer, and musician of Scottish and Irish ancestry, a member of the MacLeod clan, long recorded in oral tradition to have connections with the Sidhe. She has studied Old Irish, Scottish Gaelic, and Celtic mythology through Harvard University. She sings and plays bodran, woodwinds, and string instruments with the Moors, a Celtic medieval rock band.

Reverend Gina Pace is a Wiccan priestess and an interfaith minister with the Universal Life Church. She has been a professional tarot reader for over sixteen years, and she created a large tarot website, Wicce's Tarot Collection, located at http://www.wicce.com.

Scott Paul is a solitary eclectic Pagan with Taoist tendencies. He reads and collects books relating to Paganism, history, myth, and religion. For fun, he enjoys science fiction and cooking, and he has contributed to the Witches Voice website (www.witchvox.com).

Daniel Pharr is a writer, firewalking instructor, and Pagan who lives in the Pacific Northwest. He is an avid practioner of Wiccan and Druidic spirituality, divination, and energy work. His quests take him from seas to forests and deserts to mountains around the world. He believes in the powers of magic, love, and joyful living, and shares these beliefs in his writing and Wiccan teachings.

Robert Place is a visionary artist and illustrator, whose award-winning paintings, sculptures, and jewelry have been displayed in galleries and museums in America, Europe, and Japan. He is the creator and coauthor of two tarot decks published by Harper-Collins, and the creator and author of *The Tarot of the Saints* published by Llewellyn. He has currently completed his fourth Tarot deck and book set *The Tarot of the Buddha,* which will be published by Llewellyn in 2004.

Diana Rajchel likes books a little too much. She loves to stare at the Moon and to search strip-mall parking lots for red clover. She is a third degree priestess of Wicca and has lived the faith for eight years. She runs a website at http://www.medeaschariot.com. If you met her in person, you'd likely think of a Wiccan version of the cartoon character Daria.

Roslyn Reid is a member of the Richard P. Feynman Memorial Cabal in Princeton, New Jersey. She teaches yoga and tarot, which she has studied for over twenty-five years. She is a longtime contributor of art and articles to Llewellyn and to publications such as *Sage-Woman* and *Dalriada* (a Scottish magazine promoting Celtic heritage and spirituality). She is currently rejuvenating a former fruit farm.

Janina Renée is a scholar of diverse subjects such as material culture, foklore, mythology, ancient religion, ritual studies, psychology, medical anthropology, history, and literature. Her current research interests include the use of ritualism in nature writing, and the role and subject position of high functioning autistic persons in history, literature, and culture. When she is able to wrest time from work, studies, writing, and family duties, Renée makes forays into the American heartland to explore small towns.

Steven Repko is an elder and founding member of the Coven of NatureWise, and he has channeled the "Natural Tradition" since childhood three decades ago. An astrologer, medium, musician and poet, he and his wife are owners of Gem N' Aries, in Mays Landing, New Jersey. They provide free online horoscopes and shopping at http://www.gemnaries.com/.

Laurel Reufner has been a solitary Pagan for a while now. She writes articles and keeps an eye on bright shiny objects too interesting to resist. Southeastern Ohio has always been home for Laurel. At the moment she lives in Athens County. Laurel's website can be found at http://www.spiritrealm.com/Melinda/paganism/html.

Sheri Richerson has more than twenty years of experience in newspaper, magazine, and creative writing. She is also a lifetime member of the International Thespian Society, and is a longtime member of the Garden Writers Association of America and the American Horticultural Society. Her favorite pastimes are riding horses and motorcycles, visiting arboretums, traveling, and working in her garden. She specializes in herb gardening and in cultivating tropical, subtropical, and other exotic plants.

Michelle Santos has been a practicing Witch for over six years. Despite being solitary by choice, she is active in the Pagan community. Michelle presents various workshops and classes in Southeastern Massachusetts, and she coordinates the Massachusetts Pagan and Witch Teen Connection, an online forum and information center. She has written for *SageWoman*, *Renaissance* magazine, and *Bride's*, as well as for Llewellyn's *Magical Almanac*. Her interests include (but are not limited to) divination, yoga, fairies, elemental magic, and mythology.

Tannin Schwartzstein has dedicated a significant part of her life, both privately and professionally, to the pursuit of the spiritual arts. Tannin has studied diverse practices and paths such as chi gong, shamanistic energy techniques, Gnosticism, Afro-Caribbean religions, and even a pinch of ceremonial magic. She is the proprietor of Bones and Flowers, Worcester's only occult specialty store (www.bonesandflowers.com), and she is also a crafter in diverse media—such as acrylic, sculpture, ceramic, bone, and wood—and a legally ordained Pagan minister.

Sedwyn is a bhaird of the faery faith and a member of the Hearth of Brigid Lyceum. She leads a Pagan covenant group at a Unitarian Universalist congregation where she also hosts drumming circles.

Cerridwen Iris Shea is an urban Witch who recently relocated to the suburbs. She writes under many names in many genres. She

works in theatre, teaches tarot, loves horse racing, ice hockey, cooking, travel, and is working on her website.

Susan Sheppard is the author of three books, and is also WTAP-TV's "Daybreak Astrologer." She appears on live television on the first Friday of each month to give astrological readings to anyone who calls in. She is the creator and owner of the Haunted Parkersburg Ghost Tours in her hometown of Parkersburg, West Virginia. You can view her website at: http://magick.wirefire.com.

Maria Kay Simms, author of *The Witch's Circle, A Time for Magick,* and numerous astrology books and materials, has been an astrologer for nearly thirty years. 2004 is her sixth (and last) year as Chair of National Council for Geocosmic Research. Maria is a high priestess of the Circle of the Cosmic Muse, a New Hampshire affiliate of the Covenant of the Goddess.

Lynne Sturtevant is a freelance writer specializing in folklore, mythology, fairy tales, and the paranormal. She has been a solitary practitioner following an Eclectic path since 1970, and she holds a bachelor's degree in philosophy. Lynne is a regular contributor to Llewellyn's annuals and to *Fate* magazine.

Julianna Yau is a writer and artist residing in Toronto. She began studying Wicca in 1997, and currently maintains a website on the topic. She may be contacted through her website at http://www.transientwaters.net/btlg/.

S Y Zenith is three-quarters Chinese, one tad bit Irish, and wholly solitary Pagan. She has lived and traveled extensively in Asia—to such countries as India, Nepal, Malaysia, Thailand, Singapore, and Japan—for more than two decades. She is currently based in Sydney, Australia, where her time is divided between writing, and experimenting with alternative remedies, herb crafts, and culinary delights. She is a member of the Australian Society of Authors.

Table of Contents

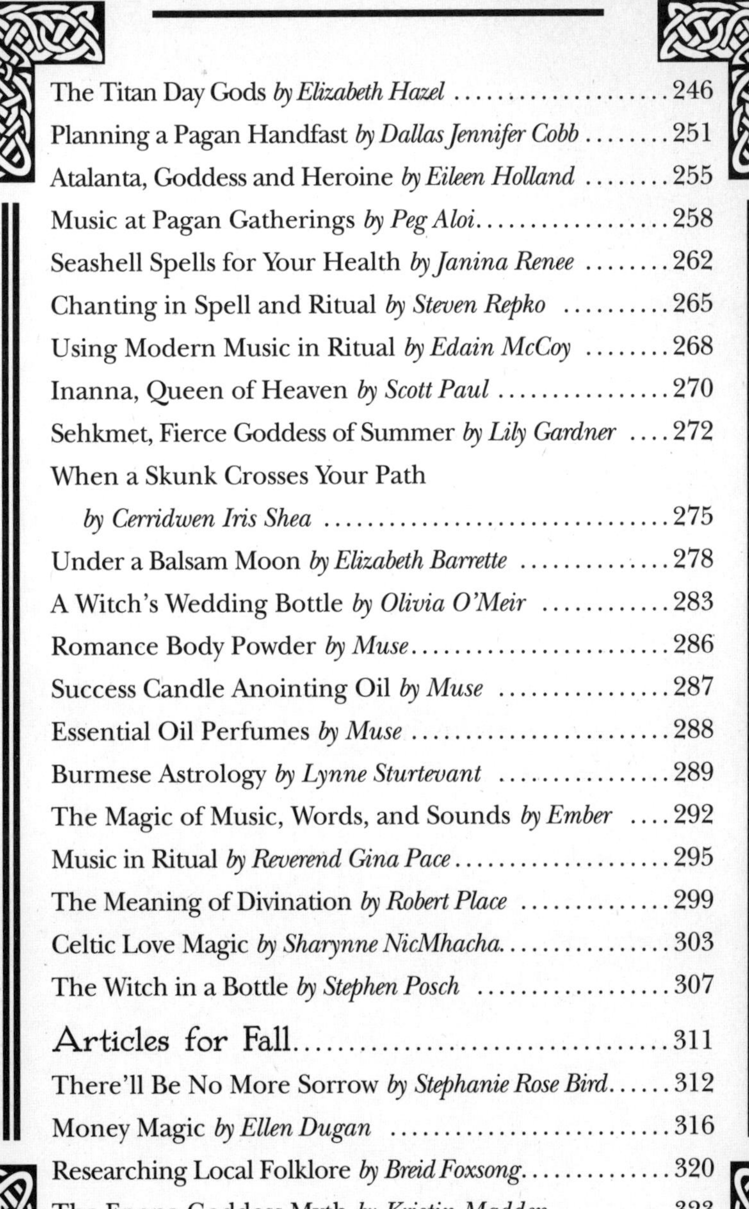

Introduction to Llewellyn's Magical Almanac

The number fourteen is very magical if you think of it in a certain way. Remember when you turned fourteen? Remember what life was like then—full of passionate highs and lows, and all the possibilities spreading out in front of you in a seemingly endless expanse of time. After fourteen years of life experience, you were ready to blossom into maturity. Or as Emely Flak writes in her article "Pathway to Adulthood" (page 149 in this edition): "In most ancient traditions, the arrival of puberty was celebrated as an important turning point . . . Just as our Pagan ancestors recognized the significance of reaching puberty, we too, can honor the teenager's maturity with celebration."

In honor of this turning point, we've come to think of this fourteenth edition of Llewellyn's *Magical Almanac* as one that finally emerges from its adolescence and finds a new maturity. In this edition, our authors are taking some newly mature looks at magic in everyday life, and tapping into some of the world's most ancient knowledge—the magic and healing power of natural forces such as stones, flowers, music, and the Moon, for instance, as well as the lore regarding birds, love, money, and an array of gods and goddesses. We bring to these pages some of the most innovative and original thinkers and writers on these subjects.

This focus on the old ways—on the lore of men and women around the world who knew and understood the power of their ancestors—is important today, as it seems the balance of the world has been thrown off-kilter; sort of like being an awkward fourteen-year-old. Terrorism, water shortages, environmental degradation, internecine battles, and simple discourtesy all seem the norm now. While we don't want to assign blame or cast any other aspersions, this state of affairs is not surprising considering so many of us—each one of us—is out of touch with the old ways. Many of us spend too much of our lives rushing about in a technological bubble—striving to make money, being everywhere but here, living life in fast-forward. We forget, at times, that all of this has happened before, and it will happen again.

Still, the news is not all bad. People are still fighting to make us all more aware of the magical, beautiful things in the world. Pagan and Wiccan communities, for instance, are thriving across the country and throughout the world. In this edition of the *Magical Almanac,* writers from far away as Australia, Canada, and England—as well as across the whole of the United States—contribute to an expanding volume of knowledge, lore, and magical ritual.

In the 2004 edition of the *Magical Almanac* we pay tribute and homage to the ideals of magic and beauty and balance of our ancestors, and to the magic of all the ages—from fourteen to ninety-four. This may sound a bit corny for some, and perhaps a bit too idealistic, too, but those who say so likely have never put what has been written in this almanac over the past fourteen years to good use.

Magic is an ancient tool whose time has come back around to help us restore balance in our lives. More and more people are using magic, celebrating the elements, praying to the Goddess and the various incarnations of the divine, and studying the myths and legends, lore and tales of the past. In the end, one person at a time, using ancient wisdom, we can make a new world.

Articles for Winter

Horns, Hands, and Eyes: Italian Charms for Protection

by Elizabeth Barrette

Mediterranean civilizations have given a great deal of culture to the world at large. This includes a rich heritage of magical concepts and artifacts that increase our ability to manage in the world. Among these are *malocchio,* or "evil eye," lore, and the many protection charms used to ward against the evil eye.

Italy is the heart of evil eye territory, both in terms of the belief and the charms associated with the belief. As a result, Venetian glassmakers create artifacts to protect against the evil eye. You can find Italian protection charms worked into jewelry, or left loose—so you can make your own jewelry.

The Horn

In all its forms, the horn represents abundance, virility, fecundity, and protection. By virtue of the many cow goddesses and bull gods found in Mediterranean cultures, the horn can stand for either masculine or feminine energy. Italians call this *cornuto* or *cornicello*—that is, "horn" or "little horn."

The most common representation of the horn in Italian artifacts is a long, gently twisted, tapered object made of gold, horn, or blood coral. Giant crowned horns that are often hung in cars are usually made of red plastic.

In America, the cornicello counts among the most popular components of a charm bracelet or charm necklace. Ironically, in Italy only men wear this symbol, because they consider it primarily masculine. It combats those aspects of the evil eye that manifest as impotence or barrenness.

The Hand

The hand symbolizes humanity, for our dexterous digits symbolically make us human. Magically, the hand can convey invisibility, strength, and protection. In Italy, the hand takes two forms. One is the *figa* or *mano fica,* also called the "fig hand." This is a fist with

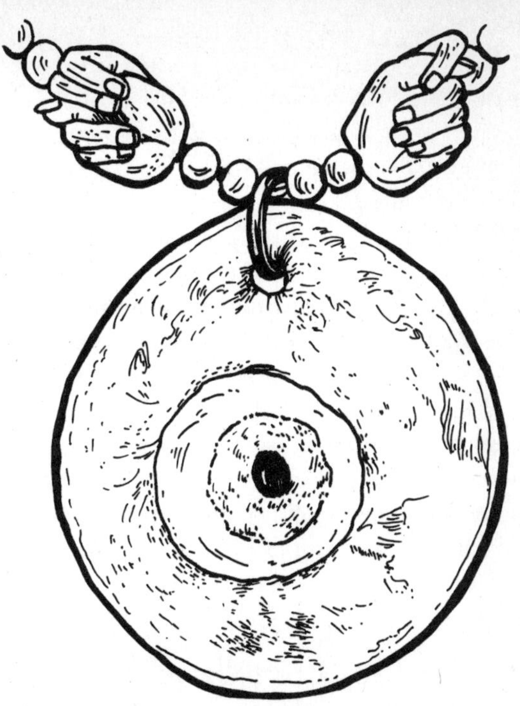

the thumb tucked between the first and second (or more rarely, between the second and third) fingers. The shape represents female genitalia.

Modern artisans make this charm of gold, but you can also find them in glass or wood. Traditionally, it was made of silver, to honor the goddess Luna, or blood coral, to honor Venus. If you hunt around, you can find these too.

A complementary charm is the *cornuta* or *mano cornu,* the "horned hand." In these, the first and last fingers extend, while the middle two fingers and thumb curl against the palm. This masculine symbol shares the same history and materials as the mano fica, but sometimes carvers make the mano cornu from bull horn. Put the two, mano fica and mano cornu, together, and you get a matched set of female-male, goddess-god symbols.

The Eye

The eye appears in many forms in Italian artifact, and it can represent an assortment of deities. Symbolically, the eye conveys thoughtfulness, vigilance, and protection. The preferred material for eyes is blue glass, either cobalt or a lighter turquoise blue. Some of the most gorgeous examples consist of Venetian glass, although Czech glass is also lovely. Eyes are engraved in metal coins and gold or silver jewelry, but the big blue eyes hung under car mirrors are usually plastic.

The eye is probably the most popular charm against the evil eye, and it can take many forms. The simplest is a "bull's-eye" pattern with a blue background, white circle, and smaller blue circle inside. Many eyes, however, are designed with exquisite delicacy so that they really resemble eyes with white, then blue, irises, and black pupils.

Eye beads and pendants appear in earrings, necklaces, keychains, and other adornments. Some jewelers also make eye rings, with the glass eye set in a silver or gold band just like a stone. In addition to wearing eye jewelry, Italians often hang the big pendants on doors, windows, cradles, and other places needing protection.

Protective Jewelry

Of the protective charms, the cornicello is the most discreet. Most people have forgotten its magical origins. Next comes the eye, which looks nifty but not necessarily magical. You can wear these anywhere. The hands are more overtly connected with mystical forces and may draw attention. Also, Italians use the mano fica and mano cornu gestures both to ward off evil and to make obscene insults.

Some jewelry designs appear often because they work well and look great. For earrings, a matched pair of horns or eyes is a favorite design of many people. If you want something definitively magical, consider a mano fica and mano cornu set, either in the same material or in silver for the feminine and gold for the masculine. Together they create a wonderful balance of polarities.

For necklaces, you can wear any of the charms alone. The large eye pendants are intended for exactly this purpose. But you can dress up the idea by combining motifs. Frame either of the hands with a pair of horns. Use eye beads as accents on a necklace on either side of a hand or horn. Create a pendant from an eye bead with a horn dangling underneath it. These patterns also work for bracelets, ankle bracelets, and so on.

If you want something really spectacular for ritual use, combine all the charms on a single necklace. Use the eye beads as accents, separated by smaller plain beads. Make the centerpiece a cornicello, flanked by a mano fica and a mano cornu. Vary the materials, too. Use a blood coral cornicello with a silver mano fica and a gold mano cornu; or use a gold cornicello with a blood coral mano fica and a horn mano cornu.

Charms that protect against the evil eye also protect against other misfortunes ranging from infertility to plain bad luck. These provide an attractive and convenient way to bring a little more magic into your life. You can find them already assembled, or you can buy the components and make your own charms. They adapt well to new purposes as well. Try using a pair of eye beads on the ties to your ritual robe or sewing a horn to dangle against a magical pouch. These also make beautiful gifts for your magical loved ones.

For Further Study

Lehner, Ernst. *The Picture Book of Symbols.* New York: Wm. Penn Pub. Corp., 1956.

Potter, Carole. *Knock on Wood and Other Superstitions.* New York: Bonanza Books, 1984.

Walker, Barbara G. *The Woman's Dictionary of Symbols and Sacred Objects.* San Francisco: HarperSanFrancisco, 1988.

Stone Magic

by Jonathan Keyes

Stones have long been used for their magical and curative powers. Each stone has a different character and personality based on an astrological association. Amber's rich red and yellow colors, for example, link it to the Sun. And so on.

When we wear stones, display them in the house or garden, or use them in ritual, we can access their healing powers. Use the following list to treat yourself when you feel yourself lacking certain elemental characteristics.

Water Stones

The water element is associated with dreams, intuition, imagination, psychic work, emotions, and transformation.

Lapis lazuli–Ruled by Venus/Neptune. This royal blue stone has an uplifting quality that can dispel depression. Also known as lazurite, this stone has a healing quality for the heart and allows for old wounds to fade away. Lapis also bolsters psychic activity, and those who use it will increase their meditative and concentrative qualities.

Moonstone–Ruled by the Moon. This stone has a milky luminous quality to it and has long been used as a symbol of lunar energy. It helps increase a receptive and meditative nature and draws forth our magical and psychic powers to give us serenity and a warmer heart.

Earth Stones

The earth element is associated with work, food, nourishment, grounding, stability, money, and gardens.

Emerald–Ruled by Venus. This well-known green stone has a strengthening and tonifying energy. It helps the wearer attract love and prosperity, and it protects from negativity. Emerald's green color nourishes our heart center and gently opens our sexual and sensual energy.

Obsidian–Ruled by Saturn/Pluto. Obsidian is created when lava rapidly cools (it is also a fire stone). It is very helpful to ground one's energy, especially when a powerful transformation is taking place. Obsidian augments a wearer's power and strengthens the will.

Turquoise–Ruled by Venus. This sky-blue stone has long been revered for its sacred power by many native peoples. Turquoise is a protective stone that wards off dark energy. It also encourages peace and prosperity in life and strengthens the wearer's purpose and willpower.

Fire Stones

The fire element is associated with playfulness, passion, sex, self-expression, vitality, creativity, and laughter.

Amber–Ruled by the Sun. This stone provides a radiant and warming energy that strengthens our overall energy, nourishes our heart and circulation, and increases our confidence and magnetism.

Ruby–Ruled by Mars. This stone is strengthening and protects by deflecting negativity. It increases the power of the wearer and helps increase sexual potency.

Rhodochrosite–Ruled by Mars. This beautiful pinkish stone helps bring a calm and gentle expression of fire. It augments energy levels, and helps open the heart. It also cleanses the blood and stimulates circulation.

Garnet–Ruled by Mars. This lovely red stone is strongly protective. It is wonderful to wear for courage going into difficult situations. It also confers strength and vitality and will bring a boost of energy when needed.

Air Stones

Air is related to communication, thought, mental acuity, intelligence, vision, the breath, and sociability.

Aventurine–Ruled by Mercury. This greenish stone has been known to augment our perceptive skills and increase the eyesight. It also increases sociability and interaction with community.

Yellow Jasper–Ruled by Mercury. Jasper comes in variety of colors, but yellow jasper is particularly suited to the air element. It strengthens our mental processes, clears the mind, and focuses our intent and vision.

Moss Agate–Ruled by Uranus. There are many varieties of agate. Moss agate opens our insight and intuition. We become more aware of messages of guidance.

Amazonite–Ruled by Uranus. This stone is helpful for increasing social connections. It also helps develop our will, composure, and sense of confidence.

Practical Application

After finding a stone that resonates with you, take time to clear its energy and welcome it into your life. There are a number of ways of preparing stones for magic and healing. One is to bathe it in salty water for a period of a few hours. Another way is to bury the rock outside in the ground overnight. Smudging with sage or incense helps remove any toxic energy it may have picked up. If the stone is in a ring, necklace, or pendant, try wearing it for a few days and notice any changes taking place. If the stone is not meant to be worn, place it in a sacred spot where you can see and feel its energy daily. Notice what happens in that space over the next week. If the changes are beneficial, the stone is resonating well with you and can be kept. If problems and misfortune start to occur, the rock may not be right for you and should either be buried or returned to the place it was found.

Spirit Guides for Healing

by Christine Jette

Even though I am best known as a tarot author, my greatest passion is working with healing energy. For me, healing is not a lucky mix of chemical processes, but it is a harmonious joining of heaven and earth. As we attune ourselves to the energy of the healing process, we become aware of receiving help from a higher frequency vibration than the physical. While this help from a higher realm has many names, I call this presence a "healing guide" or a "spirit helper." You can call upon your healing guide to give you the insight and courage needed to heal old wounds or to bring you comfort at any time.

Meeting Your Spirit Guide

Your healing guide comes out of love alone and its only motive is to help you. Ask that the guide who comes to assist you be of white light, aligned with the highest good of all and filled with universal love, truth, and wisdom. If you ever find unhelpful spirits in your aura—this will be rare if you're grounded, centered, and protected—surround yourself with white light and ask your healing guide to escort them on to their next appropriate step for their highest good.

Note: The English language does not have a personal pronoun meaning "he or she." This presents a tricky dilemma, as in my experience, a healing guide is masculine *and* feminine—a very balanced, intelligent, complete, and evolved energy. Only you can decide if your personal healing guide is a "he," a "she," a "s/he," or an "it." I have found that guides generally love to impart information. If you are uncertain, and gender is important to you, simply ask your guide.

Start the Healing

To start working with a higher realm, ask your healing guide to direct a healing through your hand chakras, the energy centers located in the palms of both hands. To begin the exercise, sit in a comfortable position. You can use a chair, but you may prefer the yoga position of sitting on a floor pillow with your legs crossed. Whatever you choose, be sure it's a comfortable position.

Take a few deep breaths and say something like this, while noting that your own words always work best: "I call upon my healing guide to assist me with my healing. I ask that only the most perfect, powerful, correct, and harmonious energies be with me, and that these be compatible with my purposes of healing. I ask that my guides come to me in the most accessible and comprehensible form possible. May my healing be for the good of all—harming no one, and according to free will. So must it be."

Now close your eyes and follow your breath in and out of your body. Take deeper and slower breaths as you become more relaxed. If you are distracted, bring your mind back to your slow, deep breathing. In your mind's eye, follow your breath into your body and all the way to the center of your heart. As your senses grow sharper, feel the energy flowing throughout your entire body.

Open up your hand chakras, the energy centers in both palms, by bringing light above you through your head, shoulders, and arms. Have the light come to rest in the palms of both hands, and visualize the centers of each palm opening. Briskly rub the palms of your hands together for several seconds to increase the energy flow. Ask your guide to enter your hand chakras and to let you feel the energy.

Allow your healing master to guide your hands around and over your body and aura. Or invite the guide into your aura, the energy field around your body, and let it work on you. Sit back and enjoy the process. Healing guides love to help. If you like, ask your guide to do a healing on you everyday.

After the Healing

At the end of the healing session, when you feel a change in the energy flow, say to yourself, in these or similar words: "This healing is over and I am thankful for it."

Thank the guide directly, and make your separations by asking the guide to move back behind you, outside of your aura. Say: "I bring all of my energy, and only my energy, back into my body."

Breathe deeply and place both hands, palms down, on the chair to ground energy. Slowly get up, stretch, and move your body. Gently shake both hands, and wash them with soap and water. Make an entry in your journal about the healing guide experience.

When to Heal, When to Stop Healing

Sometimes, the hardest part of healing isn't getting started— it's knowing when to quit. Most of the time, you'll know because the energy will just stop—there will be a cessation of energy flow through your hands. There may be times, however, when you're not sure. You can test this by slowly moving your hands away from your body. If the energy is still present, you will feel a subtle pull or pulse, and there is likely more healing to be worked.

Accept the fact that it may be difficult to know such subtleties while you are still learning about your guide and the flow of healing energy. The best suggestion is to simply end the healing when it "feels right" to do so. Trust your intuition.

I encourage you to bring your guide in to do healings on yourself, especially after any chosen healing activity such as physical therapy, shadow work, or counseling. Guides enjoy this work—it is play to them. Always work in a calm manner, letting go of preconceived notions. Allow your awareness of healing energy to develop naturally over time.

Your healing guide wants to be useful. Continue to build a relationship with your guide over the next several weeks and months. By actively engaging your healing guide in a partnership, your relationship will grow stronger and it will strengthen your connection to the divine.

Whenever you work with energy from a higher realm, thank the spirit guides and healers for their help. When you are through, release them from your grasp so that they can go where they are most needed. Despite all doubts, worries, or fears, the healing guides will come when called upon.

Guides have different purposes but they always work for your highest good. They also have their own paths to follow. When you grow and change, your healing guide may change. Ask her to tell you when it's time for her to move on. She can introduce you to your new guide when the time is right.

One final note: You may have more than one healing guide, each with a distinct purpose. If this is the case for you, ask yourself—what purpose does each guide have? Use your different guides for their individual purpose. When in doubt about this, ask the guides directly—then trust the answers you receive.

I do not write about spirit guides and help from a higher realm to impress or mystify you. I simply want to demonstrate the depth of love that always surrounds you.

The Healing Drum

by Kristin Madden

Traditionally, the drum was a main method for healers to treat psychological and physical ailments. Rhythm, not always limited to drumming, has been used in healing throughout the world for centuries. Our bodies and spirits synchronize with the rhythm and begin to resonate in a more harmonious way. This promotes healing that otherwise might not occur.

Sound as Therapy

In modern times, researcher have conducted many studies on the therapeutic use of sound, including drumming. The ideal rhythm varies according to the researcher. Psychobiological studies have found that those in meditative and shamanic trance produce greater amounts of alpha and theta frequencies than do people in normal states of consciousness. Rhythms in these ranges are preferable for inducing trance and thus promoting healing.

When we are in normal consciousness, our brain waves fall into the beta range, which occurs from fourteen to twenty-one cycles per second. The next level down is that of light trance, or the alpha state. Brain waves generally fall in the seven to fourteen cycles per second range. Below this resides the deeper trance state of theta (four to seven cycles per second). The deepest levels—normally only attained during dreaming or in comas—exist at delta, below four cycles-per-second. These deepest levels should only be used by qualified professionals.

Some healers correlate the three main sounds that may be made on many drums with the beta, alpha, and theta levels of brain activity. The deep, bass sound often found in the center of the drum is associated with the theta level. Alpha is produced by the middle sound, about halfway back to the rim. Beta corresponds to the highest sound—for instance, the slap sound on a djembe. Not only does each person have their own healthy rhythm but they also need to find their own harmony with these three sounds to align all the levels of mind and body. Of course, not all drums have these three sounds and not all people resonate with this model.

The Best Healing Rhythms

The best rhythm for your own healing really depends on several factors—including the nature of the complaint, the area of the body affected, your stage of psychic development, and your current life situation. The rhythms employed for any healing ritual may vary according to the individual, the complaint, the spirits that choose to come to heal, and several other factors. It is not always something that can be predicted. Different rhythms create or invoke different energies. Just as the same antibiotic cannot be used to clear up every bacterial infection, so too are rhythms often specific to the various conditions.

In the hands of a skilled healer, the rhythms come through naturally without interference from analytical thought. But a natural rhythm exists in any healthy energy field. Think of it this way: Most people have been aware at some time that someone they knew was upset or ill. We may say that we didn't like the "vibes" somewhere, or it just didn't "feel" right. This is an innate recognition of these natural vibrations or rhythms.

Many healers have found that each organ and each chakra is associated with a specific rhythm. When the individual is healthy, the energy flows easily throughout the body and these rhythms interact harmoniously. When using the drum, or other sound, for healing, we restore the healthy natural rhythm to the individual system. We invigorate the energy field and return the natural harmonious flow throughout all the energy bodies.

Shamanic drumming is known as an auditory driver. This means that drumming is an auditory stimulus that trains one's brain wave frequencies. Simply by hearing the rhythm of the drum, you are moved into an altered state of consciousness, and your entire energy field synchronizes with the rhythm of the drum.

Listening to the Drum

When working with drum healing, we allow the rhythm or rhythms that are right for the person in need to come through. We listen for any change in the sound of the drum that might indicate a change in the individual's energy field. However, it is vital that we stay open to intuition and spirit guides. It is quite possible to get so caught up in listening for a tonal change that you might miss something much more subtle. Sometimes the change we hear is not truly an auditory thing. It may be something we hear or feel on another level that lets us know we need to change the rhythm or stop altogether.

This intuitive listening to both the drum and your spirit guides is also important in developing your own understanding of what you are hearing and experiencing. A subtle, harmonious change may merely indicate that you are within the sphere of a new organ or chakra. But until you gain experience and allow your guides to work through you, it is possible to miss a subtle change that indicates a block or injury.

It is important for both healer and person in need of healing to be aware of what areas of the body and mind are affected during this process. Any unusual sensations, thoughts, and feelings should be noted. Each body and mind will be affected in a unique way by a given tone or rhythm. The healer must be cautioned not to assume that what worked for one person will work for any other.

Larger drums, such as the ashiko and djembe, may also be used to effect healing. In fact, the djembe is often referred to as the "healing drum."

This is usually done in two ways. The individual in need may receive healing through playing the drum alone or in a drum circle, or through non-drumming participation in a drum circle.

Experiment a bit, and see what works. Any efforts you make will not be time wasted.

One Final Note

There is one additional note I will make here, regarding the drum overtone. This is sometimes also called the drone, or the undertone, and it exists on a very extraperceptual level.

Many types of music produce a seemingly separate sound that appears to be generated on its own through the music. Often in drum circles, a musical (as opposed to percussive) sound will be heard above the drumming. Even with a single drum, an overtone can be created. These tones are useful both as healing sounds and as guiding sounds for the shamanic journey. They should be experimented with and their effects noted just as you would any rhythm.

It's in the (Hoodoo) Bag

by Stephanie Rose Bird

Nothing makes my blood boil quicker than hearing the Austin Powers character perpetuate the myth concerning *mojo* as being a metaphor for sexuality. The glazed look and sophomoric grin and gleam in his eye when he mentions his mojo, baby, is insulting. But not to blame Mike Myers too much. After all, blues singers often have included the term in their lyrics in their songs—such as the one excerpted below—and perhaps a misinterpretation of the meaning of the song is what led to this common misunderstanding.

Got My Mojo Workin'
by Preston Foster (Recorded by Ann Cole, Muddy Waters, et al)

I got my mojo workin' but it just don't work on you.
I got my mojo workin' but it just don't work on you.
I wanna love you so bad, child, but I don't know what to do.
I'm going down to Louisiana, gonna get me a mojo hand.

Going down to Louisiana, gonna get me a mojo hand.
Gonna have all you women under my command.
Got my mojo workin'. Got my mojo workin'. Got my mojo workin'.

The True Concept of the Mojo

Few people who aren't familiar with Hoodoo culture understand what a *mojo hand* is. Perhaps because of the sexual tension in much of the blues, people of African descent have been looked upon by the American culture at large as having a strong sense of sexual being. As a result, this perhaps has contributed to a general confusion about the term. But understand, mojo does not mean "sex."

Don't get me wrong. A mojo can certainly be used to enhance sexual attraction, but that is only one of its multiple purposes. To thoroughly understand the meaning of mojo it is necessary to turn away from popular culture and look instead to the root source of the term, Mother Africa.

The Key Concepts of Mojo

Ashe is the invisible power of nature. It is present in certain herbs products and natural objects. Herbal teas, incense powders, spiritual washes, healing balms, soap, charms, and even the purposefully spoken word all contain ashe. The Igala people of Nigeria, for example, consider any type of vegetation to be filled with medicinal powers. Medicines, whether designed to address spiritual or physical complaints, are believed to derive their power from ashe.

Consumable products such as tea, washes, soap, and powders are effective, yet they lack the permanency and strength encapsulated in a power object. Power objects can be shields, masks, sculptures, amulets, or charms. Each type of power object is a conglomeration of different elements of ashe. Both the Bamani Komo Society masks and Boli figurative sculptures are encrusted with feathers and quills. The mystical powers of the bird and protective nature of the porcupine are bound and coaxed to share its ashe with the object. Encrustation is the result of feeding the power object. Food is an important tool, for it sustains the life of the power object. Feeding may consist of ground stones, plants, or bones; animal skins, teeth, sexual organs, or horns; chicken blood; semen or saliva. The Yaka, Kongo, Teke, Suku, and Songhai pack a cavity in the belly of their sculptures with a wide array of ashe-providing materials: bones, fur, claws, elephant foot prints, crocodile teeth, scales, bones, and remnants of suicide victims and of warriors. The figurines are then covered with the skins of power animals: buffalo, wild cats, lizards, antelope, and birds. Snakeskins stand for transformation. Porcupine quills are protective weapons. Bird beaks, feathers, antelope horns, and snail shells indicate survival. Leopard pelts, claws, and teeth symbolize elegance, beauty, ferociousness, and nobility. These sculptures are also decorated with raffia, cloth, bells, beads, metal, and nails. Combining the animals with metals further enhances, centers, and binds the animal energy permanently to the object.

Some of the best examples of these magical figures or accumulative sculptures come from Central Africa. The Yaka, Suku, and Kongo peoples prepare sachets made from shells, baskets, pots, bottles or food tins, plastic or leather bags. The medicine bags are charged with an infinite variety of natural materials, though some, such as glass and gunpowder, are also manmade.

Kongo power figures are called *minkisi (nkisi* is plural). Nkisi incorporate elements of land, sky, or water. Nkisi are powered by nature spirits. They help people heal, and they can serve as a safe spot or hiding place for the soul. They might contain sea shells, feathers, nuts, berries, stones, bones, leaves, roots, or twigs. They are as diverse and plentiful as types of illnesses.

Nkisi nkondi are a type of figure that utilizes nails as a binder of its powers. Leaves and medicine combine, and the joining of elements increases the strength of each. Each ingredient has an action on humans—the bringing together of various natural forces the source of healing.

Ne Kongo, a cultural hero, carried the first healing medicines (nkisi) with him from heaven to earth. He prepared the medicines in a clay pot, and set them on top of three stones or termite mounds. His actions founded the expertise that a healer *(nganga)* later used as medicine. The healer's therapy involves the proper mixture of plants with natural and manmade elements.

The Bamana of the western Sudan use power objects such as medicine bags that are imbued with ashe for addressing various ills. These objects are used to express power as warriors, to fight supernatural malaise, and to foil evil intentions. The bags contain *(bilongo)* medicine and a soul *(mooyo)*.

Kongo and Angolan groups brought the concept of bilongo and mooyo together in the New World as mojo bags. The mojo bags are prepared by a specialist akin to the *banganga* (priests/priestesses), who is called a rootworker or conjurer in hoodoo practice. The objects within each bag guide the spirits to understand why their help is being sought, while also directing their actions. The idea that materials have particularly strong ashe, such as human or animal foot prints, survived slavery and are alive in American Hoodoo. Other materials encased in a mojo include ephemera associated with the dead, such as coffin nails, ground bones, or graveyard dirt. The objects—seed, pod, herb, stick, stone, bone—have corresponding spirits.

It is because the bags have a mooyo that they are alive with ashe. Hoodoo practitioners feed their mojos powdered herbs, magnetic dust, herbal oils, dusts, and foot track dirt as needed. The owner of the bag must continue to feed the bag periodically to sustain its life force. Even stones must be brought to life by charging them. To charge stones, bury them in soil for one week, soak them in a pan of salt water for a day and then Sun-dry them, or simply place them in the Sun for a week or so.

Sample Mojo Bags

In his book *Flash of the Spirit,* Robert Farris Thompson describes the interior of power bags as similar to looking through clear water at the bottom of a river. Thompson compares the bags to a miniature universe.

New World nkisi go by a variety of names—a mojo, a hand, a flannel, and a gris-gris are just a few. Whatever the name, one thing that they are not is a simple metaphor for a sexual organ or sexuality (sorry Austin). Mojos in fact have many purposes. Following are a few sample mojo medicine bags that you can make.

Fast Luck Mojo

3 white rooster feathers

1 nutmeg seed, filled with quicksilver

1 chicken wishbone

Small female lodestones

8 silver-colored coins

1 five-leaf clover (may be a metal charm)

2 tablespoons magnetic dust

⅛ cup nutmeg powder

⅛ cup five finger grass powder

Pinch of Dragon's Blood powder

Some green flannel

Wrap the first six ingredients in green drawstring flannel. Feed the Fast Luck Mojo each Sunday with a Fast Luck Powder made from remaining four ingredients.

Stay Away from Me Mojo

1 pinch of cascara sagrada

3 senna pods

1 pinch of graveyard dirt

1 piece of Dragon's Blood

1 piece of charged black onyx

¼ cup chicken bone meal (from garden center or ground yourself)

⅛ cup powdered nettles

⅛ cup powdered kaolin powder

5 drops of patchouli essential oil

1 small square of orange flannel

To fight off folks that just don't understand the meaning of "no," or to fend off evil intentions or stalkers, place the first five ingredients onto the square of flannel, and bind it up into a bag. Bury the bag for one week. After digging up the bag, mix in the chicken bone meal, nettles, and kaolin. Sprinkle the mass with patchouli essential oil.

Carry your Stay Away from Me Mojo with you at all times, especially when you are entering an unknown place. You can even place it next to your bedside if you feel it is necessary.

Peaceful Hand Mojo

- 3 myrrh tears
- 4 frankincense tears
- 1 pinch of chamomile flowers
- 1 dried angelica root
- 1 charged aquamarine stone
- ¼ cup of pulverized lavender buds
- ¼ cup of powdered violet leaves
- 2 Tbls of white kaolin powder
- 4 drops of attar of roses oil
- 1 small square of purple flannel

Bad vibes at work, tension at school, arguments at home—they all take their toll. The Peaceful Hand Mojo combines herbs, roots, and stones with peaceful correspondences to help you deal with the modern condition of stress.

Place the first five ingredients on the square of purple flannel. Mix the powdered lavender buds with the violet leaves and kaolin. Sprinkle with attar of roses. Feed the resulting powder to your Peaceful Hand Mojo each Sunday. This will enhance its power.

The Nation Sack

The nation sack is a magical item very similar to a mojo bag. Nation sacks were once only found in the Memphis, Tennessee, area, particularly in the early twentieth century. Following is a song by Robert Johnson that mentions a nation sack. Robert Johnson and Muddy Waters are two delta blues singers who frequently mention Hoodoo practices in their songs. Johnson even claimed he sold his soul to the devil to become the great singer and musician that he was. Ironically, he met with a strange death under mysterious circumstances at a juke joint.

Come on in My Kitchen
by Robert Johnson (excerpt from the first take)

You better come on
in my kitchen
babe, it's goin' to be rainin' outdoors.

Ah, the woman I love
took from my best friend.
Some joker got lucky
stole her back again.
You better come on
in my kitchen
baby, it's goin' to be rainin' outdoors

Oh-ah, she's gone
I know she won't come back.
I've taken the last nickel
out of her nation sack.
You better come on
in my kitchen
babe, it's goin' to be rainin' outdoors

Nation Sack Lore

A woman's nation sack is, as the Australian Aborigines would say, strictly "women's business." If a man should touch a woman's nation sack he will meet with ill fortune.

In general, the nation sack is full of carry-overs from Africa—even though much of West African magic is shrouded in secrecy. There are numerous secret societies, some of which negotiate between the humans and the spirit world. If anyone were to reveal the secrets, they, like the man who touches a nation sack, will live to regret it. Part of the power of the nation sack is that it is a secret pouch.

Another significant feature is that when a nation sack is used to draw love, often personal items such as a photograph, fingernails, hair clippings, pieces of clothing, and even semen from the man are included in it. This combination of secrecy, and the hunting and gathering of personal materials for the sack, creates a potent charm.

Love Draw Nation Sack

- 1 male/female pair of blue lodestones
- 1 piece of orris root (Queen Elizabeth root)
- 5 dried red rose buds
- 5 copper pennies

Personal items from the man you wish to draw to you (i.e., a tiny photograph, lock of hair, button, or any item that represents him)

1 small square of red flannel

Queen Elizabeth powder

Powdered lemon verbena

Attar of roses

Lavender essential oil

Place the first five ingredients onto the small piece of red flannel. Blend together the next four ingredients in the order given, to make a scented feeding powder. Bind the flannel up with string or thread to make a bag.

Women should keep this sack in their bras, under a garter belt, or under their pants belt. It must remain private and untouched by others. Feed the sack weekly with your powder each Friday, the day of Venus.

Always think hard before casting any sort of love spell, as it is entirely possibly you'll have difficulty getting rid of your catch after working such a potent spell.

For Further Study

Anderson, Martha G., and Christine Mullen Kreamer. *Wild Spirits, Strong Medicine: African Art and the Wilderness.* Seattle, Wash.: University of Washington Press, 1989.

Cole, Herbert M. *Icons: Ideals and Power in the Art of Africa.* Washington, D. C.: Smithsonian Institution Press, 1990.

Hyatt, Harry Middleton. *Hoodoo: Conjuration, Witchcraft, Rootwork.* Hannibal, Mo.: Western Pub., 1970.

McClusky, Pamela. *Art from Africa: Long Steps Never Broke a Back.* With a contribution by Robert Farris Thompson. Princeton, N.J.: Princeton University Press, 2002.

Mizuko Kuyo: The Japanese Rite for the Unborn

by SYZenith

Stone statues resembling children are found in abundance across Japan at temples, shrines, crossroads, roadsides, mountain passes, and graveyards.

These statues are images of the bodhisattva Jizo, who is one of the most beloved of Japanese divinities. He is esteemed as a protector of travelers—both in the physical world or in unseen realms. Also known as Mizuko Jizo Buddha, he is both guardian and representation of aborted and miscarried fetuses, stillborn babies, and prematurely deceased children. Jizo also protects expectant mothers. He is the benevolent deity who ensures the safety of fetuses during their etherworld journeys and who guides them toward birth.

Myths and Beliefs

According to one Japanese legend, fetuses or children who die prematurely are sent to the underworld to be punished for causing irreparable sorrow to parents due to their deaths. These children are deposited in a purgatorial dry bed in the "River of Souls," where they are subject to hard labors of piling stones to erect monuments to Buddha in order to receive his blessings. Tormenting demons scatters the stones and beat the children with iron clubs. It is thus common to find piles of stones laid around Jizo statues. These are offerings from compassionate humans wishing to assist the children in performing their rock-piling penance in the underworld.

Rite of Passage

In comparison with certain Eastern cultures, Western societies bestow little or no symbolic acknowledgement of miscarriage, aborted fetuses, and stillborn children. In the English language there is no word for a miscarried or aborted fetuses. There are no Western memorial services for this form of loss—no rituals to say farewell or to cleanse and assuage grief.

The Japanese are perhaps the most devoutly meticulous in their reverence for babies who remain forever unborn. In Japan, they are conferred a solemn social personhood and called *mizuko,* or "water child." The word *kuyo* means "rite." *Mizuko kuyo* then is a ritual of remembrance, honoring these spirits.

Jizo's Forms

There are innumerable images of Jizo in Japan. Over the centuries, his personifications have undergone many transformations—from a dignified adult figure to a serene child-monk. The child-monk looks about three years old and has a shaven head and gentle smile. Usually in his right hand he holds a stick with six rings. The jingles from the rings are to wake mortals from deluded dreams or warn animals of his approach. His left hand holds the bright jewel of dharma truth. The shining light from this jewel banishes all fear, and liberates people who are helplessly enmeshed in darkness.

Mizuko Kuyo Observances

There are many ways to perform Mizuko Kuyo. Women passing by Jizo statues may pause for a few moments of silence. Others may make personal offerings whenever they feel the need at shrines or other locations. These offerings consist of flowers, clothing, hats, bibs, toys, sweets, food, and so on.

Rituals are generally performed during summer and spring. Certain temples provide sections where women can purchase tombs for their mizuko and have a *kaimyo,* or a posthumous Buddhist name, inscribed upon it. The tombs are rendered from stone with a carved figure of Jizo on top. He generally wears a red bib and carries a staff with six rings or a stick with bells. To some, these temple parts are not glum graveyards but rather "happy places." Some are even outfitted with children's playgrounds.

Women and sometimes men bow and ladle water over the bodhisattva in an act of ritual cleansing. Whether male or female, some light candles, incense sticks, and they adorn the tombs and dress Jizo in garments.

Another ritual makes use of *ema,* or wooden plaques with roof-shaped tops. Each plaque is suspended by a string. Many are inscribed with prayers and personal messages to aborted or miscarried fetuses. The plaques are usually signed with the word "mother," but some fathers and entire families sign the ema to honor what they consider to be a departed family member.

A grieving mother may perform Mizuko Kuyo in the privacy of her home through a visit from a priest. The priest inscribes a posthumous Buddhist name for the unborn child on a memorial tablet or panel. This is then placed on the family altar and honored along with other ancestors

Creating an Alternative Personal Rite

Although Jizo statues are not readily available in the West, this should not deter anyone from connecting with the bodhisattva and honoring unborn children. Pictures of Jizo can be found in books or from Japanese Buddhist sources. The image can be copied, sketched, or etched on to suitable materials. Handicraft enthusiasts may try their hand at making a Jizo statue in clay. Parents who feel compelled to erect a shrine to Jizo may do so.

In honoring unborn children, parents who prefer simplicity can carve a small piece of wood in the shape of a house or plaque. Attach a string to the top of the wood, then write personal messages before suspending them in a special part of the home. Alternatively, these may be placed on a home altar.

Whichever method an individual chooses, what matters most is the sincere intent of acknowledgement toward a precious human life that could have been, but that did not physically manifest in the living world. Those who spend time in creating personal rituals are likely to find comfort, healing and for some, a sense of closure through Mizuko Kuyo.

Moon Lore

by Daniel Pharr

For thousands of years, ancient hunters, lovers, priests, farmers, and wanderers have watched the Moon for signs of what would be. Repeating patterns in the natural world were found to coincide with the changing phases and celestial position of the Moon. Once recognized, such repeating patterns became predictable, and Moon lore became common.

Moon Weather Lore

Weather was one of the most important concerns to the ancient people of our planet. Sailors relied on lunar weather predictions to guide their travels, and farmers, to time their planting and harvesting. Consider, for example, these old folk sayings.

A sallow Moon
Brings rain soon.

Shining Moon of red cast,
Calm seas will not last.

Warm days, cool nights,
A bright white Moon
And stars of light.

A full moonrise with a ring,
Clouds will rain and thunder sing.

When around the Moon a ring does glow,
The clouds will rain, and the wind will blow.

A clear Moon in spring or fall,
Soon will bring a frost to call.

A full Moon overhead in clear sight,
Nice days will reign a full fortnight.

Full Moon hidden by the noon Sun,
The coming skies will be uncertain.

Four days, no shadow is cast from the Moon,
Four days of foul weather follows soon.

Within four days a New Moon shadow is cast,
Good weather will last and last.

A blue Moon in the month of May,
Severe weather is here to stay.
Another month with a blue Moon,
Inclement weather follows soon.

An equinox Moon, full in spring,
Stormy skies it quickly brings.

Flowers in May, when spring showers stay,
First harvest is late, when spring showers wait.

The crescent Moon's horns lost in the night,
Brings wet weather before Full Moon's light.

When the Moon's obscured at her core,
The Full Moon doth rain more and more.

The Moon surrounded by a ring,
A howling storm it will bring,
Count of stars the ring does hold,
The number of days of rain and cold

The Moon, a ring does surround,
Worry and trouble will soon be found;

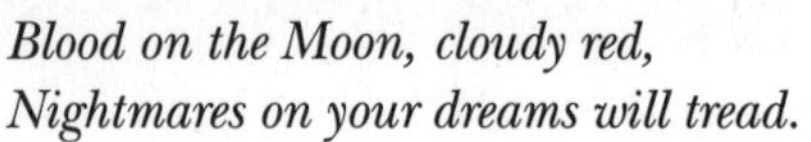

Blood on the Moon, cloudy red,
Nightmares on your dreams will tread.

An April Full Moon, so pretty and bright,
The ground will be frozen by first morning's light.

A Full Moon in winter, no clouds in sight—
Short cold days, long cold nights.

A winter Full Moon, cold snaps are long;
New Moon warming, rising at dawn.

Moon Birth Lore

Although some ancient cultures attributed masculine qualities to the Moon, most cultures considered the Sun masculine and the Moon feminine. The Moon phases followed a monthly cycle, similar to a woman's menstrual cycle. Births seemed to occur more often around Full Moons. From these observations, other correlations were added to the litany of Moon lore. These included lunar links with becoming pregnant, predetermining the sex of a child, and a baby's sleep cycle. Here are some lunar birthing rhymes.

A maiden under the Full Moon lies,
Naked, praying to the skies.
On the New Moon, a child will form,
And in nine months, she will be born.

The New Moon sets with the Sun,
The newborn's mother's work is done;
Sunset with the Full Moon rise,
All night long, the baby cries.

A newborn's mother, soon to be,
And lying naked under an apple tree,
The Full Moon light,

On the baby doth shine,
And will be born in three days time.

New Moon, sleep all night
Baby will rest, mother's delight.
Full Moon, bright and clear
Baby will dance and play and cheer.

Full Moon,
Baby soon.

Full Moon rise,
Baby no surprise.

The fourth Full Moon, and from behind,
Pregnancy is a notable sign.
A girl will be born in half a year,
The tenth Full Moon and birth is near.
The fourth full Moon and from behind,
No baby is shown, a masculine sign.
The tenth full Moon no water break,
A boy will be born and he will be late.

Moon Planting Lore

Ancient farmers considered the phases of the Moon and the Moon signs prior to planting, weeding, or harvesting. Milk production was thought to increase on the Full Moon, and the Full Moon nearest the Spring Equinox meant the first fresh milk of the season. Mating of farm animals was thought to be more productive under the Full Moon; however, the quality of farm animals was considered to best when birthed under a waxing water Moon.

Spring Full Moon, lactating ewes,
From the farmer spread the news,

Fresh milk doth come this night,
And can be had at first dawn's light.

Asparagus, broccoli, Brussels sprouts,
Leafy vegetables will grow stout,
When planted under the New Moon's light,
A bountiful harvest on Full Moon night.
Peppers, pumpkins, and peas will grow,
as will melons, garlic, squash, and tomatoes,
Sow the bounty and reap the same,
And do so in the Goddess' name.

Aries and Leo, barren and dry,
Sagittarius, Aquarius, and Gemini,
The Virgo Moon is barren and moist,
Planting is not a very good choice.
Capricorn Moon, Libra, and Taurus,
Sow not the fruit trees nor the forest,
Root crops do well, and so with vines,
But not as good as the water signs.
Cancer, Scorpio, and Pisces are best,
Lettuce, tomatoes, and all the rest,
Feminine and moist, what all plants need,
Yield voluminous fruit and plenty of seed.

Animals born under a water sign
And a waxing Moon, mature just fine,
Good breeding stock, they will be,
Healthy and happy for all to see.

The Moon's Affect on People

The Moon was thought to have power over the human experience. The light of the Full Moon was believed to make a person crazy. People became less inhibited under the Full

Moon, a condition that came to be known as lunacy. The manner in which we are affected is determined by lunar astrology and the phase of the Moon.

Under a Full Moon, do not sleep,
And your sanity you will keep.

Aries Moon, heat and fire
Set ablaze, what you desire;
Taurus Moon, solid and stable,
Only complete what you are able;
Gemini Moon, of two minds,
Will talk about the other signs;
Cancer Moon, tears will fall,
Happiness, sadness, joy, and all;
Leo Moon, center stage,
I don't believe that I have aged;
Virgo Moon, a magnifying glass,
Mine the details of your past;
Libra Moon, balanced and fair,
Let the wind blow through your hair;
Scorpio Moon, passion and sex,
The mind succumbs to the body's hex;
Sagittarius Moon, relaxed and free,
Do not tell me what will be;
Capricorn Moon, when money counts,
All distractions do renounce;
Aquarius Moon, hidden and pure,
Charisma enhances your behavior;
Pisces Moon, compassionate, caring,
Always comes before the Aries.

The Story of Mistletoe

by Scott Paul

Mistletoe. The ancients called it the golden bough. As its berries began to age they took on a golden color. In the modern age, we are most familiar with mistletoe during Christmas or Yule holiday celebrations. Tradition holds that if you hang a sprig of mistletoe over the door, those who stand beneath it must kiss. This tradition has a much more ancient origin. Mistletoe was the most sacred and magical of all plants. It was the stuff of legends and of myth.

According to Norse mythology, Frigga, the goddess of love and beauty, wished to ensure that her son Baldur would be protected from all that could harm him. To do this she traveled to each of the nine worlds and secured promises of all that she found there that nothing would harm her son. However, she failed to get such a promise from the mistletoe plant, as it was small and deemed harmless. The god Loki discovered this and plotted to kill Baldur.

Baldur's basking in his invulnerability dared the other gods to hurt him. In sport, the other gods began to throw all manner of

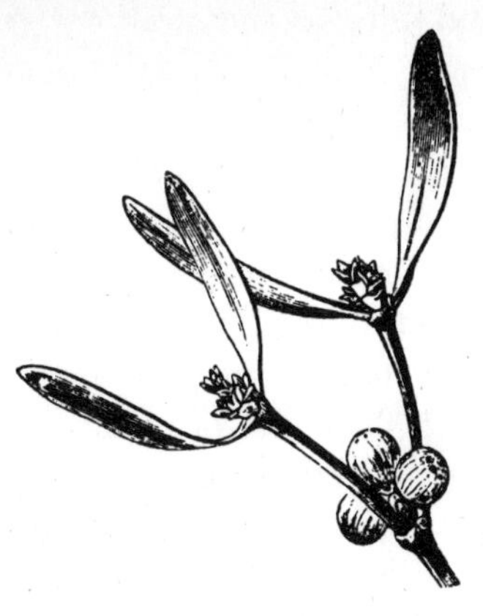

things at Baldur. Seeing this, Loki took a small branch of mistletoe and gave it to Hodr, the blind brother of Baldur. Hodr, with Loki's help, threw the branch at Baldur. The mistletoe pierced his heart and Baldur was killed. In her grief Frigga's tears became the white berries on the mistletoe plant. Later, when Baldur was rescued from the underworld, Frigga restored the reputation of mistletoe by making it a symbol of love and promising to bestow and kiss upon anyone who passed beneath it.

To the Druids, the oak tree was most sacred. Anything that grew upon it was said to have been sent from the gods and was a sign that the tree was chosen by the divine.

When mistletoe was found growing parasitically on oak trees, it received a royal treatment. A priest clad in a white robe would climb the tree. The mistletoe was cut with a gold sickle and caught in a white cloth. The Druids used the mistletoe for magical and healing purposes.

Folklore from around the world describes the uses of the plant. A sprig placed in a baby's crib will protect the baby from fairies. Warring factions meet under the mistletoe ensuring that peace would prevail. In Japan, mistletoe would be mixed with soil to ensure growth in gardens. Sometimes called the "thunder besom," mistletoe was used to protect houses from lightning strikes. Boughs of the plant were hung from the rafters of houses to protect from fire. The ancient belief that mistletoe was a "master key" and could open any lock has its origin in the myth of Aeneas.

According to Greek myth, Aenaes spurned Dido of Carthage and went in search of his father Anchises in the underworld. The poet Virgil describes how Aenaes was counseled by Sybil to follow two doves into the forest in search of the golden bough. At the height of winter some species of mistletoe have berries that turn gold. Taking the mistletoe with him Aenaes descended into the land of the dead. The Ferryman refused him passage until Aneas took out the bough. Thus the gates to the underworld were opened for Aenaes.

Healers and doctors prescribed mistletoe as a cure-all for illness. The Druids called mistletoe "heal-all." Until the eighteenth century, potions and medicines made from mistletoe were used to treat sterility, epilepsy and other nervous disorders, childhood diseases, and, ironically enough, for cases of poisoning. Modern studies have shown that most of the 1,500 species of mistletoe found worldwide are highly toxic. Some of the European species are used in the treatment of cancer or in experimental drug treatments. But as a rule, mistletoe should always be kept away from small children and should never be eaten or taken internally.

Folklore and myth join as one when mistletoe is used to brighten our lives and to celebrate the seasons of joy and giving.

A Ritual for Yule: Calling on Ancient Power

by Sedwyn

The items needed for this ritual consist of three strands of gold garland (found in most stores that carry Christmas tree trimmings)—the longer, the better; and also some tea light candles in holders to protect the flame. More specifically, these candles will be placed on the floor and you want to protect anyone wearing long clothing from catching it on fire.

Use the garland to create three spirals in the center of the floor, making the space within each spiral wide enough to form a path on which to walk. Lay the spirals in such a way that the "entrances" to them are away from each other. Place the candles along the perimeter of each spiral.

The Ritual

A priest or priestess will lead a gathering in speaking the following words.

> Leader: *Now is the time of greatest darkness, but soon the dark will give way to light. Time is suspended; the Old King (the old year) is transformed into the Infant Sun (the new year). At dawn the Great Mother will give birth to the Divine Light, and the wheel of the year will begin turning anew. We wait and watch for the Sun to arise from the dark womb of the night. Hand to hand the circle is cast.*
>
> All (joining hands): *Hand to hand the circle is cast. With this very circle*
> *we now have created a sacred space where two worlds can flow together.*
>
> Leader: *Come ye spirits of the north; powers of earth. Your bounty*

sustains us through the winter. Be with us as the silent cavern; place of renewal.

All: *Be with us this night. Blessed be.*

Leader: *Come ye spirits of the east; powers of air. Sail on crisp winter wings as you bring the golden dawn. Be with us as a clear night sky.*

All: *Be with us this night. Blessed be.*

Leader: *Come ye spirits of the south; powers of fire. Bring the heat of a flame to warm our hearts. Be with us as a welcoming hearth.*

All: *Be with us this night. Blessed be.*

Leader: *Come ye spirits of the west; powers of water. You nourish the earth and bathe us in sweet rains. Be with us as a quiet snowfall.*

All: *Be with us this night. Blessed be.*

Leader: *Great Mother Goddess, provider of all life, bring forth your son; transform the light.*

All: *Be with us this night. Blessed be.*

Leader: *Tomorrow the Sun begins its journey back to us. Tonight we celebrate the rebirth of light. A common component of the Yule ritual when done outdoors is to jump a bonfire and a make wish for in the coming year. Tonight we combine this basic idea with the spiral, which is associated with the Goddess, winter, and the Winter Solstice.*

The spiral is a fundamental form found in nature. To ancient people, the spiral was a sacred symbol of the Goddess and her transformative powers. Our ancestor knew and we are only rediscovering the vortex of energy in a spiral that allows us to connect with our deepest selves, the web of life and the divine.

At the ancient site of Newgrange in Ireland there is a set of three spirals on the back wall of the inner chamber, sixty-five feet from the entrance. On the Winter Solstice, as well as the day before and after, the rising Sun illuminates these spirals.

The spiral is also symbolic of winter hibernation. During the cold months we turn inward for a time of reflection. But the same spiral of energy that leads us downward, inside ourselves in winter eventually leads us up toward the light in spring.

Tonight we use the spiral in making our wishes for the new year.

Think of what you want to manifest in your life. When you are ready, walk one of the spirals. When you get to the center, pause and then step over the inner-most coil. As you do this, say your wish aloud.

While some are walking the spirals, the rest of us will do a circle dance around the spirals while chanting.

All: *Let it begin with each step we take,*
And let it begin with each wish we make.
Let it begin with each breath we take,
And let is begin every time we awake.

Leader (after everyone has walked the spiral): *May our wishes and intentions manifest into the physical world. As above, so below.*

All: *Blessed be.*

Leader: *It is time to center ourselves as we move back to the everyday world. Close your eyes; let your energy spiral down. Feel it touch the Earth. Be at peace this winter night. As darkness is followed by light, so winter is followed by spring. The wheel of the year turns ever onward.* (Pause) *When you are ready, open your eyes.*

Great Mother who gives birth to the light and gives our world form, we thank you for your presence this night and ask for your blessings as you depart.

All: *Hail and farewell. Blessed be.*

Leader: *Spirits of east, of waters that fill the rivers in spring. Stay if you will; go if you must.*

All: *Hail and farewell. Blessed be.*

Leader: *Spirits of south, of fire that provides new beginnings. Stay if you will; go if you must.*

All: *Hail and farewell. Blessed be.*

Leader: *Spirits of east, of air and the precious breath of life. Stay if you will; go if you must.*

All: *Hail and farewell. Blessed be.*

Leader: *Spirits of north, of earth that sustains us. Stay if you will; go if you must.*

All: *Hail and farewell. Blessed be.*

Leader: *Our circle is open, but unbroken. May the peace of the Goddess remain in our hearts.*

All: *Merry meet, merry part, and merry meet again.*

For Further Study

Ferguson, Diana. *The Magickal Year.* York Beach, Maine: Samuel Weiser, 1996.

Morrison, Dorothy. *Yule: A Celebration of Light and Warmth.* St. Paul, Minn.: Llewellyn Publications, 2000.

What Is a Wicked Witch?

by Elizabeth Hazel

The wicked Witch is an intriguing character. Her ugliness, threatening manner, and maliciousness are uncontestable, yet there is more substance beneath the obvious and hideous outer shell. Following many threads of literature, film, and art, I've sought to find the truth of this character behind the tattered robes and striped socks.

A Quick History of the Wicked Witch

In the early literature of the Greeks and Romans, Witches were young and sexy and got away with murder, literally. The tales of Medea's brews and incantations, and Circe's allure to seafaring men, make for fascinating reading. These two were dangerous, tricky, and sometimes evil, but they had absolutely no warts on their lovely noses. The Greeks and Romans had a fuller appreciation for powerful women, possibly because they were still conversant with various forms of the Goddess.

But time and religion distanced Western culture from a healthy spectrum of feminine images. By the fifteenth century, wicked and ugly Witches began to appear in primitive woodcuts. They are angular and grim, yet paradoxically they engage in lascivious activities with a goat-like master. These surreal presentations seem silly until the next page reveals a picture of a Witch being sizzled at the stake. They must have been very, very wicked, indeed.

Some Ideas about Wickedness

What is wickedness exactly? Is it the embodiment of malice and threat in feminine form? Or is it merely a derogatory label for women who did what they bloody well wanted in spite of pressure to conform? A legacy of religious persecution passed from the Romans to the Inquisitors, and many dissenters and heretics were burned. But the loss of the full spectrum of feminine images caused Witches to elicit an especially fierce variety of harassment.

The traditional Anglo-Euro wicked Witch is a specialized offshoot of the dark feminine image portrayed in the folklore and myths of many cultures. This feminine image, once respected in early civilizations, became demonized in a culture obsessed with virgins. Literature from the Middle Ages to the current era paints her as the enemy of the lauded hero. She is his polar opposite. Her blood mysteries and ecstatic wildness are anathema to his pristine, rational, masculine persona. She evokes a crisis, an imperative mission for the knight to defeat or overcome her traps, lures, artifices, and spells. The hero must mobilize his resources and allies to win.

The Grimm Brothers wrote many tales that follow this plot line, only varying to the extent that a couple of snotty older brothers run into her first and go down hard. The irony of Grimm is that the hero often possesses his own magic to put an end to the Witch's design. Apparently it is acceptable if the heroes use it, but not Witches. That is, being wicked evidently isn't about the magic—so it could only be about two things: thwarting the hero, or being a woman.

Modern Witch Visions

Contemporary works presents the full flowering of the wicked Witch. In *The Wizard of Oz,* Frank L. Baum created the Wicked Witch of the West, whose winged monkeys terrorize the skies of Oz and good old Dorothy. Dorothy joins forces with the Scarecrow, Lion, and Tin Man, and destroys the Witch. The Witches in Disney's *Snow White* (1952) and *Sleeping Beauty* (1959) are also out to kill the title characters. Disney drafted the tales from Grimm and Perrault, but crafted a modern view of wicked Witches in animated films. Snow White's stepmother is conniving and treacherous; but Maleficent in Sleeping Beauty is a maelstrom of evil powers. She can teleport, curse, terrorize, abduct, engulf an entire castle with thorns, and finally morph into a dragoness of monstrous proportions. Disney makes clear the line between good magic and bad in his films. His Witches have no redeeming features, and are obstacles to true love in both stories.

In these tales, the juxtaposition of the dark feminine with bright masculine reaches its greatest extreme: as the hero gets brighter, the Witch gets darker. Yet in modern literature, the pendulum of bright and dark becomes more muted. In Gregory Maguire's book, *Wicked* (1995), the Witch character is attempting to restore justice by combating a tyrant. She is angry, defiled, and trivialized, and blooms into magnificent vengeful rage. Yet Maguire gives her the burden of inexorable fate, writing: "When the times are a crucible, when the air is full of crisis, those who are most themselves are the victims."

Perhaps Maguire is correct. The individual driven by righteous fury is soon catapulted into ego oblivion. The wicked Witch can arise, but her vengefulness leads to a doom of her own making—a sacrifice for the forces of light. The wickedness that is her greatest strength is also her greatest liability, leaving her vulnerable to the socially acceptable hero.

In a culture of youth and beauty, the wicked Witch, the old hag or crone, is the antithesis of desirability. She is unwanted by men and feared by all. Her capacity for polarizing the hero archetype is decried as evil, but who else will activate his destiny? The wicked Witch antagonizes human intellect into motion, single-handedly compelling a protagonist into asserting his courage. She makes a man into a hero, but is not thanked for it.

The lonely exception to this attitude is found in Carlos Castaneda's wicked Witch, La Catalina. She stalks Carlos, and attempts to kill him. Don Juan points out to Carlos how he should appreciate her efforts on his behalf. Carlos screws up every encounter with her and barely escapes through dumb luck. Juan tells Carlos, "There are some people who are very careful about the nature of their acts. Their happiness is to act with the full knowledge that they don't have time; therefore, their acts have a peculiar power." Carlos is not allowed to indulge in hatred toward his opponent. Don Juan insists that La Catalina is necessary for his development as a sorcerer.

Much like Maguire, Castaneda blurs the lines between wickedness and nonwickedness. They have found a place and a meaning for the dark feminine image, shifting away from revulsion and rejection to a more thoughtful assessment of the wicked Witch's role. They are not liked, for no amount of storytelling can change a wicked Witch into a lap cat. But they are respected as a source of causality, a mechanism of greater destiny. Perhaps this is a sign that Witches have come full circle, back to the place they held in the days of Homer some 3,000 years ago.

The wicked Witch cannot be released with impunity: her realm of authority is fearsome. Her actions result in heroic efforts, a battle for survival. To encounter the wicked Witch within the psyche unleashes seething emotions from the restraints of ethics and rationalism. Opposing the wicked Witch is a catalyst for resourcefulness, ingenuity, and bravery in the face of danger. Both are exhausting experiences, but without her the wheels of fate cannot grind on toward the goal.

Each October, the wicked Witch resurfaces in the mass consciousness as Samhain approaches. Cartoons of the hag in black on a broom appear on doors and in yards. This commercialized image obscures her real meaning and power. But this year I'll see those images with new respect, and honor her for the part she may play in a life filled with mundane chores and daily grinds. When she is doing her worst she is at her best. She is the hard corner around which glorious fate turns.

Jack Parsons: Man of Science, Man of Magic

by Denise Dumars

Freedom is a two-edged sword of which one edge is liberty and the other responsibility; on which both edges are exceedingly sharp, and which is not easily handled by casual, cowardly, or treacherous hands.
—Jack Parsons

Jack Parsons was cofounder of NASA's Jet Propulsion Laboratory (JPL); he invented solid rocket fuel. He is a pivotal figure in the history of southern California's aerospace industry, and on the dark side of the Moon there is a crater that bears his name. Every year on Halloween, JPL holds a "Nativity Day" honoring him and his inventions.

Is this the same Jack Parsons who was a follower of Aleister Crowley, and who tried to create a homunculus, or a magical child? Who was this mystery man of science—and of magic? His death at the age of thirty-seven is as mysterious as was his life, which was very mysterious indeed. Born in 1914 as Marvel Whiteside Parsons, he could not have had a more appropriate name for magic, though he later changed his name to John W. Parsons and was known to friends as "Jack." The reason for the name change is that his mother left his father, the original "Marvel" Parsons, and she raised her son to

loathe his allegedly adulterous father. Parsons spent the rest of his life with an admitted "Oedipal complex" and an unconscious desire to find a father figure.

And find one he did—in Aleister Crowley. He ran across one of the aging occultist's books at a friend's house and immediately decided to become a member of Crowley's magical lodge, the famed Ordo Templi Orientis (OTO). Eventually Parsons began a correspondence with Crowley, who saw him as a very promising student. Parsons, however, did not follow OTO degrees of initiation to the letter. He always improvised on his rituals, and he sometimes gave himself "degrees" not granted by the organization. Perhaps this was his way of substituting his magical degrees for the university degree he never completed.

Parsons called Crowley "father," but Crowley became disenchanted with Parsons' recklessness in pursuit of magical goals. He warned Parsons more than once that the magic he was working might have dangerous consequences. During one magical working, a roof in another part of Parsons' property caught fire. Parsons said that every time he did a ritual, something vanished from his home. Of course, these events could have a more prosaic cause for this: Parsons ran his house like a commune or artists' colony, accepting very idiosyncratic people as boarders.

Meanwhile, Parsons' leaps of faith about science were paying off. His genius was widely known; he and his friends were allowed a lab at CalTech even though Parsons had no affiliation with the school. Parsons had attended Pasadena City College and the University of Southern California, but he did not graduate. His group was called the "Suicide Squad" due to its reckless use of high explosives. This nickname would prove, unfortunately, prophetic.

Parsons befriended numerous men as mentors in the magical realm. One of his earliest took up with Parsons' wife. He lost his next girlfriend (and a sum of money) to L. Ron Hubbard.

Science fiction had fueled Parsons' imagination since childhood, and in both his professional and avocational life he looked to science-fiction writers as his inspiration. He attended meetings of the Los Angeles Science Fantasy Society (LASFS), and at least two science fiction writers used Parsons as model for characters.

On display in the Smithsonian is Parsons' original Jet-Assisted Take-off (JATL) canister, the invention that gained him fame and, for a short time, fortune. Parsons' success did not last long after WWII, and it is perhaps not surprising that he was a victim of McCarthyism's "witch hunts." However, it was not his celebrated magical excess that caused his government security clearance to be revoked; rather, it was the fact that he had friends affiliated with the Communist Party. Parsons eventually got his security clearance back, only to lose it again near the end of his life.

What of the magical child? At one point, Parsons began an extended magical working called the "Babalon project." In the midst of this, a young artist named Cameron showed up. Parsons was immediately smitten with her and felt at first that she was the magical goddess-figure Babalon. According to people who knew the couple, for a time Parsons and Cameron attempted to create a magical child through an elemental spirit. However, Cameron had no children until she remarried after Parsons' death.

On June 17, 1952, Parsons and Cameron were packing for a trip to Mexico. Parsons was in his garage when a tremendous explosion occurred. The blast was heard blocks away and shattered windows in the neighborhood. Parsons himself was engulfed in flames, and the explosion blew off his right arm, broke his other arm and both legs, and tore a hole through his jaw. Incredibly, Parsons was awake and aware when help arrived. He died at Huntington Memorial Hospital thirty-seven minutes after the explosion. When Parsons' mother heard of his death, she committed suicide in front of a horrified wheelchair-bound houseguest who was unable to stop her.

Parsons' death was ruled an accident by the Pasadena police. It was theorized that he had dropped a canister of fulminate of mercury. While it is true that he stored explosives in the garage, many think it is unlikely that he would be so careless in handing them, and speculated that he might have been murdered.

Though both Parsons' life and death were tainted by scandal, this remarkable figure remains an indelible part of southern California history and the development of the U.S. space program. Most of his magical writings have not seen print, save for a slim volume edited by his former wife in 1989. Subsequent publication of his writings may prove whether his magical experiments were as valuable to the occult community as his inventions were to the sciences.

A New Moon Purification Bath

by Ember

On the night of the New Moon, sprinkle a few drops of rosemary oil into a warm bath. Light a black candle in a safe container, and set it on the edge of the bathtub. Place a clear and charged quartz crystal near the candle so the light shines upon it. Use rosemary herbal soap to bathe, and visualize the water refreshing you physically, mentally, emotionally, and spiritually. As you soak and breathe the rosemary essence, gaze upon the candlelight and the crystal.

When you're ready, hold the crystal in your hand, or place it in the water with you. Breathe deeply. As you inhale, visualize your entire being as clear as crystal. As you exhale, sense the black candle absorbing and dispelling the old as you draw in the new with each new breath. Feel yourself being revived and renewed as you chant either aloud or to yourself:

Begin again and cleanse my flesh,
Begin again and cleanse my mind,
Begin again and cleanse my heart,
Begin again and cleanse my soul.
New Moon darkness bathe me. Make me new again.

After bathing, allow the candle to burn completely. Keep the crystal near your bedside or in your pillowcase while you sleep that night, then carry it with you for a couple days to continue feeling its cleansing energy.

Space Cleansing and Purification

by Reverend Gina Pace

Space cleansing is a subject that most people these days are familiar with nowadays. Space cleansing can be performed for any number of reasons. You may be about to perform a ritual, and you need to clear your circle area of distracting, disturbing, or disconcordant engeries. How to go about doing it, however, is an entirely different matter.

Space cleansing is mentioned in many books, yet is explained fully in very few of them. In fact, my own system, which is a combination of techniques culled from different cultures, is one that I arrived at only after a lot of trial and error.

Once you determine the reasons to perform a space cleansing and purification ritual, decide what materials you want to include. Traditional space cleansing rituals typically involve smudging with sage or other smoking herbs. For many people, however, a cloud of purifying smoke may cause more trouble than it cures (especially in cases of allergies).

I like to begin my ceremony with a prayer and a bell of some sort. Sound is an especially good tool in the cleansing ritual. My own personal favorite are the *tingsha,* a pair of brass cymbal-shaped bells strung on a leather thong and held in one hand so that they dangle. With practice, they can be manipulated with your thumb and one finger to ring at will. These are a tool of Chinese feng shui and Buddhist meditation practitioners, so they are probably not difficult to find. Tibetan singing bowls are another option, though these can be expensive. You must make the decision whether or not to include sound based on your comfort in investing in an instrument.

I also use a sage wand for smudging as the first major step of my purification ritual. There are several types of sage and of preprepared sage wands available. I tend to purchase smaller wands rather than one large one. I'd rather start a new wand each time, as opposed to relighting a used one. Most smudge wands are made of white sage, which looks like a bundled roll of dried whole leaves of very pale grayish-green color, or of sagebrush, which looks like a bundled roll of brownish-gray twigs. Most people associate this last type with their idea of what a smudge stick looks like, but in reality sagebrush is a different species of sage entirely from white sage. While all varieties of sage will provide a cleansing energy, I do find that white sage is a much stronger and purer energy for cleansing, and thus I prefer it for my rituals. Sagebrush smells sweeter, but white sage smells more like a ritual smoke. You can make the choice based on your own preference.

Another important cleansing devise is a sweetgrass braid. Sweetgrass brings in a positive energy of prosperity and happiness into a space. While not mandatory, it is always nice following a sage smudging. Imagine that you are removing the negative energies from a space or home; if you do not follow this with something that welcomes in a more positive, blessed energy, you are basically leaving yourself with a void. Sweetgrass is most often found in a long green, dried-grass braid. Look for the freshest, greenest grass you can find. The fresher the dried grass is, the more it will smoke.

The last ingredient you may choose to incorporate into your smudging ritual is cedar incense. This is the least essential ingredient, but it has the highest spiritual property of all ritual smoke used in purification. It is used to bring in the connection with the divine during the ritual itself. I tend to use it in between the sage and the sweetgrass. I like to cleanse the area of negative energies; then, when it is pure and new and open, I consecrate the area to the higher power with cedar. I finally bring in the sweetgrass to welcome the positive energies.

Before performing a space cleansing, always cleanse yourself first. If I am able to plan in advance, I time my ritual for when I am freshly bathed. I never perform a cleansing after work or other frustrations. A long, hot bath with sea salts and a few drops of cedar oil are appropriate for this. Don clean, fresh, comfortable clothing, and then spend a few moments in meditation when you have arrived at the area to be cleansed. set up a small area where you can light all of the smudges, using a shell or fire-proof bowl to hold the items so they do not burn anything. Light the sage, then light the sweetgrass braid, and blow out the flame once the grasses and leaves begin to smolder and glow. When you are ready to begin your smudging ritual, ring the bell or chime, then begin by saying a prayer such as this one which I recently wrote for a wedding cleansing:

Mother Earth, Father Sky, I offer you this sage today.
Bless it and infuse it with your grace,
That it may cleanse this sacred space.

I offer you this cedar pine as a symbol of the Divine.
Bless it and touch it with your love;
What is below is reflected above.

I offer you this grassy braid, sweet and richly made.
Bless it with abundance and peace;
Let this space be filled with happiness.

Ring the bell or chime again with three successive strikes. Let each chime ring till it faces from hearing before ringing the next time. This gives a clear signal that you are about to begin.

Once the third chime has faded, take up the sage wand. If you are cleansing an entire home, begin at the main entrance to the house. Take the smoking wand, and carry it around the perimeter of the home in a counterclockwise direction. As you pass the wand around the inside of the walls, move it in small circles constantly to keep the smoke flowing and moving. It is very important that you move counterclockwise with the sage, as it is the direction for banishing.

Move about the entire space. If the house has more than one floor, move around the entire main floor first, then move to your other floors till you return to your main entrance. If you are cleansing anything other than a house, simply apply the same method, starting with your entry point into the area, and cleansing in a counterclockwise motion. In the case of a ritual circle, your entry point is usually either in the north or east, depending on your magical tradition. Do not change your normal entry point for this cleansing ritual.

Follow this by lighting the cedar in the area to be cleansed. It is fine if all you have for this is cedar incense. I begin by carrying the cedar into the center of the space and lifting it up as high as I can without losing control over it. This is to consecrate the space to the higher power and to raise the energy center of the space as high as possible. Imagine that as you do this you fill the entire space with love and light. Then carry the cedar in a spiraling motion clockwise from the center of the space out to the entry point and back again. This is generally the shortest part of the ritual.

Once this is completed, you are ready to bring in the sweetgrass braid. Carry the lighted braid into the area at the entry point. Smudge the entire area around its perimeter; this time, however, go in a clockwise motion around the inside walls. Make a circling, clockwise motion in the air with the sweetgrass as you carry it around. When you return to the point of entry, you are finished. Put out the sweetgrass, then take up the bell or chime and perform another set of three long clear rings. Let each ring fade out naturally before ringing the following.

I usually end by standing in the center of the space and clapping my hands three times, saying: "This space is now ready to be used in love, light, and happiness. Blessed be!"

A note for house blessings: at this point, if you have blessed a house for someone, make sure they re-enter the house at this time, one at a time. They should carry a purse with them to ensure prosperity in the newly cleansed home. A luncheon or party is an appropriate celebration to follow the cleansing.

When you are finished with this, make sure you get something to eat as you will need to ground your energy.

If you are allergic to smoke, or for any other reasons do not wish to use smudge wands to cleanse and purify the space, you have some other options.

Sage oil is available from herbal or New Age shops. Choose an essential oil if possible, or one that is as pure and close to essential oil as you can get. Try not to get an alcohol-based tincture. A small bottle of distilled or pure water combined with fifty drops of sage oil can be used in an atomizer to "sage" an area without smoke. This is especially effective for cleansing a very small space—such as a car. I have sold bottles of preprepared sage spray in my shop for years and no one has ever reported any trouble with allergies or other sensitivities.

Holy water, used for centuries in many mainstream churches, is essentially a pure or distilled water that is blessed by a member of the clergy. I tend to make my own using a sea salt and rainwater mixture. I dissolved the salt in the collected rain water, and then say a purification prayer over the water to consecrate it for ritual purposes.

Many books refer to "Florida water" as an appropriate ritual cleansing agent. Florida water is actually a type of cologne water comprised of water and citrus oils. I keep a bottle of this myself for when I need it. You can often find small bottles of this at outlandish prices in New Age catalogs and shops. I purchased mine for under two dollars in the local supermarket. It is produced by Goya, a vendor of beans, olives, oils, and foods for ethnic cooking. Goya also makes many products that can be used for magical purposes. Almost every supermarket has a section of Goya products. If you decide to use a Florida water for your ritual purposes, I recommend you get it in this way rather than spend fifteen dollars for a bottle elsewhere.

With these alternative materials, follow the directions above for the cleansing ceremony, substituting the sage spray for the sage smudge wand. Sprinkle the area next with the holy water. The Florida water can be used as a substitute for the sweetgrass. Use the bell the same way as in the smudging ceremony and clap your hands at the end. You will still need to ground yourself afterward even though you are not using smoke.

The first time you perform these ceremonies, they may feel a little strange; however, they are designed out of much trial and error. As such, I have found that they become second nature very quickly. Try them for yourself and see.

Rune Divination

by Michelle Santos

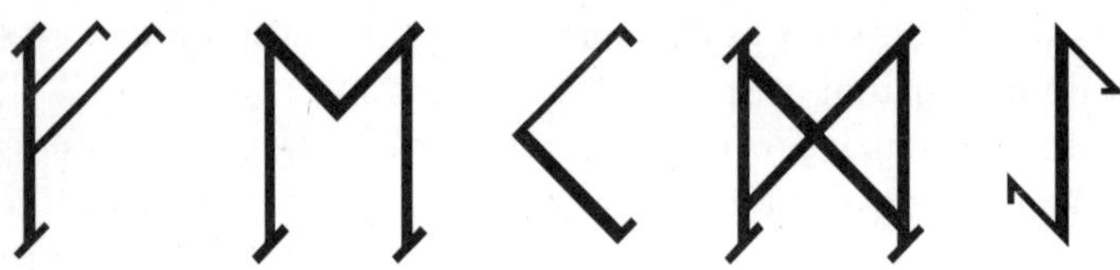

Rune work is not as easy as it looks. Many people, when looking into divination systems, compare the seventy-eight cards in the tarot deck to the twenty-four runes in the elder futhark, and automatically lean toward the runes as the simpler choice. And at first glance, there does appear to be less to remember and memorize with runes. But beware—this is an illusion. The depth of the runes is actually very immense.

A Norse Alphabet

For those unfamiliar with the runes, they are a Norse magical alphabet, a divination system, a link to the gods, a spellcaster's tool, a poem, and a song. They are, in short, magic.

In legend, the runes were given to the god Odin, or Wodan, when he sacrificed himself on the world tree, Yggdrasil. In history, there has been little hard-and-fast evidence to suggest exactly where and when the runes evolved. Severaltheories have been put forward but none have been proven completely. I think this is yet another indication of the mystical quality of the runes.

All work with the runes takes time, focus, and energy. Understanding and knowing the runes fully is not a task to be rushed. A rune master once instructed me to use caution when using runes in spellwork, for their power could not be harnessed easily. He suggested that a spellcaster needed knowledge of all the aspects of the rune even before attempting magic.

Today, I agree with him. And I know that the only way to know the runes is to work with them. Divination is the best pathway to runic knowledge.

Finding a Rune Set

Traditionally, runes have been carved into small pieces of flat wood (usually yew or birch) of similar size and shape. The runic sigils are carved into the wood and then painted red. Often the blood of the rune maker is included in the paint, in order to mark the runes as the user's own, and to bind them to him or her.

When I attained my rune set, I did not follow this traditional method. Instead, I bought twenty-four fairly flat, similar-sized tiger's-eye stones from my local science store. (I chose tiger's-eye because it was a stone that resonated with me; but for you any stone will do, as long as it feels right.) Then, using permanent silver marker, I drew the sigils on each of the stones and sealed them with clear lacquer. River stones or sea stones would also work very well. Naturally, the color of the paint or marker is up to you.

There are several commercial rune sets made of stones or bone that you could easily buy. Should you choose to purchase a rune set, I recommend clearing it by putting it under running water or burying it in salt, and then charging it by setting it out in the light of the Full Moon. (This should be done for any stones bought in a store as well.)

After removing negativity through clearing and charging, allow your energy to seep into the runes. Carry them around with you in a briefcase, pocketbook, or book bag, sleep with them under your pillow, or take one at a time and carry it in your pocket.

Runic Spreads

The two most commonly used runic spreads are the one-rune and three-rune spreads. I will briefly describe these spreads before explaining a more complicated, multi-rune spread.

One-Rune

The one-rune spread is excellent for quick yes-or-no questions. The querent thinks of such a question and then reaches into the rune bag and pulls out a rune. The querent then shows the reader the rune and receives an answer from the reader. This is also a great spread to see what kind of day you are going to have. As soon as you get up, pull a rune and see what the day will bring, generally speaking.

Three-Rune

The three-rune spread is for more detailed and involves more questions. The querent thinks of a question and pulls three runes out of the bag. He hands them to the rune reader who lays them out left to right. Any three-rune reading has a relationship to the three Norns in Norse mythology, so the rune reader should understand who they are and how they function. Knowledge of the triple god Odin-Villi-Ve is also important.

A past-present-future reading would be for the querent who wants to know what will happen if he or she stays in a certain situation. The first rune would be the past rune. The second rune would be the present rune, and the third would show the future. If a querent is unhappy with the outcome as depicted by the future rune, he or she might want to draw three more runes out of the bag.

This second reading would be a situation-action-outcome spread. This reading would be for the querent who is uncertain if he or she should undertake a certain action. The first rune is the querent's current situation in life. This rune will give the reader clues about what aspect of life the querent is concerned with—i.e. work, home, family, or love life. The second rune is the action that the querent could possibly take in the future, and the third rune is the result or consequence of that action. A situation-action-outcome spread can be done as many times as the querent wants, as long as the question is different each time.

Multi-Rune

There are many different kinds of multi-rune spreads, and all of them take time and knowledge to master. I recommend using the first two runic spreads until you are comfortable with them and with the runes. Otherwise, a multi-rune spread can be overwhelming.

The following multi-rune spread is one that is rarely, if ever, mentioned in books. I automatically started doing it when I began working with the runes years ago. The concept is derived from the bone-throwers of ancient times.

The querent begins by holding all twenty-four runes in hand. The querent then thinks of a question and throws the runes onto the floor or table. The reader has the choice of reading the runes as they face the querent, or as they face the reader. I usually sit across from the querent and read them as they face me. However, the choice is up to the individual reader and may change with each reading.

At this point, the rune reader must read the pattern of the runes as well as the individual sigils that fall face up. The easiest way to do this is to look for a path in the way the runes fell. Try to determine the beginning of the path. Where does the eye automatically fall, and where does it travel? Are there any runes that have fallen off by themselves? Are there any that appear to be blocked in by upside-down stones? Use your intuition, and start your reading where it feels right.

Look at the way the runes fell. Is there a natural progression? Does any way seem blocked? Allow your eyes to blur slightly and move over the runes toward the way of least resistance. Don't force anything. Often the meanings of the sigils will cause you to move in a certain way because it is obvious that they are linked. Other times, the placement of the runes will form an obvious stream or path.

Once you have derived a pathway, begin with the first rune, continuing to the next rune or grouping of runes, until you have reached the end of the path. Each rune may be read by itself or it may form meaning with a group of runes. Your knowledge of the rune sigils is essential here, as is your intuition or psychic ability. Trust yourself. If you feel that certain runes are grouped together for a reason, then they undoubtedly are. Follow the runes, reading them as you go, until you reach the end of the pathway. At that point, you should be able to formulate an overall understanding of the message given you by the runes.

If the querent has questions that were raised by the multi-rune spread, you can follow up with a one-rune or three-rune spread. These will help the querent address specific concerns, and will help him or her leave with a definite action plan. Undoubtedly, this will also affirm the multi-rune spread, as similar runes will continue to pop up.

Rune work is challenging. The hard-and-fast answers of the modern world do not apply to learning the runes. However, if you want to delve into a fascinating divination system, steeped in history, legend, and myth, then the runes are for you. They are a reward unto themselves.

For Further Study

Aswynn, Freya. *Northern Mysteries and Magick: Runes, Gods, and Feminine Powers.* St. Paul, Minn.: Llewellyn Publications, 1998.

Thorsson, Edred. *At the Well of Wyrd: A Handbook of Runic Divination.* York Beach, Maine: Red Wheel/Weiser Publications, 1988.

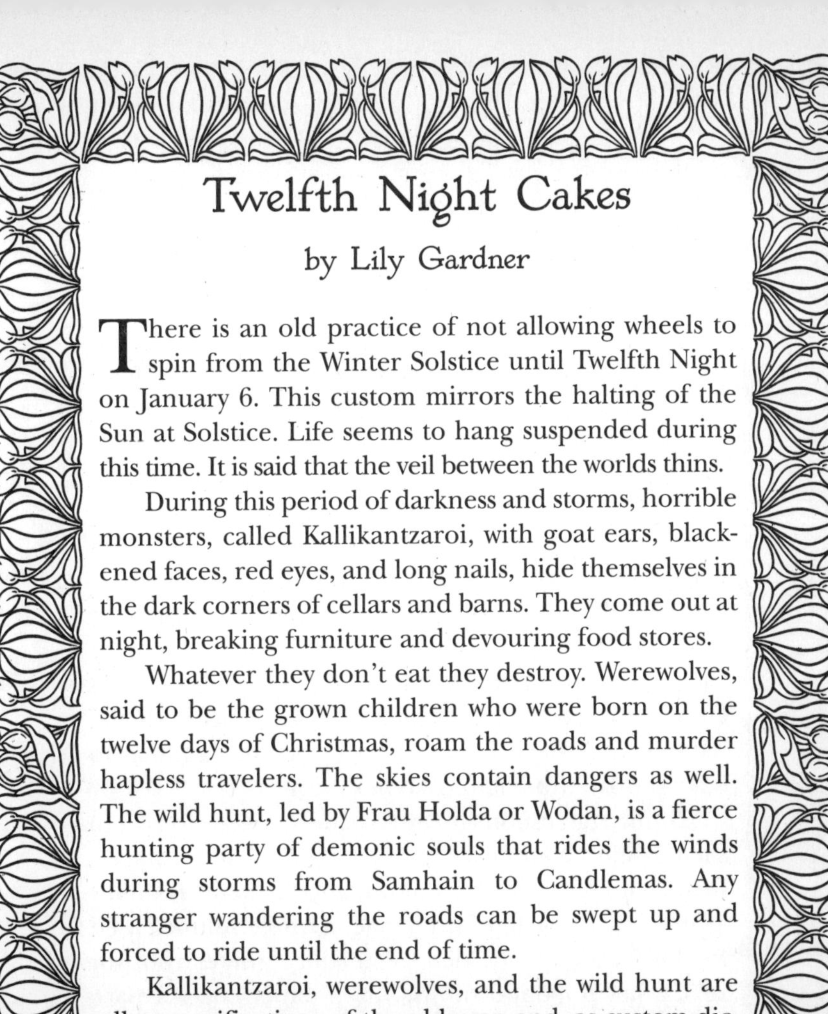

Twelfth Night Cakes

by Lily Gardner

There is an old practice of not allowing wheels to spin from the Winter Solstice until Twelfth Night on January 6. This custom mirrors the halting of the Sun at Solstice. Life seems to hang suspended during this time. It is said that the veil between the worlds thins.

During this period of darkness and storms, horrible monsters, called Kallikantzaroi, with goat ears, blackened faces, red eyes, and long nails, hide themselves in the dark corners of cellars and barns. They come out at night, breaking furniture and devouring food stores.

Whatever they don't eat they destroy. Werewolves, said to be the grown children who were born on the twelve days of Christmas, roam the roads and murder hapless travelers. The skies contain dangers as well. The wild hunt, led by Frau Holda or Wodan, is a fierce hunting party of demonic souls that rides the winds during storms from Samhain to Candlemas. Any stranger wandering the roads can be swept up and forced to ride until the end of time.

Kallikantzaroi, werewolves, and the wild hunt are all personifications of the old year, and, as custom dictates, we have to banish the old year now. When the old year is disposed of, traditionalists perform ceremonies to ensure good luck for the New Year, with the principle that "well begun is well ended."

One practice to ensure good luck is to make a Twelfth Night cake. Twelfth Night ends the Christmas festivities for many people. For the most luck, everyone in the household, from eldest to youngest, must stir the

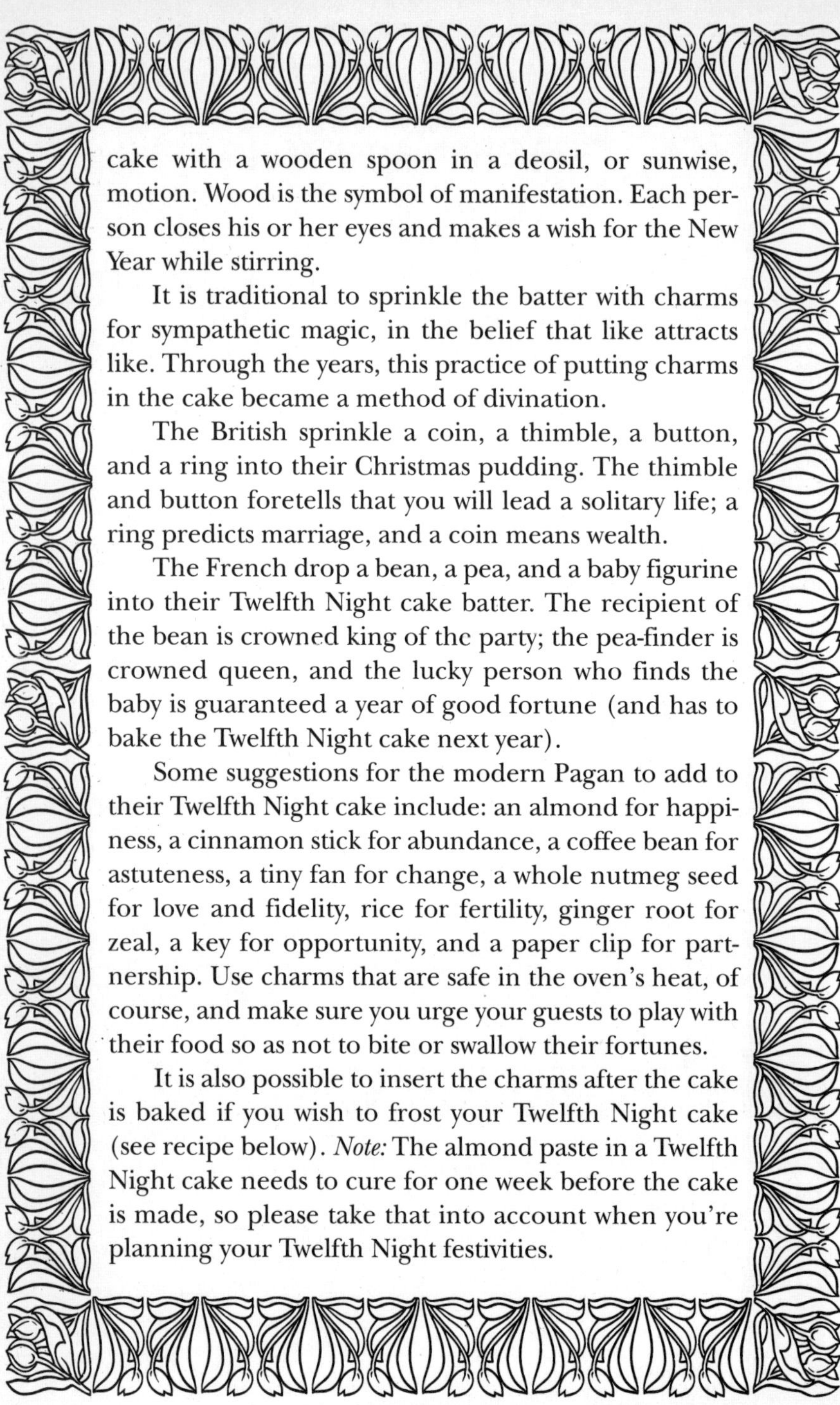

cake with a wooden spoon in a deosil, or sunwise, motion. Wood is the symbol of manifestation. Each person closes his or her eyes and makes a wish for the New Year while stirring.

It is traditional to sprinkle the batter with charms for sympathetic magic, in the belief that like attracts like. Through the years, this practice of putting charms in the cake became a method of divination.

The British sprinkle a coin, a thimble, a button, and a ring into their Christmas pudding. The thimble and button foretells that you will lead a solitary life; a ring predicts marriage, and a coin means wealth.

The French drop a bean, a pea, and a baby figurine into their Twelfth Night cake batter. The recipient of the bean is crowned king of the party; the pea-finder is crowned queen, and the lucky person who finds the baby is guaranteed a year of good fortune (and has to bake the Twelfth Night cake next year).

Some suggestions for the modern Pagan to add to their Twelfth Night cake include: an almond for happiness, a cinnamon stick for abundance, a coffee bean for astuteness, a tiny fan for change, a whole nutmeg seed for love and fidelity, rice for fertility, ginger root for zeal, a key for opportunity, and a paper clip for partnership. Use charms that are safe in the oven's heat, of course, and make sure you urge your guests to play with their food so as not to bite or swallow their fortunes.

It is also possible to insert the charms after the cake is baked if you wish to frost your Twelfth Night cake (see recipe below). *Note:* The almond paste in a Twelfth Night cake needs to cure for one week before the cake is made, so please take that into account when you're planning your Twelfth Night festivities.

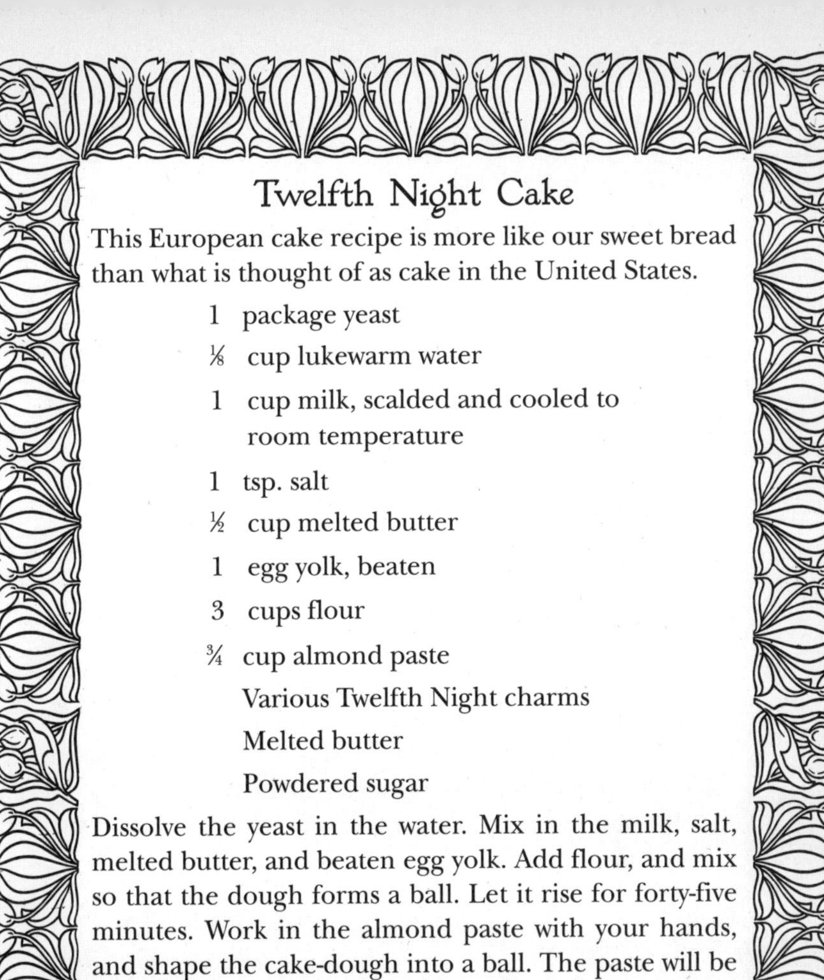

Twelfth Night Cake

This European cake recipe is more like our sweet bread than what is thought of as cake in the United States.

- 1 package yeast
- ⅛ cup lukewarm water
- 1 cup milk, scalded and cooled to room temperature
- 1 tsp. salt
- ½ cup melted butter
- 1 egg yolk, beaten
- 3 cups flour
- ¾ cup almond paste
- Various Twelfth Night charms
- Melted butter
- Powdered sugar

Dissolve the yeast in the water. Mix in the milk, salt, melted butter, and beaten egg yolk. Add flour, and mix so that the dough forms a ball. Let it rise for forty-five minutes. Work in the almond paste with your hands, and shape the cake-dough into a ball. The paste will be stiff, so mix as thoroughly as you can. Stuff the charms into the dough at this time. Place the ball of dough onto a parchment-lined cookie sheet, cover with plastic wrap, and let rise for another thirty minutes. With a sharp knife, cut a pentacle across the top of the ball of dough, then bake the cake for 25 minutes in a 375°F oven until the surface is golden brown. Let it cool off and brush the cake's top with melted butter. Sprinkle powdered sugar in the carved pentacle. (Or you can add your favorite frosting if you prefer.)

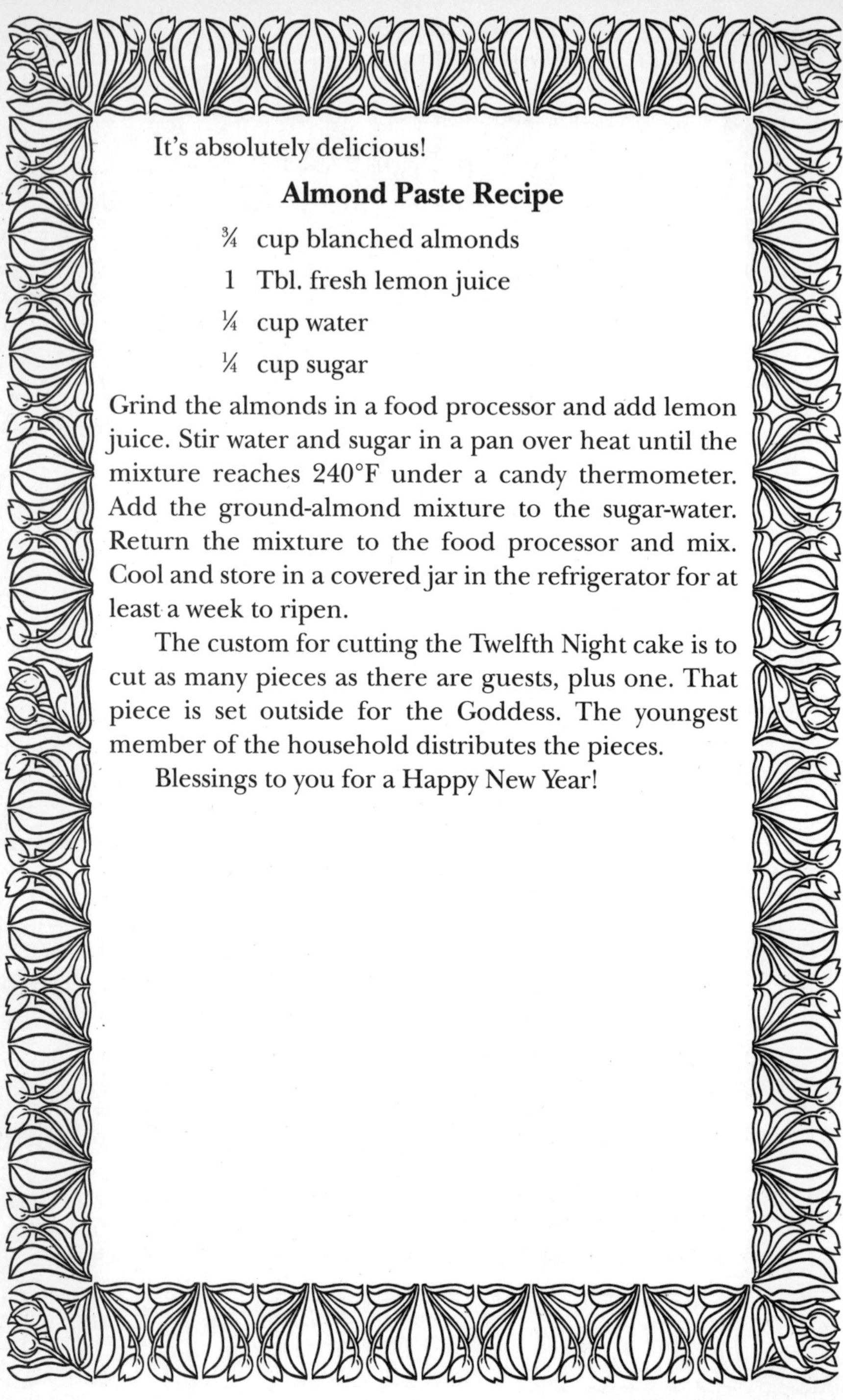

It's absolutely delicious!

Almond Paste Recipe

¾ cup blanched almonds

1 Tbl. fresh lemon juice

¼ cup water

¼ cup sugar

Grind the almonds in a food processor and add lemon juice. Stir water and sugar in a pan over heat until the mixture reaches 240°F under a candy thermometer. Add the ground-almond mixture to the sugar-water. Return the mixture to the food processor and mix. Cool and store in a covered jar in the refrigerator for at least a week to ripen.

The custom for cutting the Twelfth Night cake is to cut as many pieces as there are guests, plus one. That piece is set outside for the Goddess. The youngest member of the household distributes the pieces.

Blessings to you for a Happy New Year!

Activating Your Psychic Awareness

by Karen Follett

Psychic ability has a long history. Much of this history engulfed in mysticism and secrecy. Palmists, mediums, crystal gazers, and those who read divinatory tools have been involved in this history since its origins. Still, while psychic ability is a part of society, it is often viewed, unfortunately, as separate from the mainstream, and this dictates a "those who can" versus "those who cannot" mentality, regarding accessing the knowledge that exists beyond our tangible world.

The Truth about Psychic Ability

While the concept of the "extraordinary" and "unique" ability regarding the psychic realm is a fabulous marketing strategy, it is inaccurate to think that only a "special few" people have the ability to perceive psychic information. The ability to see, hear, feel, and know the psychic realm is extraordinary, unique, and special.

But this ability is no more extraordinary than the ability of every living creature on this planet to perceive the world around us.

Psychic ability, which is also known as precognition, clairvoyance, and intuition, was gifted to our ancient ancestors by the divine creators. The ancient's wisdom regarding the perception of the oneness that exists between themselves, their universe, and the divine opened their psychic awareness. The ancient's day-to-day incorporation of spiritual beliefs into mundane existence furthered their psychic skills and perceptions.

Since that time, eons of "evolution" have brought us into the "civilized" world of today. Our encapsulated existence in cities, suburbs, and housing tracts has caused us to separate ourselves from nature. The grind of work, social and personal responsibilities, and daily modern living all too often tend to leave us with little time to attune to the universe and it's creators. As a result of this "evolution," we have become more accustomed to using our analytical skills and less accustomed to tuning into our psychic skills.

Regardless of this conditioning, psychic ability remains a part of our genetic code. While some people seem to be more naturally plugged into the psychic circuit, it is important to know that the wiring is present in all of us. It just may need reconnecting.

Rewriting Yourself for the Psychic Realm

The fact that you possess a (perhaps latent) psychic ability is the first step in developing your psychic potential. The next step is to ask the universe to help you reconnect your psychic circuits.

Since we exist in a tangible, visual world, it is helpful to state to the universe an action that will initiate your "psychic circuitry." This action could be the visualization of flipping on a switch or turning a dial. Or it could be an actual physical act such as anointing or touching your third eye.

The creation of such a switch connects the physical world and our basic selves to the spiritual world and our higher selves. The "switch" also helps in turning off or toning down the psychic circuit when you are in situations of psychic overload. Two tools that are essential to aid in your reconnection to the universal "oneness" of our ancestors are guided imagery and meditation.

Guided imagery is communicating to the universe. By imaging a mind's eye scene with focused intent, you communicate your desires to the universe. Utilize guided imagery to state your intent and create the environment that will be conducive to the second tool of meditation.

While guided imagery is communicating to the universe; meditation is listening to the universe. Relax your body and open your quiet mind. "Listen" to the universe and the messages that are being sent. Open the "message centers" of seeing, hearing, feeling, and knowing.

Psychic communication can come in a variety of forms. You may see images or symbols. You may hear words or sounds; you may feel emotional or physical sensations. Or you may have a "gut" feeling that just informs you of something.

Particularly in the early stages of reconnection, some of this communication may seem confusing or insignificant. Don't worry about interpretations at this point, just accept the perceptions as they are given. As mentioned before, the guided imagery and meditation act to reunite you to the universal oneness.

Once you feel comfortable with your reestablished relationship with the universe, you will be able to ask for and receive symbolic interpretations of this information. You will also notice that you can set your psychic circuit to the "comfortably on" mode, and receive perceptions without constant use of formal guided imagery and meditation.

Psychic Journaling

Please note that I intentionally used the words of "constant" and "formal" in the previous statement. Regardless of how tuned in you become to your psychic ability, there will be times when guided imagery and meditation are priceless.

The next step in the psychic reconnection process is to begin a "psychic development journal." Your initial use of the journal will be to document any perceptions that you received during the meditation session. To begin your journal, keep your "psychic circuit" connected and record what you visualized, heard, felt, and suddenly knew. Again, don't analyze, but ask the universe if there are any interpretations that it would like to send to you at this time.

After you have completed your journal entry, thank the universe for your reconnection and close your psychic circuits. As tedious as it may sound, writing in your journal will prove to be an invaluable tool, regardless of how adept you become in your psychic development. The act of writing tends to occupy the analytical brain and leave the the perceptive brain open to receiving messages.

In the end, your journal will provide tangible proof of your progress in psychic development. You will also be able to refine your perceptive abilities by documenting perceptions and outcomes.

Reality, both tangible and psychic, is a matter of personal perception. The psychic messages sent from the universe are pure. We are human. As humans we have the innate ability to take a pure perception and alter the interpretation to meet our own perceptions of reality (or desired reality). By documenting perceptions and sensations noticed with your senses, you will be able to discern a true psychic interpretation.

Keep in mind that psychic hits and misses are just a part of life. I once read that even the psychic cream of the crop experiences only about 80 percent accuracy. More often than not, this 80 percent reflects the most important element of the universal reconnection process. Meaning, that since psychic perceptions reflect a static situation in a universe that is ever flowing and changing, there is no absolute accuracy in perception. Any action or inaction can set the flow to alter outcome.

Psychic ability is an ever-changing gift from an ever-changing universe. The assimilation of this concept is the last step in psychic development. Reconnecting your "oneness" to the universe and the acceptance of her psychic gifts will ensure that you will flow as she flows, you will grow as she grows, and you will respect her laws of karma and balance in the use of her gifts.

A Ritual for Planetary Healing

by Maria Kay Simms

The sabbats are ideal times to do rites of planetary healing, as these are when the Sun resides on the cardinal axes of the Earth, synergizing the energy necessary to life. This ritual of healing is especially effective at any or all of the sabbats.

Below are exact times for 2004 sabbats in the Eastern time zone (EST is Eastern Standard Time; EDT is Daylight Saving Time). *Note:* These times are based on actual planetary locations and may not coincide with more generally accepted dates for sabbat holidays.

Winter Solstice/Yule: December 21, 2003; 2:05 am EST.
Imbolc: February 5, 2004, 6:45 am EST.
Spring Equinox/Ostara: March 20, 2004, 1:50 am EST.
Beltane: May 4, 2004, 11:50 pm EDT.
Summer Solstice/Litha: June 20, 2004, 8:58 pm EDT.
Lammas: August 7, 2004, 12:08 am EDT.
Fall Equinox/Mabon: September 22, 2004, 12:31 pm EDT.
Samhain: November 6, 2004, 8:47 pm EST.

With only minor adaptations, this ritual will work for solitary use or in groups. Work outdoors, or indoors with appropriate caution in using candles.

Place candles on your altar at the four directions, and add two altar candles; one silver or green for Goddess, the other gold or yellow for God. On or near altar place a fan or large feather, a red candle, a spray bottle of water, a container of soil, a container of salt, a censer, and luminaries (tea candles in small paper cups). Gather sound-makers for each element: tinkling bells for air, loud a rattle for fire, a rainstick for water, a drum for earth. Use multiples of twelve for the tea candles—one for each person involved.

Cast the circle according to your tradition, and speak as follows.

At this time of turning of the great wheel of the year, be reminded of the eternal circle of life. The seeds of life germinate within, sprout, grow stronger, bud, flower, fruit, ripen and fall. And so is the eternity of nature. Everything is born again in a new form, at a new time. Abundant is our Great Mother the Earth, warmed and energized by Father Sun. But we are not appreciative. Our Mother's life-sustaining environment is polluted and ravished. Her people fail to see that we are all her children and should work together for the good of all. I charge that this sabbat rite be a magical act of healing. O Great Mother Earth and Father Sun, bless and consecrate this circle. Let the Spirit flow within. (Light the Goddess and God candles.) *As it is willed, so mote it be!*

It is my (our) will and intent within this magical rite to heal and protect the Earth, and to send energy of peace to all Earth's children, knowing full well this must begin within.

Power of air, our Mother's breath, blow from the east and bring clarity. Bless this space and bless this rite; I (we) greet thee, blessed be! (Wave the fan and ring bells once, in a sunwise direction around the circle.)

Power of fire, our Mother's passion, flame from the south with spirit free. Bless this space and bless this rite; I (we) greet thee, blessed be! (Carry the red candle and shake the rattle once, in a sunwise direction around the circle.)

Power of water, our Mother's womb, flow from the west in dark mystery. Bless this space and bless this rite. I (we) greet thee, blessed be! (Spray water mist and turn the rainstick once, moving in a sunwise direction around the circle.)

Power of earth, our Mother's body, sound from the north, evoking stability. Bless this space and bless this rite. I (we) greet thee, blessed be! Behold the earth (sift soil through your fingers), *and behold the heartbeat of the Mother* (walk once sunwise around the circle while beating a steady heartbeat on the drum).

Pass the elemental symbols sunwise as each person speaks the following promises.

Direct my mind, O power of air, in ways to keep you clean and free. I pledge to heal and serve you. This is my will, so mote it be!

Rouse my courage, power of fire. Charge my spirit energy; with passion will I heal and serve. This is my will, so mote it be!

Charge my insight, power of water—in ways to keep you clean and free. I pledge to heal and serve you. This is my will, so mote it be!

Charge my strength, O power of earth, to help and heal, to grow and see how best to serve our Mother. This is my will, so mote it be!

Now, chant the final words below as you light the tea candle luminaries and place them in a circle around you. Sing an appropriate song, or play meditative music as you form the circle of light. Meditate within for a time. Groups may wish to share experiences afterward.

We create a spirit of peace with this circle of light,
Knowing full well in our hearts and souls
That peace begins with each of us.

May this magic ring of light
Send outward peaceful energy.
May it flow throughout the Earth,
Healing and unifying minds and hearts.

Peace to all Earth's children;
With light and love, so mote it be!

Before closing thank Mother Earth, Father Sun, and the Guardians of the Watchtowers for their presence and assistance in this rite.

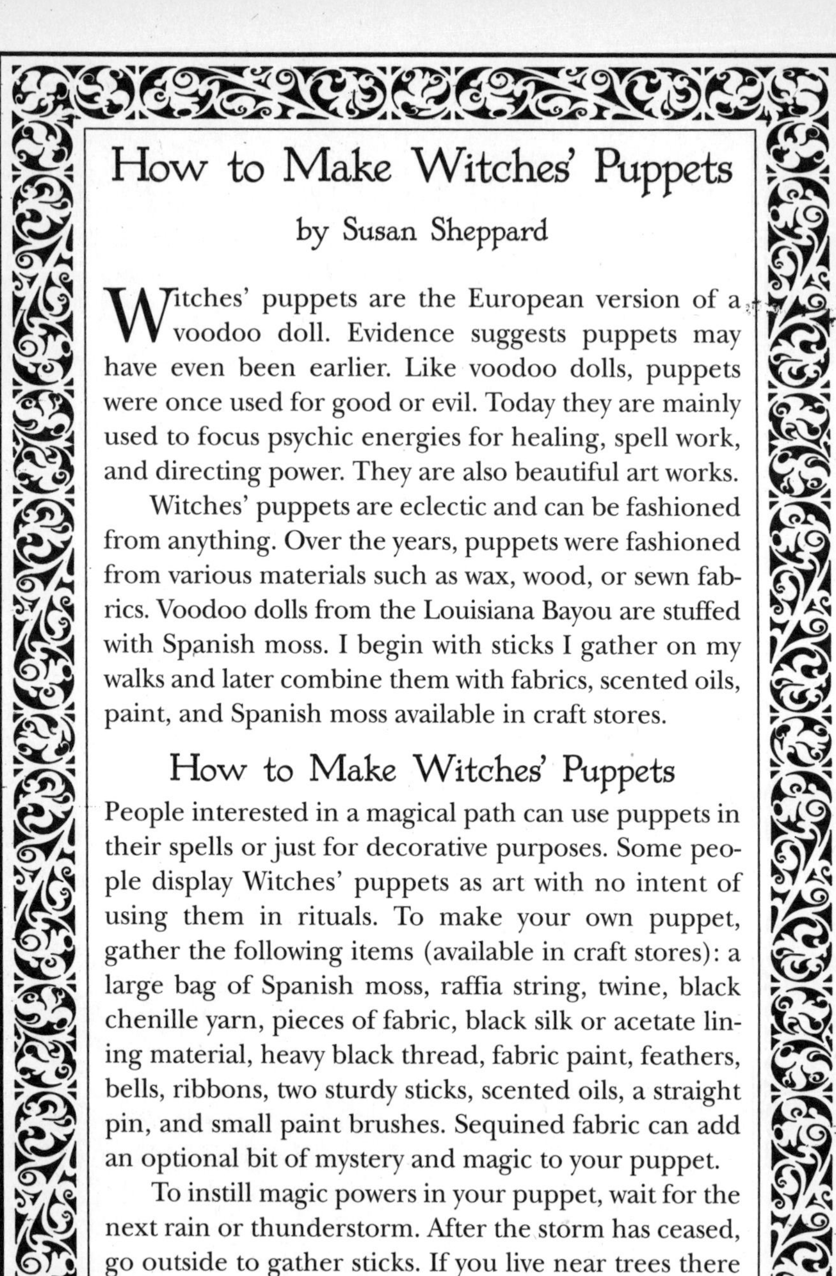

How to Make Witches' Puppets

by Susan Sheppard

Witches' puppets are the European version of a voodoo doll. Evidence suggests puppets may have even been earlier. Like voodoo dolls, puppets were once used for good or evil. Today they are mainly used to focus psychic energies for healing, spell work, and directing power. They are also beautiful art works.

Witches' puppets are eclectic and can be fashioned from anything. Over the years, puppets were fashioned from various materials such as wax, wood, or sewn fabrics. Voodoo dolls from the Louisiana Bayou are stuffed with Spanish moss. I begin with sticks I gather on my walks and later combine them with fabrics, scented oils, paint, and Spanish moss available in craft stores.

How to Make Witches' Puppets

People interested in a magical path can use puppets in their spells or just for decorative purposes. Some people display Witches' puppets as art with no intent of using them in rituals. To make your own puppet, gather the following items (available in craft stores): a large bag of Spanish moss, raffia string, twine, black chenille yarn, pieces of fabric, black silk or acetate lining material, heavy black thread, fabric paint, feathers, bells, ribbons, two sturdy sticks, scented oils, a straight pin, and small paint brushes. Sequined fabric can add an optional bit of mystery and magic to your puppet.

To instill magic powers in your puppet, wait for the next rain or thunderstorm. After the storm has ceased, go outside to gather sticks. If you live near trees there should be numerous branches left in the grass.

Locate the straightest sticks that you can find. Pick up several. Break your sticks evenly. The first stick should measure about a foot. The next one should be around seven inches long.

Take all of your materials inside or to your work area. With a piece of twine, tie the two sticks together to form a cross. Tie them tightly. Make certain your sticks are sturdy and don't wobble. Once they are secure, move on to the next step.

Take moss from the bag. Pull out a string two or three feet long. Wrap the moss around the top of the stick cross the way a food vendor wraps cotton candy on a stick. Go up and down the body. Wrap moss around the areas that will make the arms. Use the moss liberally as it shrinks over a period of time.

Tie raffia crisscross over the moss body of the doll, until your doll has the likeness to a person. Cut a four-by-seven-inch rectangle of fabric. Sew a "hood" on your doll. Leave the top open. Make certain this hood is tight around the head, pulling your thread tightly. Shape the head. Now imagine a face on your puppet. If the face area is bumpy, with your fingertips smooth out the surface as best you can.

Take a fine brush. It is time to add features to your doll. When you are painting your puppet's face, think of light on shadow. Lightly, map out your doll's features by drawing a straight line down the middle of the face, then three lines across to form the mouth, nose, and eyes. Choose your base color. Outline the doll's face as an oval. Starting with forehead and going down the nose, draw a T to create the forehead and the nose. Paint in cheekbones. Leave the eye sockets black. Add a chin with a daub of paint.

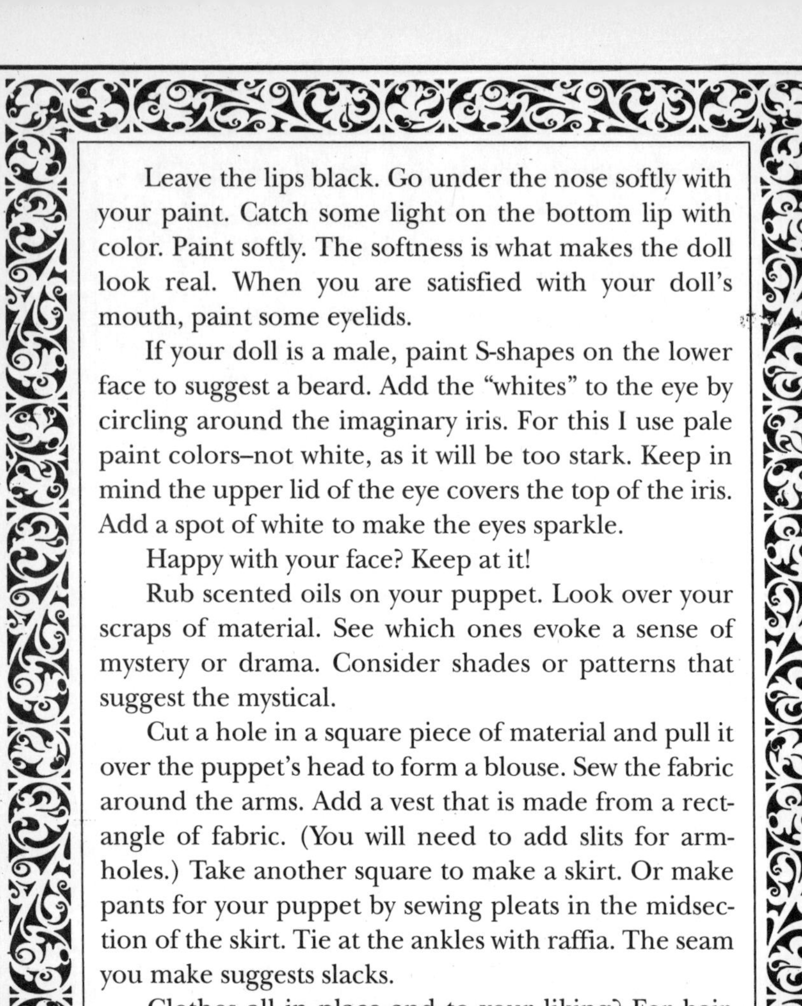

Leave the lips black. Go under the nose softly with your paint. Catch some light on the bottom lip with color. Paint softly. The softness is what makes the doll look real. When you are satisfied with your doll's mouth, paint some eyelids.

If your doll is a male, paint S-shapes on the lower face to suggest a beard. Add the "whites" to the eye by circling around the imaginary iris. For this I use pale paint colors–not white, as it will be too stark. Keep in mind the upper lid of the eye covers the top of the iris. Add a spot of white to make the eyes sparkle.

Happy with your face? Keep at it!

Rub scented oils on your puppet. Look over your scraps of material. See which ones evoke a sense of mystery or drama. Consider shades or patterns that suggest the mystical.

Cut a hole in a square piece of material and pull it over the puppet's head to form a blouse. Sew the fabric around the arms. Add a vest that is made from a rectangle of fabric. (You will need to add slits for armholes.) Take another square to make a skirt. Or make pants for your puppet by sewing pleats in the midsection of the skirt. Tie at the ankles with raffia. The seam you make suggests slacks.

Clothes all in place and to your liking? For hair, take some yarn (chenille looks great, but any yarn is fine), and wrap it around the extended fingers of your opposite hand three or four times. With a piece of yarn, tie the other pieces of yarn together. Cut one end of the yarn. Keep doing this until you have eight or nine bunches of yarn for your puppet's hair. With needle and thread, sew bunches of yarn to the doll's head. Start at the back and work your way around. This should take six pieces or so. Sew extra pieces under

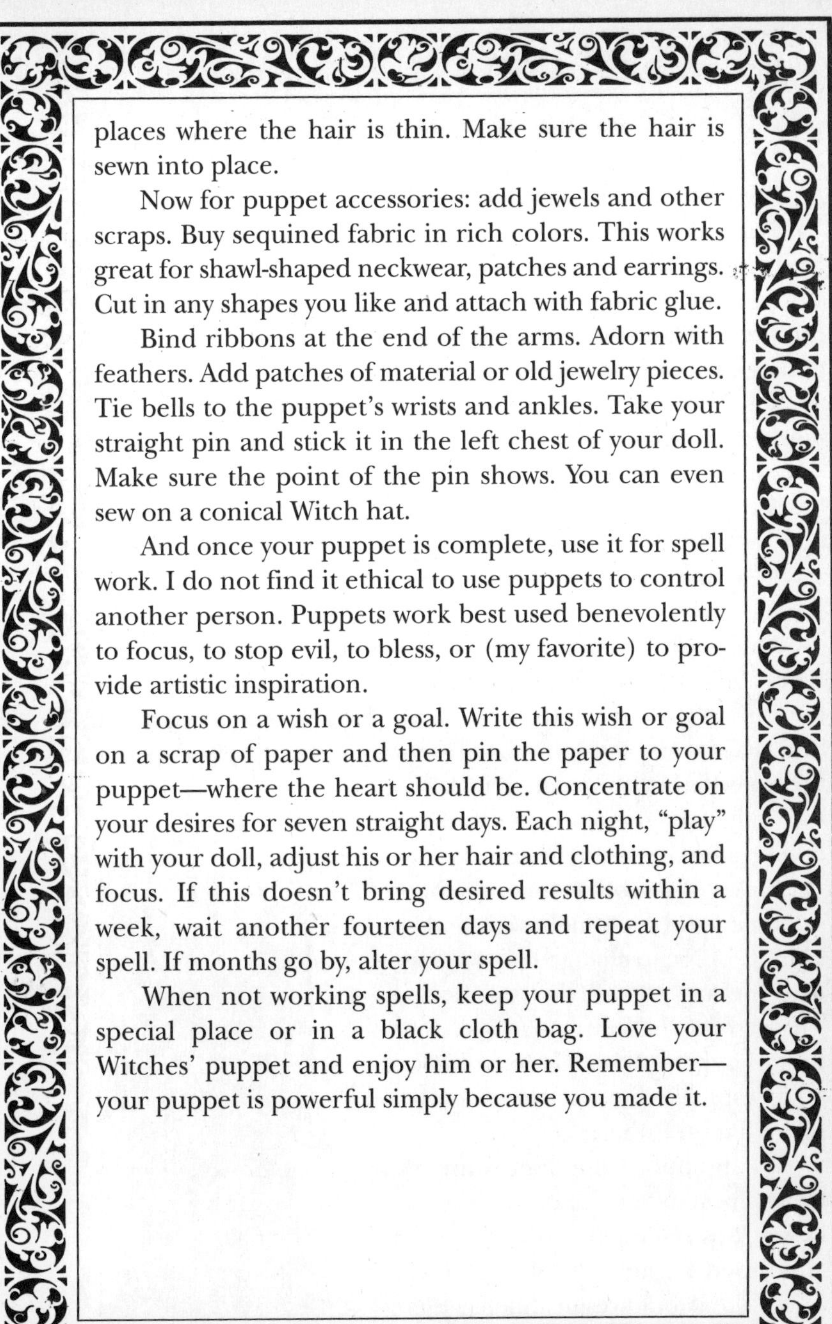

places where the hair is thin. Make sure the hair is sewn into place.

Now for puppet accessories: add jewels and other scraps. Buy sequined fabric in rich colors. This works great for shawl-shaped neckwear, patches and earrings. Cut in any shapes you like and attach with fabric glue.

Bind ribbons at the end of the arms. Adorn with feathers. Add patches of material or old jewelry pieces. Tie bells to the puppet's wrists and ankles. Take your straight pin and stick it in the left chest of your doll. Make sure the point of the pin shows. You can even sew on a conical Witch hat.

And once your puppet is complete, use it for spell work. I do not find it ethical to use puppets to control another person. Puppets work best used benevolently to focus, to stop evil, to bless, or (my favorite) to provide artistic inspiration.

Focus on a wish or a goal. Write this wish or goal on a scrap of paper and then pin the paper to your puppet—where the heart should be. Concentrate on your desires for seven straight days. Each night, "play" with your doll, adjust his or her hair and clothing, and focus. If this doesn't bring desired results within a week, wait another fourteen days and repeat your spell. If months go by, alter your spell.

When not working spells, keep your puppet in a special place or in a black cloth bag. Love your Witches' puppet and enjoy him or her. Remember—your puppet is powerful simply because you made it.

The Ghosts of Key West

by Sheri Richerson

What is it about an old town with a history of pirates and rum-runners that makes it a perfect place for spirits to dwell? The Florida Keys, especially Key West, have long been a favorite stopping place for the young and old alike as well as a hideaway for the famous and not so famous. Some of these visitors are ghosts, or so the stories go.

Key West has long been known as a place that attracts fishermen, pirates, and artists who work in a wide range of fields. Throughout the years, many of these local ghost stories have been captured and written down so that future generations can continue to research and possibly even see the ghosts for themselves. Other stories are kept hush-hush and known only among the natives.

One such ghost story revolves around a house located on Eaton Street in Key West. As rumor has it, Robert "Gene" Otto grew up in this house. In 1904 when Robert was four years old, a doll that resembled him was presented as a gift. Whether it was his grandfather or a native girl from the Bahamas girl who gave him the doll remains a mystery to this day.

Since the doll came to Robert unnamed and yet somehow resembled him, he chose to change his own name to Gene and to call the doll Robert. Throughout his life whenever something happened that Gene needed to take responsibility for, he always had blamed it on Robert.

As an adult, Gene met Anne and they were married. Upon their arrival in Key West, Gene took his bride to his childhood home and told her this is where they would reside. Shortly thereafter, Gene began work on an attic room that was built specifically for Robert. He even had miniature furniture constructed for the doll's comfort.

Through the years that the Ottos resided in the house, many of the neighborhood children claim they saw Robert move. Upon the death of Gene, Anne left the homestead. When Anne died in 1976, the house was sold. From this point on, workers in the home as well as guests claim that they have seen the doll move and heard noise from the attic room.

Although Robert has since been moved to Von Philster Street for safekeeping in a museum, it is said that Robert's influence can still be heard in the house. It has also been rumored that Anne Otto returns to the house to protect the inhabitants. Her ghost has been seen in various locations including the famous attic room that was built for Robert.

While many of the ghost stories circulating around Key West are so strange that you will need to take a ghost tour to understand, there is another one about the Colours Guest House that I think is worth sharing.

Enriquetta Marrero was married to a man who sold cigars. Their home was located in the middle of the Key West business district. Her husband, Francisco, had left for a trip to Cuba to purchase supplies for his business.

While he was gone, Enriquetta heard a loud rap on the door. She asked one of her eight children to answer the door since she knew Francisco was still not due back from the trip. By the time she heard the second set of raps, she knew she would have to answer the door herself. Upon coming down the steps she noticed the chandelier shaking. When she answered the door, she was informed that her husband had died of unknown causes.

During the next six months, the situation worsened for Enriquetta and her children. Francisco had never mentioned that he was previously married, and that he had never divorced. Once rumor of Francisco's death circulated, his first wife appeared in Key West.

A bitter court battle ensued with the outcome being that the first wife, Maria Ignacia Garcia de Marrero, was awarded the title of estate administrator. Enriquetta lost not only her home, but the cigar business as well.

The day she was forced from her home—June 16, 1891—she stood outside on the steps and told the crowd that was surrounding the home that they were witnessing a great injustice. She also said that with God as her witness she would always remain in the home in spirit.

In the following years all of her family's lives were taken either from diphtheria or consumption. However, Enriquetta has kept her word and according to many her spirit does remain in the home.

When a guest arrives that she does not approve of, the chandelier begins to shake just as it did on that fateful day so many years ago.

The owners claim that wakes them up regularly. And guests claim that they have seen her in their room, smelled strange perfume, and even seen an employee pushed into the pool by an unseen person.

Other well-known places in Key West have great stories of hauntings as well. These places include the Hard Rock Café, the

Audubon House and Gardens, Fort Zachary Taylor, the Hemingway House, and (believe it or not) the Ripley's Believe It or Not Odditorium.

Are these ghost stories real? For the most accurate information, the Key West Library has a file that is three-and-a-half inches thick with newspaper clippings and other documentation that the curious can look at.

However, if you are really intrigued by these stories and would like to hear more or simply see for yourself, David Sloan runs the Original Key West Ghost Tours. Not only is his staff full of great stories but you can book a spot on his tours to go to these places and judge for yourself. After all, seeing is believing.

The Ancient Irish Year Wheel

by Sharynne NicMhacha

Years ago, I began my exploration of the Celtic tradition to honor my Scottish grandmother, a vibrant and spirited woman who was extremely proud of her heritage. My journey led me into the realm of folklore and magic, and eventually into the world of Celtic Paganism and earth religion. As my quest delved further into the traditions of my Scottish and Irish ancestors, my experiences deepened and a whole new world of spiritual connection opened up. The Celtic gods have become part of daily life, and my seasonal rituals have evolved to focus on the ways of the ancestors.

A question I ask myself now is: What did the holidays mean to the Pagan Celts? Early Greek and Roman writers describe the society and customs of ancient Gaul. Information about seasonal activities of early Ireland was recorded by monks, scribes, and historians. In addition, we have evidence from archeology and a large body of folklore from Ireland, Scotland, Wales, Cornwall, Brittany, and the Isle of Man. Below is a guide to the earliest meaning of the holidays based on my research (as well as animals that were likely venerated at these sacred points of the year wheel).

Samhain (the Boar or Raven): In Ireland (as well as Gaul), the year was divided into two main seasons—the warm and the cold, called *sam* and *gam.* In Ireland, at least, the year was further divided, creating four festivals that marked the turning points of the year. The greatest festival was Samhain (pronounced SAH–ven in Old Irish), held on the first of November. This was the Celtic New Year, which marked the end of one year and the beginning of the next. The night before Samhain was the most important point of this festival and may have been considered an independent point in time that belonged neither to the old year or the new.

Because of this quality, the gateways between this world and the Otherworld were easily crossed and communications and interactions between the worlds could took place. Gods and magical figures emerged from caves and *síd-mounds,* and many significant or supernatural events occurred. It was a time of danger, as well as a time of potential. Just as the Celtic day began at night, the New Year also began in darkness (similar to the dark period before the New Moon). This was a spiritual or cosmic darkness from which life would eventually emerge. Thus, Samhain was associated with life as well as death.

In order to ensure the success of the tribe in the coming year, religious ceremonies focused on the renewal of prosperity. The deities, ancestors, and the spirits of the land were honored in ritual. As well, offerings would have been made to the gods, and a recitation or enactment of the tribe's religious beliefs pertaining to creation (common in New Year's rites around the world) would have also taken place. Samhain rituals may also have commemorated the union of the tribal deity with the earth goddess of the local territory.

One example of this is the union between the Dagda and the Mórrigan at Samhain. According to this belief, Dagda stands with one foot on either side of a river (symbolizing a place and point that is "neither this nor that"). This kind of divine union was very important in Celtic religion and was reflected in the rites of the mortal realm. Within the tribe or territory, it was important that the king unite with the goddess of the land in order for his reign to be successful. Without her blessing and aid, the people, crops, and herds would not prosper.

The feast days of the early Celts focused on herding practices rather than agriculture and farming. While the Druids or other wisdom-keepers would have maintained records of various astrological events, there is no evidence that they celebrated holidays such as the solstices and equinoxes. Samhain was the end of the grazing season, when the herds and flocks were brought back to the village after enjoying rich summer pasture. Only those animals necessary for breeding were kept throughout the winter. The others provided meat and hides to sustain the people during the cold season.This is an ancient practice which dates back to the Neolithic era. It was a custom of necessity and also helped provide a great feast for this most sacred time of the year.

Samhain also coincides with the breeding season of the wild boar. Animals were not hunted during their breeding period.

Therefore, a sacred boar hunt would have taken place prior to Samhain in preparation for the great festival. Numerous myths and stories tell of the adventures associated with hunting the wild boar at this time of year. In addition, it was customary that all crops be harvested or gathered, and stored before the holiday. We can see that the customs and traditions associated with the feast of Samhain were both practical and spiritual in nature, in tune with both the seasons and the land and in harmony with the cycles of the natural world.

Beltane (Cow): The most important holiday after Samhain was the first of May, the beginning of the warm season. This was known as Beltane (pronounced BEL-tih-nuh) or *Cétshamain* (KAYT-hah-vin). Cétshamain means "the beginning of summer." Beltane means either '"bright fire" (from the Indo-European word *bhel,* "to shine, flash or burn") or "the fire of Bel." Bel is not the same as Baal, of course, but we don't know much else about this figure. He may be similar to a widely worshiped Celtic deity called Belenus who was venerated from northern Italy to the British Isles. Belenus was often associated with healing waters, and sometimes likened to Apollo (who had an aspect as a healer and a Sun god).

Beltane was also associated with herding practices. As the weather improved, animals could be led out to summer pasture. Great fires were lit and the cattle were driven between them to protect them from disease and misfortune. The lighting of fires at this time of year continued well into the Christian era. The coming of warm weather was heralded by the appearance of singing birds, blooming flowers, and the greening of the land—elements that contributed to a joyful celebration of life and fertility. However, in ancient times, Beltane was also a period of great uncertainty. People did not yet know if their crops or animals would survive, so rituals of propitiation and protection were extremely important.

Beltane marked the beginning of hunting season, which lasted until Samhain (although the period from July to September was peak hunting season). It was the end of the traditional marriage season, and an unlucky day to marry. Temporary or trial marriages could end on this day. In modern folk tradition, May is still considered an unlucky month to marry (hence the popularity of the June wedding).

Imbolc (Sheep): This festival took place on the first of February and was, once again, associated with animals. Imbolc is when the sheep gave birth and started to produce milk. During the winter, any remaining stores of dairy (in the form of cheese) would have given out. When the sheep began to give fresh milk again it was a time of joy and plenty.

Imbolc was associated with the goddess Bríg (pronounced BREEGH) who may be similar to the British goddess Brigantia. She was said to have two sisters also named Brighid, and was a triple goddess of healing, smithcraft, and poetry. In Christian times, the holiday became associated with St. Bridget. Through her connection with the birth of young, she became a protectress of women in the childbed. There seems to be a focus on feminine energy at this point in the year wheel (in the focus on birth, the renewal of milk, and so on). It may also have been associated with rituals of purification. Imbolc is the Celtic holiday about which we have the least information (perhaps due to its association with women's concerns, and the fact that it is commemorated in the home and during the winter).

Lugnasad or Lammas (Horse or Stag): This feast day may have been the last holiday to be introduced into the Irish seasonal calendar. While the other holidays focus on herding (the primary method of sustenance for the Celts and other European peoples), this festival is associated with the harvest. This may be reflected in the traditional stories of the god Lugh (who is connected with this holiday). In these myths he is portrayed as a newcomer to the Irish pantheon, a young multiskilled god who obtains knowledge of agriculture from Bres, the husband of Bríg. Lugh instituted this feast day to honor his beloved foster-mother Tailtiu, who died as the result of clearing many great plains (probably in preparation for planting). The name of the holiday means the festival or funeral games *(nasad)* of the god Lugh.

In addition to Tailtiu, other divine ancestresses or goddesses were also associated with Lammas in different parts of Ireland. The Festival of Carmun was celebrated in Leinster, while the goddess Macha was honored in the north (Ulster). Goddesses of the land and of sovereignty, such as Macha, were often associated with horses. Horses continue to play a prominent role in later Lammas folklore and folk celebrations. Shortly after taking my magical name (NicMhacha, "daughter of Macha"), I discovered that Macha was associated with this holiday, which is also my birthday. I also found out years later that my Irish ancestors were from the north of Ireland.

July was considered a time of great scarcity, as the crops were not yet ripe. In order to ensure the success of the harvest, harvest ceremonies took place and the gods of the land and the harvest were honored and propitiated. After the rites of Lammas, farmers began to reap their grain (wheat, spelt, and barley) during the months of August and September. The importance of this festival continued well into Christian times. The name Lammas comes from the Anglo-Saxon *hlafmass,* which means "loaf-mass."

Lammas fairs are still held in Ireland, Scotland, and other areas where the Celts once lived. Trial marriages known as Tell-town marriages (from the name of Lugh's fostermother Tailtiu) sometimes take place at the fairs. This custom continued well into the twentieth century.

For Further Study

McNeill, Florence Marian. *The Silver Bough: A Study of the National and Local Festivals of Scotland.* Glasgow: W. Maclellan, 1957.

Patterson, Nerys Thomas. *Cattle-lords and Clansmen: Kinship and Rank in Early Ireland.* New York: Garland Pub., 1991.

Powell, Thomas George Eyre. *The Celts.* New York: Thames and Hudson, 1980.

Articles for Spring

The Magical Properties of Wood

by Magenta Griffith

There are many books and articles on the various magical properties of herbs and other plants, but there are few on the magical uses of trees and their woods. Here are some odds and ends of tree lore that might prove useful to you.

Wood Lore

The **alder** is considered a tree of the element fire. From the alder, you can make three different dyes—red from its bark, green from its flowers, and brown from its twigs. This symbolizes the elements of fire, water, and earth. The alder is sometimes called the wood of the Witches. It is said that whistles made of this wood can summon and control the four winds, so it is an excellent wood for making magical pipes and flutes.

Apple trees are magical because of all the associations of its fruit. The wood not especially magical, though it is very useful for burning, producing sweet-smelling fires. The apple harvest comes around Lammas on August 1, so the apple is associated with that holiday. If you cut an apple in half cross-wise, the seeds form a pentagram, and so the fruit is considered a token of Witches.

The **ash,** in Norse myth, is the most important tree, as Yggdrasil, the Tree of Life from which all the worlds spring, is a giant ash. Yggdrasil is the bridge between the worlds that the gods, and some chosen mortals, may traverse. Beneath Yggdrasil, the three Norns dispense judgment over gods and men. A dragon lives in the roots of the World Ash and an eagle in its branches. Odin hung nine days on Yggdrasil to gain wisdom, in the form of a drink from a spring at the foot of the tree. Ash is still considered a tree of wisdom in parts of Europe, and therefore ash branches are used for dowsing, especially to find lost objects.

Birch is a tree of beginnings, partly because it is often the first tree to have new leaves in the spring. Since it is quick growing, it is usually one of the first trees to grow in a new forest, or to return after a fire. Therefore, a birch forest is young, and birch is linked to youth and all things new. The birch is used in cleansing rituals. In Europe, birch twigs are used to expel evil spirits and to drive out the spirits of the old year.

Cedar is an evergreen like juniper, to which it is related. Therefore, it is symbolic of the promise of eternal renewal. Cedar of Lebanon was the wood from which the great Jewish Temple of Solomon was built. Associations with Solomon are, of course, magical, since he is known for his powers of magic and an ability to bind spirits to his service. Cedar is a wood of protection and preservation; it is also called arbor vitae, or "tree of life." Cedar oil is an insect repellent; this is why cedar chests keep out moths. Cedar is especially powerful for banishing an area prior to magical work.

Elder, in Norse mythology, was the abode of the goddess Freya. In medieval times, people thought Witches lived in elder trees, and therefore it was considered dangerous to sleep under an elder or to cut it down. Also, Witches were thought to ride on elder branches to the Sabbat. Elder is said to symbolize the end in the beginning and the beginning in the end—life in death and death in life.

Hawthorn can be used for protection, love, and marriage spells. It is associated with Beltane, May Eve. Songs tell of going out to gather branches of the "May Tree," the hawthorn, to bring back to the village as tokens of spring. The Greeks and Romans saw the hawthorn as a symbol of marriage, but in medieval Europe it was associated with witchcraft and considered to be unlucky. It is a tree of contradictions, with beautiful, strongly scented flowers, but dangerous thorns. The wood burns with a fierce heat, but the tree is small, almost a shrub.

Hazel is a tree of wisdom. In England, eating hazel nuts was supposed to bring knowledge. A forked branch of hazel is the most popular form of divining or dowsing rod. In medieval Europe, such a branch was sometimes used to determine the guilt of people accused of murder. More recently, hazel has been used to locate treasure, valuable metallic ores such as silver or gold, and to find water. Water dowsing is still practiced in parts of the United States.

Holly is the tree of winter. It is associated with the death and rebirth symbolism of winter. The word *holly* is derived from "holy." The Holly

King defeats the Oak King at Lammas, and thus reigns until Winter Solstice. The rune most associated with the holly is *tyr,* which means spear; holly was traditionally used for spear shafts by the ancient Celts. Therefore, this tree is considered male by nature, and associated with the phallic spear. Holly is a fine-grained, very pale wood, and is considered excellent for wands.

Juniper berries are the primary flavoring in gin, which derives its name from the Dutch word for juniper. It is a short, evergreen shrub, and the berries are actually used for a variety of culinary and medicinal purposes. The wood is used for furniture. Because its wood contains oil that deters moths, it is often used to line chests.

Oak is the tree of Zeus, Jupiter, Thor, and other thunder gods. The Oak King defeats the Holly King at Yule, and thus rules over the light half of the year. The Midsummer fire is always oak, and the "need fire" is always kindled in an oak log. It is an excellent wood for wands and other tools, especially if endurance and wisdom are desired. Oak is associated with kingship and wise rule, personal sovereignty, authority, power, and protection. The oak is the tree of endurance and triumph, and like the ash, is said to withstand lightning. Oak is a male wood, which is ideal for the construction of any tool that needs the male influence (athames, wands, staffs). Oak traditionally provided not only one of the most durable woods for construction and fuel, but also acorns for winter pig-feed.

Pine, an evergreen, is a symbol of life and immortality. It is one of the few trees that is considered androgynous. It was worshiped by the ancients as a symbol of fire because of its resemblance to a spiral of flame. The resin from the pine tree can be used as incense to clear negative energies, and pine is regarded these days as a very soothing tree. The wand of Bacchus was tipped with a pine cone; this sort of wand is thought to bring fertility and sexual vigor. Pine branches placed at doors and windows are thought to keep out evil.

Rowan is also called the mountain ash. The rowan's flowers and bright-orange berries display a pentagram, the symbol of the five elements. The berries, because they are often retained through winter, symbolize the endurance of life through the dark of the year. Also called witchen or witchbane, rowan has been considered the enemy of all evil Witchery, and protects against one's being carried off to the fairy realm against one's will. Rowan traditionally is said to avert storms and lightning, and to bring peace and astral vision. The fondness of songbirds for rowan berries gives the tree a link to the bards, and to the goddess Brigid in her role as muse of poets.

Willow is sacred to the Moon, and to Diana and the feminine principle in general. It is also associated with Beltane. Willow is the foremost tree of the element of water, and is especially suited to works of the New Moon. It is a tree of renewal of fertility and creativity, of spells of glamour and bewitchment, and of sexual passion and relationship. Because of its association with water, willow is sometimes used for water dowsing.

Yew is associated with death and graveyards in most of Europe, and it is sacred to Hecate. As such, this evergreen governs travel between the worlds. It is associated with spells of illusion, astral travel, necromancy, and the conjuring of spirits. Most parts of this tree are poisonous. While it is good for bows, yew should never be used for magical tools.

Combining woods can produce interesting results. Dion Fortune, in her book *The Sea Priestess* (Samuel Weiser, 1981), describes what she calls the Fire of Azrael. Composed of cedar, juniper, and sandalwood, this is a fire for scrying that is supposed to produce true visions.

Robert Graves' masterwork *The White Goddess: A Historical Grammar of Poetic Myth* (Carcanet, 1997) is an excellent source of information on tree lore as well as Celtic folklore in general; I strongly recommend it for further reading.

Fertility Deities of the Near East

by Laurel Reufner

Let us step back in time, to the Near and Middle East and the beginnings of civilization. The *en-priestess* slowly climbs the pyramidal ziggurat steps, up to the temple atop it. Once there, she makes the appropriate ministrations to her goddess, and looks out over the Sumerian city below. Women waiting anxiously below have given offerings of gold and votives, which are placed near the altar. As the priestess returns to the bottom of the ziggurat, the women slowly turn toward home to await the goddess' answer and the stirring of new life within their bodies.

There is no way around the fact that early civilized life was hard work. Mainly barren desert, the harsh, serene beauty of the Near Eastern region did offer early humans some definite areas of fertile, watered ground to build on. But irrigation from underground springs was vital for crops to survive.

These springs ensured the survival of all lived nearby. And our forebears not only survived, but also thrived—carving out cities of beauty and creating cultures lush and colorful.

These people came to value their children even more, as it was through them that they passed along their family heritage and wealth. Woman's worth, while in opposition to our modern philosophies, was often measured in her ability to produce children—especially sons—for her husband's family. As a result, we have a rich legacy of beloved fertility deities who may be found

not only in the Near East and Fertile Crescent, but all the world over. Something as important as producing children could not be left to mere chance, but instead demanded the favor and protection of the gods themselves.

Inanna and Other Goddesses

Inanna, queen of heaven, ruled over fertility, love, and war in ancient Sumeria. She managed to get her way in just about any matter she was involved with. Inanna had a way with those around her, in spite of her occassionally wild, and always fickle, approach to life. Or maybe it is because of her approach to life that she was so well loved. She was definitely one to color outside the lines and get you to like it.

Once a year, in a sacred ceremony, the high priestess and the king of the city-state would consummate a sacred marriage between the queen of heaven and the city itself. This would help ensure her blessings and the fertility of the city for the coming year. Like most love goddesses, Inanna loves jewelry and rich clothing. A piece of lapis lazuli, or perhaps some jewelry fashioned from the gem, would be quite appropriate on an altar dedicated to her.

Like many powerful ancient goddesses, Inanna was widely worshiped under other names. As a different culture adopted her for themselves, they often changed her name to better reflect their language and culture. In Babylon, Inanna was known as Ishtar and possessed almost identical aspects to the Sumerian deity. In many cases, only the name was changed. Mylitta was yet another Babylonian/Assyrian goddess representing fertility, though not much is known of her.

Another of the earliest Near Eastern fertility deities was Anahita, a Persian and Babylonian goddess of flowing waters and human procreation. Many of the fertility gods and goddesses have a connection to water, as water is crucial to fertile fields (think of the yearly inundation of the Nile). Also known as the "Immaculate One," Anahita is often depicted as a virgin garbed in a golden cloak with a diamond crown atop her head. If you call upon Anahita, wear flowing garments, place a water pitcher upon your altar along with some green candles, and make offerings of gold, water, and peacock or dove feathers.

As often happens with beloved and responsive deities, worship of Anahita spread to many of the surrounding states. In Armenia, she became Anahit, the much-loved mother goddess of fertility. She was associated with a triad including Aramazd (father of the gods) and Vahagn (a war god.)

At some time, temple prostitution was introduced into the worship, so Anahita's worshippers participated in orgiastic rites probably intended to increase the overall fertility of the state. February 10 is a day sacred to Anahit, as is the silvery light of the waxing Moon.

Worship of this goddess also spread to Kemet, which would later become Egypt. Here, her warlike aspects would take precedence over her procreative assistance. Deities local to this region—including Heket, a frog-headed goddess who oversaw fertility and birth, and Muyt, and abstract figure personifying seeds and their fertility—already occupied the realm of fertility.

In Greece, Anahita, like Inanna, was associated with Aphrodite and possibly Athena. Some scholars argue that Aphrodite and Anahita are indeed the same goddess absorbed and renamed by the Greek people who discovered and fell in love with her. Others argue that her origins may be found in Inanna and Ishtar. Whatever the case, we can easily add Aphrodite to our list of fertility figures. Seeing Athena as a goddess of procreation may be a bit of a stretch, but she was appointed with overseeing the welfare of the Athens city-state, which would have included the fertility of its citizens. There is also her connection as a goddess of wisdom.

By now you're probably asking yourself what the differences are between the goddesses. It is the variations that make and keep life interesting. All of the diverse cultural shading keep us from getting too bored and offer us ever-new horizons to explore and understand. It's my belief that once a new culture noticed a goddess and claimed her, she was immediately transformed into a new being. While the aspects of the new goddess are similar to the one that inspired her, the new one still became her own distinct divinity.

As we have seen, in spite of their differences many fertility deities for the Near East share attributes. They are all associated with the planet Venus or the Moon and the day of Friday. Most of the goddesses prefer the color white or green. Jewelry is always popular with ancient Near Eastern goddesses, as are rich, often embroidered fabrics. For foodstuffs, think of things that pleasure the senses: figs, dates, pomegranates, and grains. These goddesses are all very sensual, so nearly anything that brings sensory pleasure is fair game in drawing their blessings to you and your home.

As a final note: There are many hymns, myths, and poems dedicated to and dealing with the queen of heaven. You should be able to find translations easily online, if they aren't available at your local library or bookstore.

For Further Study

Coulter, Charles Russell, and Patricia Turner. *The Encyclopedia of Ancient Deities.* Jefferson, N.C.: McFarland, 2000.

Online, check out *Encycolpedia Mythica* at http://www.pantheon.org/mythica.html.

The Once and Future Wand

by Sedwyn

For many years I had not used a wand in ritual, nor even given it a thought, until I was one day confronted by a mysterious visit. That is, one day while minding my own business, I happened to glance on a fallen tree branch and was struck with a vision. Suddenly, it was as if I were looking at one picture superimposed over another: a wand was inside the branch.

Knowing that it is important to be open to information received during magic work as well as everyday life, I didn't ignore the image that popped into my mind. Instead, I picked up the branch and continued my walk, getting a feel for the branch in my hand. There were no leaves attached to it and only a few tiny side twigs. When I returned home I wasn't quite sure what to do with it. I knew very little about wand making, but I had a feeling this branch would "tell" me what I needed to know.

Shaping Your Wand

When in doubt about your wand, you should always let your intuition guide you. My branch was longer than needed, but somehow it seemed just about the right length below where it curved. I vaguely recalled reading that the ideal length of a wand should measure from your elbow to the tip of your middle finger. Even though this wand would be a little shorter than the "prescribed" length, I thought it best to do what seemed right.

Putting a new sharp blade in my X-acto knife, I set to work. First I shortened the branch just below where it curved, and then trimmed the jagged bottom end. After removing the small side twigs, I carefully peeled off the bark to reveal the light, almost white, maple wood underneath. It was smooth and pleasant to the touch.

The branch had been thin to begin with and now without its bark it was indeed smaller. My idea of attaching a crystal point at the end was a fleeting thought. Instead, I carefully tapered the end of the branch into a point. This little wand was destined to direct energy on its own.

With fine-grade sandpaper I smoothed the areas I had whittled with the knife. I sanded down the remnants of the side twigs, but left enough of a bump to indicate where each had once grown. It seemed important to keep the wand as natural as possible and not strive for perfection. This process took several days, and at this point the bare wood seemed dry. To finish the wand and nourish the wood, I rubbed lemon oil over its entire surface, which gave it rich patina.

One thing I did know about wands—and magic tools in general—is that they must be consecrated in ritual before actual use. Since this was a small wand (that I had already taken to calling my Fairy Wand), it seemed appropriate to dedicate it to the goddess Danu on Litha.

Each of the four magical tools corresponds with a particular element, direction, and conceptual use. The wands represent fire, the south, and the will. It is our "will" that we use to direct energy and magic; will flows from us through a wand and then out into the world to manifest intention. Using my wand for the first time on Litha, a day that also corresponds with fire and the direction south, has made this a potent tool for me.

Different traditions vary in the assignment of element and direction, and several associate the wand with air and the east. The prescribed length of a wand also varies according to one's practice. Work with whatever fits your background.

To consecrate a wand you may want to use an oil that corresponds with the current season, sabbat, or purpose. Dip your finger into the oil, and then draw a rune or sacred symbol on the wand. Next, pass the wand through the smoke of sage or mugwort or carefully through the flame of a candle. While doing this, ask the Goddess and God to bless it.

Since acquiring my first wand, I have experimented with making and been presented with other wands. The willow tree outside my front door presented me with a straight, sturdy branch. This wand I use for dark Moon and Samhain rituals, as willow is associated with death and transformation. I experimented with a linden branch, and while the wood was easy to carve it has a tendency to shred when handled frequently.

Wands can be natural and simple, or as elaborately decorated as you like. You may want to carve or paint sacred symbols and runes to inscribe a chant or spell on it. Some people like to wrap ribbon, yarn, or strips of leather at one end to create a handle. Crystal or other objects can be attached if you feel these will enhance your own energy as it passes through the wand.

If you cut a branch from a tree, seek its permission first, and leave an offering. When making a wand, you may want to consider the type of wood. The four sacred trees that are most frequently used for wands include elder, hazel, oak, and rowan. Different trees are associated with certain gods and goddesses as well as particular attributes.

Ash: Odin; divination, healing, inner conflicts, general magic

Birch: Cerridwen; beginnings, purification, creativity, good luck

Elder: Hel, Isis; awareness, love, protection, healing, wish-fulfillment

Hazel: Danu, Diana, Arianrhod; fertility, wisdom, marriage, divination, healing, protection

Holly: Inanna, Odin; luck, prosperity, protection (especially against uninvited spirits)

Maple: Brigid, Hathor; love, abundance, binding, attraction, communication, positivity

Oak: Cernunnes, Herne, Dagda; wisdom, strength, protection, endurance, abundance, fertility

Pine: Danu, nature spirits; healing, cleansing, longevity, divination

Rowan: Celi, Brigid; healing, protection, blessings

Willow: Morrigan, Hecate, Hera; balance, intuition, transformation.

For Further Study

Stepanich, Kisma. *Faery Wicca: Book One*. St. Paul, Minn.: Llewellyn Publications, 1994.

McCoy, Edain. *Witta: An Irish Pagan Tradition*. St. Paul, Minn.: Llewellyn Publications, 1993.

Creating Sacred Space for Tarot Readings

by Reverend Gina Pace

I have been doing readings for the past sixteen years, working professionally both in and out of my home, and I've learned over the years how important it is to have a sacred space for a reading. While many people actually do their tarot readings in their homes, I have actually created a tarot "office" where I hold my readings. Clients come to me and I have a special place (not in my home) where I can receive them. The reasons for this are three-fold, and explained each in turn below.

First off, when there is a specially designated space for tarot readings, the space can be cleansed on a regular basis but does not need to be cleansed specifically each time you are going to do a reading. If you have a place in your house that you do your readings (such as your living room), and then other people are

trucking through the place all the time. You will often find distracting energies in this space—even if you can limit the amount of time your family visits it. It isn't really a good idea to be doing a reading when something predictable, such as having the family dog bound in unannounced, can happen. And you don't have to worry about clearing off the coffee table so you can make room for your cards.

Even if you're just reading for yourself, it's good to have at the very least a designated corner of a room that is not used much and off the beaten path, so that you have less chance of being disturbed. My tarot office is actually not even in my home, but rather it is attached to the classroom space of the New Age bookstore where I work. This way, it is close and convenient, but separate and protected from the energies of the home which can obviously be quite hectic.

The second reason for a separate "reading" space is the office is separate from my living quarters and therefore safer for me to have clients come in for readings. To be perfectly honest, you don't always know the people you are going to read for, and it isn't always a good idea to have strangers come into your home. On a magical level, it's true that you can always smudge afterwards, but safety is not always just a magical concern. It can be a physical one as well. Not everyone has this option, but there are other ways of making sure your regular living areas are protected from strangers' energies.

Finally, the point of having a sacred space where you do your readings is that once you have consecrated the space and cleansed it and made it yours. You have a subconscious mental association that the space is "sacred" and "meant for divination," and thus the simple act of entering and sitting in that space puts you in the right frame of mind to do readings. You will be able to go into much deeper levels of divination if you are in a sacred space, than if you are in your kitchen and you're watching the roast while you read your cards.

Many times, the accoutrements of your tarot reading room are what make you feel most like you have made the space sacred for divination. A special table, for example, which is only used for readings, is a perfect example of this. Likewise, some people will use only a certain incense when they do readings, This helps to put them in that sacred frame of mind for divination.

Aside from my tarot office being geographically separate from my living space, the following five factors also mark my sacred space as particularly sacred.

First, my office has two Victorian style antique brass torchieres with cut glass shades that give indirect soft lighting. I put sixty-watt *pink* bulbs in them as well. (These can be found in the supermarket, though you may have to dig around.) They offer softer, warmer light than regular white bulbs. The torchieres, while they may look expensive and elegant, actually only cost $15 at Walmart—a very small price to pay in order to make a special ambience in your sacred space.

Second, I have hung one of those lovely tapestry afghans on the wall—the kind you can buy everywhere nowadays which have scenic pictures on them. Mine has a beautiful Temperance Angel on it designed by Amy Zerner (she's the Zerner half of the Zerner-Farber tarot team). You can use any scene you like. I have found that hanging textiles on the wall instead of flat pictures softens the room's ambience further, and also soundproofs the space to some degree. It also makes the room feel warmer, and induces people to feel more at ease.

Third, I use two votive candles, one at each side of the large round table that I have in my room for readings. I prefer round tables because I often get caught on the corners walking around a rectangular table, but there's no reason you can't use any table you like. I have my table covered with a purple topper over a green tablecloth. I sit on one side, and the client sits opposite me with two votive candles to our left and right. These are used more for atmosphere than anything else.

Fourth, I use a clay lamp ring in one of the lamps, and I place several drops of rosemary oil on the ring before each reading. Rosemary gives off a strong but healing scent that I love. Additionally, rosemary allows a stronger connection to past memories that are always helpful in a reading. I like to think that it helps people access their memories on a subconscious level so they just feel relaxed and comfortable. Many people have painful memories from their past, and I have noticed that rosemary eases the pain while allowing the memories to come through more clearly. An additional benefit is that it helps the person remember their reading later with more clarity.

Fifth, I have a CD player that always plays soft and gentle background music. Actually, I always use the same CD—called "The Eternal Om." It's essentially sixty minutes of monks chanting the Om mantra softly and quietly, yet powerfully. If you have never heard "The Eternal Om" then you should definitely check it out; it puts me in the right frame of mind for a reading within just about sixty seconds. Really good stuff. And all my clients always comment on it positively. Your local New Age bookseller should have a copy of it, or can order it for you.

My space gets smudged on a regular basis, approximately once a month during the waning Moon, so that any negative energies can be banished. I begin by smudging with white sage and I go around the room in a widdershins (counterclockwise) direction, befitting the release of negative energies.

White sage is cleansing and removes any energies that are not conducive to good workings. I then use a cedar resin incense to purify the space. Cedar is a sacred wood and burning it produces a very high spiritual energy that blesses and purifies the space. Lastly, I burn some sweetgrass (I have a braid of it and just burn as much as I need off the ends) to bring in the positive energies and spirits of abundance. (See page 65 of this edition for more details on space purification.)

I move around the room in a deosil (clockwise) manner, because moving in this direction promotes positive energies. Always make sure your room is properly ventilated when you do this, or else make sure to take the battery out of the smoke alarm. The smoke quickly vanishes afterward, but the energies (and the blessings) remain, and your space remains sacred and ready for your readings.

Lighting the Fires of Spring

by Laura LaVoie

The long Celtic winter was drawing to a close across the island of Erin. As the gods began the work toward thawing the land they learned that the fires of spring were missing. The gods convened and chose the young Maiden of Ireland, Brigid, to embark on a journey to find the fires.

So Brigid set out across her land to bring the fires back to the gods.

As she journeyed eastward, she happened upon a beautiful dragonfly. The little winged creature buzzed about her head and tickled her ears.

Brigid decided to ask for help: "Dragonfly, can you tell me where the fires of spring can be found?"

The dragonfly replied, "I know of many things. I am the spirit of curiosity. Yet I do not know where these fires are. Perhaps the horse of the south will have an answer for you."

Brigid thanked the dragonfly for her help and hurried on to find the horse.

After a time, she came across a graceful mare, and she said to her: "The dragonfly told me that you may know where I could find the fires of spring."

To which the horse replied, "I know of many things. I am the passion of humankind. Yet I do not know where you might find these fires. Perhaps you should ask the bear in the west."

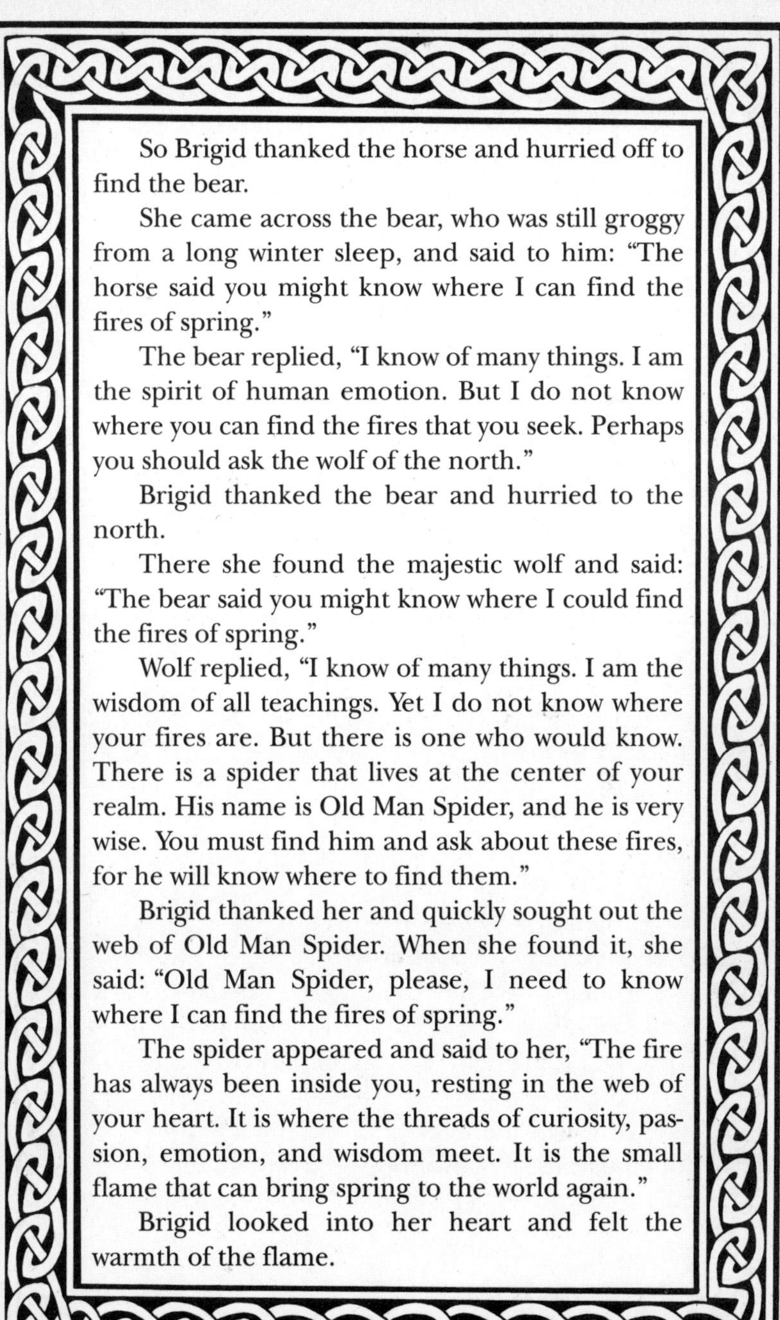

So Brigid thanked the horse and hurried off to find the bear.

She came across the bear, who was still groggy from a long winter sleep, and said to him: "The horse said you might know where I can find the fires of spring."

The bear replied, "I know of many things. I am the spirit of human emotion. But I do not know where you can find the fires that you seek. Perhaps you should ask the wolf of the north."

Brigid thanked the bear and hurried to the north.

There she found the majestic wolf and said: "The bear said you might know where I could find the fires of spring."

Wolf replied, "I know of many things. I am the wisdom of all teachings. Yet I do not know where your fires are. But there is one who would know. There is a spider that lives at the center of your realm. His name is Old Man Spider, and he is very wise. You must find him and ask about these fires, for he will know where to find them."

Brigid thanked her and quickly sought out the web of Old Man Spider. When she found it, she said: "Old Man Spider, please, I need to know where I can find the fires of spring."

The spider appeared and said to her, "The fire has always been inside you, resting in the web of your heart. It is where the threads of curiosity, passion, emotion, and wisdom meet. It is the small flame that can bring spring to the world again."

Brigid looked into her heart and felt the warmth of the flame.

The curiosity of the dragonfly led her on, and the passion of the horse brought her strength. The bear gave her the emotion to care for her people, and the wisdom of the wolf brought her to the answer.

The flame was indeed right where Old Man Spider said it would be.

She returned to the gods and shared her discovery. Each god lit a candle from the flame in Brigid's heart, and winter melted away.

A Child-Welcoming Ritual

by Dallas Jennifer Cobb

The rite of Baptism is not original to Christianity, but was adapted from Norse and Celtic Druid water ceremonies. Formally, baptism holds three purposes: to wash away original sin, to protect the child from the devil, and to enroll the child in the church of the parents.

For most Pagans, baptism makes little sense. Still, they may still want to mark this important event. We can formally welcome newborn children even if we don't believe in the concept of original sin, the devil, and we belong to no church.

A Welcoming Ritual

Holding a ceremony of welcoming can be a memorable event to introduce your child to your community, bestow blessings and gifts upon the child and parents, and formally give thanks to the

gods, goddesses, and elements for the arrival of the child. Such a ritual is suitable for all children.

This rite of passage centers around your new child, so let them be the guiding energy in planning the ritual. Cater to the specific needs of your infant. Hold the ritual at a time of day following usual naptime. Feed your child upon waking, and dress them in the outfit you have chosen for the ritual. A contented child will be alert and aware throughout the ceremony.

Smile with your baby and tell her or him how much you love them, and how many wishes you have for them. Ask a community member to make garlands for the parents and child to wear, with protective herbs, flowers, and ribbons. Plan on a small, intimate gathering. No more than twenty minutes in total is advisable. The child will not be able to stay alert and attentive for too long. Limit the number of people attending to less than twenty as well. Make sure the familiar faces of parents are always close by.

Parents can offer a gift, perhaps a family treasure, to the child. The simplest Child-Welcoming Ceremony involves an introduction of the child, a parent blessing, and a child blessing. Use a quick method of casting a circle. A spirit parent is an ideal choice to introduce the child. Then while holding the child, the spirit parent can speak about parenting. Acknowledge that everyone attending the ceremony will contribute to the life of the child. Introduce the parents now, and say: "Let us bless these parents."

The child is held by one parent who speaks blessings then passes the child to the other parent. The parents may speak of their wishes and dreams for the child. Blessings are as varied as those who bestow them. Seek out your own meaningful blessings, or write one specifically for the occasion. Ask others to offer their blessings to the child as well.

When the blessings are done and there is a quiet lull in the circle, the circle can be opened and the ritual finished. Take the good energy from the ritual with you into the long and blessed life you will share with your child.

Go now. Feast, celebrate, and enjoy.

Aphrodite

by Ellen Dugan

Who is Aphrodite? Is she a daughter of Zeus and Dionne? Is she the "foam-born goddess" that appeared full grown from the sea? Is she a cute, giggling blonde wearing sheer pink as on the television series *Hercules* and *Xena?* Or is she more than all of these thing?

Aphrodite was the ancient Greek goddess of love, lust, beauty, fertility, and procreation. She actually predates Zeus and the other Olympians by many centuries. She rose from the sea foam, created when Cronus—the father of the Olympians—threw

Uranus's severed genitals into the sea. One of the most popular images of Aphrodite is from Botticelli's famous painting. The golden haired and curvy goddess is riding on a sea shell over the sea, from where she was born.

At the same time, there is more to Aphrodite than meets the eye. She was more than a captivating and beautiful goddess of sexual love. She was also a mother and a grandmother. Aphrodite bore several children from different partners. Her most long-standing lover was Ares, the god of war. She produced three children by him—Phobus (god of panic), Deimus (fear), and Harmonia.

She also had a child with Dionysus, who was named Priapus, and a child with Hermes called Hermaphroditus. She also hooked up with mortal men from time to time and did have a son by one of them. Her son was called Aeneas, a mortal and a Trojan leader. Probably the most well-known of Aphrodite's offspring was Eros, the god of love. Eros and his wife Psyche produced a child named Volupta (goddess of pleasure).

Mighty Aphrodite

Aphrodite was by all accounts a celebrated goddess of her time. Her cult was popular throughout most of the Greek world. The interesting part about Aphrodite is that she was not of Greek origin. Her followers came to Greece from Cyprus, where she was known as Kypris, or the lady of Cyprus. Aphrodite may well have been the local Cypriot version of the great mother.

She was described in her day as being both an awful and lovely goddess, at whose feet grass sprang up and grew. She is a goddess of the sea and gardens and was associated with the three graces and with the Horae, the goddesses of the seasons. But no matter how you look at it, this ancient goddess of love and pleasure was one very busy lady.

Aphrodite was well-known for her charms and beguiling ways. When the mood struck her she could make the gods and mortals alike fall in love (or lust) with each other. No one was immune nor safe. This is a goddess that you would definitely want to keep happy.

It wasn't until I began the research for writing this article that I realized that representations of Aphrodite had been in my home for quite a long time. Staggering into the kitchen to fix myself a cup of tea early one morning, I automatically reached for my favorite mug. I stopped and stared at Botticelli's vision of Aphrodite gazing back at me. I've had that goddess mug for years, and now I suddenly felt like I was seeing it for the first time. I opened the refrigerator door to get the milk and noticed that my daughter's report card was anchored to the door with a goddess magnet. Which goddess you wonder? Aphrodite again. I laughed at myself and wondered if this was her way of reminding me to get busy and to write the darn article. I almost expected to hear Aphrodite tapping her foot at me.

So how does a modern Witch relate to Aphrodite? Well if anyone can appreciate the rush and craziness of modern life—kids, work, your relationships, and so on—I think that she would be the one. After all, Aphrodite did manage to juggle numerous partners, watch over her children, and keep up with her goddess duties. She even found the opportunity to play and stir up a little trouble from time to time. What a gal.

Glamouries, Love Spells, and Beauty Magic

Aphrodite is the one to call on when you feel the need to enhance your appearance magically. Technically this would be called glamoury. If you ask for Aphrodite's help with a simple beauty-enhancing glamoury, you will see results. But I warn you, glamouries can be a double-edged sword. Casting any glamoury will draw attention to yourself. And you may accidentally attract some interest that you weren't looking for. (Like your newly married boss or your best friend's boyfriend.) I would be cautious and consider exactly what you are hoping to achieve—the tone of the glamour, so to speak—before slinging around a glamour.

As to love spells, even more caution is called for. If you want to encourage more passion between yourself and an existing partner, Aphrodite is a logical choice. However, ask for magical sexiness of allure only for yourself. Do not magically zap your partner, as that is manipulation.

Probably your safest bet is to work instead for an inner beauty. The kind of loveliness that just shines right through—sort of a magical sparkle. With this thought of inner beauty in mind, Aphrodite can help you to learn to love yourself and your body just as you are. Also, take a look at those old statues and paintings of the goddesses sometime. Notice anything? They have curves! Real women have curves. Learn to embrace yours, and don't worry so much about your dress size. I don't care if you are a size 4 or a size 24, beautiful and bewitching women come in all different shapes, colors, and sizes.

Popular Aphrodite images show a woman with rounded thighs, full breasts, and a curved tummy. And she is a knockout. So take a hint from Aphrodite and be voluptuous, sexy, and proud of who you are.

A Beauty Ritual

Start off your Aphrodite beauty ritual by taking a tub bath. Toss a few tablespoons of sea salt into your bath water. Light some floral scented candles, and sprinkle a few rose petals on the water. Soak in the tub for a while and relax.

When the water starts to cool, step out of the tub and dry off. Slip on a favorite robe or a comfortable outfit. Gather together as many things from the following correspondence list as you can, and go settle down in your favorite outdoor space.

Magical correspondences for Aphrodite

Planetary association: Venus
Moon phase: Full Moon
Oils: Rose or any other type of floral scent that you find pleasing
Places: The seashore or a garden
Plants: Red and white roses, blue flowers
Images: A dolphin, an owl, or a seashell
Crystals and stones: Rose quartz, pearls, abalone, and coral
Candle colors: Pink and aqua green
Incense: Rose or any type of floral scent that you find pleasing

Set up your working area with a pretty arrangement of your Aphrodite items. Calm and center yourself, then when you feel that you are ready, begin. Light the candle or the incense and repeat Aphrodite's charm three times.

Aphrodite's Beauty Charm

Sea foam, white roses, and a rope of pearls,
Aid my magic; hear the plea of this girl.

Cause my eyes to sparkle, bring a glow to my skin,
As I deepen the beauty that comes from within.

When you are finished with your ritual, allow your candles to burn out in a safe place. Keep one of the items from your ritual with you for one week.

You may repeat this charm at every Full Moon or whenever the mood strikes you. Have fun with this "inner beauty" ritual. And may you walk through life as Aphrodite herself, proudly and with beauty.

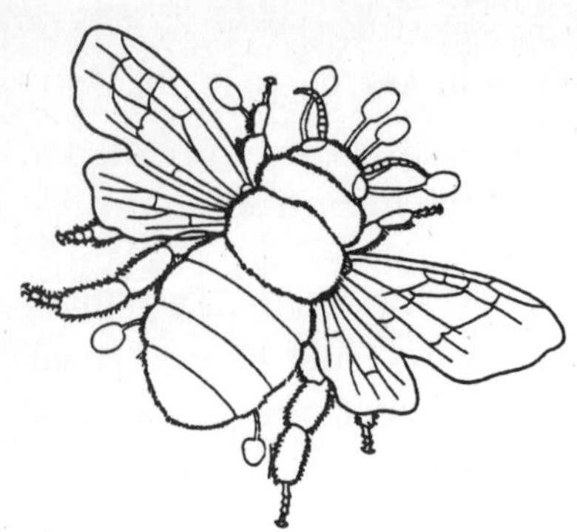

The Magic of the Hive

by Nuala Drago

Throughout the ancient world, it was believed that honeybees were a divine gift, bequeathed to humans from days when gods and goddesses walked the earth as mortal beings do. That was an age when pristine forests and fields of wildflowers sheltered the earth, and nectar was plentiful so that the bees produced vast stores of honey to eat and for brewing honey wine, or mead. Honey and mead imparted to the deities their extraordinary sexual prowess and the ability to regenerate, the greatest secrets of their immortality.

In ancient Greece, the honeycomb was the symbol of Aphrodite, goddess of love and beauty, known to her worshippers as the queen bee. The social structure of the hive was the pattern for her cult. Priestesses who served in her temples were called bees. The high priestess was Aphrodite's earthly representative and the only member of the sect who was allowed to mate. She would choose a male consort to remain with her for the duration of a year. When the year ended, her lover, who represented the drone of the hive, was killed in ritual sacrifice to Aphrodite.

The Greek philosopher, Plato, studied honeybees extensively. He associated them with reincarnation, the female potency of nature, and the geometric mysteries of the universe. Plato's student, Aristotle, was tutor to Alexander the Great. On Alexander's death, Aristotle had him embalmed in an earthen jar filled with honey.

To Pythagoras, another Greek philosopher, the honeycomb represented the fundamental symmetry of the cosmos. Because each cell of a honeycomb is a perfect hexagon, he believed that the universe, like the honeycomb, was a manifestation of mathematical ratios.

Among the dynastic Egyptians, the potency of symbols was a basic tenet of religion. To them, the honeybee represented immortality and rebirth. Images of honeybees often adorned the walls of their burial places, and pots of honey and honey wine were entombed with the dead to nourish them and speed their spirits to their next incarnation.

In ancient Rome, honey was highly valued and often accepted in place of gold to pay taxes. Surgeons to the legions dressed wounds with honey to prevent infection and promote healing. Honey and mead were rationed to soldiers to provide energy, lift sagging spirits, and to medicate. Honey and mead were remedies in themselves, but because of their sweet flavor they were also the vehicles to deliver herbs that would have been too bitter to drink on their own. No wedding celebration in Rome would have taken place without honey and mead. Honey cakes were eaten for sexual potency at wedding feasts, and newlyweds drank mead for a month after the wedding, a practice that gave rise to the term honeymoon.

It was also believed that eating honey cakes and drinking mead would increase longevity. In fact, because of this belief, wild orgies would often be held by the rich and powerful at which guests gorged on all manner of honey-rich foods and beverages.

The medicinal use of honey and other bee products—such as royal jelly, beeswax, and propolis—has long been an art in China. In ages past, victims of small pox would be covered with honey. The practice seemed to thwart infection, offer relief from pain, and minimize the hideous scarring most survivors were forced to endure. Along with this, bee venom therapy was also practiced.

In Celtic countries, honeybees were considered too sacred to be purchased with currency, so they were acquired through the barter system. Druids of Britain and Ireland revered honeybees to the extent that their legal authorities, the Brehons, established laws to regulate the keeping of bees, the production of honey, and the brewing of mead. In fact, Britain was at one time called the Honey Isle because of the enormous quantity of mead that was brewed and consumed there.

In medieval times, honeybees were adopted into European heraldry to incite fear and admiration. They also came to symbolize social order and ideals such as courage and loyalty. Beekeeping and mead making were elevated to the highest of arts. It was common for each wealthy landowner to employ a resident

Bee Master to oversee a private honeybee garden and to consult with a favorite brewer of mead.

Today we know of the importance of bees as pollinators and as a sign of a healthy planet. Healers around the globe are employing honey and bee venom therapy to cure all manner of diseases such as arthritis and other inflammatory and degenerative diseases. Natural honey, bee pollen, royal jelly, propolis, beeswax, and honey-based beverages are all in demand again.

Honeybees have been around for more than 180 million years. In these modern times, just as in ages past, they are recognized as symbols of regal power—feared and venerated by some, and, in general, still identified with gods, spirits, and the supernatural realm. Any beekeeper will tell you that there is mystery in the hive and that honeybees possess a magic uniquely their own.

Honey makes an excellent replacement for sugar when baking. Just remember that honey is much sweeter than sugar, so you will have to use slightly less than the recipe calls for. And because honey is liquid, you will also have to decrease the amount of other liquids. You will learn what works through trial and error, since there is no set rule.

While the following recipe may not endow you with immortality, it is a delicious way to celebrate the magic of the hive.

The Queen Bee's Gingerbread

Line the bottom of a nine-inch square pan with parchment and set aside. Next, sift together 1¼ cups of all-purpose flour, ½ teaspoon each of allspice, cloves, nutmeg, ginger, baking powder, and baking soda, and 1 teaspoon cinnamon. (Add a pinch of salt, if desired.) In a medium bowl, beat ½ cup of softened butter with ½ cup of firmly packed dark brown sugar until fluffy. Beat in one large egg and ½ cup of your favorite dark honey. Blend in the flour mixture alternately with ½ cup of plain yogurt until well combined. Turn the batter into the prepared pan, and bake in a preheated 350°F oven for about thirty minutes or until done. Cool on a rack and enjoy it plain, iced, or served with fresh fruit and dollops of whipped cream. Depending on the season, enjoy the bread with a glass of well-chilled mead or a mug of honey-sweetened tea with your cake.

The Magic of Herbs

by Jonathan Keyes

In the summertime, my wife and I like to go herb collecting. One of our favorite, but hard-to-find, herbs is mugwort. We love this herb not only for its soothing properties, but also for its more mystical and magical properties. We will often use it in healings, laying a stick of mugwort on our altar, or we honor the spirit of mugwort in our rituals and ask for its assistance in our task. Mugwort can be used to make dream pillows that help to open up and assist our psychic abilities.

For thousands of years, herbs have been used not only for their curative properties but for their magical properties as well. When a South American *curandero* uses a rattle of plantain leaves or a Native American healer smudges with sage, they are working with herbs to conduct and transform energy magically.

What Makes an Herb Magical?

When you travel through the countryside, you may see wild herbs such as dandelion or mullein growing freely on the side of roads, by streambeds or in high rocky plains. Each plant is adapted to a certain region where it is best suited. Certain herbs love the sunlight and others love the shade. Some herbs need a rich moist ground while others like rocky arid soil. Each herb's adaptation gives us clues to their nature and their magical properties. A field of sunflowers standing tall and craning their necks toward the Sun may remind you of the joy and exuberance of the summertime and the radiant glow of the Sun. If you are walking near a small stream and you spy a little gathering of violets nestled underneath a Douglas fir, you may be reminded of the quieter, more introspective side of yourself. Each herb we encounter tells us a story by where it likes to live, the

color of its flowers, its height and width, and if it has a strong scent. These attributes point not only to their medicinal qualities but to their magical properties as well.

Herbs and the Four Elements

One way to classify herbs magically is to organize them according to the four elements. Herbs associated with the fire element often draw out our creative and expressive capabilities. They are helpful for moving stagnant energy and increasing our courage and playfulness. Herbs associated with the water element (such as mugwort) help draw out our more receptive and psychic potentials. Herbs associated with the air element increase our mental and cognitive abilities, and they stimulate our communicative functions. Herbs associated with the earth element are helpful for keeping us grounded and for attracting wealth and prosperity.

Here are examples of a few herbs associated with each element that can be used magically. There are numerous ways to connect to magical herbs. Try sitting with the herb in its natural state and watch its evolution over the seasons. Use your five senses—touch it, taste it, observe it, listen to it, and smell it.

If it is a medicine, try drinking an infusion of it or try a tincture of it. These methods will all help you connect to its essence. Then work with these herbs in your rituals, put them on your altar, and grow them in your backyard. Soon some of these friendly herbs may turn into your magical allies.

Fire Herbs

Sunflower

Sunflower is a supreme solar plant and can be called on when our inner Sun, our inner glow, is diminished. Sunflower helps to broaden, magnify, and externalize our expression. We become more dynamic, healthy, and happy beings with sunflower around.

Ginger

When we are listless, drained, and sapped by our lifestyle and the people around us, ginger helps to enliven us and remove the stagnation from our lives. There is a rawness to the root that helps draw out creativity and sexual energy.

Nettle

Nettle is a powerful healer and rejuvenator. It picks the worst wastelands in which to grow strong. It provides a rich mineral and nutrient base for other plants and trees to grow on. Nettle energy is proud warrior energy—strong, clear, and glowing green.

Air Herbs

Chamomile

Chamomile has a light and pleasing appearance. It is gentle and refined and offers clarity and ease of vision. Chamomile relaxes our energy.

Lavender

Lavender's sweet and refreshing scent, as well as its lively and beautiful purple flowers, help us to access our highest selves. We feel refreshed and calm with this herb. Lavender opens our hearts and sweetens our connections with each other. It brings us serenity and joy.

Mullein

Mullein is a proud creature that stands very tall and erect (sometimes up to nine feet in height). Its firmness of character and its soft velvety leaves give it a nobility of character. Mullein is a charming gentleman who can help us stand firm and see clearly.

Water Herbs

Lemon Balm

Lemon balm is a dear friend. Her relaxed and jovial manner attract friendship and success. She helps put us in touch with serenity, joy, and simple pleasure.

Mugwort

Mugwort is a very powerful shamanic herb, capable of tremendous healing. It is used as a smudge to purify and enliven an environment. It is also very helpful for those needing to seek a vision or to gain psychic skills. It has the power to move and channel energy like almost no other herb.

Raspberry

Raspberry is a beautiful tangled herb with delicious berries. Its interwoven physical form represents the web of life and shows the beauty of our interconnectedness. Raspberry emits a powerful feminine force that is beautiful, rich, complex, and deep.

Earth Herbs

Comfrey

Comfrey is used for regeneration in times of extreme weakness and debility. It helps to make things whole again when we feel fragmented and confused. Comfrey knits the parts back together.

Dandelion

Dandelion is a great plant totem. Its nobility, strength, and sweet optimism make it a delight to know. It helps relieve stress and strain in the body and the emotions, and it returns one to a state of childlike simplicity.

Oregon Grape

Oregon grape is a prickly creature and a great defender. If negative energy is being thrown at someone, Oregon grape can ward it off and send it away. It is also helpful for keeping us grounded and relaxed.

The Great Pan

by Scott Paul

. . . That dismal cry rose slowly
And sank slowly through the air,
Full of spirits melancholy
And eternity's despair;
And they heard the words it said—
Pan is dead—Great Pan is dead,
Pan, Pan is dead.

"A Musical Instrument," 1859

It has been almost 150 years since poet Elizabeth Barrett Browning wrote that Great Pan is dead. Pan has long been a symbol of the wild-at-heart and the carefree. But just who is Pan, where did he come from, and why does he evoke such thoughts?

Among the most recognized of all the Greek gods, Pan is described as a satyr. Dion Fortune called Pan the "Goat Foot God." He has the body of a man, and the hindquarters of a goat. Pan was an Arcadian god of shepherds. With the arrival of the Olympian gods, new myths were told to explain his presence. Pan's relationship to the gods is varied. One myth tells that Pan is a son of Kronos and foster brother of

Zeus. In another story, he is the son of Hermes and the nymph Dryope. Some have said that his mother was Queen Penelope, the wife of Odysseus, and that his father was all of her suitors. Whatever Pan's origins, he is associated with bee keeping, music, fertility, and dance. He is also god of prophecy. He is best known, however, for his sexual escapades.

The nymph Syrinx escaped his passion for her by having herself turned into a clump of reeds by the gods. Pan plucked a handful of the reeds and created his panpipes. He remembers her with his music. Pan seduced the nymph Pitys away from Boreas, the north wind. The goddess Gaia changed Pitys into a pine tree to save her from Boreas's wrath. Pan seduced the goddess Selene when he changed into a white ram and lured her into the forest.

The worship of Pan centered on the region of Arcadia until the Battle of Marathon in 490 BC. Greece was being invaded by the Persians, and Athens sent a runner to Sparta for help. On his return trip, the runner Pheidippides encountered Pan in Arcadia. Making his presence known, Pan told Pheidippides that if the Athenians would worship him he would aid them in battle. It is said that Pan's cry caused a panic amongst the Persian army. In Athens a shrine to Pan was built in the wild places below the acropolis.

Pan is unique among the other Greek gods in that he is the only one with a story of his death. Plutarch wrote of a merchant ship that was plying its trade amongst the Greek isles. When the ship neared the isle of Paxi, a great voice called, asking the captain to tell a neighboring island that "Great Pan is dead." The death of Pan seemed to signal the death of all of the gods. In Greek, Pan literally means "all."

But Pan is not dead. Authors have immortalized him up to present day. He even was a cartoon sidekick to Hercules in a popular Walt Disney movie. Pan has become the embodiment of all things wild and carefree. He is now a cultural icon in the modern age. In short, Pan lives.

Edible Flowers

by Shira Bee

Flowers enhance our lives. They are not only beautiful to observe, but they are also an integral component of fairy lore and religious ceremonies. Flowers hold symbolic significance in both ancient and modern cultures and have appeared in countless myths and folkloric accounts.

Flowers grace our gardens and altars, and we identify personally with them. Flowers are so revered by human beings they have become popular female namesakes (Rose, Iris, Daisy, and so on) in virtually every language on Earth. Floral essences are also integral components of aromatherapy and many of the cosmetic and herbal preparations we use. How delightful then that some of the most beautiful flowers are edible, delicious, and readily available for adding to our diet.

Mother Earth blesses us with an array of edible flowers that can be served during rituals or festive gatherings, or integrated with meals on a daily basis. Edible flowers make irresistible additions to salads. Peppery nasturtiums add a bright splash of color to a plate of greens, as do squash blossoms, a popular garnish in Latin and Italian regions. Zucchini flowers, tangy dandelion greens, silky pansies, sweet bachelor buttons, spicy marigolds, and a host of other flora pack punch into conventional salad arrangements.

Historical accounts of edible flora date back thousands of years. Lavender and magnolia blossoms were used as natural sweeteners before the widespread availability of sugar (the French still utilize lavender as a sweetener and garnish). Before the advent of artificial flavors and colors, flowers were used almost exclusively to add color and texture to dishes. Roses have long been valued for their culinary usage. They have been utilized in the preparation of vinegar, jam, tea, sauces, and wine by Middle Eastern, Eastern European, Indian, and Asian cultures since prebiblical times. Rose water, consumed liberally by the ancient Romans, is still widely used as flavoring in Eurasian regions. Rose petal sandwiches, a favored eighteenth-century delicacy, continue to appear in modern recipes. The Chinese have even carried into modern times their long-standing tradition of serving rose fritters during their New Year celebrations.

Flowers are superb garnishes on sweet dishes as well. Candying violets, pansies, and rose petals is an old fashioned technique that was widely practiced throughout western Europe during the eighteenth and nineteenth centuries. Violets are historically known for their sentimental symbolism and culinary usage by the Victorians of England, who employed them as garnish and flavor-

ing for sweet dishes. The use of violets in food preparation can be traced as far back as the ancient Greeks. And old-fashioned wisdom translates into modern day. To add irresistible touches to your desserts such as cakes, cookies, puddings, and ice cream dishes you can add edible flowers. Freeze small flower heads or petals into ice cubes for a whimsical touch to cold beverages. Or do as confectioners and bakers do and candy them. Edible flower dishes make for an enchanting, eye-catching presentation at parties and gatherings.

Edible blooms are perhaps best known in teas. Adding flowers to tea is an ancient Chinese tradition that later spread into Europe and other parts of the world. Asian cultures, notably the Chinese and Japanese, have drunk floral-based teas for thousands of years. You might never guess from the daisylike appearance of tiny chamomile blooms that they were once revered by the ancient Egyptians and used in Roman remedies. The calming, therapeutic effects of floral teas have been extensively documented in scientific literature. Fragrant jasmine blooms, bitter-sweet chrysanthemums, aromatic roses, and hibiscus flowers are among those flowers widely used today in tea blends. Flowers are alluring additions to cold drinks as well. Adding lavender and elder flowers to lemonade and iced tea preparations is common practice in Europe.

Spring is the ideal time to collect and wild-craft edible flora. Take caution to eat only those flowers you are certain are edible and pesticide-free. Reference your local library or bookstore for current edible herb and flower field guides. And as with other greens, be sure to wash flowers in cold water before consuming them. If wild crafting is not an option, you can purchase edible flowers at gourmet and specialty markets.

Edible flowers add color and zest to soups, salads, sandwiches, sauces, marinades, oils, vinaigrettes, and desserts. As garnishes, they beautify meals and captivate guests. Edible flora can be sprinkled onto virtually any dish. Have fun experimenting with all the possible colors and taste combinations.

Sex Magic Basics

by Diana Rajchel

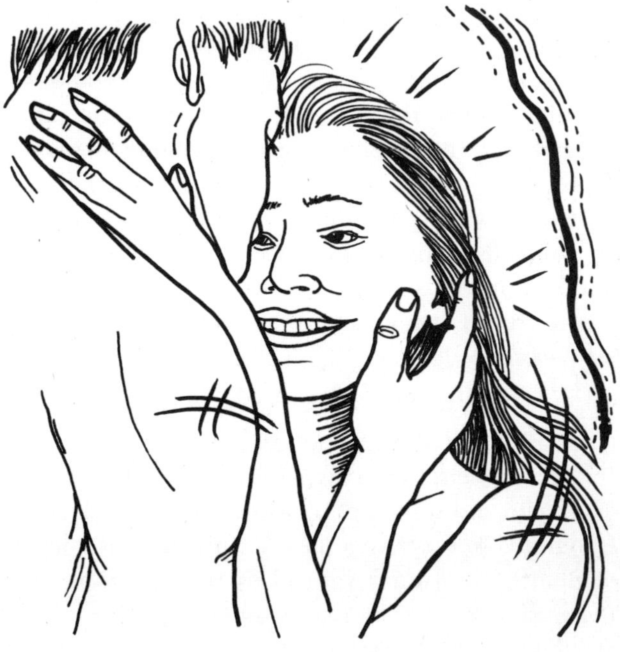

The average reader may have flipped to this entry because its title includes the word "sex." Good move, though really this article covers aspects of sex far prior to foreplay—so only the really creative may find this information prurient.

Generally speaking, interest in sex comes from a combination of human nature and cultural programming: people like to have sex, yes, but we are also told this over and over to the point of saturation. Occultists, being people, like sex as much as anyone, and as they often use materials and actions to raise energy occultists have found that sex works really well for producing the emotional and metaphysical state necessary to alter the structure of internal and external reality.

Sex magic works according to the same principles of other forms of magic. The sexual act raises energy and intention toward a purpose, and at the right moment, usually during orgasm, this energy is released. But there are rules.

Basic Rules for Sex Magic

1. Know Yourself

Spend time examining your attitudes about sex and why you harbor the attitudes. You may want to invest in the game *Scruples* or the *What If?* books as a means of bringing forward deeply held beliefs. The act of ritual sex bares a person completely; you must know what lies underneath your skin so you can fully involve yourself in the sexual act. If you discover you are affected by a previous trauma, seek treatment. Sex magic can bring forward old attitudes and fears in a negative way if not properly acknowledged.

2. Practice Psychic Protection

A shield is a bubble of protection that you create through visualization. This shield forms the basis of most ritual acts outside a magic circle, and some people continue to use shields while inside a circle. If you have a partner, practice visualizing bubbles of blue light around yourselves (many people conceive blue more easily than protective white light). Use these visualizations while connected and while not connected, and practice dropping these shields when physically close. Use this connection to practice concentrating on the same ideas and holding thoughts together for as long as possible.

3. Examine Physical Details

Develop a regular exercise program, and take a close look at your diet and habits. While you need not hire a personal trainer to prepare for sex ritual, simple activity can benefit both the pleasure of the ritual and its effects. You may want to explore gentler forms of exercise that align body and spirit—such as yoga or aikido—or in activities that help you build comfort with your sensuality—such as belly-dancing. Physical activity enhances your self-awareness. The more comfortable you feel in your body, the more comfortable you feel during sex. No one needs to try every position—or even half the positions—listed in the Kama Sutra. Sex magicians just need to move their bodies in the most beneficial manner possible.

The Reasons for Sex Magic

Ritual sex is not used simply for pleasure alone. Sex among Pagans does not happen for procreation only, but within a ritual setting it does not happen as a trivial activity, either. This does not in any way suggest that consensual pleasure has no place in Pagan religion; however, sex during ritual has serious implications beyond the physical sharing.

Wiccans use the great rite as a symbolic celebration of the union of male and female; this helps adherents meditate upon the significance of fertility cycles. A sex rite may create a sort of magical child in the astral plane. This creation usually manifests some spiritual quality or guardianship as designated by those involved in the ritual. I have used sex magic for extremely potent healing rituals—sex raised within a Wiccan circle and then sent to the person in need of the energy has been very effective and enjoyable.

The Great Rite

Wicca centers its religious philosophy around the sacred union between the primal god and goddess forces. Most covens recognize this union symbolically by placing an athame to represent the male organ into the chalice to represent the female organ. Isolated groups may use actual sex as part of totally experiencing the energy of god and goddess. Participants describe this process as a deeply spiritual experience.

Magical Child

The creation of a "magical child"—more commonly known as a thought form—comes from ceremonial magic. Ceremonials may want to create a nonphysical (or other-dimensional) being to act as a guardian of an area, to relay a message, or to assist in some other ritual purpose. This form of sex magic bases itself upon the theory that when a couple physically unites, the energy above them coalesces into its own life force. This life force, if not used to impregnate the female, can be directed to other purposes based upon the focused intention of the couple.

Sexual Healing

Healthy, pleasurable sex can relieve headaches, seal holes in the auric body, and relax physical tension. In a monogamous relationship, part of this healing comes from a loving, safe connection to another person. This powerful connection, through sex magic, can be transferred to others in need of healing. A typical cone of power such as that used in Wiccan ritual can direct the energy to a person in need. If the person receiving the energy might disrupt the rhythm of the ritual, naming that person and identifying the intent on a candle or other symbol of that person will suffice for creating a target for the energy. This way, you and your partner can concentrate on the act itself.

Sex magic can cause positive changes. Mature and responsible legal adults can certainly benefit themselves by exploring this aspect of ritual. It also can contribute to the betterment of the world.

The cautions about sex magic are usually slightly exaggerated, but there are also good reasons for these warnings. Sex is a powerful act with or without a ritual context. Engage in sex magic with joy and wisdom and with full acceptance of all consequences.

Equine Magic

by Cerridwen Iris Shea

Horses are fascinating creatures. The image of a horse running at full speed, with mane and tail streaming out behind, is a vision of beauty, freedom, and skill. Horses have distinct personalities, and most of them are quite intelligent. As with many animals, they sometimes get exasperated at the slowness of human understanding.

Horse Folklore

There is a great amount of folklore involving horses. Several tales connect white horses with red-haired women. One tale claims if you see a white horse, you will soon meet a red-haired woman. Another tale claims if you see a red-haired woman, you will soon meet a white horse. (I wonder how many white horses people have seen after meeting me in New York City.)

I am rather skeptical of these tales. Another one says if you don't meet a red-haired woman after you meet a white horse, it is bad luck. Of course, the origins of these tales are obscure. There's a saying that seeing a white horse will bring you bad luck, and for good luck you should stamp a white horse. Huh? When in doubt, I say give the horse a carrot. Then you'll be friends for at least the next four minutes. A gentler tale says that a white horse can warn you of danger, and, because a white horse lives longer than a dark horse, it is considered a living amulet against an early death. Yet another white horse tale says you must cross your fingers until you meet a dog after seeing a white horse. The mere thought causes hand cramp.

The legends of Rhiannon, Epona, and Macha all include horses as major characters. According to the Medicine Cards, Horse represents power and the wisdom and understanding that come from walking someone else's path. In the Druid Animal Oracle, Horse calls us to travel, and brings the querent closer to the power of the land and the Sun. Horse power helps us travel through our life cycles.

There's a tale that suggests you should never buy a horse with four white feet, comparing them to outlaws who stay on the move. A more sensible tale tells that you must not buy a horse that shows the white of his eyes, or you will not be able to do anything with him. That makes sense. If he's rolling his eyes at you, and perhaps baring his teeth, then chances are that he doesn't like you.

Horse's breath was supposed to cure whooping cough. Horses are also associated with fertility, which is celebrated by riding the hobbyhorse every year on Beltane. Walking a horse through the house was considered good luck (but probably difficult on your knick-knacks).

A few years ago, I saw a documentary about a couple who took their injured horse into the house to take care of her. They housetrained her—to the point where she undid the latch on the kitchen door to let herself into the yard when she needed to relieve herself, and she ate spaghetti at the table with them. They did, however, have to put away all their collectibles because her tail kept sweeping them to the floor.

Horseshoes are considered magical. Since many are made of iron, they are a protection against enchantment. Horseshoes were also believed to cure hiccups. Hung over the doorway, horseshoes are believed to encourage good luck. However, there is a debate about whether to hang them facing downward, or if that causes the luck to run out. A horseshoe hung in the bedroom is supposed to keep nightmares away.

Putting Equine Magic to Use

With all these conflicting tales, how can you perform your own equine magic? Well, to start find a picture of a horse which appeals to you. It can be a mythical depiction, from a book of fairy tales or your favorite tarot deck, or perhaps a photograph of a horse. Or find a small sculpture of a horse which you find enticing. Of course, if you live with a horse, you can communicate directly with it. You can ask the horse if he or she wishes to act as your familiar when you work magic.

Most of us, however, don't have that option, and we have to use pictures or statues of horses. The important thing is to find a representation of horse to which you connect.

Next, make time where you won't be disturbed, and light a candle. White always works, but I usually prefer green for this work.

Sit quietly, staring at the image of the horse. Let yourself go into soft focus. Allow yourself to enter a meditative state, imagining yourself in the horse's territory. Let the horse approach you and initiate contact. Perhaps you will touch the horse, feed it, groom it, and pick dirt out of its hooves. Perhaps, eventually, you will ride the horse. The key here is patience. Let the horse set the tone. If you try to control the horse, the horse will leave and the magic won't work. When you work with an entity, it is important to let the relationship develop. As with human relationships, every relationship has its own rhythm, and if you try to force it or rush it, you can destroy it.

In my own magic, I use horse power as a messenger. When I need to communicate with someone—whether via e-mail, phone, or letter, I image Horse guiding the message. I consider Horse a psychic Pony Express. I also use horse magic for energy. When I feel depleted, I think of the racehorse in the starting gate. He is alert, on his toes, ready to take off at top speed. The image revitalizes me.

Horse magic is also good for self-esteem work. When a horse is brushed and bathed, he knows how handsome and gorgeous he is. He tosses his mane, he prances, and every line in his body is filled with self-confidence. If you're feeling uncertain about your appearance, imagine yourself as a sleek, healthy, and beautifully groomed horse. You will see and feel how the people around you respond positively.

Horse magic can also be used to encourage healthy eating habits. The phrase "he eats like a horse" means a healthy appeti-

tive. And that's the key—healthy. Horses instinctively know that they are what they eat. A well-fed, healthy horse has a variety of feeds, mashes, alfalfas, grasses, and even sometimes molasses in his diet. If you have problems with eating, horse magic can help guide you to a healthy diet that will leave you feeling fit, confident, and fully prepared for endurance.

With a little imagination and patience, you can discover your own type of horse magic, and integrate the power of Horse into your daily life. And, while you're at it, why not make a donation to your local horse-related charity? Time matters more than cash. Even if you can't own a horse yourself, you can support those who rescue and find homes for these magnificent, magical creatures.

For Further Study

Carr-Gomm, Philip and Stephanie. *The Druid Animal Oracle: Working With the Sacred Animals of the Druid Tradition.* New York: Simon and Schuster, 1994.

Sams, Jamie, and David Carson. *Medicine Cards.* New York: St. Martin's Press, 1999.

Pathway to Adulthood

by Emely Flak

In most ancient traditions, the arrival of puberty was celebrated as an important turning point. This rite of passage from adolescence to puberty took place at the onset of menstruation for young women and when signs of physical maturity were evident in young men. Its purpose was to acknowledge the new adult identity of these young people with an elaborate celebration.

In Western society today, we regularly perform rituals for births, marriages, and deaths. Some religions celebrate "coming of age" events—such as the Jewish *bar mitzvah* for boys and *bat mitzvah* for girls. In many communities, however, a ceremony for the onset of puberty is missing. Somewhere, in humankind's perennial quest for advancement, we lost touch with some of our own physical and emotional milestones.

The Scourge of Adolescence

Adolescence for many young women and men can be a difficult time. Along with the challenges of physical and hormonal changes, there is pressure of academic achievement, peer approval, and the search for a sense of identity. Teenagers today also tend to spend more time at school and college, meaning that the adolescent phase is prolonged and adulthood is postponed.

With a meaningful rite of passage to puberty, this transition can be eased. For a young woman, it should be a reminder of her sacred connection to the Moon cycle; for the male, it's an opportunity to connect with his warrior energy and magic within. Teenagers, without reliable adult guidance or role models, risk seeking their own wisdom and acceptance through unwise sources such as misguided friends. Those who crave a sense of belonging may look to gangs that offer initiation rites and group markings such as tattoos and piercings.

Just as our Pagan ancestors recognized the significance of reaching puberty, we too, can honor the teenager's maturity with celebration. The challenge is to integrate elements of ancient ritual with modern sensibilities to make the ceremony relevant today. Tribal societies recognized the young person's emerging maturity by acknowledging their fertility and ability to carry out adult tasks and responsibilities. In a hunting and gathering society, youths were required to undergo an ordeal to prove their new status as young adults. The adolescent males joined the men on the hunt, and the females were sent on missions—such as a search for sacred herbs and plants. Afterward, the village or tribe welcomed them back as adults.

Today, we need a way to bid farewell to the child and welcome the adult. A rite of passage to puberty sends a strong message that this transitional phase in their lives deserves celebration.

The Benefits of a Puberty Rite of Passage

The benefits of acknowledging this difficult passage from childhood to adulthood are not only evident for the family and an extended network of friends, but also for the teenager. The rite of passage helps them accept their emerging sexuality as a positive and natural force. This reinforces their self-belief and confidence, as they are taught to welcome the changes to their bodies rather than resent them.

For females, celebrating the maiden phase is a way for them to welcome menstruation as a blessing, not a curse. Today, many pubescent girls fear the arrival of their first Moon flow. For a young man, this rite allows him to accept his physical and hormonal changes as a way of releasing the emerging warrior within.

In the absence of a community-sanctioned ceremony for the passage through puberty, many parents are devising rituals for their teenage children to help minimize the confusion and loneliness often associated with the adolescent years. Along with establishing a support network of adults, the ritual can reduce the risk of teenagers seeking other ways to deal with the stresses of this time.

Preparing for this Rite of Passage

There is no set way to perform the ceremony. The format and level of formality depends on spiritual and family preferences. Any ritual tailored to the individual will be empowering and memorable. Below are some basic tips for preparing for this rite of passage.

The Ceremony

Agree on a ceremony format with the initiate. Check that he or she is happy with the location, time of day, date, and type of ceremony. Ensure that the initiate is comfortable presenting a short reading or a self-dedication (this can intimidate some teenagers). Consider selecting their favorite spiritual music for the ritual.

Adult Support Network

Identify family members and friends of the same gender who will participate in the ceremony and agree to continue their role as "mentor" throughout the transition period to adulthood. In the spirit of a tribe, aim to create a climate of perfect love and trust.

A Memento of the Occasion

Give a gift or memento of the occasion to the initiate. This may have a spiritual theme (symbolic jewelry or an icon), or it may be a personally oriented gift. The music used at the ceremony can be compiled on a CD or cassette tape as a memento.

Affirmation of Adulthood

Choose an activity that the initiate can undertake to mark the start of adulthood. This might include having the young adult take greater responsibility in caring for a younger sibling or participating in volunteer work.

Ritual Outline

A well-planned ritual includes a clear beginning and end to the ceremony. Use these steps as a guide for creating your own ritual. You can include any other elements that you, or your teenager, feel are appropriate.

Preparation of the site or sacred space

Period of seclusion of initiate, who will be joined by other friends and family members afterward during the celebration

Ritual bathing or purification

Casting circle, calling quarters

Invocation of chosen god or goddess

Stating of purpose of ceremony

Raising energy through chanting, drumming, music

Circle of men or of women—for sharing wisdom and telling stories

Affirmation (by initiate) of his or her goals, and a reading by initiate (and others, if appropriate)

Choosing (by initiate) of a magical name

Sharing the chalice, and cakes and ale

Farewell quarters, open circle

Like all of us, adolescents have an innate need to belong to a tribe or a community. As the urban goddesses and urban warriors of the new millennium, they are our future. For nature-based worshippers, a rite of passage through puberty reinforces the message to our young adults that we are all connected and that they belong to a caring community. It clearly identifies a new beginning and rebirth in their life cycle. And it acknowledges the growing responsibility that this young adult has in their intellectual, emotional, and spiritual development.

Making Your Own Magical Crochet Rune Set

by Karen Follett

As with any instrument of divination, the runes are tools of communication. The era of their origins has been speculated and disputed time and time again. Personally, I agree that runes, and their origins, are mysterious and secretive. But I feel that the mysteries and secrets pertain mostly to the hidden vault of knowledge that is unlocked by the runes.

The Runes in Early Times

I hold the opinion that early humankind's view of self was one of complete unity with universal forces. It is also my opinion that early humankind relied on their intuitive abilities to communicate to each other and to interpret the natural forces of the universe.

They based their perceptions on what they intuitively knew—the inner knowing of the collective unconscious, or the Akashic library. As the conscious analytical skills evolved in these people, the intuitive knowledge of their creators dimmed with each passing generation. Telepathic (or intuitive) communication gave way to written communication. The runic sigils were a portion of that written communication, but they also provided the bridge between the intuitive, Akashic wisdom to the conscious knowing—the connection between the mystery of intangible perception to the senses of the tangible world.

Crocheting an Ancient Divination Device

After generations of repression, the runes are now reclaiming their rightful place as a tool of divine communication. True to their historical use, the runic symbols create a bridge to give readers access to lost ancient wisdom.

My crochet pattern for the rune set begs for a rune assembly line type of production, but before you give in to the assembly line, please remember that the runes are tools of communication that is highly individual and based on individual perception. To enhance the communication process, I have included a list of the runic names and a very brief description of their traditional meanings.

As you work through the repetitive pattern of the crochet, your left brain will be occupied by the manual construction while your right brain (or the intuitive brain) will be opened by the mantra of working the pattern.

When crocheting, allow your mind to focus on the intent and the traditional meaning of each rune. Relax your mind with the pattern of creating each rune. As you work through the creation process with the individual runes, you will begin to perceive the individualistic nuances of communication that will bridge your personal pathways between your intuitive unconscious and your actively knowing conscious.

The choice of when to begin and finish your rune set is individual. The fact that you are beginning a new path of communication and that your focused intent of creation is energetically charging the runes with the forces of the universe should factor into your choice of timing. You will want to pick a start and finish time that allows for successive completion of each rune and that takes advantage of your natural rhythms with the universe. The optimal time frame would be to begin the set with the New Moon and have the set ready for consecration with the Full Moon.

Beginning Crocheting

Gather the following materials for constructing your runes.

Size 10 crochet cotton thread in main color

Size 10 crochet cotton thread in complimentary color

Cotton balls

Size 7 steel crochet hook

Mugwort (or other herb or oil for divination)

Fabric glue (optional for securing knots)

Tapestry (or large eye) needle

When you are ready to begin the pattern, start by shredding the cotton balls while mixing in your divination herb. Visualize yourself being attuned to the web of fate or the strands of time. Set aside the mixture until you are ready to stuff the runes.

Question each rune as you begin to work. How does its traditional meaning play into your life (see below). What is the "light" aspect of the meaning? What is the "shadow" aspect of the meaning? This begins your communication as you now are ready to begin the pattern.

Traditional Runic Messages

Feoh (ᚠ): Money, wealth
Eoh (ᛇ): Resilience, endurance
Ur (ᚢ): Strength, physicality
Peordh (ᛈ): Change, evolution
Thorn (ᚦ): Destruction, power
Eolh (ᛉ): Luck, protection
Os (ᚨ): Wisdom, insight
Sigil (ᛊ): Success, honor
Rad (ᚱ): Travel, change
Tyr (ᛏ): Courage, victory, justice
Ken (ᚲ): Energy, creativity, change
Beorc (ᛒ): Healing, renewal
Gyfu (ᚷ): Gift, sacrifice
Eh (ᛖ): Journeys, work
Wynn (ᚹ): Joy, harmony
Mann (ᛗ): Man, self, intelligence
Haegl (ᚺ): Union, completion
Lagu (ᛚ): Healing, protection, life
Nyd (ᚾ): Need, deliverance
Ing (ᛜ): Fertility, energy
Is (ᛁ): Ice, barrenness
Daeg (ᛞ): Opportunity, change
Jera (ᛃ): Bounty, fruition, reward
Ethel (ᛟ): Land, prosperity, power
Wyrd: This is the "blank" rune. Apparently not a member of the original futhark set, Wyrd, is still used, however,

by some diviners today. In my mind, Wyrd is the summation of one's web of fate. As such, I associate this rune with the idea that the issue is "In the hands of the gods." The querent has chosen his or her path and lessons that need to be learned regard less of the outcome.

The Crochet Pattern

The stitches that you will use in this pattern include: Single crochet (marked as *sc* in the text), slip stitch *(ss)*, and chain *(ch)*.

Rune Set Backgrounds

With main color, *ch* 10, row 1, *sc* in 2nd chain from hook and in each *ch* across (9 *ss*), turn. Row 2–9, *ch* 1, *sc* in each *sc* across (9 *ss*), turn. At the end of the 9th row, cut and secure thread. Using double strands of the complimentary color (either two strands or one strand doubled over the tapestry needle), follow in an embroidered backstitch. Cut threads and secure with a knot. You may want to use fabric glue to further secure the threads.

Finishing the Runes

With the main color, hold two rune backgrounds together, with right sides facing out and inscribed side facing toward you. Attach thread with a single crochet to the top right-hand corner. Work seven single crochet stitches across the straight edges to corners. In the corners, work three single crochet stitches. Repeat the last two steps to the fourth side of the rune. Stuff rune with cotton and herb mixture. Resume closing the rune as per instructions to the last corner.

Work two single crochet stitches in last corner (which is the same stitch as the beginning single crochet). Join thread to first single crochet with a slip stitch.

Cut and Secure Thread

With the complementary color, attach thread to top right stitch (2nd *sc* in the corner of the previous row) with a single crochet. Work *sc* in each of nine *sc* across rune side. Work 3 *sc* in 2nd *sc* in corner of previous row. Work nine *sc* along next two sides, then repeat the last step. Work nine *sc* along last side to corner. Work two *sc* in last corner and join to beginning.

Single crochet with a slip stitch. Cut and secure threads. Weave in ends. Each rune measures about one and a half inches.

Consecrating Your Crochet Runes

Set up your altar with the representations of the elements. Place your rune set in the middle of the altar. Cast a circle, and lay your hands on your rune set. Center your energy and allow the energy to open your chakras. Visualize your energy exchanging with and charging the energy of the runes.

You can call any deity that you feel comfortable with and whose energy you associate with divination. Since the runes of the elder futhark are associated with the Nordic pantheon, Freya, Odin, and the Wyrd sisters are excellent choices for this.

Beginning at the north, present your rune set to the elements. Say these or similar words:

> *I present this rune set for your blessing. Made from the natural riches of the Earth, may these runes retain their vibrations of the abundant earth.*

Sprinkle with salt or a purifying herb. Move to the east, and say:

> *I present this rune set for your blessing. May these runes communicate the knowledge of their mysteries and their messages.*

Pass the rune set through a purifying incense (such as cedar). Move to the south:

> *I present this rune set for your blessing. May I have the strength to clearly see your truths. The courage to change my path or to strive on course.*

Pass the rune set above a candle flame. Move to the west, and say:

> *I present this rune set for your blessing. May they clearly speak their flow of messages to my intuition.*

Sprinkle the rune set with water. Return your rune set to the middle of your altar. Suspend your hands over the set with thumbs and forefingers touching to form a triangle. Visualize a divine ray traveling through your crown to your hands and to the runes. Say these or similar words:

Wisdom of the divine
Circle around the web of fate,
Clearly lighting the torch of time.
These runes are blessed by your light,
Their messages clearly seen by my sight.

Thank deity and dismiss the elements. Open the circle.

Using Your Runes

You used intent to create and consecrate your runes, and this intent imprinted your runes to you. It also charged your runes with the energy of the universe. You will use intent as you speak to your runes. Whether you use a tarot spread, choose your runes from a pouch, or cast your entire set of runes on a cloth, it is your focus on the matter at hand that will speak the energy of intent to the runes.

Any spread that is chosen creates the puzzle. The runes provide the pieces to that puzzle. Interpreting the pieces involves relaxation of mind and body, allowing the runes to speak to your inner conscious. Interpreting involves watching the flow of runes in relation to each other. And finally, interpreting involves the willingness and strength to learn what you need to know, not just what you want to know.

It is written that the ancients viewed their runic divinatory practices as "seeking counsel from the gods." Think about this. Our ancient ancestors were closer to the creator gods. They treated the runes with reverence. They understood the runic sigils and their relevance.

Generations of people have come and passed, yet the runes have survived to link us back to the wisdom of the gods—honored wisdom that can lead us to the life that we were born to have.

Making Your Own Drum

by Danny Pharr

The drum has been the centerpiece of ritual and ceremony for thousands of years. Like a mother's heartbeat comforting a newborn baby, we are drawn to the beat of the drum and affected by its rhythm. A steady drumbeat holds us in a close embrace, a rapid drumbeat sends us dancing.

Every drum reflects its builder in a personal way. A drum can be made in a very complex fashion, as would have been done centuries ago by people well versed in woodsmanship, hunting and tracking, and hide curing and tanning. A drum-maker in those days would have first hunted and killed a deer, stretched its hide in the Sun to dry, and then felled a tree, cut a round from the trunk, hollowed the round, and built the drum. This process could still be followed today if someone had the time, skills, and proper licenses. Another method, much less complex and more popular today, is buying a drum kit.

A drum-making kit will include the round, the rawhide, and the lacing, and can be purchased online at stores catering to the magical, New Age, and spiritual marketplace, or at Native American drum stores. Either method of drum-making will produce a drum that you will cherish for years.

Building the Drum

Start this process just after the appearance of the New Moon. Building a drum requires one day for soaking the rawhide, one day to assemble the drum, and up to a week for drying and tightening.These activities should occur during the waxing moon.

Cast a circle and create a sacred work space by walking clockwise three times around the perimeter and chanting:

Earth, air, water, fire,
Create this space as I desire.
Goddess, join me, as I've asked,
Bless me to complete this task.
A drum I'll make to honor thee,
So help me, Goddess, and blessed be.

Spread out the rawhide, rough side up, and identify the spine region of the hide—the area in the center, between the legs of the animal. Trace the outline of the round spine area of the rawhide with a pencil. Outside the pencil circle, draw a line in the shape of a sine wave (see illustration) with thirteen evenly spaced hills and valleys. Draw two lace slots side by side, one-half inch apart, in each of the thirteen humps (each about three-quarters inch from the edges). Use scissors to cut out the drumhead from the rawhide following the wavy line. Punch a circular hole, about one-eighth to one-quarter inch in diameter, at the outside end of each slot—so that the slot extends from the punched hole toward the center of the drum. Cut the lace slots into the thirteen humps.

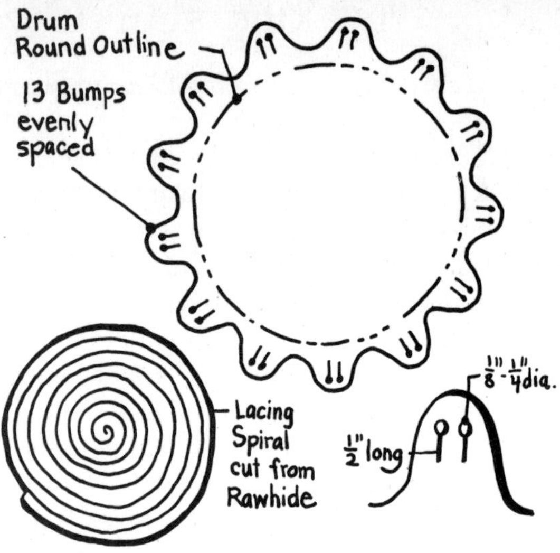

Draw a twelve-inch diameter circle on the remaining rawhide, and cut out the circle with scissors. Next, cut fifty feet of lacing from the circle by starting at an outside edge and cutting a three-eighths inch strip spiraling into the center. When complete, cut the lace into two twenty-five foot pieces.

Soak the rawhide drumhead and the lacing in water overnight—at least twelve hours (twenty-four hours is better). A magical drum should be consecrated during this soaking process. If the drum is for personal use, add small quantities of one or many bodily secretions—such as saliva, sweat, tears, mucus, or ear wax—to the soaking water. If for coven use, each member of the coven should add to the mix. While consecrating the drum, say:

Bless this drum and bond to me
By the earth, air, fire, and sea.
Its percussion shall travel across the oceans

And bring to me all that I've chosen.
With each drumbeat, molecules align,
Manifesting the desires of me and mine.
This drum is hallowed for me and thee,
And together we shall blessed be.

After soaking the rawhide overnight, it will be ready for stretching. A second person will be required to help in the stretching of the drumhead.

To begin this, light a candle during a waxing Moon. Anoint yourselves with cinnamon and sandalwood in an invoking pentagram blessing (touch the herb or oil to the third eye, right breast, left shoulder, right shoulder, left breast, and third eye). Collect some candle light in the palms of the hands while saying:

From materials collected across the land
We'll build a drum with these hands—
The beat of which will honor thee,
So help me Goddess and blessed be.

Then cover your eyes with your palms and visualize purity, spiritual intention, and the finished drum.

Inside the circle, both drum-makers should sit on their legs with their knees touching each other. Grip the wet rawhide with both hands and stretch it by leaning backward and pulling. Release, turn the rawhide a few degrees clockwise, and stretch it again. Repeat this process until the rawhide is large enough to come at least halfway down the sides of the drum round. Stretching squeezes the moisture from the rawhide, so be sure to pour a little water on the hide with each stretch. If the rawhide does become really dry, submerge it for one minute.

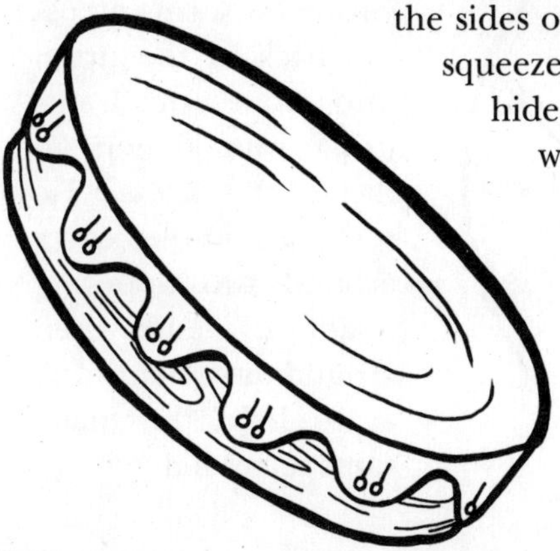

When the rawhide has been stretched to its desired size, it must be laced on to the round. Place the rawhide on the ground, rough side up, and center the round in the middle of the rawhide. Tie one end of the lace to one of the lace slots using a square knot. Thread the other end of the lace through a lace slot on the opposite side of the drum. Pull the lace tight, drawing opposing lace slots together.

Thread the lace through the slot immediately to the left (clockwise) of the square knot, and tighten. Thread the lace through the slot immediately clockwise of the laced slot on the opposite side of the drum and tighten. Continue lacing across the drum clockwise, through each subsequent lace slot, and tighten. Note that the slots will stretch and enlarge but they will not tear out. When completely laced, tie off the lacing at the slot opposite the last hole.

Further tension must now be added by tying the drum in accordance with the four directions. Group the lacing across the back of the drum into four quadrants using your fingers to divide the areas. Tie some lace in the center around two opposing quadrants and then around the other two so as to hold the quadrants separated.

The Four Directions

Fire and earth, south and north,
Elemental powers, come ye forth.
Air and water, east and west,
May this magical drum be blessed.
The sound of this drum will call forth and free,
The power of lightning, wind, land, and sea.
For my use, as I desire.
Earth, air, sea, and fire.

While chanting, wrap the lacing up one of the lace quadrants toward the drum edge, bundling the laces into a single thick cord and then wrap back down to the middle. Wrap the lace up the opposite lace quadrant and back to the center. Wrap the lace up one of the two remaining quadrants and back to the center and then up the opposite and back. Tie the lace in the middle.

The drum is complete, though it must dry. Hang the drum in a tree, if possible, or any area inside or out with good air circulation. Avoid hanging the drum directly over a heat source. The drum is dry when the wad of laces has completely dried. This may take several days, depending on the heat and humidity. Test the drum by tapping on the drumhead. If the drum rings, it is ready, if it thuds, use a hair dryer and add tension by further drying the head of the drum. Store the drum in a dry place in cloth.

The Drum Beater

When making a beater, use the same techniques of cutting, soaking, and lacing the rawhide. Mark a five-inch diameter circle on the remaining piece of rawhide. Cut the out beater head and soak it for twenty-four hours. Cut some lacing and soak it as well. Select a stick for a beater handle.

Shape the rawhide head of the beater with the rough side of the rawhide out and smooth side in. Stuff the rawhide with sand until the rawhide has stretched to the desired size. Wrap the end of the beater handle with cotton cloth and insert it into the head, working it into the center of the sand. Wrap the head around the stick, and tie it in place with many layers of lacing. Hang the beater to dry.

Unfamiliar Familiars

by Breid Foxsong

The concept of the familiar is spread throughout various cultures. The Romans, for example, believed that each household was protected by a familiar whose job it was to keep the family from harm. Shamans and medicine people of various tribal traditions on several continents honored the spirits of animals for their wisdom and assistance in magical workings. This includes rabbits, dogs, mice, even lowly insects.

In the Middle Ages, the familiar took on the role of Witch's companions and assistant, aiding her in diagnosing illnesses, divining for lost objects, and helping with spells and charms. Familiars usually assumed animal forms; nearly any animal in the vicinity was a possible collaborator.

Today's Witches view their familiars in an altogether different light. For the modern Witch, a familiar can be any animal that the individual feels an affinity for. These animals are far from being just household pets—they are treated as partners in the practice of magic. Animals are believed to be more sensitive to vibrations from the unseen world, and so act as a kind of psychic radar, indicating negative energy by their behavior. Familiars also bring added energy to magic workings through their affinity with the spirit world and attunement with their Witch.

Some Witches also use the term "familiar" to describe thought forms created magically and empowered to carry out a certain task on the astral plane. Although they play the same role as animal familiars, these spirit familiars are more versatile. Their presence is often experienced as a voice, vision, or strong feeling of peace. If necessary, they can be associated with inanimate objects, such as a stone, piece of jewelry, or other talisman.

A question at this point: Why has the cat become the most well-known familiar? Why not some of the more esoteric animals? Especially since the familiar was supposed to be able to take any form? Some scholars believe that the cat, being both plentiful and self-sufficient, was an easy scapegoat for suspicions by nonmagical people. Anyone who has tried to keep a cat out of anywhere it wants to be knows that cats can magically appear where they are least wanted. Also, the cat's association with the mysteries of Egypt and the magic of foreign lands made it easy for people to believe that they were involved in bewitchments.

Let's take a look at some of the less-familiar familiars through history. Toads were common familiars in the Roman days. They were thought to confer invisibility and detect poison. It was also believed that they could influence the weather. Today toads are welcomed into a Witch's garden since they will eat pests that eat the plants.

Bees were popular as well, since they produced honey (which could be magically changed into alcohol), and required little maintenance. Legends say, if a Witch or sorceress managed to eat a queen bee before she was arrested, she would be able to withstand torture and trial without confessing.

In Suffolk, chicken named Nan was charged with being a familiar in the seventeenth century. Three other chickens were also cited as imps in the case. In the same trials, a Witch was accused of having flies for her familiars. Another unusual familiar was the snail. John Bysack, an accused Witch, confessed to having six snail familiars.

Mice were another common familiar in the sixteenth and seventeenth centuries. Easy to keep and tame, mice were quiet companions who would keep an elderly lady entertained and amused. Rats, although not as amiable as mice, are also easy to train and require little care. Both can be affectionate without being as pushy as a larger animal.

Hares and rabbits were also associated with witchcraft. A number of superstitions surround the hare—such as its association with fertility and luck. Spiders are another small creature that is common and self-sufficient. The strength of a spiderweb is legendary, and the spider's ability to escape swatting gave them the illusion of immortality. Killing a spider in the fall is said to bring rain, something that could mean disaster to a farm-based economy.

Dogs got their share of bad press as well, especially black ones. The Black Dog was often sited as the proceeder or associate of many a ghostly vision in the English Moors. The Black Dog of Cornwall was a beneficent dog who warned sailors of dangerous tides. White dogs with red ears belonged to the Sidhe.

Snakes have gotten bad press since the Garden of Eden, but in Rome they were revered not only as protectors but also as oracles—since they were believed to communicate directly to the goddess Hertha. Snakes also served the same purpose as cats in removing pests, even though their flat unblinking gaze makes some uncomfortable.

The finding of an animal familiar is a very personal thing, and often the Witch will send out a psychic call to attract a suitable one. An immediate and overwhelming feeling of kinship between the Witch and the animal usually signifies the discovery of the new familiar.

Johnny Appleseed

by Susan Sheppard

In Ellen Cannon Reed's *Witches Tarot Kit* (Llewellyn, 1995), the mythic figure in the Fool card is none other than Johnny Appleseed. This is a quite apt figure, since the card represents a leap of faith—stepping into darkness in order to comprehend the light, trusting in the unknown. It is also somewhat amusing given the fact that Johnny Appleseed was a real person who laughed and loved, with perfectly human dreams and desires. That is, he was a modest man on the American frontier whose selfless acts of kindness were so unusual, his name was eventually elevated into myth.

Although John Chapman was a Christian in the most genuine sense of the word, one can easily connect him to the Fool card in the tarot, as well as to the Green Man, Cernunnos, the Wild Man, Herne the Hunter, Dionysus, and even John the Baptist. Johnny Appleseed personified mythology more than any American.

But before making such mythic comparisons, it is important to look at the man. John Chapman was born on September 26, 1774, near Leomister, Massachusetts, at the time of year when apples show their most intense blush as they ripen. John was the only child of Nathaniel and Elizabeth Chapman. John's mother died when he was small, and by the time he was a teen his father had remarried and moved to western Pennsylvania. It is here that Johnny first gathered apple seeds from cider presses, cleaning and collecting the most viable seeds and filling his famous knapsack. By the time Johnny was twenty-five years old, he was already planting apple orchards throughout the Pennsylvania and Ohio wilderness. He accomplished this by planting the seeds, then building a fence around the trees that he wove from dense brush.

Disney cartoons show a gawky, freckled, red-haired Johnny Appleseed with a tin pan on his head. In fact, Johnny was a small, thin man with wild black hair and intense hazel eyes. Generally, he wore no shoes but would fashion a type of crude sandal for winter. His jacket was a burlap sack with slits for his arms and his head.

Johnny was a pacifist and a vegetarian, refusing to kill in order to eat. Yet Johnny Appleseed was not destitute and he certainly was

not poor. He had guardianship over fertile lands on islands along the West Virginia and Ohio border, and he planted hundreds of apple orchards between the Ohio and Mississippi Rivers. But John Chapman was never one to feather his own nest. He gave what he had to others, asking very little in return.

John Chapman walked easily among, and was accepted by, warring Native American tribes. The Shawnee, especially, considered Johnny sacred, protected by the spirit world. To harm him would bring certain doom upon them. Johnny Appleseed spoke the Shawnee language and often slept in Shawnee camps. He once overheard his Shawnee friends planning an attack on Fort Wayne. John slipped away during the night and warned the settlers. The attack was thwarted and no one was killed.

What set John's heart aflame was an inborn spiritual fire. He became a follower of the Swedish mystic Emmanuel Swedenborg and believed that his true mate was an angel in heaven who awaited him in the afterlife. Although Johnny Appleseed could not read the Bible very well, he carried one and memorized long passages.

Because of his deep reverence of nature and its cycles, Johnny Appleseed was a Pagan at heart. He did not believe that human beings were superior to other creatures. He also believed the humble apple represented the most superb creation on Earth.

Apples are important symbols of fertility and growth in Paganism, as the Roman festival of Pomona celebrates. The biblical tale of Adam and Eve suggests apples also represent sexual pleasure and forbidden knowledge. When the Romans conquered Britain, they brought with them the apple tree. Eventually, a reverence for apples became a part of the Celtic festival of Samhain.

If you cut an apple in half, you will notice the seeds form a perfect pentagram. In Michael Pollan's *Botany of Desire: A Plant's Eye View of the World* (Random House, 2001), he likens Johnny Appleseed to an American Dionysus, and points out that it was John Chapman's apples were something sweet and rare on the early frontier.

Johnny Appleseed knew that to be separated from nature is what divides us from what is truly divine: nature's cycles, seasons, creatures, and the Earth. To make claims on rivers and lands makes an unnatural prison out of our earthly paradise.

Often in mid to late September I am asked to help celebrate the life and deeds of Johnny Appleseed with school children in my area. As a descendent of John's first cousin, William Chapman, I suppose I am as fitting a representative of Johnny Appleseed as anyone. After all, he had no direct descendants. We usually end the festivities by planting an apple tree together.

After the ceremony, I can count on getting a thick lump in my throat as the school children wait in line to "shake the hand of Johnny Appleseed's cousin." In doing this, I help honor the one who gave so much yet asked for so little. Whether John was a devout Christian or a perfect Pagan really makes no difference. Like all great people, the life and deeds of John Chapman transcends all categories. As the modest epitaph on his gravestone in Fort Wayne, Indiana reads: "John Chapman 1774–1845. He Lived for Others."

Eating Like the Ancestors: A Pagan Diet

by Peg Aloi

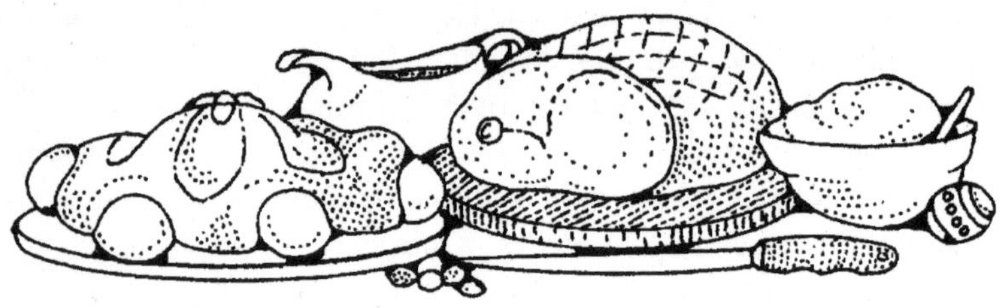

In this modern world, many of us do not have a healthy relationship with food. Despite so many choices, many of us hurry through meals or simply eat the quickest thing available. Our European ancestors had a deep reverence and respect for the land and its inhabitants, and their relationship to food was a very conscientious one.

Modern Pagans try to enhance their relationship to the natural world, and one good way to do this is by paying special attention to the food we eat. This article will look at the ways we can enjoy better health by aligning our eating habits with those of our ancestors.

Although we have been told for years by the medical establishment that we need to cut down on fats and red meat, many Americans are losing weight on trendy high-protein, low-carbohydrate diets. Obviously such an extreme diet is not healthy in the long run. But the principle behind it actually has its roots in our early evolution.

Prior to the advent of agriculture, humans were hunters and gatherers. That meant eating animals and green plants, and whatever fruits or nuts could be foraged. The consumption of grains, which form the basis of the starchy, agriculture-based foods—such a bread, pasta, potatoes, and cereals—in our diets began relatively recently in our history. It is believed that humans are designed to digest grains efficiently, because they are made of both protein and carbohydrates, and the stomach utilizes different enzymes to digest these foods. So ingesting them at the same time can lead to poor absorption of nutrients and faulty digestion. This principle forms the basis of the popular "food-combining" diets, as found in many contemporary books.

The human body is designed to eat meat and plants; our teeth are made for tearing into flesh and for grinding down plant material. There is growing interest these days in so-called "caveman diets," which emphasize leaner meat than what we find in grain-fed cattle—such as elk, deer, or buffalo.

The healthiest humans in the world (with virtually no cardiovascular or heart disease, nor cancer) are the Masai tribe of Africa. These people are nomadic cattle herders who eat almost nothing but the meat, marrow, and milk of their cattle, along with green plants. They also get a lot of exercise—walking and running up to twenty miles a day as they herd their cattle.

Clearly their healthy hearts and lungs are helped by the fresh air and exercise, but the quality of the food they eat is also significant. In the Western world, much of the meat we eat is raised for slaughter, and animals are pumped full of antibiotics and hormones for more efficient production. The health dangers of a high-meat diet are not just due to the low fiber, high-fat content, but also to the traces of these toxic substances that remain in our tissues.

So what do we eat to stay healthy—especially if we can't walk twenty miles each day? I propose a lifestyle that attempts to eat as our ancestors did: simple, healthy foods in reasonable amounts that are, where appropriate, specific to our ethnic background or our region.

In earlier generations, foods were not full of pesticide residue or hormones and antibiotics. Our oceans and lakes were not laden with chemicals. Fruit and vegetables were not tainted.

Today, therefore, there is no better way to spend our food dollars than to buy organically grown produce and naturally raised meat and fish. Unfortunately, in some areas organic foods are expensive and hard to find. The greater the demand for these products, the more widely available, and cheaper, they will become—so ask for them. We may raise our eyebrows at the higher price on apples grown without pesticides, but isn't better health and a cleaner environment worth a few extra pennies?

Our ancestors did not have grocery stores, microwave ovens, or refrigerators. They hunted and gathered from season to season, and they stored what they could to get them through winter. Fruits and vegetables, nuts and seeds were eaten raw, and so kept all of their nutritional value. One of the best ways to align ourselves with the natural rhythms of the seasons, as our ancestors lived, is to eat locally grown raw foods.

Most cities, and towns have a farmers' market in late summer or early autumn when so much of the harvest is available. Depending on your area, you could get wonderful fresh fruits and vegetables from April through November. Local grocery stores will also make an effort to sell this local produce so look for the signs that identify foods as "locally grown." Think of how a tomato that you eat in the middle of winter is tasteless, or how store-bought apples in spring are mealy—they have usually been picked prematurely and shipped a long way. We can enhance our health and get great pleasure from our food if we take advantage of the growing seasons in our area.

It is believed by holistic healers that the human body stays healthiest by eating foods grown in our natural climate. These foods protect us from infections and enhance our natural immunity because of pollination and other environmental factors. So even though I love Florida oranges and grapefruit in winter, they are not as health-giving for me as summer raspberries grown in Massachusetts.

We are also products of our ethnic heritage. Being half Italian and half Irish, I notice tastes and preferences, not to mention food sensitivities, particular to my background. Traditional cultural food preferences develop over centuries, based on climate and availability. As customs form, that particular group's genetic make-up is affected by the foods eaten over many generations. My Italian half prefers to cook with olive oil (much healthier than other oils), while the Irish side likes butter (still better for us than margarine or other partially hydrogenated fats). The Italian likes savory herbs such as basil and rosemary and thyme; the Irish likes good old salt and pepper. Neither of these influences has allowed me to stomach hot spicy food—but someone of Mexican or Spanish descent would have no problem eating lots of red hot chilies.

You can find out which foods might aggravate certain chronic conditions (headache, fatigue, indigestion, insomnia, and so on) by finding out as much as you can about your mother's natal nutritional habits. When my mother was carrying me, she broke out in hives whenever she ate cheese—so even though my Italian and Irish ancestors were great cheese lovers, I need to eat it in moderation.

It is believed that the current rise in peanut allergies in children is due to an increase in peanut consumption by pregnant and nursing mothers (maybe trying to get their protein from nonmeat sources). Understanding our personal nutritional needs, including what we are allergic or sensitive to, helps us choose foods that enhance our immunity and align our health in subtle ways. In this way, we can then avoid any self-medicating with painkillers, sleep aids, caffeine, or toxic substances such as cigarettes, alcohol, or prescription medications.

Many health complaints can be traced to a nutritional deficiency, yet nutrition is not a required field of study in medical school. Is it any wonder then that the Western world is plagued by so many lifestyle-related disorders directly linked to poor diet?

As modern Pagans, we seek a closer relationship to nature, and we feel a need to be stewards of the Earth. By following a spiritual path that emphasizes personal responsibility and self-transformation, we make our way in the larger community by choosing to make the world a better place.

By choosing naturally raised meats and fish over factory-farmed products, we show our support for humane methods of animal husbandry. By choosing organically grown local produce, we show our support for small, noncorporate farms that choose not to poison our environment with pesticides. Food need not be a political issue, but by aligning our lifestyle choices with the eating patterns of our ancestors, we can not only honor our past but help to preserve our future.

The Gods of the Celts

by Sharynne NicMhacha

Who were the gods and goddesses of the Celts, and when were they honored or invoked during the year? These are the questions that sometimes keep me up at night.

To the ancient Celts, Samhain was the end of the old year and beginning of the next, when the otherworld was near and many sacred and supernatural events occurred. The sacred union between the tribal god and the goddess of the land may have been commemorated at this time of year. One Irish story tells of the sexual union between the Dagda and the Mórrigan at Samhain. The Dagda is a great tribal father deity associated with Druidical wisdom, magic, the harvest and the weather, and the powers of life and death. The Mórrigan was associated with battle, conflict, and death, as well as sexuality, fertility, sovereignty, and the land. Their union results in her bestowing her blessing and assistance on the gods, leading them to victory in a great battle.

Another divine female associated with Samhain is a female magician known as Tlachtga. She was associated with the site where the early Irish celebrated the Feast of Samhain (the Hill of Ward, known as Tlachtga in earlier times). Another text refers to the holiday of Samhain as the feast of Mongfind, a divine female figure whose name may mean "she of the bright hair." Some Pagans feel connected to the Welsh witch Cerridwen at Samhain, and they honor her at this time of year.

In Celtic tradition, there may have been an association between women and the dark half of the year and men with the bright half of the year. For this reason, I honor the Cailleach (a folkloric figure known from Ireland and Scotland) at the darkest point of winter. I also invoke Goibhniu, the Irish smith god, for his association with fire and mastery over the elements. There are a number of British and continental Celtic gods and goddesses who may have a solar aspect due to their association with warm healing waters. One of these is the British goddess Sulis whose name is either associated with a word for "Sun" or for "eye" (a euphemism for the Sun). Many people like to include Herne the Hunter in their Winter Solstice rites and festivities.

As far as we know, the Celts celebrated Samhain and Beltane, and in Ireland, at least, Imbolc as well. We don't have any evidence that they held celebrations at the solstices and equinoxes, although their people of wisdom would have been aware of these points of the year wheel.

Imbolc took place on February 1, and was a holiday associated with the birth of the first lambs of the year and the return of fresh milk. It was also connected with childbirth, purification, and possibly with the preparation of the earth for spring planting in March. Imbolc was associated with the goddess Bridget (Bríg, in early Irish tradition), a triple goddess of healing, poetry, and smithcraft. In Christian times she was known as St. Bridget and was invoked to protect women in child bed. Imbolc is connected with the birth of lambs, the return of milk, and women's interests.

At the Spring Equinox, I like to honor Oengus Mac Óc, the young god of love and beauty, as well as Rhiannon with her magical singing birds. Cliodna is another divine female figure from Ireland, an otherworld queen who also possessed beautiful songbirds. Other Celtic deities include Damona, a continental Celtic goddess associated with healing and regeneration. Mabon from Wales and Maponus from Britain may be similar in aspect to Oengus, and therefore appropriate to invoke in your equinox rituals and celebrations.

Beltane took place on May 1. Like Samhain, it was a point outside of time and a period of potential danger, as well as blessings and prosperity. Great fires were lit, and the cattle were run between them to protect them from disease and harm. The Pagan Irish celebrated Beltane at Uisneach, a sacred hill located near the cosmological center of Ireland. This síd-mound was where the Dagda was said to reside. Beltane heralded the start of the bright half of the year, when there may have been an increased focus on male deities. The hunting season ran from Beltane to Samhain, and a figure such as Cernunnos, the Lord of the Animals, may also have been honored at this time.

I like to show reverence for the Irish god Ogma at the Summer Solstice. He was a great warrior and poet whose epithet *Grianainech* means "Sun-face." He was also credited with the invention of the ogam alphabet. It also seems appropriate to honor Taranis the thunderer at this time of year, when powerful thunderstorms abound. Ériu represents the land of Ireland and is connected with the concept of sovereignty.

Many practitioners of earth religions celebrate the bounty of the earth at this time at the Fall Equinox. In Irish tradition, the Dagda was responsible for the weather and the harvest. Irish and Scottish folklore tells how the last sheaf of the harvest was bound into the form of a woman and called the Cailleach, or Hag.

At the Autumn Equinox I honor the Cailleach and the beginning of her reign, as I prepare for the coming shift in focus towards female energies which takes place at Samhain. There was a Christian holiday known as Michaelmas, which took place around the time of the equinox. A number of similarities exist between St. Michael and the Irish god Manannán Mac Lir. They are both associated with the sea and with horses. For many Celtic peoples, the concept of harvest would have included the produce of the sea. Epona was a widely worshiped deity in Britain and Gaul. She was associated with horses and passages to the otherworld, and she is represented with symbols of plenty and abundance such as grain, fruit, and bread.

I hope this inspires you to read about the Celtic deities and the folklore of the Celtic countries, meditating on their meaning and symbolism and exploring their nature and possibilities in terms of personal seasonal celebrations. May you find your own resonance with these powerful gods and goddesses who have such a deep connection with the land and the world of spirit.

Almanac Section

Calendar

Time Changes

Lunar Phases

Moon Signs

Full Moons

Sabbats

World Holidays

Incense of the Day

Color of the Day

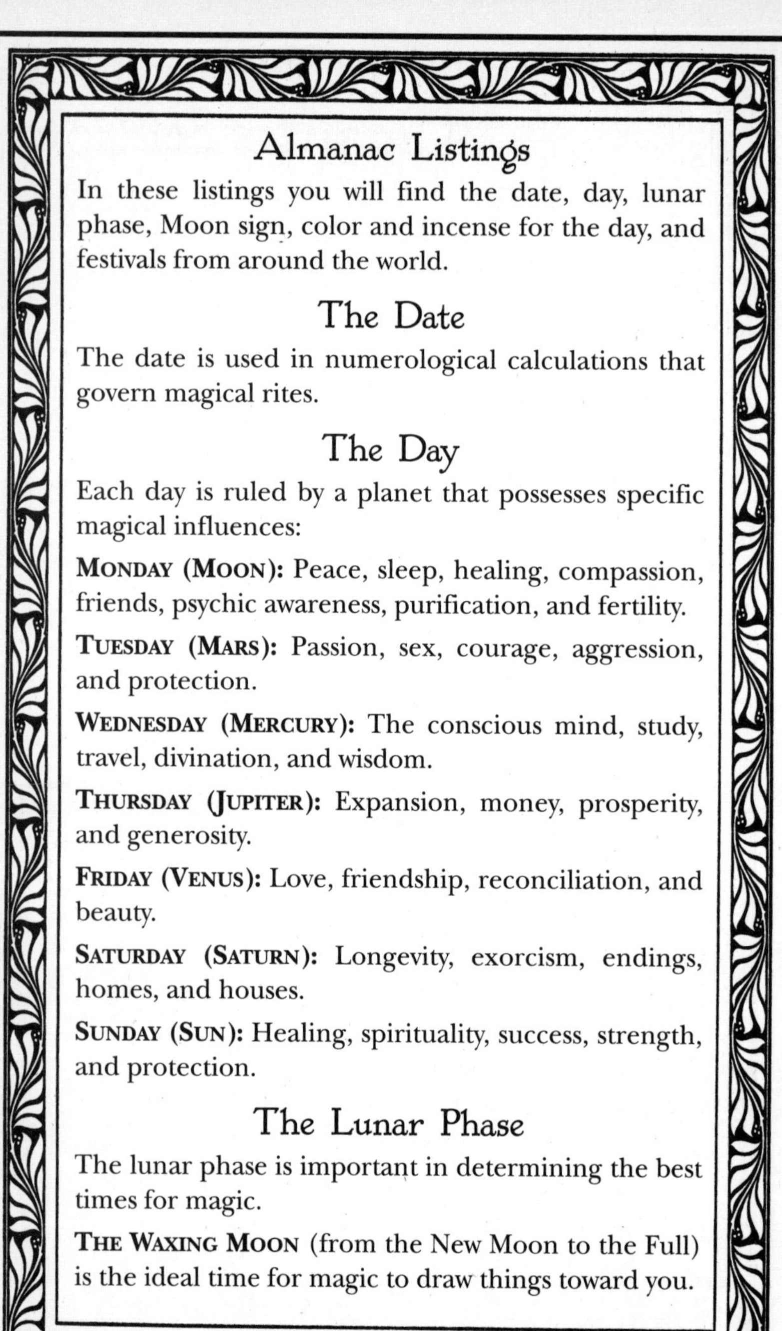

Almanac Listings

In these listings you will find the date, day, lunar phase, Moon sign, color and incense for the day, and festivals from around the world.

The Date

The date is used in numerological calculations that govern magical rites.

The Day

Each day is ruled by a planet that possesses specific magical influences:

Monday (Moon): Peace, sleep, healing, compassion, friends, psychic awareness, purification, and fertility.

Tuesday (Mars): Passion, sex, courage, aggression, and protection.

Wednesday (Mercury): The conscious mind, study, travel, divination, and wisdom.

Thursday (Jupiter): Expansion, money, prosperity, and generosity.

Friday (Venus): Love, friendship, reconciliation, and beauty.

Saturday (Saturn): Longevity, exorcism, endings, homes, and houses.

Sunday (Sun): Healing, spirituality, success, strength, and protection.

The Lunar Phase

The lunar phase is important in determining the best times for magic.

The Waxing Moon (from the New Moon to the Full) is the ideal time for magic to draw things toward you.

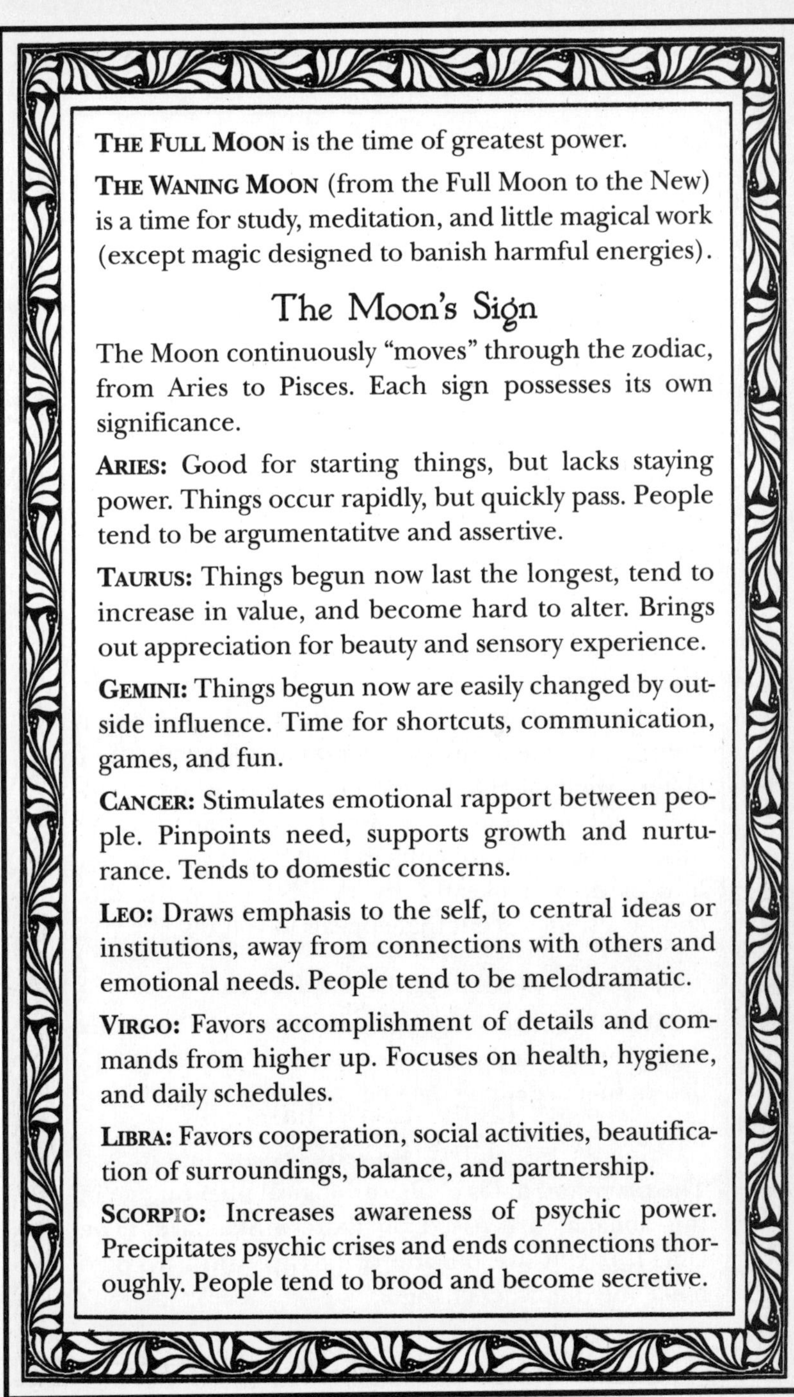

The Full Moon is the time of greatest power.

The Waning Moon (from the Full Moon to the New) is a time for study, meditation, and little magical work (except magic designed to banish harmful energies).

The Moon's Sign

The Moon continuously "moves" through the zodiac, from Aries to Pisces. Each sign possesses its own significance.

Aries: Good for starting things, but lacks staying power. Things occur rapidly, but quickly pass. People tend to be argumentatitve and assertive.

Taurus: Things begun now last the longest, tend to increase in value, and become hard to alter. Brings out appreciation for beauty and sensory experience.

Gemini: Things begun now are easily changed by outside influence. Time for shortcuts, communication, games, and fun.

Cancer: Stimulates emotional rapport between people. Pinpoints need, supports growth and nurturance. Tends to domestic concerns.

Leo: Draws emphasis to the self, to central ideas or institutions, away from connections with others and emotional needs. People tend to be melodramatic.

Virgo: Favors accomplishment of details and commands from higher up. Focuses on health, hygiene, and daily schedules.

Libra: Favors cooperation, social activities, beautification of surroundings, balance, and partnership.

Scorpio: Increases awareness of psychic power. Precipitates psychic crises and ends connections thoroughly. People tend to brood and become secretive.

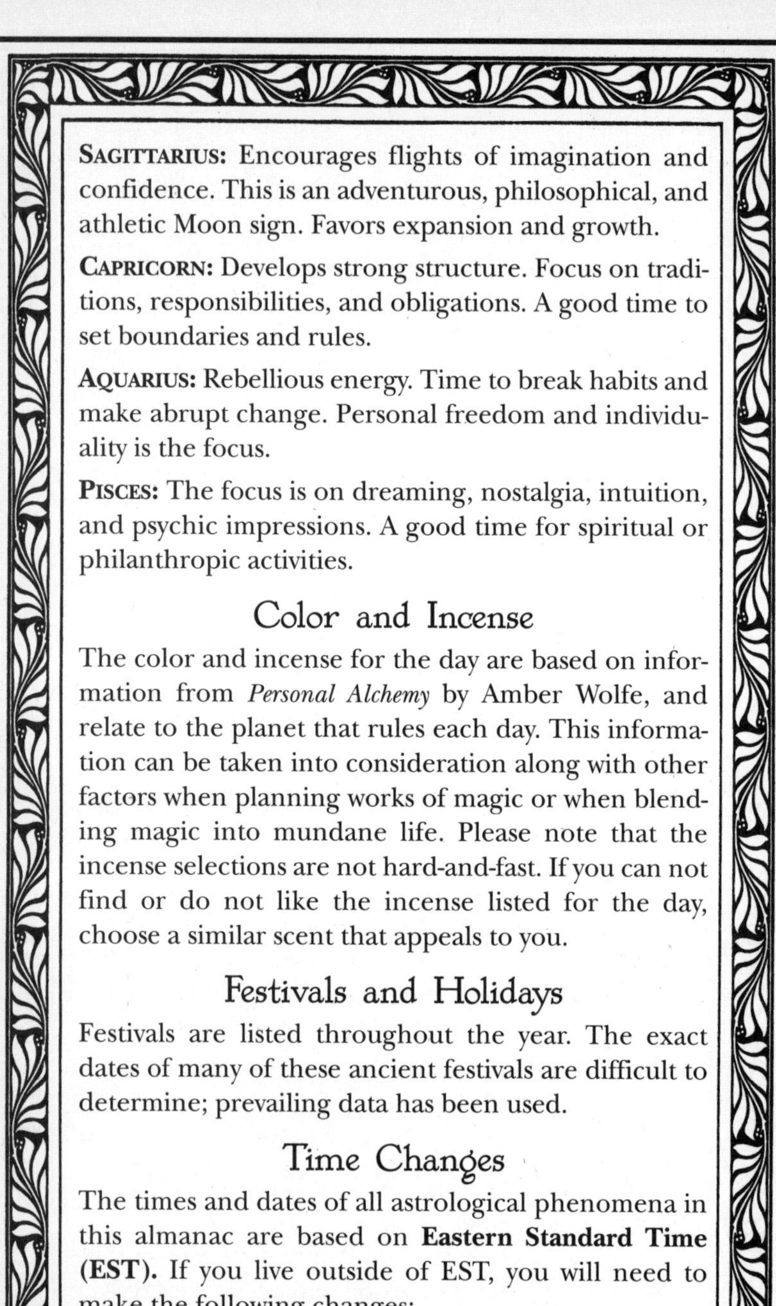

Sagittarius: Encourages flights of imagination and confidence. This is an adventurous, philosophical, and athletic Moon sign. Favors expansion and growth.

Capricorn: Develops strong structure. Focus on traditions, responsibilities, and obligations. A good time to set boundaries and rules.

Aquarius: Rebellious energy. Time to break habits and make abrupt change. Personal freedom and individuality is the focus.

Pisces: The focus is on dreaming, nostalgia, intuition, and psychic impressions. A good time for spiritual or philanthropic activities.

Color and Incense

The color and incense for the day are based on information from *Personal Alchemy* by Amber Wolfe, and relate to the planet that rules each day. This information can be taken into consideration along with other factors when planning works of magic or when blending magic into mundane life. Please note that the incense selections are not hard-and-fast. If you can not find or do not like the incense listed for the day, choose a similar scent that appeals to you.

Festivals and Holidays

Festivals are listed throughout the year. The exact dates of many of these ancient festivals are difficult to determine; prevailing data has been used.

Time Changes

The times and dates of all astrological phenomena in this almanac are based on **Eastern Standard Time (EST).** If you live outside of EST, you will need to make the following changes:

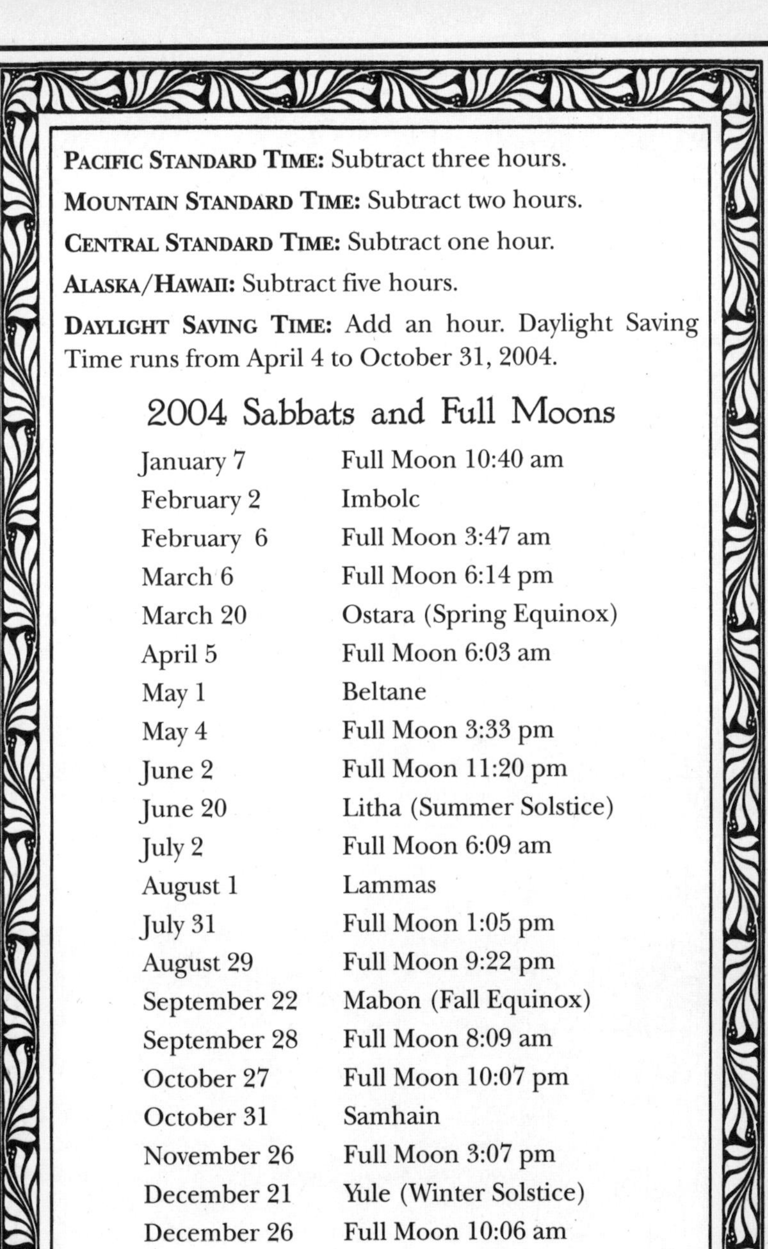

Pacific Standard Time: Subtract three hours.

Mountain Standard Time: Subtract two hours.

Central Standard Time: Subtract one hour.

Alaska/Hawaii: Subtract five hours.

Daylight Saving Time: Add an hour. Daylight Saving Time runs from April 4 to October 31, 2004.

2004 Sabbats and Full Moons

January 7	Full Moon 10:40 am
February 2	Imbolc
February 6	Full Moon 3:47 am
March 6	Full Moon 6:14 pm
March 20	Ostara (Spring Equinox)
April 5	Full Moon 6:03 am
May 1	Beltane
May 4	Full Moon 3:33 pm
June 2	Full Moon 11:20 pm
June 20	Litha (Summer Solstice)
July 2	Full Moon 6:09 am
August 1	Lammas
July 31	Full Moon 1:05 pm
August 29	Full Moon 9:22 pm
September 22	Mabon (Fall Equinox)
September 28	Full Moon 8:09 am
October 27	Full Moon 10:07 pm
October 31	Samhain
November 26	Full Moon 3:07 pm
December 21	Yule (Winter Solstice)
December 26	Full Moon 10:06 am

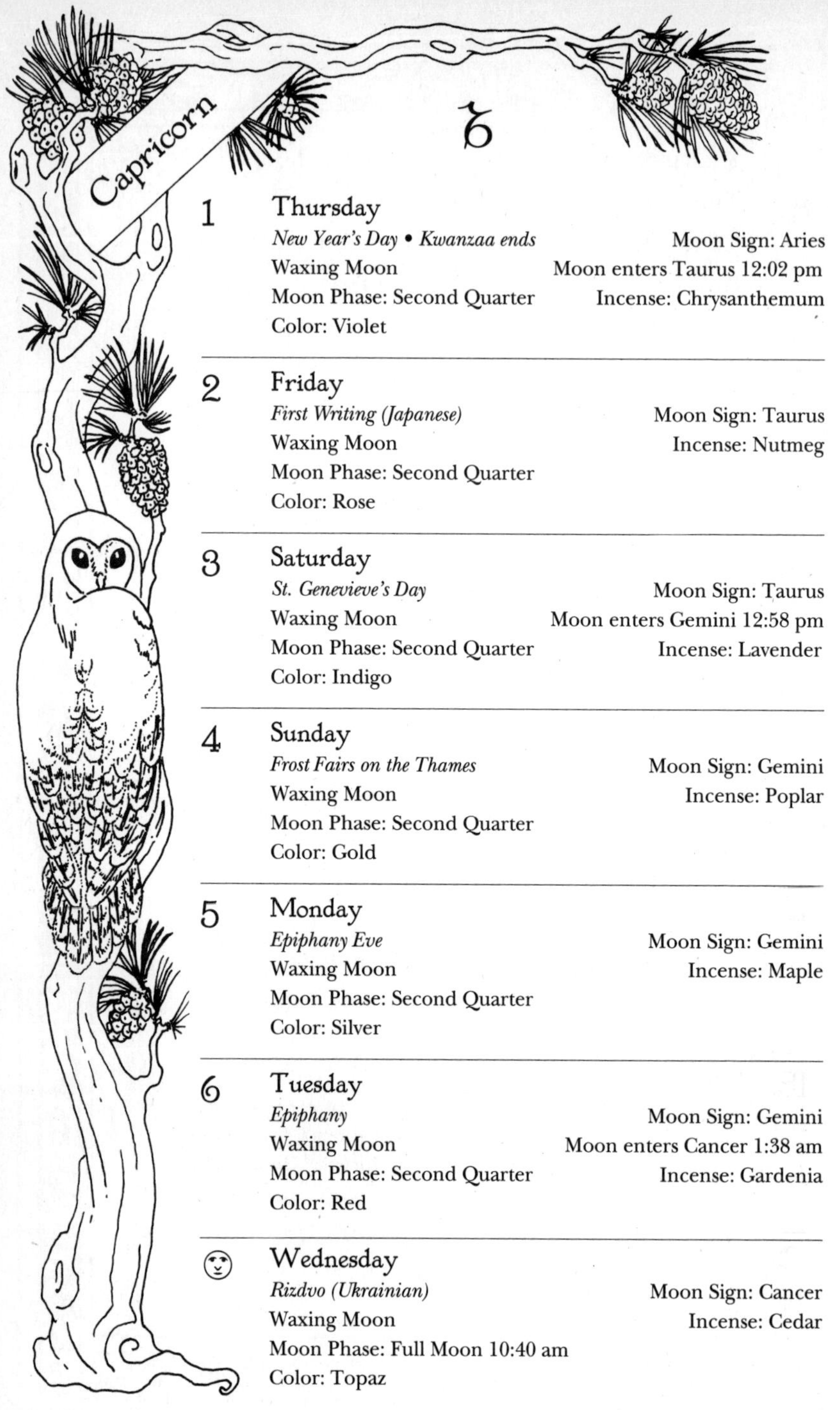

1 **Thursday**
New Year's Day • Kwanzaa ends
Waxing Moon
Moon Phase: Second Quarter
Color: Violet

Moon Sign: Aries
Moon enters Taurus 12:02 pm
Incense: Chrysanthemum

---

2 **Friday**
First Writing (Japanese)
Waxing Moon
Moon Phase: Second Quarter
Color: Rose

Moon Sign: Taurus
Incense: Nutmeg

---

3 **Saturday**
St. Genevieve's Day
Waxing Moon
Moon Phase: Second Quarter
Color: Indigo

Moon Sign: Taurus
Moon enters Gemini 12:58 pm
Incense: Lavender

---

4 **Sunday**
Frost Fairs on the Thames
Waxing Moon
Moon Phase: Second Quarter
Color: Gold

Moon Sign: Gemini
Incense: Poplar

---

5 **Monday**
Epiphany Eve
Waxing Moon
Moon Phase: Second Quarter
Color: Silver

Moon Sign: Gemini
Incense: Maple

---

6 **Tuesday**
Epiphany
Waxing Moon
Moon Phase: Second Quarter
Color: Red

Moon Sign: Gemini
Moon enters Cancer 1:38 am
Incense: Gardenia

---

7 **Wednesday**
Rizdvo (Ukrainian)
Waxing Moon
Moon Phase: Full Moon 10:40 am
Color: Topaz

Moon Sign: Cancer
Incense: Cedar

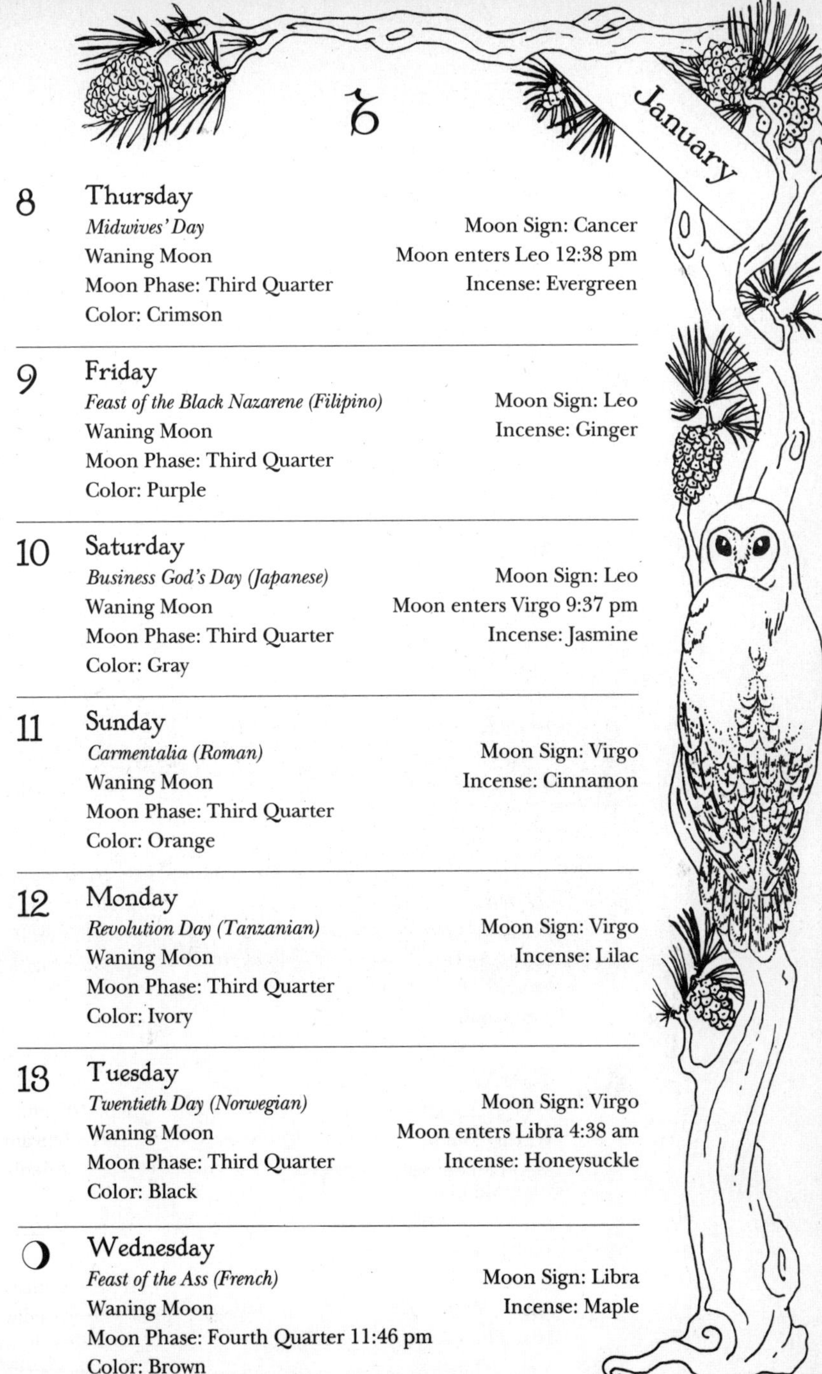

♑

8 Thursday
Midwives' Day
Waning Moon
Moon Phase: Third Quarter
Color: Crimson

Moon Sign: Cancer
Moon enters Leo 12:38 pm
Incense: Evergreen

---

9 Friday
Feast of the Black Nazarene (Filipino)
Waning Moon
Moon Phase: Third Quarter
Color: Purple

Moon Sign: Leo
Incense: Ginger

---

10 Saturday
Business God's Day (Japanese)
Waning Moon
Moon Phase: Third Quarter
Color: Gray

Moon Sign: Leo
Moon enters Virgo 9:37 pm
Incense: Jasmine

---

11 Sunday
Carmentalia (Roman)
Waning Moon
Moon Phase: Third Quarter
Color: Orange

Moon Sign: Virgo
Incense: Cinnamon

---

12 Monday
Revolution Day (Tanzanian)
Waning Moon
Moon Phase: Third Quarter
Color: Ivory

Moon Sign: Virgo
Incense: Lilac

---

13 Tuesday
Twentieth Day (Norwegian)
Waning Moon
Moon Phase: Third Quarter
Color: Black

Moon Sign: Virgo
Moon enters Libra 4:38 am
Incense: Honeysuckle

☾ Wednesday
Feast of the Ass (French)
Waning Moon
Moon Phase: Fourth Quarter 11:46 pm
Color: Brown

Moon Sign: Libra
Incense: Maple

15 Thursday

Martin Luther King, Jr.'s Birthday (actual) Moon Sign: Libra
Waning Moon Moon enters Scorpio 9:33 am
Moon Phase: Fourth Quarter Incense: Vanilla
Color: Turquoise

16 Friday

Apprentices' Day Moon Sign: Scorpio
Waning Moon Incense: Parsley
Moon Phase: Fourth Quarter
Color: Coral

17 Saturday

St. Anthony's Day (Mexican) Moon Sign: Scorpio
Waning Moon Moon enters Sagittarius 12:18 pm
Moon Phase: Fourth Quarter Incense: Violet
Color: Blue

18 Sunday

Assumption Day Moon Sign: Sagittarius
Waning Moon Incense: Sage
Moon Phase: Fourth Quarter
Color: Amber

19 Monday

Birthday of Martin Luther King, Jr. (observed) Moon Sign: Sagittarius
Waning Moon Moon enters Capricorn 1:24 pm
Moon Phase: Fourth Quarter Incense: Coriander
Color: Gray

20 Tuesday

Sun enters Aquarius Moon Sign: Capricorn
Waning Moon Incense: Poplar
Moon Phase: Fourth Quarter
Color: Maroon

☽ Wednesday

St. Agnes Day Moon Sign: Capricorn
Waning Moon Moon enters Aquarius 2:11 pm
Moon Phase: New Moon 4:05 pm Incense: Pine
Color: Yellow

♒

22 Thursday

Chinese New Year (monkey)
Waxing Moon
Moon Phase: First Quarter
Color: White

Moon Sign: Aquarius
Incense: Sandalwood

---

23 Friday

St. Ildefonso's Day
Waxing Moon
Moon Phase: First Quarter
Color: Pink

Moon Sign: Aquarius
Moon enters Pisces 4:29 pm
Incense: Rose

---

24 Saturday

Alasitas Fair (Bolivian)
Waxing Moon
Moon Phase: First Quarter
Color: Indigo

Moon Sign: Pisces
Incense: Cedar

---

25 Sunday

Burns' Night (Scottish)
Waxing Moon
Moon Phase: First Quarter
Color: Gold

Moon Sign: Pisces
Moon enters Aries 10:06 pm
Incense: Basil

---

26 Monday

Republic Day (Indian)
Waxing Moon
Moon Phase: First Quarter
Color: White

Moon Sign: Aries
Incense: Myrrh

---

27 Tuesday

Vogelgruff (Swiss)
Waxing Moon
Moon Phase: First Quarter
Color: Gray

Moon Sign: Aries
Incense: Juniper

---

28 Wednesday

St. Charlemagne's Day
Waxing Moon
Moon Phase: First Quarter
Color: Topaz

Moon Sign: Aries
Moon enters Taurus 7:46 am
Incense: Neroli

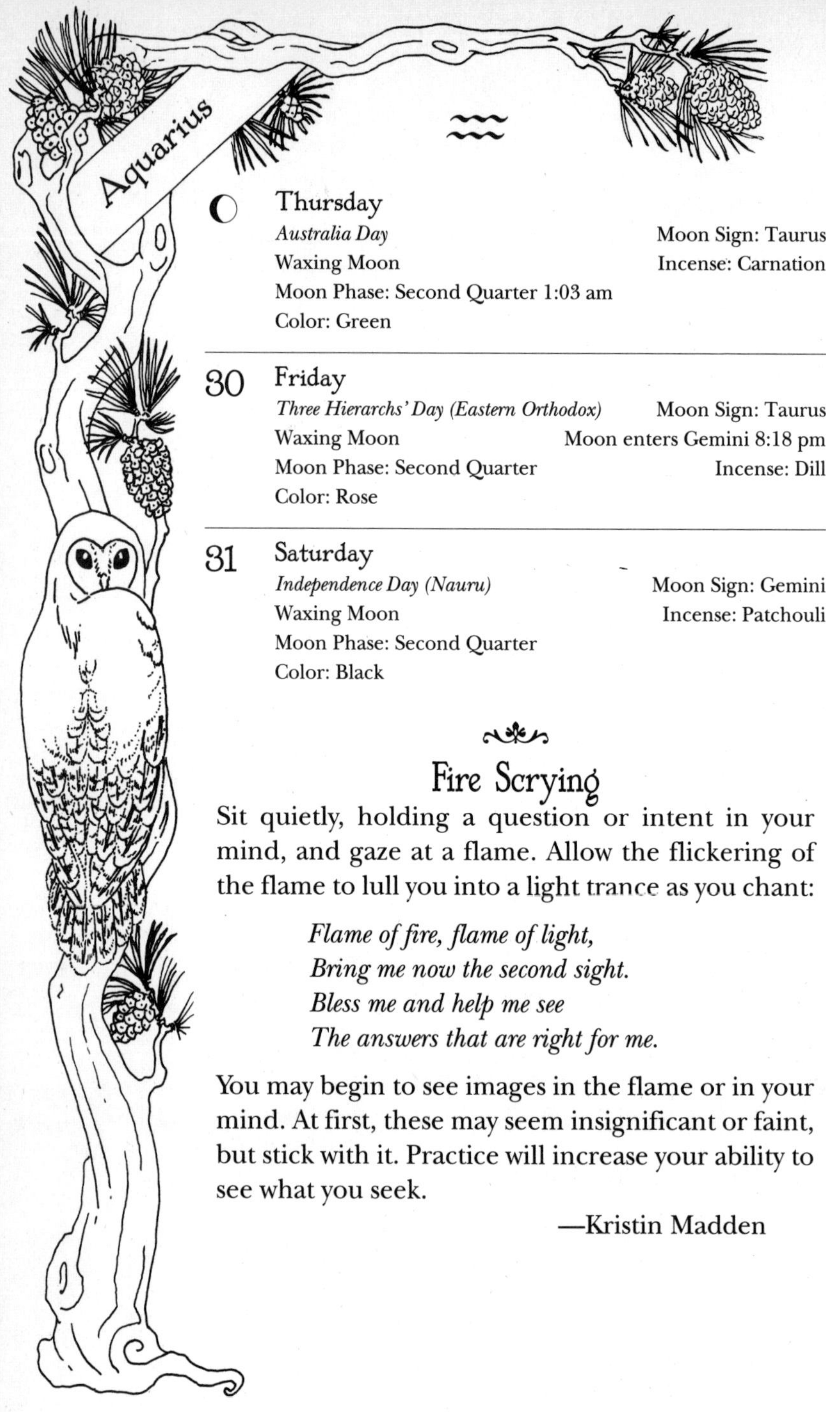

Thursday
Australia Day
Waxing Moon
Moon Phase: Second Quarter 1:03 am
Color: Green
Moon Sign: Taurus
Incense: Carnation

---

30 Friday
Three Hierarchs' Day (Eastern Orthodox)
Waxing Moon
Moon Phase: Second Quarter
Color: Rose
Moon Sign: Taurus
Moon enters Gemini 8:18 pm
Incense: Dill

---

31 Saturday
Independence Day (Nauru)
Waxing Moon
Moon Phase: Second Quarter
Color: Black
Moon Sign: Gemini
Incense: Patchouli

Fire Scrying

Sit quietly, holding a question or intent in your mind, and gaze at a flame. Allow the flickering of the flame to lull you into a light trance as you chant:

Flame of fire, flame of light,
Bring me now the second sight.
Bless me and help me see
The answers that are right for me.

You may begin to see images in the flame or in your mind. At first, these may seem insignificant or faint, but stick with it. Practice will increase your ability to see what you seek.

—Kristin Madden

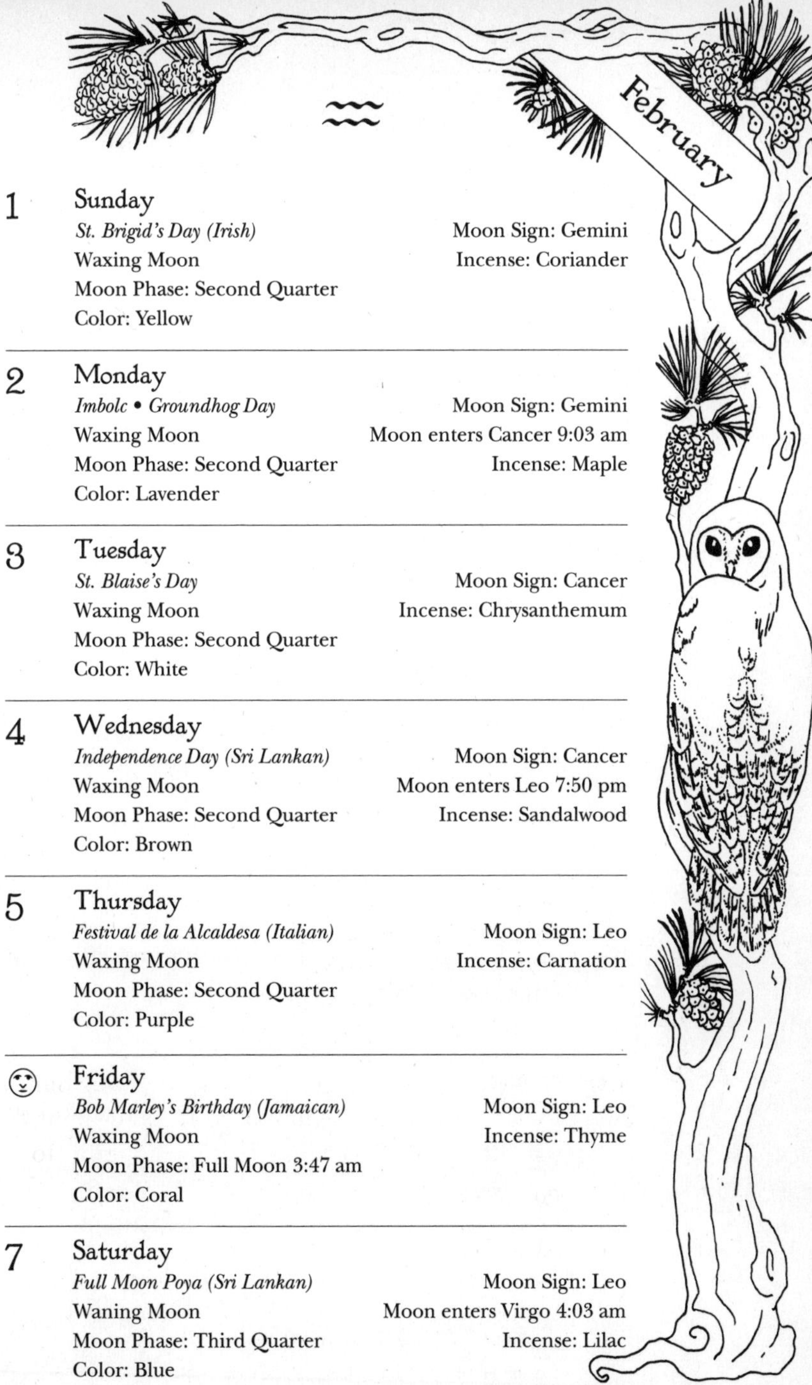

♒

1 Sunday
St. Brigid's Day (Irish) Moon Sign: Gemini
Waxing Moon Incense: Coriander
Moon Phase: Second Quarter
Color: Yellow

---

2 Monday
Imbolc • Groundhog Day Moon Sign: Gemini
Waxing Moon Moon enters Cancer 9:03 am
Moon Phase: Second Quarter Incense: Maple
Color: Lavender

---

3 Tuesday
St. Blaise's Day Moon Sign: Cancer
Waxing Moon Incense: Chrysanthemum
Moon Phase: Second Quarter
Color: White

---

4 Wednesday
Independence Day (Sri Lankan) Moon Sign: Cancer
Waxing Moon Moon enters Leo 7:50 pm
Moon Phase: Second Quarter Incense: Sandalwood
Color: Brown

---

5 Thursday
Festival de la Alcaldesa (Italian) Moon Sign: Leo
Waxing Moon Incense: Carnation
Moon Phase: Second Quarter
Color: Purple

---

6 Friday
Bob Marley's Birthday (Jamaican) Moon Sign: Leo
Waxing Moon Incense: Thyme
Moon Phase: Full Moon 3:47 am
Color: Coral

---

7 Saturday
Full Moon Poya (Sri Lankan) Moon Sign: Leo
Waning Moon Moon enters Virgo 4:03 am
Moon Phase: Third Quarter Incense: Lilac
Color: Blue

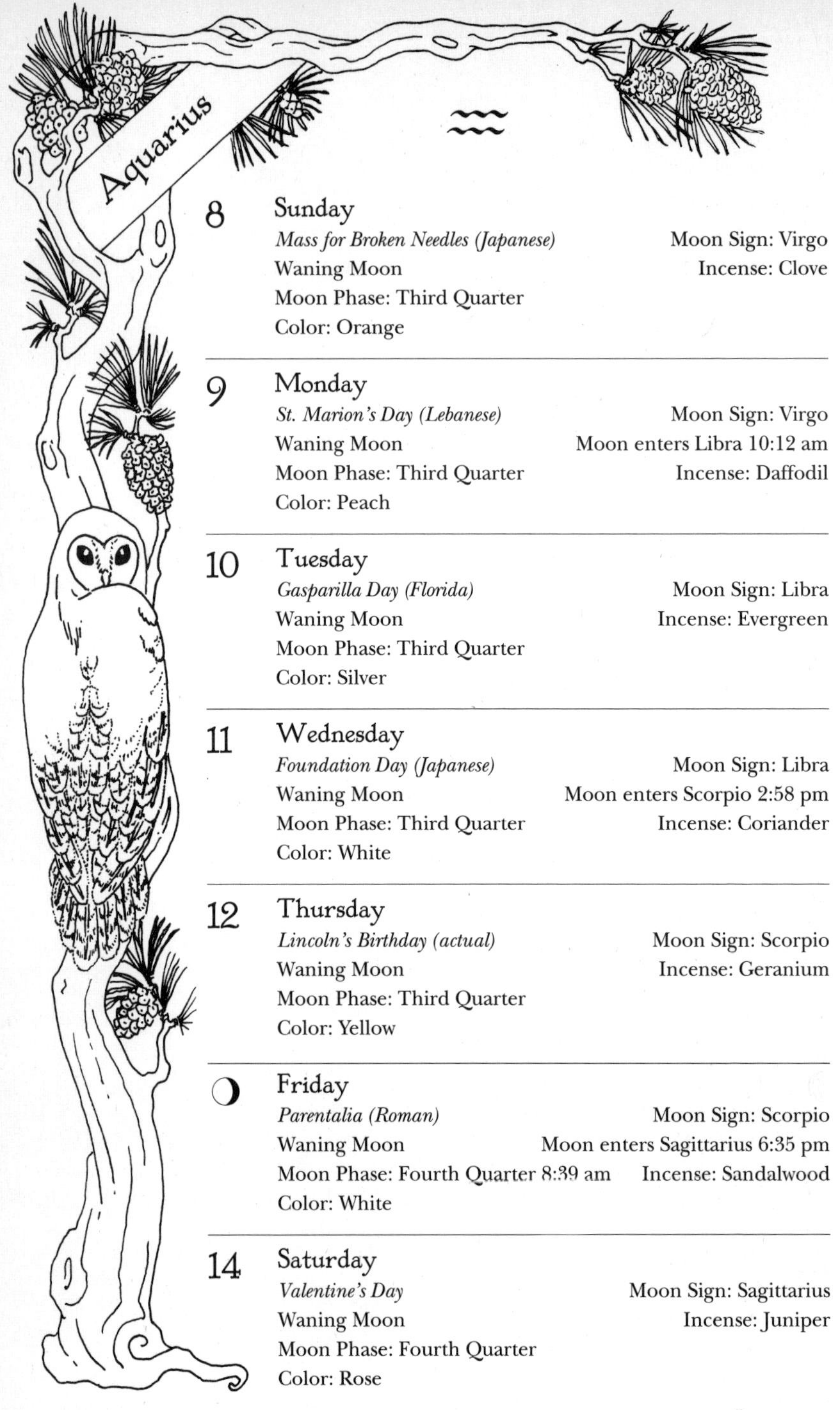

♒

8 **Sunday**
Mass for Broken Needles (Japanese) — Moon Sign: Virgo
Waning Moon — Incense: Clove
Moon Phase: Third Quarter
Color: Orange

---

9 **Monday**
St. Marion's Day (Lebanese) — Moon Sign: Virgo
Waning Moon — Moon enters Libra 10:12 am
Moon Phase: Third Quarter — Incense: Daffodil
Color: Peach

---

10 **Tuesday**
Gasparilla Day (Florida) — Moon Sign: Libra
Waning Moon — Incense: Evergreen
Moon Phase: Third Quarter
Color: Silver

---

11 **Wednesday**
Foundation Day (Japanese) — Moon Sign: Libra
Waning Moon — Moon enters Scorpio 2:58 pm
Moon Phase: Third Quarter — Incense: Coriander
Color: White

---

12 **Thursday**
Lincoln's Birthday (actual) — Moon Sign: Scorpio
Waning Moon — Incense: Geranium
Moon Phase: Third Quarter
Color: Yellow

◑ **Friday**
Parentalia (Roman) — Moon Sign: Scorpio
Waning Moon — Moon enters Sagittarius 6:35 pm
Moon Phase: Fourth Quarter 8:39 am — Incense: Sandalwood
Color: White

---

14 **Saturday**
Valentine's Day — Moon Sign: Sagittarius
Waning Moon — Incense: Juniper
Moon Phase: Fourth Quarter
Color: Rose

15 **Sunday**

Lupercalia (Roman) — Moon Sign: Sagittarius
Waning Moon — Moon enters Capricorn 9:14 pm
Moon Phase: Fourth Quarter — Incense: Poplar
Color: Amber

---

16 **Monday**

President's Day (observed) — Moon Sign: Capricorn
Waning Moon — Incense: Rose
Moon Phase: Fourth Quarter
Color: White

---

17 **Tuesday**

Quirinalia (Roman) — Moon Sign: Capricorn
Waning Moon — Moon enters Aquarius 11:27 pm
Moon Phase: Fourth Quarter — Incense: Sage
Color: Black

---

18 **Wednesday**

Saint Bernadette's Second Vision — Moon Sign: Aquarius
Waning Moon — Incense: Coriander
Moon Phase: Fourth Quarter
Color: Topaz

---

19 **Thursday**

Sun enters Pisces — Moon Sign: Aquarius
Waning Moon — Incense: Musk
Moon Phase: Fourth Quarter
Color: Crimson

Friday

Installation of the New Lama (Tibetan) — Moon Sign: Aquarius
Waning Moon — Moon enters Pisces 2:27 am
Moon Phase: New Moon 4:18 am — Incense: Ylang ylang
Color: Purple

---

21 **Saturday**

Feast of Lanterns (Chinese) — Moon Sign: Pisces
Waxing Moon — Incense: Pine
Moon Phase: First Quarter
Color: Brown

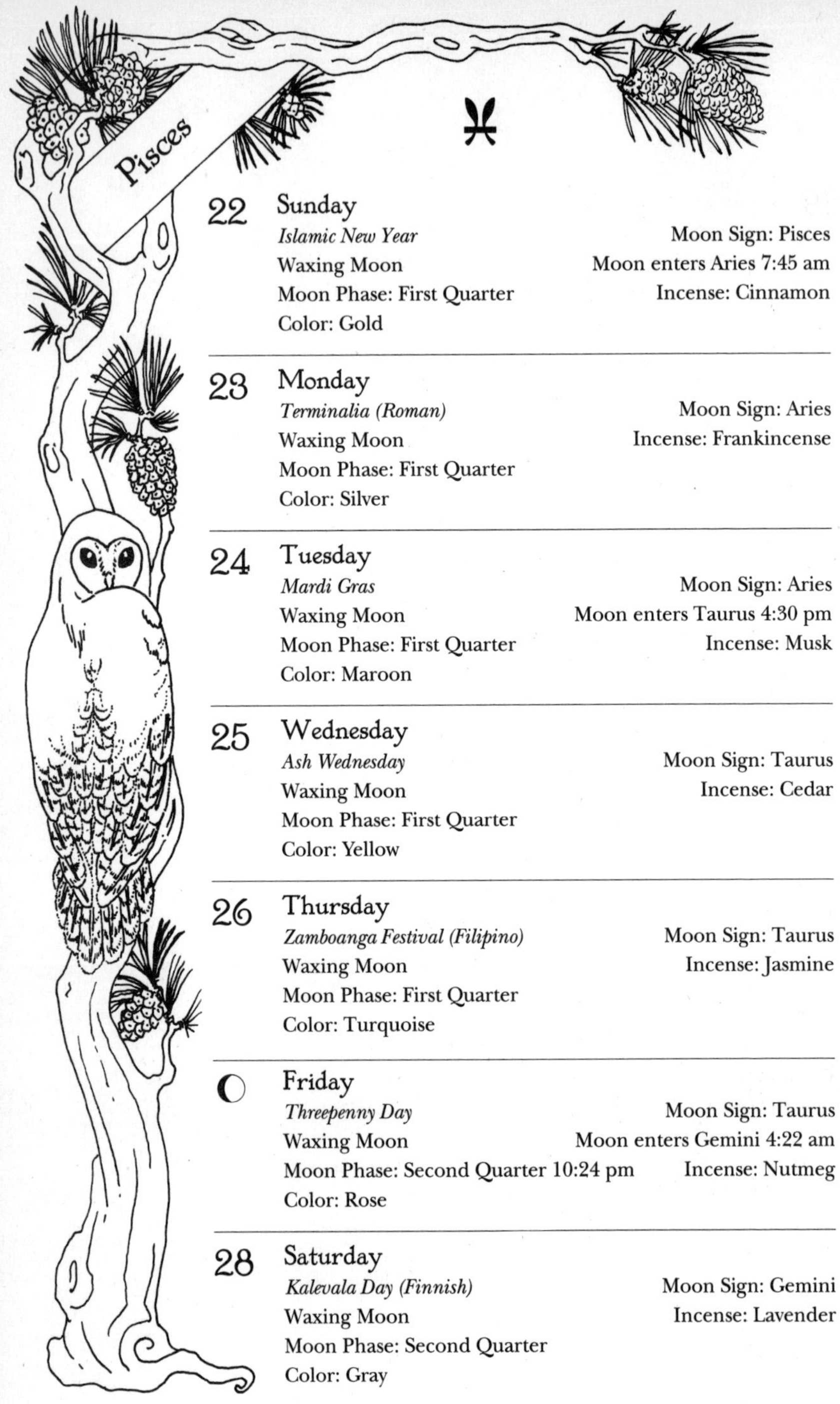

22 Sunday
Islamic New Year
Waxing Moon
Moon Phase: First Quarter
Color: Gold

Moon Sign: Pisces
Moon enters Aries 7:45 am
Incense: Cinnamon

---

23 Monday
Terminalia (Roman)
Waxing Moon
Moon Phase: First Quarter
Color: Silver

Moon Sign: Aries
Incense: Frankincense

---

24 Tuesday
Mardi Gras
Waxing Moon
Moon Phase: First Quarter
Color: Maroon

Moon Sign: Aries
Moon enters Taurus 4:30 pm
Incense: Musk

---

25 Wednesday
Ash Wednesday
Waxing Moon
Moon Phase: First Quarter
Color: Yellow

Moon Sign: Taurus
Incense: Cedar

---

26 Thursday
Zamboanga Festival (Filipino)
Waxing Moon
Moon Phase: First Quarter
Color: Turquoise

Moon Sign: Taurus
Incense: Jasmine

◐ Friday
Threepenny Day
Waxing Moon
Moon Phase: Second Quarter 10:24 pm
Color: Rose

Moon Sign: Taurus
Moon enters Gemini 4:22 am
Incense: Nutmeg

---

28 Saturday
Kalevala Day (Finnish)
Waxing Moon
Moon Phase: Second Quarter
Color: Gray

Moon Sign: Gemini
Incense: Lavender

♓

29 **Sunday**
Leap Day
Moon Sign: Gemini
Waxing Moon
Moon enters Cancer 5:12 pm
Moon Phase: Second Quarter
Incense: Basil
Color: Orange

---

1 **Monday**
Matronalia (Roman)
Moon Sign: Cancer
Waxing Moon
Incense: Peony
Moon Phase: Second Quarter
Color: Lavender

---

2 **Tuesday**
St. Chad's Day (English)
Moon Sign: Cancer
Waxing Moon
Incense: Gardenia
Moon Phase: Second Quarter
Color: Red

---

3 **Wednesday**
Doll Festival (Japanese)
Moon Sign: Cancer
Waxing Moon
Moon enters Leo 4:18 am
Moon Phase: Second Quarter
Incense: Maple
Color: Brown

---

4 **Thursday**
St. Casimir's Day (Polish)
Moon Sign: Leo
Waxing Moon
Incense: Vanilla
Moon Phase: Second Quarter
Color: Green

---

5 **Friday**
Isis Festival (Roman)
Moon Sign: Leo
Waxing Moon
Moon enters Virgo 12:18 pm
Moon Phase: Second Quarter
Incense: Ginger
Color: Pink

---

6 **Saturday**
Alamo Day
Moon Sign: Virgo
Waxing Moon
Incense: Patchouli
Moon Phase: Full Moon 6:14 pm
Color: Blue

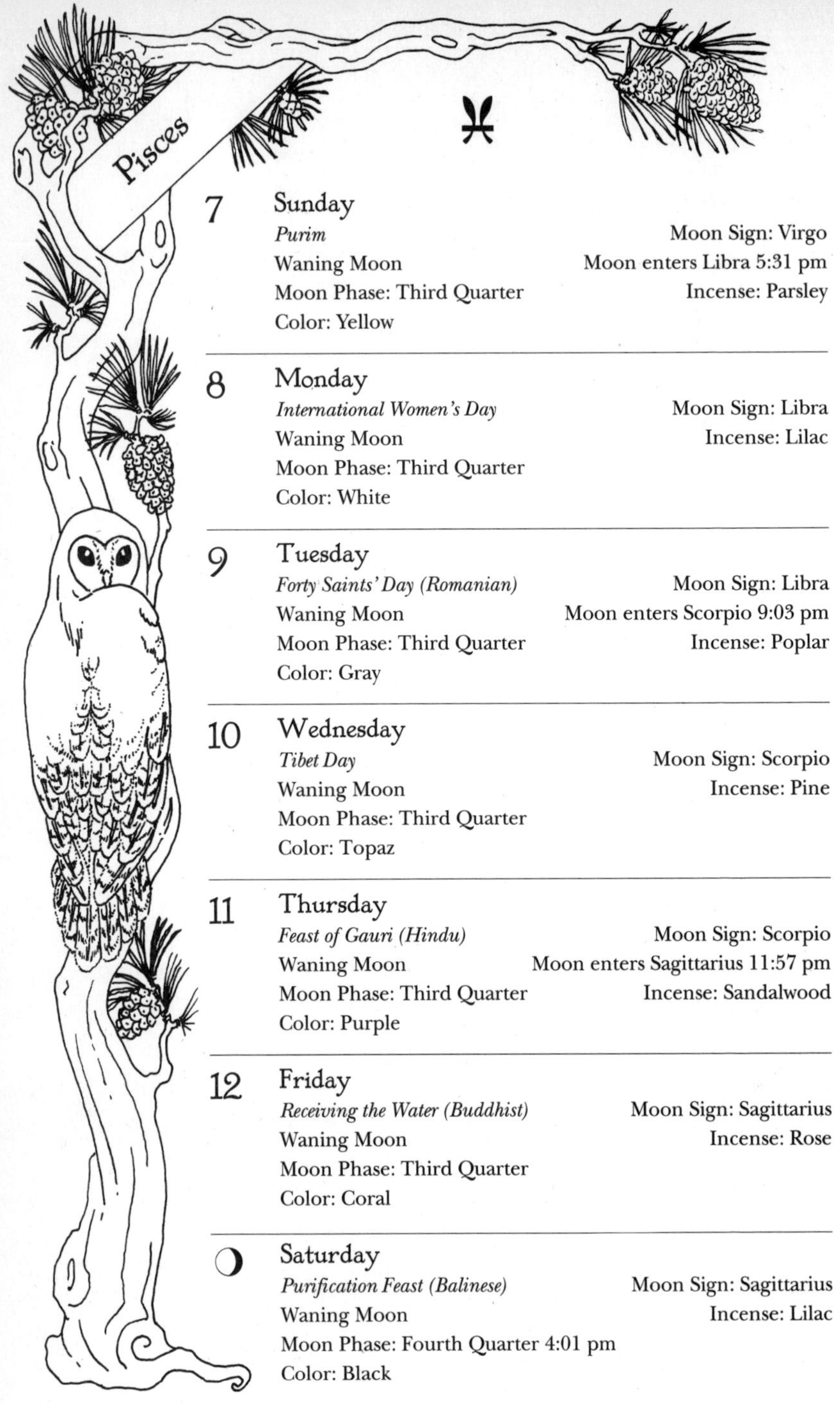

♓

7 Sunday

Purim
Waning Moon
Moon Phase: Third Quarter
Color: Yellow

Moon Sign: Virgo
Moon enters Libra 5:31 pm
Incense: Parsley

---

8 Monday

International Women's Day
Waning Moon
Moon Phase: Third Quarter
Color: White

Moon Sign: Libra
Incense: Lilac

---

9 Tuesday

Forty Saints' Day (Romanian)
Waning Moon
Moon Phase: Third Quarter
Color: Gray

Moon Sign: Libra
Moon enters Scorpio 9:03 pm
Incense: Poplar

---

10 Wednesday

Tibet Day
Waning Moon
Moon Phase: Third Quarter
Color: Topaz

Moon Sign: Scorpio
Incense: Pine

---

11 Thursday

Feast of Gauri (Hindu)
Waning Moon
Moon Phase: Third Quarter
Color: Purple

Moon Sign: Scorpio
Moon enters Sagittarius 11:57 pm
Incense: Sandalwood

---

12 Friday

Receiving the Water (Buddhist)
Waning Moon
Moon Phase: Third Quarter
Color: Coral

Moon Sign: Sagittarius
Incense: Rose

◑ Saturday

Purification Feast (Balinese)
Waning Moon
Moon Phase: Fourth Quarter 4:01 pm
Color: Black

Moon Sign: Sagittarius
Incense: Lilac

14 Sunday
Mamuralia (Roman) Moon Sign: Sagittarius
Waning Moon Moon enters Capricorn 2:51 am
Moon Phase: Fourth Quarter Incense: Cinnamon
Color: Amber

---

15 Monday
Phallus Festival (Japanese) Moon Sign: Capricorn
Waning Moon Incense: Chrysanthemum
Moon Phase: Fourth Quarter
Color: Silver

---

16 Tuesday
St. Urho's Day (Finnish) Moon Sign: Capricorn
Waning Moon Moon enters Aquarius 6:10 am
Moon Phase: Fourth Quarter Incense: Juniper
Color: Black

---

17 Wednesday
St. Patrick's Day Moon Sign: Aquarius
Waning Moon Incense: Neroli
Moon Phase: Fourth Quarter
Color: White

---

18 Thursday
Sheelah's Day (Irish) Moon Sign: Aquarius
Waning Moon Moon enters Pisces 10:26 am
Moon Phase: Fourth Quarter Incense: Carnation
Color: Crimson

---

19 Friday
St. Joseph's Day (Sicilian) Moon Sign: Pisces
Waning Moon Incense: Dill
Moon Phase: Fourth Quarter
Color: Rose

Saturday
Ostara • Spring Equinox • Int'l Astrology Day Moon Sign: Pisces
Waning Moon Sun enters Aries
Moon Phase: New Moon 5:41 pm Moon enters Aries 4:29 pm
Color: Indigo Incense: Pine

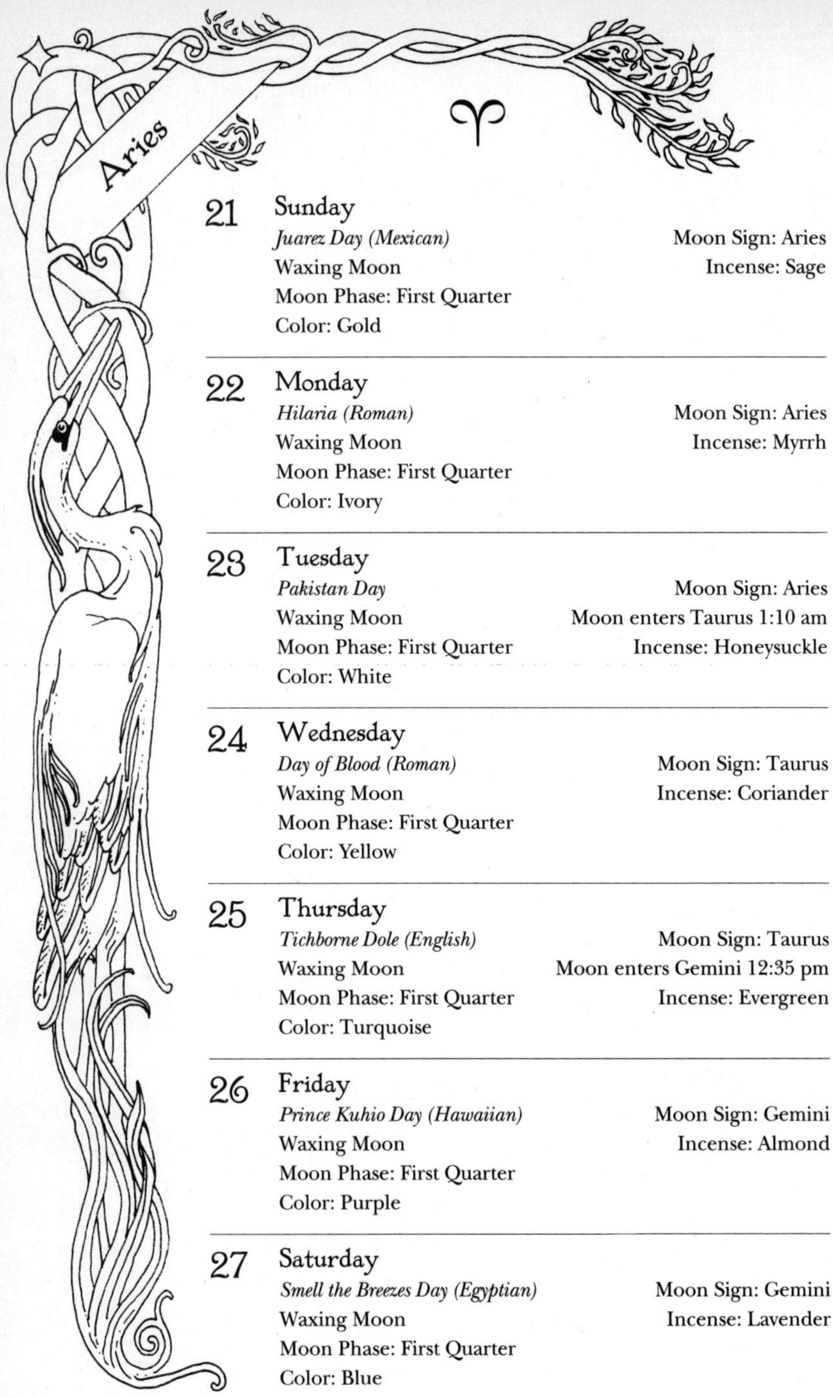

♈

21 Sunday

Juarez Day (Mexican)
Waxing Moon
Moon Phase: First Quarter
Color: Gold

Moon Sign: Aries
Incense: Sage

---

22 Monday

Hilaria (Roman)
Waxing Moon
Moon Phase: First Quarter
Color: Ivory

Moon Sign: Aries
Incense: Myrrh

---

23 Tuesday

Pakistan Day
Waxing Moon
Moon Phase: First Quarter
Color: White

Moon Sign: Aries
Moon enters Taurus 1:10 am
Incense: Honeysuckle

---

24 Wednesday

Day of Blood (Roman)
Waxing Moon
Moon Phase: First Quarter
Color: Yellow

Moon Sign: Taurus
Incense: Coriander

---

25 Thursday

Tichborne Dole (English)
Waxing Moon
Moon Phase: First Quarter
Color: Turquoise

Moon Sign: Taurus
Moon enters Gemini 12:35 pm
Incense: Evergreen

---

26 Friday

Prince Kuhio Day (Hawaiian)
Waxing Moon
Moon Phase: First Quarter
Color: Purple

Moon Sign: Gemini
Incense: Almond

---

27 Saturday

Smell the Breezes Day (Egyptian)
Waxing Moon
Moon Phase: First Quarter
Color: Blue

Moon Sign: Gemini
Incense: Lavender

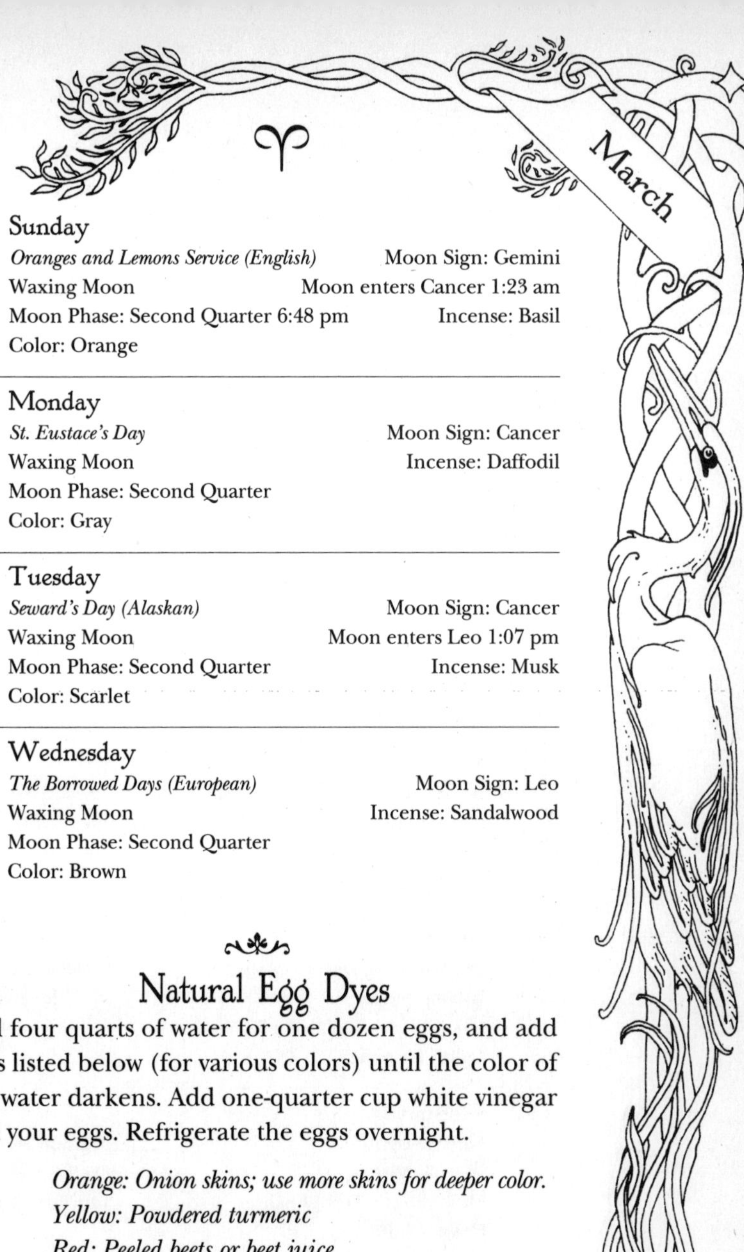

♈

◐ Sunday
Oranges and Lemons Service (English) Moon Sign: Gemini
Waxing Moon Moon enters Cancer 1:23 am
Moon Phase: Second Quarter 6:48 pm Incense: Basil
Color: Orange

---

29 Monday
St. Eustace's Day Moon Sign: Cancer
Waxing Moon Incense: Daffodil
Moon Phase: Second Quarter
Color: Gray

---

30 Tuesday
Seward's Day (Alaskan) Moon Sign: Cancer
Waxing Moon Moon enters Leo 1:07 pm
Moon Phase: Second Quarter Incense: Musk
Color: Scarlet

---

31 Wednesday
The Borrowed Days (European) Moon Sign: Leo
Waxing Moon Incense: Sandalwood
Moon Phase: Second Quarter
Color: Brown

Natural Egg Dyes

Boil four quarts of water for one dozen eggs, and add dyes listed below (for various colors) until the color of the water darkens. Add one-quarter cup white vinegar and your eggs. Refrigerate the eggs overnight.

Orange: Onion skins; use more skins for deeper color.
Yellow: Powdered turmeric
Red: Peeled beets or beet juice
Purple: Sliced inner leaves from red cabbage
Light Blue: Outer leaves from red cabbage
Brown: Strong coffee in place of the water

—Kristin Madden

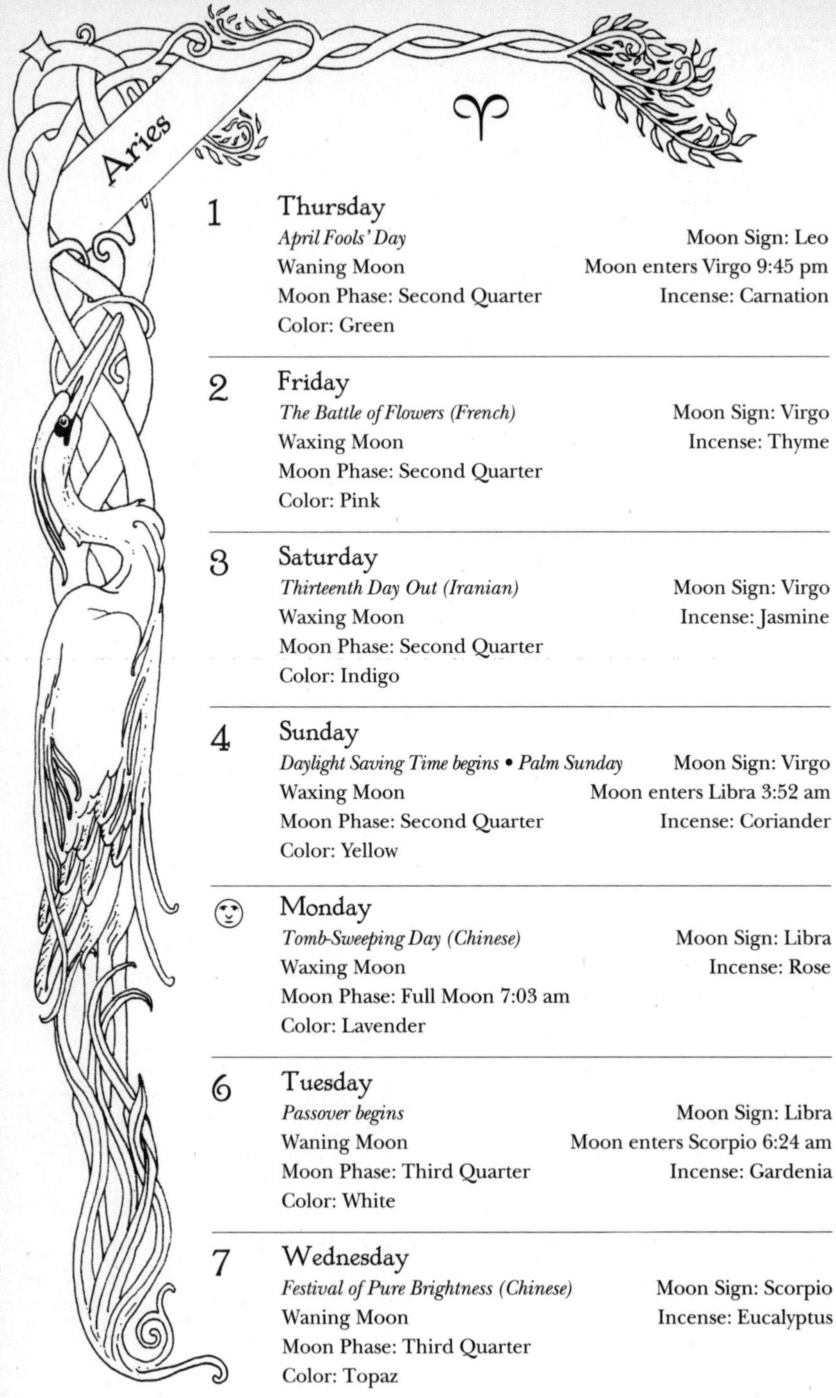

♈

1 Thursday
April Fools' Day
Moon Sign: Leo
Waning Moon
Moon enters Virgo 9:45 pm
Moon Phase: Second Quarter
Incense: Carnation
Color: Green

---

2 Friday
The Battle of Flowers (French)
Moon Sign: Virgo
Waxing Moon
Incense: Thyme
Moon Phase: Second Quarter
Color: Pink

---

3 Saturday
Thirteenth Day Out (Iranian)
Moon Sign: Virgo
Waxing Moon
Incense: Jasmine
Moon Phase: Second Quarter
Color: Indigo

---

4 Sunday
Daylight Saving Time begins • Palm Sunday
Moon Sign: Virgo
Waxing Moon
Moon enters Libra 3:52 am
Moon Phase: Second Quarter
Incense: Coriander
Color: Yellow

Monday
Tomb-Sweeping Day (Chinese)
Moon Sign: Libra
Waxing Moon
Incense: Rose
Moon Phase: Full Moon 7:03 am
Color: Lavender

---

6 Tuesday
Passover begins
Moon Sign: Libra
Waning Moon
Moon enters Scorpio 6:24 am
Moon Phase: Third Quarter
Incense: Gardenia
Color: White

---

7 Wednesday
Festival of Pure Brightness (Chinese)
Moon Sign: Scorpio
Waning Moon
Incense: Eucalyptus
Moon Phase: Third Quarter
Color: Topaz

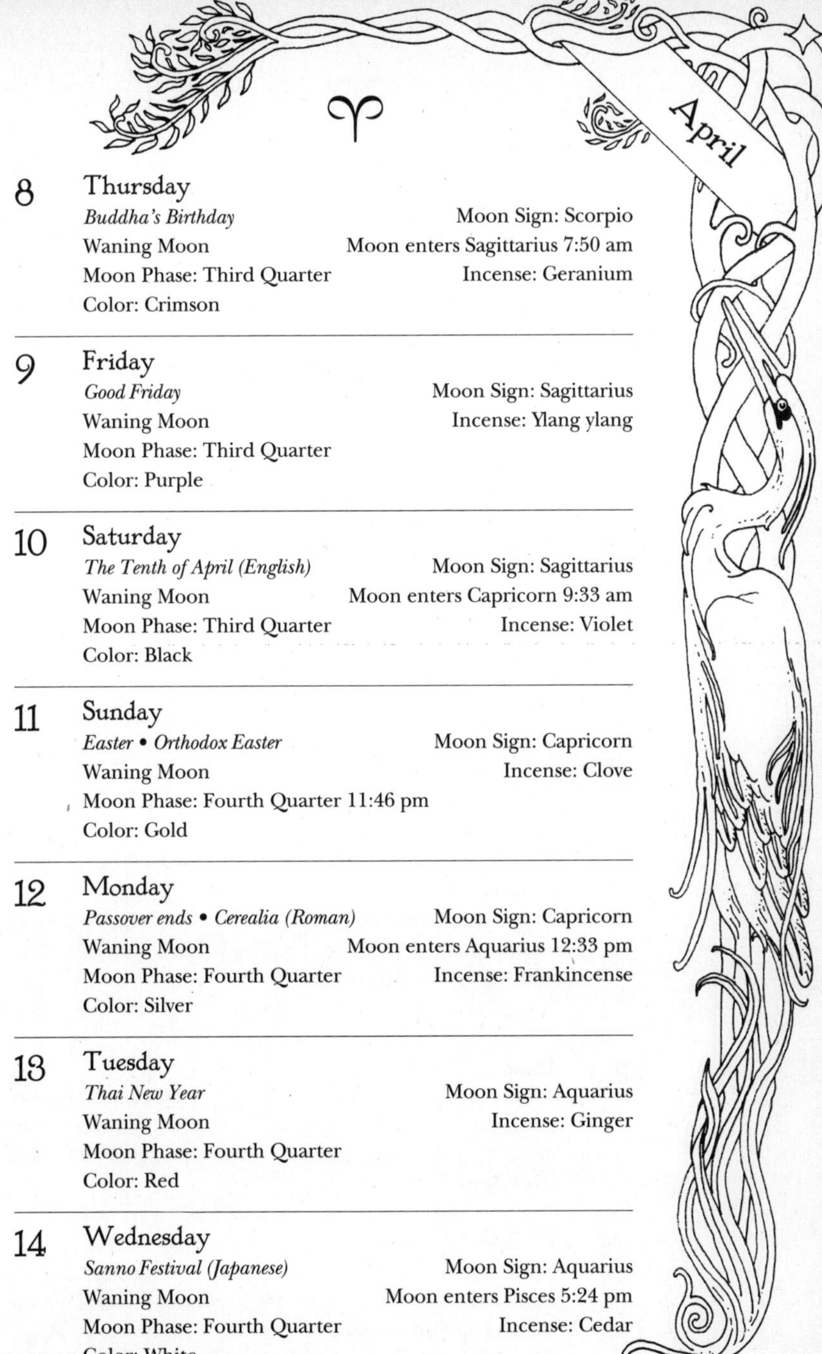

♈

8 Thursday

Buddha's Birthday — Moon Sign: Scorpio
Waning Moon — Moon enters Sagittarius 7:50 am
Moon Phase: Third Quarter — Incense: Geranium
Color: Crimson

---

9 Friday

Good Friday — Moon Sign: Sagittarius
Waning Moon — Incense: Ylang ylang
Moon Phase: Third Quarter
Color: Purple

---

10 Saturday

The Tenth of April (English) — Moon Sign: Sagittarius
Waning Moon — Moon enters Capricorn 9:33 am
Moon Phase: Third Quarter — Incense: Violet
Color: Black

---

11 Sunday

Easter • Orthodox Easter — Moon Sign: Capricorn
Waning Moon — Incense: Clove
Moon Phase: Fourth Quarter 11:46 pm
Color: Gold

---

12 Monday

Passover ends • Cerealia (Roman) — Moon Sign: Capricorn
Waning Moon — Moon enters Aquarius 12:33 pm
Moon Phase: Fourth Quarter — Incense: Frankincense
Color: Silver

---

13 Tuesday

Thai New Year — Moon Sign: Aquarius
Waning Moon — Incense: Ginger
Moon Phase: Fourth Quarter
Color: Red

---

14 Wednesday

Sanno Festival (Japanese) — Moon Sign: Aquarius
Waning Moon — Moon enters Pisces 5:24 pm
Moon Phase: Fourth Quarter — Incense: Cedar
Color: White

♈

15 Thursday

Plowing Festival (Chinese)
Waning Moon
Moon Phase: Fourth Quarter
Color: Purple

Moon Sign: Pisces
Incense: Musk

---

16 Friday

Zurich Spring Festival (Swiss)
Waning Moon
Moon Phase: Fourth Quarter
Color: Coral

Moon Sign: Pisces
Incense: Nutmeg

---

17 Saturday

Yayoi Matsuri (Japanese)
Waning Moon
Moon Phase: Fourth Quarter
Color: Gray

Moon Sign: Pisces
Moon enters Aries 12:24 am
Incense: Patchouli

---

18 Sunday

Flower Festival (Japanese)
Waning Moon
Moon Phase: Fourth Quarter
Color: Orange

Moon Sign: Aries
Incense: Poplar

☽ Monday

Cerealia last day (Roman)
Waning Moon
Moon Phase: New Moon 9:21 am
Color: Ivory

Moon Sign: Aries
Moon enters Taurus 9:43 am
Sun enters Taurus 1:50 pm
Incense: Peony

---

20 Tuesday

Drum Festival (Japanese)
Waxing Moon
Moon Phase: First Quarter
Color: Black

Moon Sign: Taurus
Incense: Pine

---

21 Wednesday

Tiradentes Day (Brazilian)
Waxing Moon
Moon Phase: First Quarter
Color: Brown

Moon Sign: Taurus
Moon enters Gemini 9:10 pm
Incense: Maple

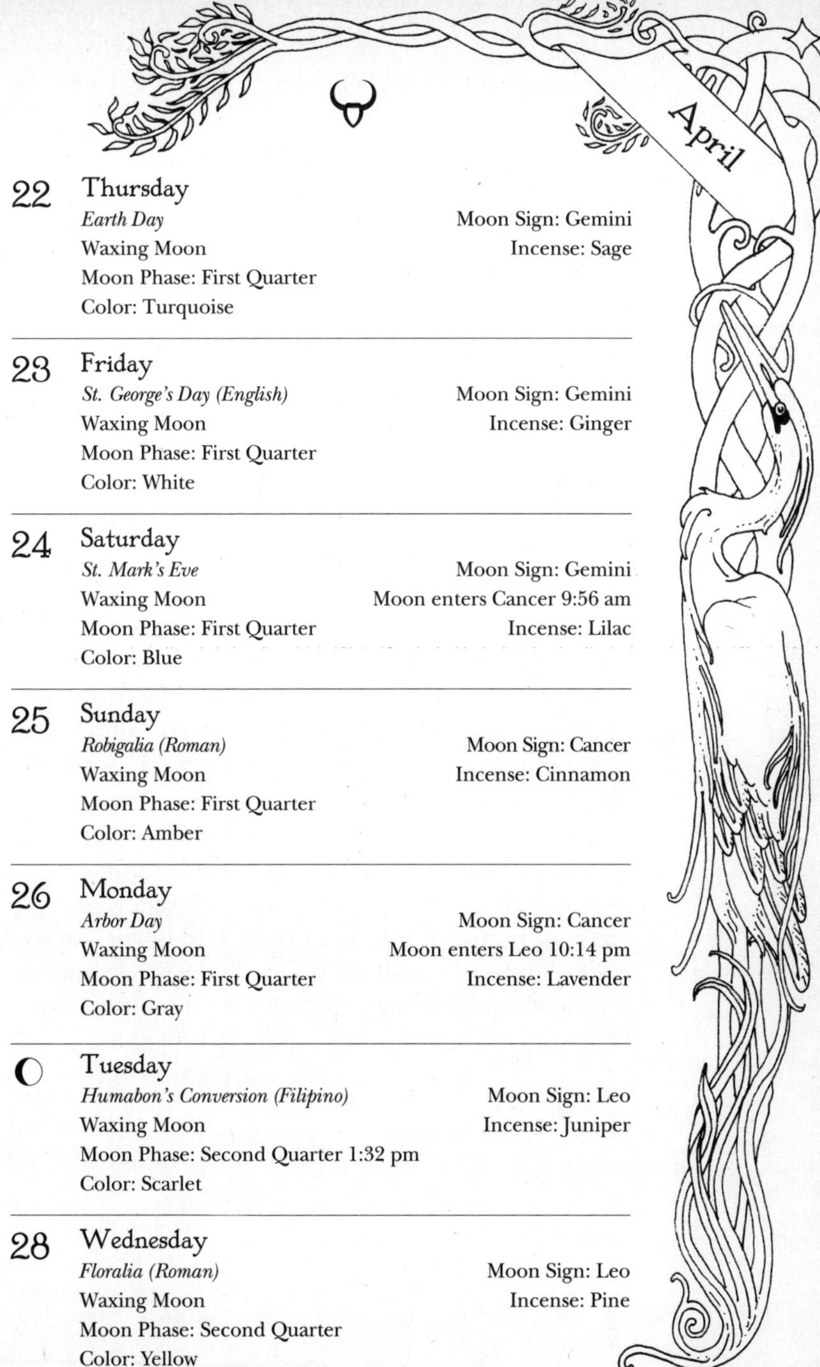

22 Thursday

Earth Day
Waxing Moon
Moon Phase: First Quarter
Color: Turquoise

Moon Sign: Gemini
Incense: Sage

---

23 Friday

St. George's Day (English)
Waxing Moon
Moon Phase: First Quarter
Color: White

Moon Sign: Gemini
Incense: Ginger

---

24 Saturday

St. Mark's Eve
Waxing Moon
Moon Phase: First Quarter
Color: Blue

Moon Sign: Gemini
Moon enters Cancer 9:56 am
Incense: Lilac

---

25 Sunday

Robigalia (Roman)
Waxing Moon
Moon Phase: First Quarter
Color: Amber

Moon Sign: Cancer
Incense: Cinnamon

---

26 Monday

Arbor Day
Waxing Moon
Moon Phase: First Quarter
Color: Gray

Moon Sign: Cancer
Moon enters Leo 10:14 pm
Incense: Lavender

◐ Tuesday

Humabon's Conversion (Filipino)
Waxing Moon
Moon Phase: Second Quarter 1:32 pm
Color: Scarlet

Moon Sign: Leo
Incense: Juniper

---

28 Wednesday

Floralia (Roman)
Waxing Moon
Moon Phase: Second Quarter
Color: Yellow

Moon Sign: Leo
Incense: Pine

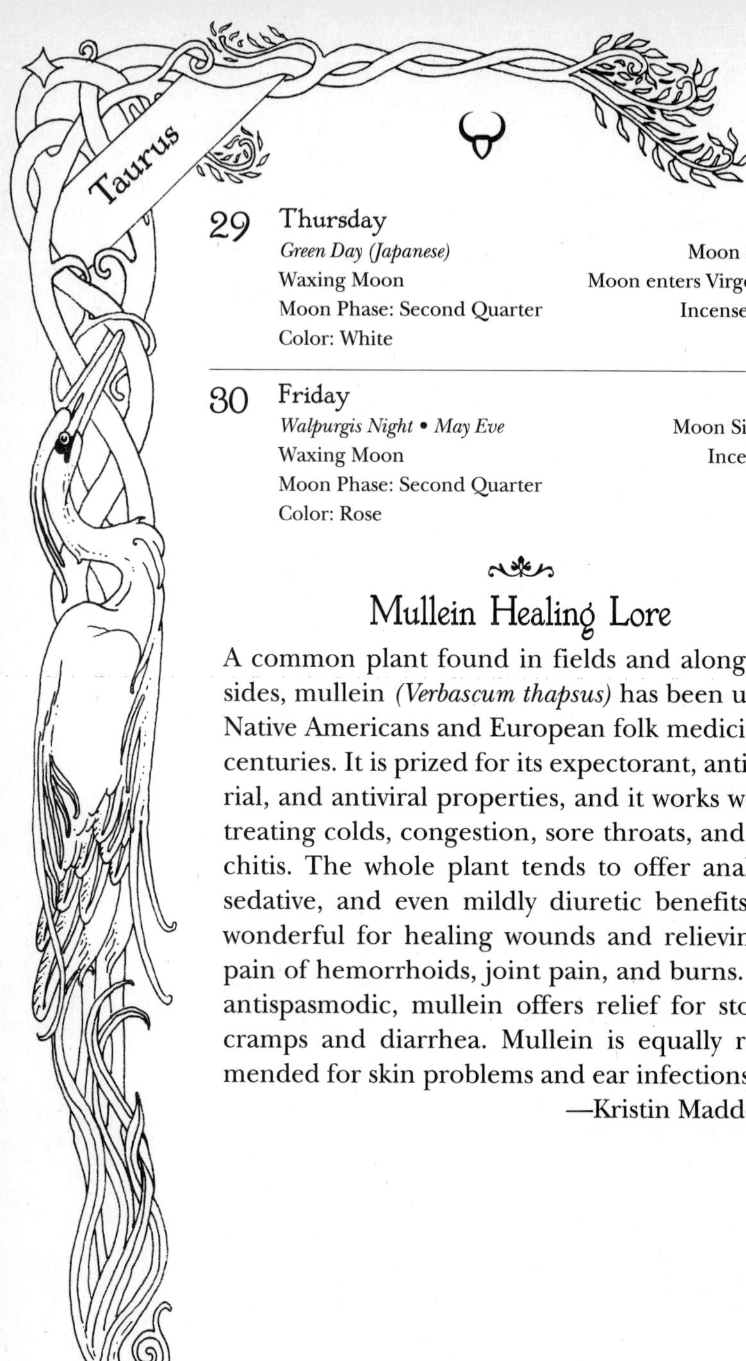

29 Thursday

Green Day (Japanese)
Waxing Moon
Moon Phase: Second Quarter
Color: White

Moon Sign: Leo
Moon enters Virgo 8:00 am
Incense: Jasmine

---

30 Friday

Walpurgis Night • May Eve
Waxing Moon
Moon Phase: Second Quarter
Color: Rose

Moon Sign: Virgo
Incense: Rose

Mullein Healing Lore

A common plant found in fields and along roadsides, mullein *(Verbascum thapsus)* has been used in Native Americans and European folk medicine for centuries. It is prized for its expectorant, antibacterial, and antiviral properties, and it works well for treating colds, congestion, sore throats, and bronchitis. The whole plant tends to offer analgesic, sedative, and even mildly diuretic benefits. It is wonderful for healing wounds and relieving the pain of hemorrhoids, joint pain, and burns. As an antispasmodic, mullein offers relief for stomach cramps and diarrhea. Mullein is equally recommended for skin problems and ear infections.

—Kristin Madden

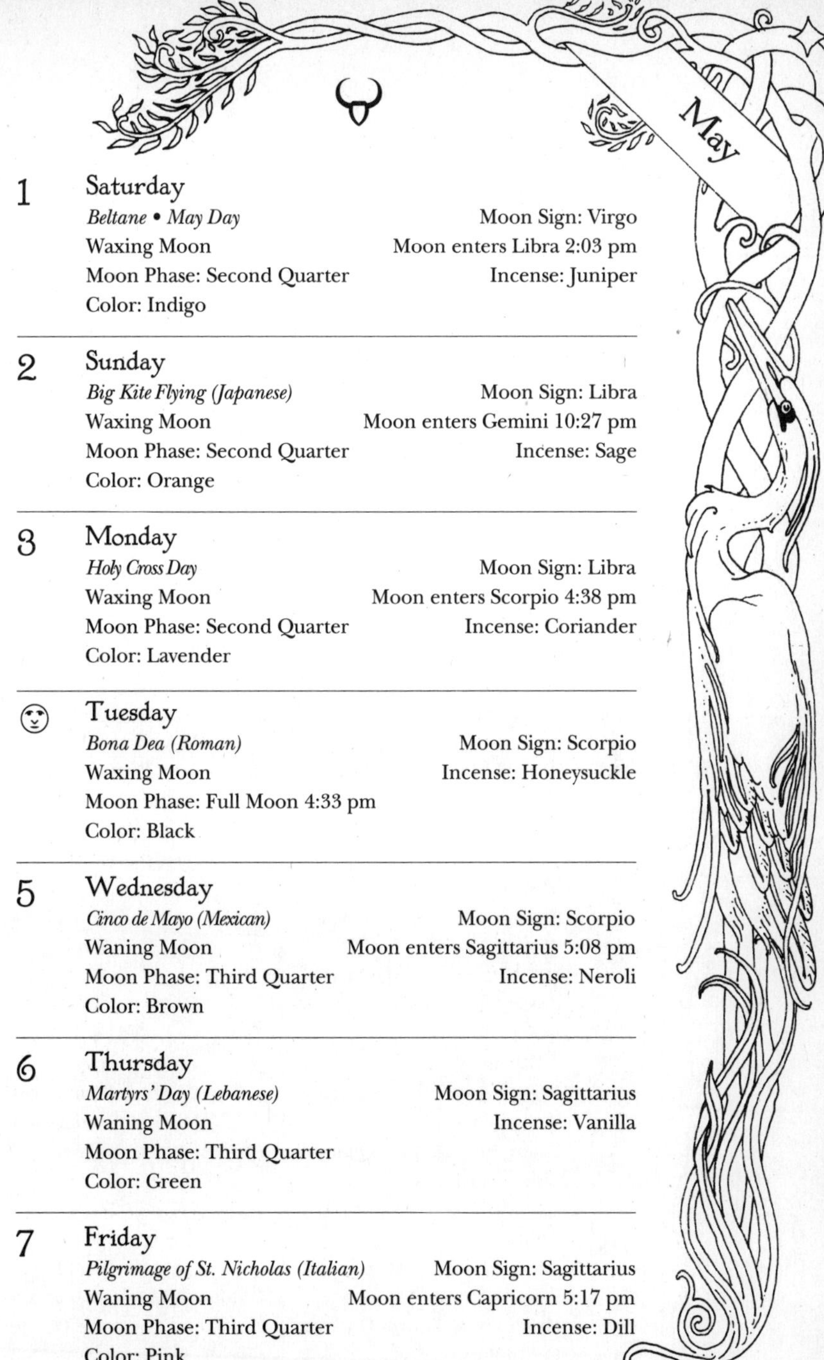

1 **Saturday**
Beltane • May Day — Moon Sign: Virgo
Waxing Moon — Moon enters Libra 2:03 pm
Moon Phase: Second Quarter — Incense: Juniper
Color: Indigo

---

2 **Sunday**
Big Kite Flying (Japanese) — Moon Sign: Libra
Waxing Moon — Moon enters Gemini 10:27 pm
Moon Phase: Second Quarter — Incense: Sage
Color: Orange

---

3 **Monday**
Holy Cross Day — Moon Sign: Libra
Waxing Moon — Moon enters Scorpio 4:38 pm
Moon Phase: Second Quarter — Incense: Coriander
Color: Lavender

---

4 **Tuesday**
Bona Dea (Roman) — Moon Sign: Scorpio
Waxing Moon — Incense: Honeysuckle
Moon Phase: Full Moon 4:33 pm
Color: Black

---

5 **Wednesday**
Cinco de Mayo (Mexican) — Moon Sign: Scorpio
Waning Moon — Moon enters Sagittarius 5:08 pm
Moon Phase: Third Quarter — Incense: Neroli
Color: Brown

---

6 **Thursday**
Martyrs' Day (Lebanese) — Moon Sign: Sagittarius
Waning Moon — Incense: Vanilla
Moon Phase: Third Quarter
Color: Green

---

7 **Friday**
Pilgrimage of St. Nicholas (Italian) — Moon Sign: Sagittarius
Waning Moon — Moon enters Capricorn 5:17 pm
Moon Phase: Third Quarter — Incense: Dill
Color: Pink

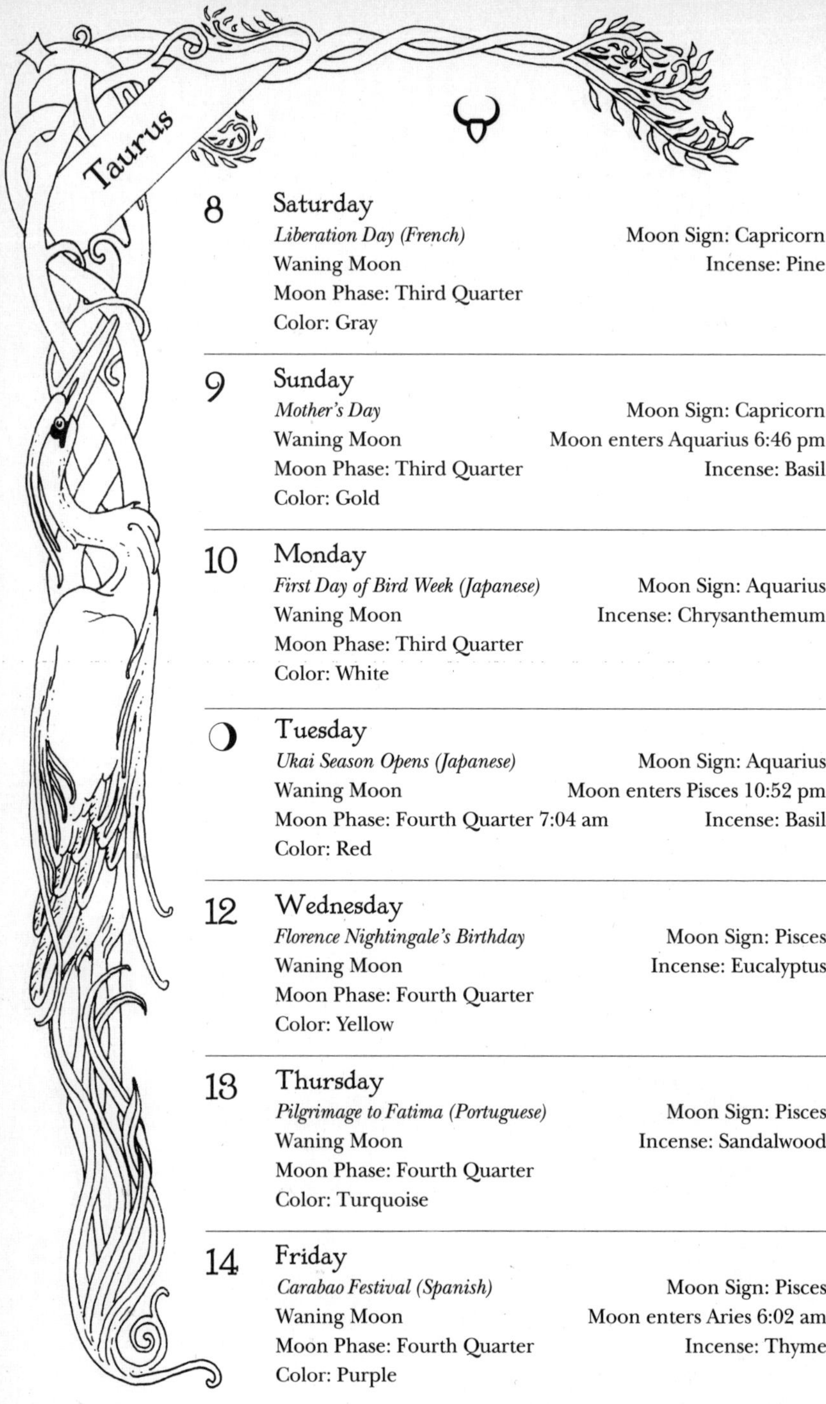

8 **Saturday**
Liberation Day (French) — Moon Sign: Capricorn
Waning Moon — Incense: Pine
Moon Phase: Third Quarter
Color: Gray

9 **Sunday**
Mother's Day — Moon Sign: Capricorn
Waning Moon — Moon enters Aquarius 6:46 pm
Moon Phase: Third Quarter — Incense: Basil
Color: Gold

10 **Monday**
First Day of Bird Week (Japanese) — Moon Sign: Aquarius
Waning Moon — Incense: Chrysanthemum
Moon Phase: Third Quarter
Color: White

◑ **Tuesday**
Ukai Season Opens (Japanese) — Moon Sign: Aquarius
Waning Moon — Moon enters Pisces 10:52 pm
Moon Phase: Fourth Quarter 7:04 am — Incense: Basil
Color: Red

12 **Wednesday**
Florence Nightingale's Birthday — Moon Sign: Pisces
Waning Moon — Incense: Eucalyptus
Moon Phase: Fourth Quarter
Color: Yellow

13 **Thursday**
Pilgrimage to Fatima (Portuguese) — Moon Sign: Pisces
Waning Moon — Incense: Sandalwood
Moon Phase: Fourth Quarter
Color: Turquoise

14 **Friday**
Carabao Festival (Spanish) — Moon Sign: Pisces
Waning Moon — Moon enters Aries 6:02 am
Moon Phase: Fourth Quarter — Incense: Thyme
Color: Purple

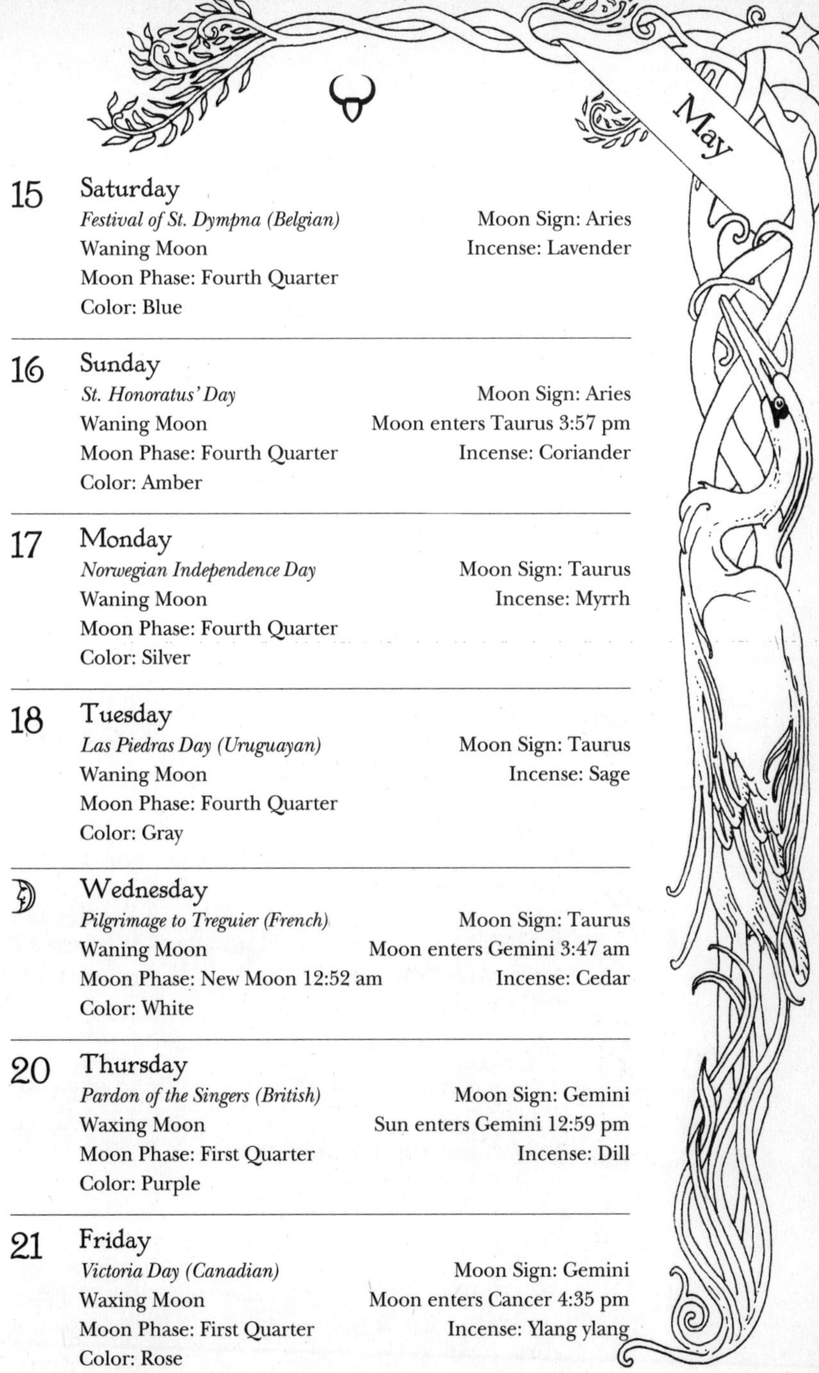

15 Saturday

Festival of St. Dympna (Belgian)
Waning Moon
Moon Phase: Fourth Quarter
Color: Blue

Moon Sign: Aries
Incense: Lavender

---

16 Sunday

St. Honoratus' Day
Waning Moon
Moon Phase: Fourth Quarter
Color: Amber

Moon Sign: Aries
Moon enters Taurus 3:57 pm
Incense: Coriander

---

17 Monday

Norwegian Independence Day
Waning Moon
Moon Phase: Fourth Quarter
Color: Silver

Moon Sign: Taurus
Incense: Myrrh

---

18 Tuesday

Las Piedras Day (Uruguayan)
Waning Moon
Moon Phase: Fourth Quarter
Color: Gray

Moon Sign: Taurus
Incense: Sage

☽ Wednesday

Pilgrimage to Treguier (French)
Waning Moon
Moon Phase: New Moon 12:52 am
Color: White

Moon Sign: Taurus
Moon enters Gemini 3:47 am
Incense: Cedar

---

20 Thursday

Pardon of the Singers (British)
Waxing Moon
Moon Phase: First Quarter
Color: Purple

Moon Sign: Gemini
Sun enters Gemini 12:59 pm
Incense: Dill

---

21 Friday

Victoria Day (Canadian)
Waxing Moon
Moon Phase: First Quarter
Color: Rose

Moon Sign: Gemini
Moon enters Cancer 4:35 pm
Incense: Ylang ylang

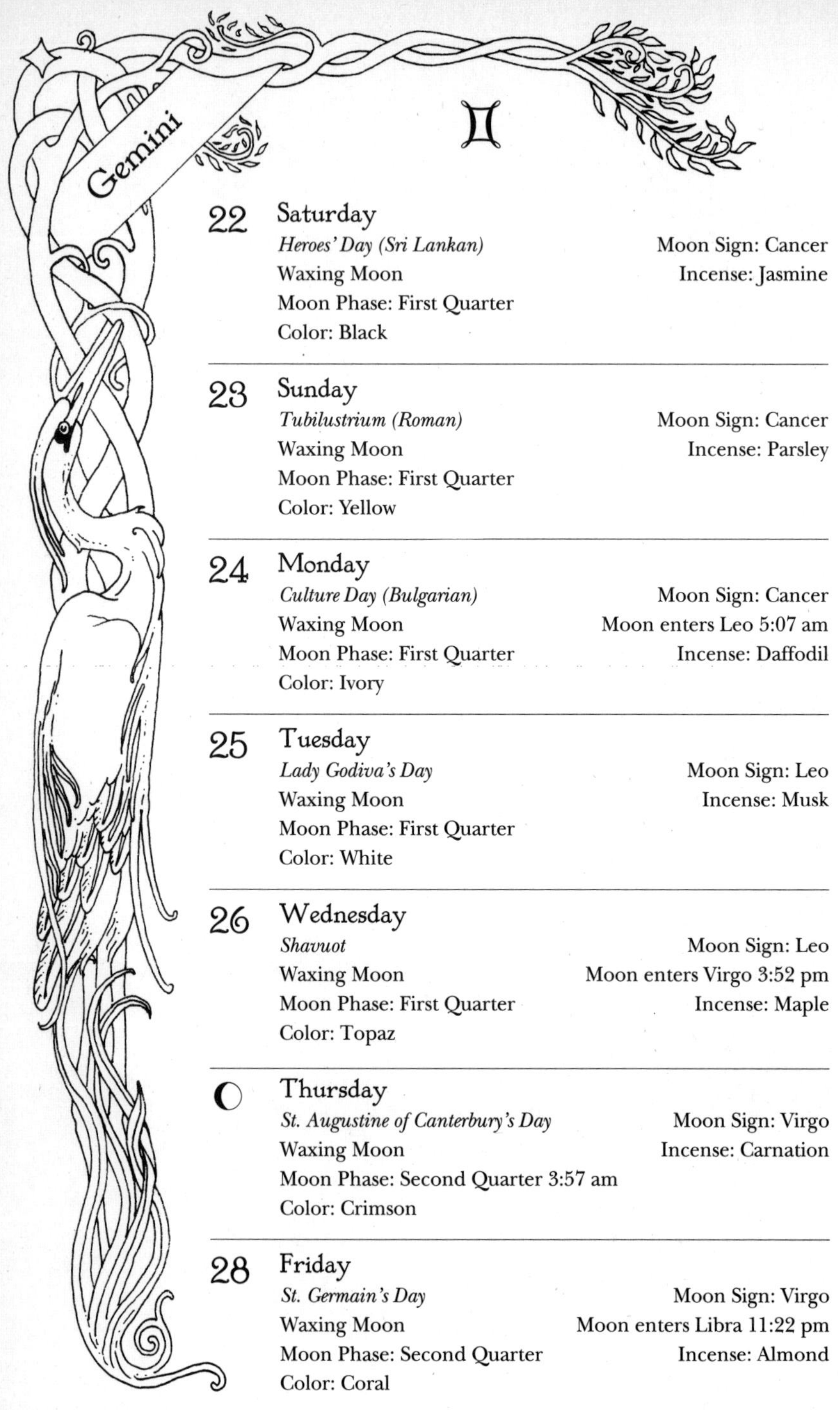

22 Saturday
Heroes' Day (Sri Lankan)
Waxing Moon
Moon Phase: First Quarter
Color: Black

Moon Sign: Cancer
Incense: Jasmine

---

23 Sunday
Tubilustrium (Roman)
Waxing Moon
Moon Phase: First Quarter
Color: Yellow

Moon Sign: Cancer
Incense: Parsley

---

24 Monday
Culture Day (Bulgarian)
Waxing Moon
Moon Phase: First Quarter
Color: Ivory

Moon Sign: Cancer
Moon enters Leo 5:07 am
Incense: Daffodil

---

25 Tuesday
Lady Godiva's Day
Waxing Moon
Moon Phase: First Quarter
Color: White

Moon Sign: Leo
Incense: Musk

---

26 Wednesday
Shavuot
Waxing Moon
Moon Phase: First Quarter
Color: Topaz

Moon Sign: Leo
Moon enters Virgo 3:52 pm
Incense: Maple

◐ Thursday
St. Augustine of Canterbury's Day
Waxing Moon
Moon Phase: Second Quarter 3:57 am
Color: Crimson

Moon Sign: Virgo
Incense: Carnation

---

28 Friday
St. Germain's Day
Waxing Moon
Moon Phase: Second Quarter
Color: Coral

Moon Sign: Virgo
Moon enters Libra 11:22 pm
Incense: Almond

29 Saturday
Royal Oak Day (English)
Waxing Moon
Moon Phase: Second Quarter
Color: Indigo

Moon Sign: Libra
Incense: Violet

---

30 Sunday
Pentecost
Waxing Moon
Moon Phase: Second Quarter
Color: Gold

Moon Sign: Libra
Incense: Clove

---

31 Monday
Memorial Day (observed)
Waxing Moon
Moon Phase: Second Quarter
Color: Gray

Moon Sign: Libra
Moon enters Scorpio 3:08 am
Incense: Rose

Butterfly Lore

To some native peoples of Mexico and the American Southwest, the butterfly represents the fertility of the earth. To people throughout the globe, butterflies have come to represent transformation and rebirth. Butterflies have been associated with the immortal soul and the transformation that occurs in physical death. For many, the chrysalis stage shows us that change is inevitable and we may experience it more easily when we turn inward to seek guidance. But more than that, butterflies bring joy and beauty, the lightness of air, and divine inspiration.

—Kristin Madden

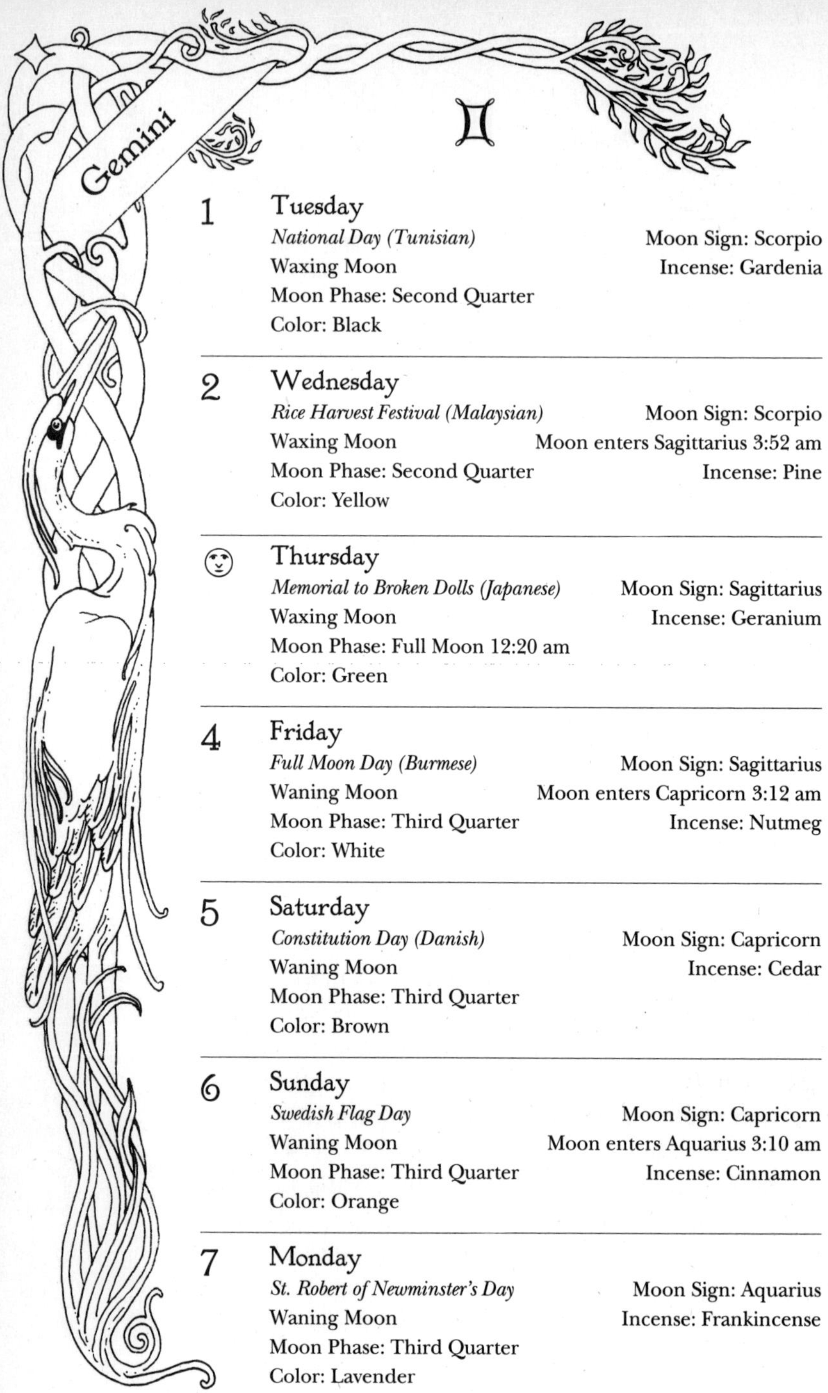

1 Tuesday
National Day (Tunisian)
Moon Sign: Scorpio
Waxing Moon
Incense: Gardenia
Moon Phase: Second Quarter
Color: Black

---

2 Wednesday
Rice Harvest Festival (Malaysian)
Moon Sign: Scorpio
Waxing Moon
Moon enters Sagittarius 3:52 am
Moon Phase: Second Quarter
Incense: Pine
Color: Yellow

Thursday
Memorial to Broken Dolls (Japanese)
Moon Sign: Sagittarius
Waxing Moon
Incense: Geranium
Moon Phase: Full Moon 12:20 am
Color: Green

---

4 Friday
Full Moon Day (Burmese)
Moon Sign: Sagittarius
Waning Moon
Moon enters Capricorn 3:12 am
Moon Phase: Third Quarter
Incense: Nutmeg
Color: White

---

5 Saturday
Constitution Day (Danish)
Moon Sign: Capricorn
Waning Moon
Incense: Cedar
Moon Phase: Third Quarter
Color: Brown

---

6 Sunday
Swedish Flag Day
Moon Sign: Capricorn
Waning Moon
Moon enters Aquarius 3:10 am
Moon Phase: Third Quarter
Incense: Cinnamon
Color: Orange

---

7 Monday
St. Robert of Newminster's Day
Moon Sign: Aquarius
Waning Moon
Incense: Frankincense
Moon Phase: Third Quarter
Color: Lavender

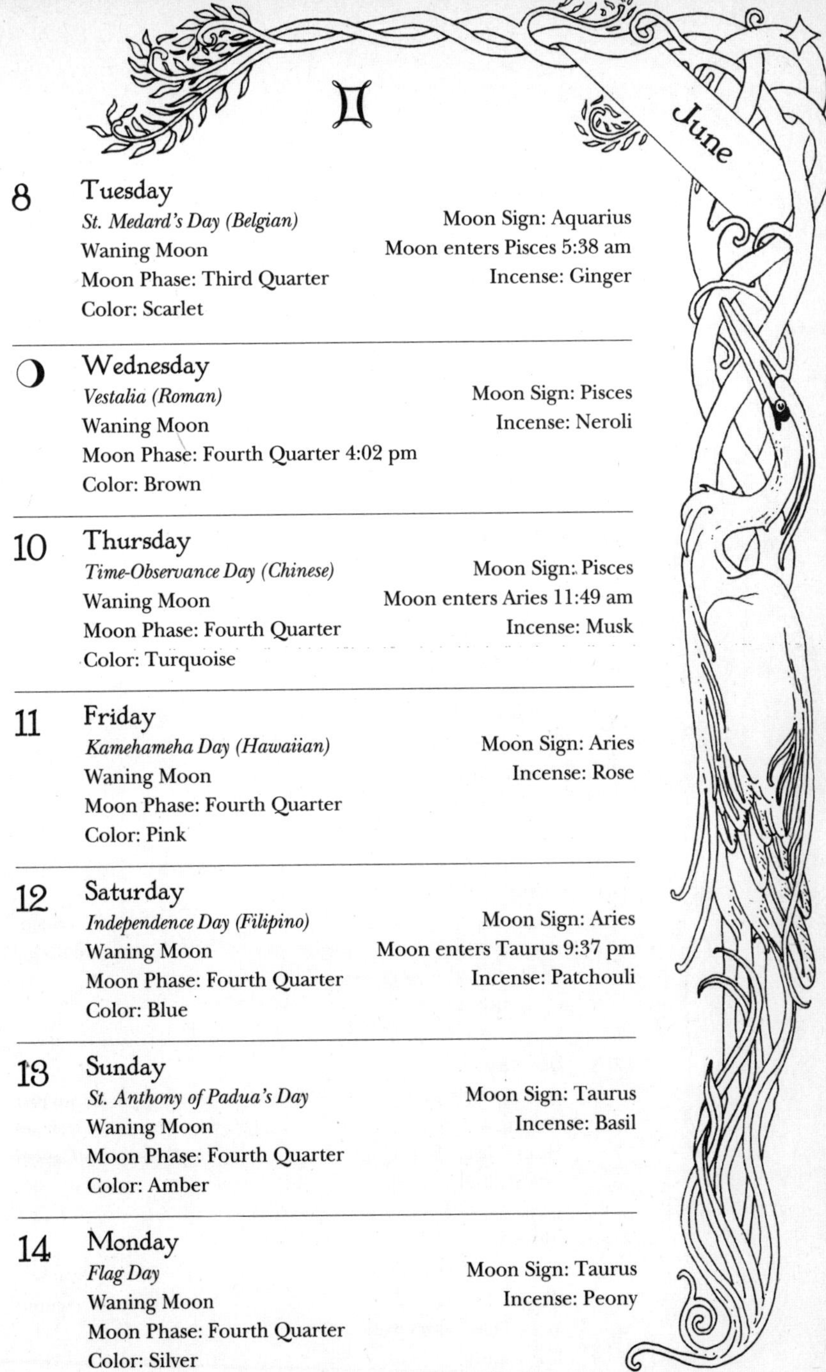

♊

8 **Tuesday**
St. Medard's Day (Belgian)
Waning Moon
Moon Phase: Third Quarter
Color: Scarlet

Moon Sign: Aquarius
Moon enters Pisces 5:38 am
Incense: Ginger

☽ **Wednesday**
Vestalia (Roman)
Waning Moon
Moon Phase: Fourth Quarter 4:02 pm
Color: Brown

Moon Sign: Pisces
Incense: Neroli

---

10 **Thursday**
Time-Observance Day (Chinese)
Waning Moon
Moon Phase: Fourth Quarter
Color: Turquoise

Moon Sign: Pisces
Moon enters Aries 11:49 am
Incense: Musk

---

11 **Friday**
Kamehameha Day (Hawaiian)
Waning Moon
Moon Phase: Fourth Quarter
Color: Pink

Moon Sign: Aries
Incense: Rose

---

12 **Saturday**
Independence Day (Filipino)
Waning Moon
Moon Phase: Fourth Quarter
Color: Blue

Moon Sign: Aries
Moon enters Taurus 9:37 pm
Incense: Patchouli

---

13 **Sunday**
St. Anthony of Padua's Day
Waning Moon
Moon Phase: Fourth Quarter
Color: Amber

Moon Sign: Taurus
Incense: Basil

---

14 **Monday**
Flag Day
Waning Moon
Moon Phase: Fourth Quarter
Color: Silver

Moon Sign: Taurus
Incense: Peony

15 Tuesday

St. Vitus's Day Fires
Waning Moon
Moon Phase: Fourth Quarter
Color: Gray

Moon Sign: Taurus
Moon enters Gemini 9:44 am
Incense: Poplar

---

16 Wednesday

Bloomsday (Irish)
Waning Moon
Moon Phase: Fourth Quarter
Color: White

Moon Sign: Gemini
Incense: Coriander

Thursday

Bunker Hill Day
Waning Moon
Moon Phase: New Moon 4:27 pm
Color: Purple

Moon Sign: Gemini
Moon enters Cancer 10:37 pm
Incense: Sage

---

18 Friday

Independence Day (Egyptian)
Waxing Moon
Moon Phase: First Quarter
Color: Rose

Moon Sign: Cancer
Incense: Dill

---

19 Saturday

Juneteenth
Waxing Moon
Moon Phase: First Quarter
Color: Black

Moon Sign: Cancer
Incense: Maple

---

20 Sunday

Father's Day • *Litha* • *Summer Solstice*
Waxing Moon
Moon Phase: First Quarter
Color: Gold

Moon Sign: Cancer
Moon enters Leo 11:05 am
Sun enters Cancer
Incense: Parsley

---

21 Monday

U.S. Constitution ratified
Waxing Moon
Moon Phase: First Quarter
Color: Ivory

Moon Sign: Leo
Incense: Lavender

22 Tuesday
Rose Festival (English)
Waxing Moon
Moon Phase: First Quarter
Color: Orange

Moon Sign: Leo
Moon enters Virgo 10:10 pm
Incense: Juniper

---

23 Wednesday
St. John's Eve
Waxing Moon
Moon Phase: First Quarter
Color: Topaz

Moon Sign: Virgo
Incense: Sandalwood

---

24 Thursday
St. John's Day
Waxing Moon
Moon Phase: First Quarter
Color: Crimson

Moon Sign: Virgo
Incense: Carnation

◐ Friday
Fiesta of Santa Orosia (Spanish)
Waxing Moon
Moon Phase: Second Quarter 3:08 pm
Color: Coral

Moon Sign: Virgo
Moon enters Libra 6:40 am
Incense: Thyme

---

26 Saturday
Pied Piper Day (German)
Waxing Moon
Moon Phase: Second Quarter
Color: Indigo

Moon Sign: Libra
Incense: Lilac

---

27 Sunday
Day of the Seven Sleepers (Islamic)
Waxing Moon
Moon Phase: Second Quarter
Color: Yellow

Moon Sign: Libra
Moon enters Scorpio 12:13 pm
Incense: Cinnamon

---

28 Monday
Paul Bunyan Day
Waxing Moon
Moon Phase: Second Quarter
Color: Gray

Moon Sign: Scorpio
Incense: Chrysanthemum

♋

29 Tuesday
Saint Peter and Paul's Day
Waxing Moon
Moon Phase: Second Quarter
Color: Red

Moon Sign: Scorpio
Moon enters Sagittarius 2:15 pm
Incense: Honeysuckle

---

30 Wednesday
The Burning of the Three Firs (French)
Waxing Moon
Moon Phase: Second Quarter
Color: Brown

Moon Sign: Sagittarius
Incense: Eucalyptus

Prickly Pear Healing Lore

Prickly Pear *(Opuntia* spp.) is rich in ascorbic acid, vitamin C, bioflavonoids, potassium, calcium, and seventeen essential amino acids. The pads of this fruit are wonderful drawing poultices and are used in swelling, bruises, and burns. The juice helps balance blood sugar and functions as an anti-inflammatory and diuretic. It is often used in conjunction with antibiotics to soothe urinary tract infections and cystitis. The flowers are useful in fighting colitis, asthma, and bronchitis. Most of all, the fruit is very delicious—just beware of the spiny hairs if you happen to be picking them fresh.

—Kristin Madden

1 **Thursday**
Climbing Mount Fuji (Japanese) Moon Sign: Sagittarius
Waxing Moon Moon enters Capricorn 2:01 pm
Moon Phase: Second Quarter Incense: Geranium
Color: White

Friday
Heroes' Day (Zambian) Moon Sign: Capricorn
Waxing Moon Incense: Sandalwood
Moon Phase: Full Moon 7:09 pm
Color: Purple

---

3 **Saturday**
Indian Sun Dance (Native American) Moon Sign: Capricorn
Waning Moon Moon enters Aquarius 1:22 pm
Moon Phase: Third Quarter Incense: Juniper
Color: Black

---

4 **Sunday**
Independence Day Moon Sign: Aquarius
Waning Moon Incense: Sage
Moon Phase: Third Quarter
Color: Orange

---

5 **Monday**
Tynwald (Nordic) Moon Sign: Aquarius
Waning Moon Moon enters Pisces 2:25 pm
Moon Phase: Third Quarter Incense: Myrrh
Color: Ivory

---

6 **Tuesday**
Khao Phansa Day (Thai) Moon Sign: Pisces
Waning Moon Incense: Evergreen
Moon Phase: Third Quarter
Color: Scarlet

---

7 **Wednesday**
Weaver's Festival (Japanese) Moon Sign: Pisces
Waning Moon Moon enters Aries 7:03 pm
Moon Phase: Third Quarter Incense: Cedar
Color: Yellow

♋

8 Thursday
St. Elizabeth's Day (Portuguese)
Waning Moon
Moon Phase: Third Quarter
Color: Green

Moon Sign: Aries
Incense: Musk

---

9 Friday
Battle of Sempach Day (Swiss)
Waning Moon
Moon Phase: Fourth Quarter 3:34 am
Color: Pink

Moon Sign: Aries
Incense: Ylang ylang

---

10 Saturday
Lady Godiva Day (English)
Waning Moon
Moon Phase: Fourth Quarter
Color: Indigo

Moon Sign: Aries
Moon enters Taurus 3:51 am
Incense: Pine

---

11 Sunday
Revolution Day (Mongolian)
Waning Moon
Moon Phase: Fourth Quarter
Color: Gold

Moon Sign: Taurus
Incense: Clove

---

12 Monday
Lobster Carnival (Nova Scotian)
Waning Moon
Moon Phase: Fourth Quarter
Color: Gray

Moon Sign: Taurus
Moon enters Gemini 3:45 pm
Incense: Rose

---

13 Tuesday
Festival of the Three Cows (Spanish)
Waning Moon
Moon Phase: Fourth Quarter
Color: Black

Moon Sign: Gemini
Incense: Sage

---

14 Wednesday
Bastille Day (French)
Waning Moon
Moon Phase: Fourth Quarter
Color: Brown

Moon Sign: Gemini
Incense: Maple

♋

15 Thursday
St. Swithin's Day
Waning Moon
Moon Phase: Fourth Quarter
Color: Purple

Moon Sign: Gemini
Moon enters Cancer 4:40 am
Incense: Jasmine

---

16 Friday
Our Lady of Carmel
Waning Moon
Moon Phase: Fourth Quarter
Color: White

Moon Sign: Cancer
Incense: Nutmeg

☽ Saturday
Rivera Day (Puerto Rican)
Waning Moon
Moon Phase: New Moon 7:24 am
Color: Blue

Moon Sign: Cancer
Moon enters Leo 4:56 pm
Incense: Lavender

---

18 Sunday
Gion Matsuri Festival (Japanese)
Waxing Moon
Moon Phase: First Quarter
Color: Amber

Moon Sign: Leo
Incense: Basil

---

19 Monday
Flitch Day (English)
Waxing Moon
Moon Phase: First Quarter
Color: Silver

Moon Sign: Leo
Incense: Daffodil

---

20 Tuesday
Binding of Wreaths (Lithuanian)
Waxing Moon
Moon Phase: First Quarter
Color: Gray

Moon Sign: Leo
Moon enters Virgo 3:44 am
Incense: Musk

---

21 Wednesday
National Day (Belgian)
Waxing Moon
Moon Phase: First Quarter
Color: White

Moon Sign: Virgo
Incense: Pine

22 Thursday
St. Mary Magdalene's Day — Moon Sign: Virgo
Waxing Moon — Sun enters Leo 7:50 am
Moon Phase: First Quarter — Moon enters Libra 12:39 pm
Color: Crimson — Incense: Chrysanthemum

23 Friday
Mysteries of Santa Cristina (Italian) — Moon Sign: Libra
Waxing Moon — Sun enters Leo 1:04 am
Moon Phase: First Quarter — Incense: Ginger
Color: Coral

◐ Saturday
Pioneer Day (Mormon) — Moon Sign: Libra
Waxing Moon — Moon enters Scorpio 7:08 pm
Moon Phase: Second Quarter 11:37 pm — Incense: Violet
Color: Brown

25 Sunday
St. James' Day — Moon Sign: Scorpio
Waxing Moon — Incense: Coriander
Moon Phase: Second Quarter
Color: Yellow

26 Monday
St. Anne's Day — Moon Sign: Scorpio
Waxing Moon — Moon enters Sagittarius 10:48 pm
Moon Phase: Second Quarter — Incense: Peony
Color: White

27 Tuesday
Sleepyhead Day (Finnish) — Moon Sign: Sagittarius
Waxing Moon — Incense: Gardenia
Moon Phase: Second Quarter
Color: Red

28 Wednesday
Independence Day (Peruvian) — Moon Sign: Sagittarius
Waxing Moon — Moon enters Capricorn 11:57 pm
Moon Phase: Second Quarter — Incense: Neroli
Color: Topaz

29 Thursday

Pardon of the Birds (French)
Waxing Moon
Moon Phase: Second Quarter
Color: Turquoise

Moon Sign: Capricorn
Incense: Evergreen

---

30 Friday

Micmac Festival of St. Ann
Waxing Moon
Moon Phase: Second Quarter
Color: Rose

Moon Sign: Capricorn
Moon enters Aquarius 11:54 pm
Incense: Parsley

---

31 Saturday

Weighing of the Aga Khan
Waxing Moon
Moon Phase: Full Moon 2:05 pm
Color: Gray

Moon Sign: Aquarius
Incense: Cedar

Sagebrush Healing Lore

Best known for its use in sacred saunas, sweat lodges, and smudge sticks, sagebrush is *Artemisia* spp., not *Salvia* spp., which is true sage. Sagebrush is one of the Navajo life medicines, and it is highly prized for its healing properties. Sagebrush is considered to be a general stimulant and possesses antimicrobial properties. It is used as a disinfectant wash, to kill intestinal worms, and for dysentery, both as a preventive and as a cure. Powdered leaves of dried sagebrush ease diaper rash and chafing as well as digestive problems, headache, colds, sore throats, fevers, and even childbirth pain.

—Kristin Madden

♌

1 **Sunday**
Lammas
Waning Moon
Moon Phase: Third Quarter
Color: Gold

Moon Sign: Aquarius
Incense: Poplar

---

2 **Monday**
Porcingula (Native American)
Waning Moon
Moon Phase: Third Quarter
Color: Lavender

Moon Sign: Aquarius
Moon enters Pisces 12:34 am
Incense: Lavender

---

3 **Tuesday**
Drimes (Greek)
Waning Moon
Moon Phase: Third Quarter
Color: Black

Moon Sign: Pisces
Incense: Ginger

---

4 **Wednesday**
Cook Islands Constitution Celebration
Waning Moon
Moon Phase: Third Quarter
Color: Yellow

Moon Sign: Pisces
Moon enters Aries 3:59 am
Incense: Coriander

---

5 **Thursday**
Benediction of the Sea (French)
Waning Moon
Moon Phase: Third Quarter
Color: Crimson

Moon Sign: Aries
Incense: Dill

---

6 **Friday**
Hiroshima Peace Ceremony
Waning Moon
Moon Phase: Third Quarter
Color: Purple

Moon Sign: Aries
Moon enters Taurus 11:25 am
Incense: Rose

◑ **Saturday**
Republic Day (Ivory Coast)
Waning Moon
Moon Phase: Fourth Quarter 6:01 pm
Color: Brown

Moon Sign: Taurus
Incense: Patchouli

♌

8 **Sunday**

Dog Days (Japanese) Moon Sign: Taurus
Waning Moon Moon enters Gemini 10:33 pm
Moon Phase: Fourth Quarter Incense: Cinnamon
Color: Amber

---

9 **Monday**

Nagasaki Peace Ceremony Moon Sign: Gemini
Waning Moon Incense: Maple
Moon Phase: Fourth Quarter
Color: White

---

10 **Tuesday**

St. Lawrence's Day Moon Sign: Gemini
Waning Moon Incense: Juniper
Moon Phase: Fourth Quarter
Color: Gray

---

11 **Wednesday**

Puck Fair (Irish) Moon Sign: Gemini
Waning Moon Moon enters Cancer 11:20 am
Moon Phase: Fourth Quarter Incense: Sandalwood
Color: Topaz

---

12 **Thursday**

Fiesta of Santa Clara Moon Sign: Cancer
Waning Moon Incense: Carnation
Moon Phase: Fourth Quarter
Color: Green

---

13 **Friday**

Women's Day (Tunisian) Moon Sign: Cancer
Waning Moon Moon enters Leo 11:30 pm
Moon Phase: Fourth Quarter Incense: Thyme
Color: Rose

---

14 **Saturday**

Festival at Sassari Moon Sign: Leo
Waning Moon Incense: Lilac
Moon Phase: Fourth Quarter
Color: Blue

♌

15 Sunday
Assumption Day
Waning Moon
Moon Phase: New Moon 9:24 pm
Color: Yellow

Moon Sign: Leo
Incense: Sage

---

16 Monday
Festival of Minstrels (European)
Waxing Moon
Moon Phase: First Quarter
Color: Silver

Moon Sign: Leo
Moon enters Virgo 9:49 am
Incense: Chrysanthemum

---

17 Tuesday
Feast of the Hungry Ghosts (Chinese)
Waxing Moon
Moon Phase: First Quarter
Color: White

Moon Sign: Virgo
Incense: Honeysuckle

---

18 Wednesday
St. Helen's Day
Waxing Moon
Moon Phase: First Quarter
Color: Brown

Moon Sign: Virgo
Moon enters Libra6:09 pm
Incense: Eucalyptus

---

19 Thursday
Rustic Vinalia (Roman)
Waxing Moon
Moon Phase: First Quarter
Color: Turquoise

Moon Sign: Libra
Incense: Geranium

---

20 Friday
Constitution Day (Hungarian)
Waxing Moon
Moon Phase: First Quarter
Color: Pink

Moon Sign: Libra
Incense: Sandalwood

---

21 Saturday
Consualia (Roman)
Waxing Moon
Moon Phase: First Quarter
Color: Gray

Moon Sign: Libra
Moon enters Scorpio 12:37 am
Incense: Juniper

22 Sunday

Feast of the Queenship of Mary (English) Moon Sign: Scorpio
Waxing Moon Sun enters Virgo 2:53 pm
Moon Phase: First Quarter Incense: Clove
Color: Orange

---

23 Monday

National Day (Romanian) Moon Sign: Scorpio
Waxing Moon Moon enters Sagittarius 5:08 am
Moon Phase: Second Quarter 6:12 am Incense: Frankincense
Color: Ivory

---

24 Tuesday

St. Bartholomew's Day Moon Sign: Sagittarius
Waxing Moon Incense: Evergreen
Moon Phase: Second Quarter
Color: Scarlet

---

25 Wednesday

Feast of the Green Corn (Native American) Moon Sign: Sagittarius
Waxing Moon Moon enters Capricorn 7:46 am
Moon Phase: Second Quarter Incense: Cedar
Color: White

---

26 Thursday

Pardon of the Sea (French) Moon Sign: Capricorn
Waxing Moon Incense: Musk
Moon Phase: Second Quarter
Color: Purple

---

27 Friday

Summer Break (English) Moon Sign: Capricorn
Waxing Moon Moon enters Aquarius 9:08 am
Moon Phase: Second Quarter Incense: Ylang ylang
Color: Coral

---

28 Saturday

St. Augustine's Day Moon Sign: Aquarius
Waxing Moon Incense: Pine
Moon Phase: Second Quarter
Color: Indigo

♍

29 Sunday
St. John's Beheading — Moon Sign: Aquarius
Waxing Moon — Moon enters Pisces 10:33 am
Moon Phase: Full Moon 10:22 pm — Incense: Basil
Color: Amber

---

30 Monday
St. Rose of Lima Day (Peruvian) — Moon Sign: Pisces
Waning Moon — Incense: Myrrh
Moon Phase: Third Quarter
Color: Gray

---

31 Tuesday
Unto These Hills Pageant (Cherokee) — Moon Sign: Pisces
Waning Moon — Moon enters Aries 1:46 pm
Moon Phase: Third Quarter — Incense: Sage
Color: Black

Magical Salsa Recipe

For this recipe, you will need:

- 3 ripe tomatoes
- 1 onion, red or Vidalia
- 3 cloves garlic
- ½ tsp. salt
- ¼ tsp. cumin
- ½ cup chopped red peppers
- 1 small can of diced green chilies

Mix all ingredients, including the juice from the tomatoes. Store in a refrigerator for at least one hour before serving. Add the hot chilies (substitute jalapenos for a spicier salsa). This can be frozen for two months or kept in the refrigerator for two weeks.

—Kristin Madden

1 Wednesday
Greek New Year
Waning Moon
Moon Phase: Third Quarter
Color: Brown

Moon Sign: Aries
Incense: Maple

---

2 Thursday
St. Mamas's Day
Waning Moon
Moon Phase: Third Quarter
Color: Crimson

Moon Sign: Aries
Moon enters Taurus 8:16 pm
Incense: Jasmine

◐ Friday
Founder's Day (San Marino)
Waning Moon
Moon Phase: Third Quarter
Color: Rose

Moon Sign: Taurus
Incense: Almond

---

4 Saturday
Los Angeles' Birthday
Waning Moon
Moon Phase: Third Quarter
Color: Blue

Moon Sign: Taurus
Incense: Lavender

---

5 Sunday
Roman Circus • First Labor Day (1882)
Waning Moon
Moon Phase: Third Quarter
Color: Yellow

Moon Sign: Taurus
Moon enters Gemini 6:24 am
Incense: Coriander

---

6 Monday
Labor Day (observed)
Waning Moon
Moon Phase: Fourth Quarter 11:10 am
Color: Lavender

Moon Sign: Gemini
Incense: Rose

---

7 Tuesday
Festival of the Durga (Hindu)
Waning Moon
Moon Phase: Fourth Quarter
Color: Red

Moon Sign: Aquarius
Moon enters Cancer 6:50 pm
Incense: Musk

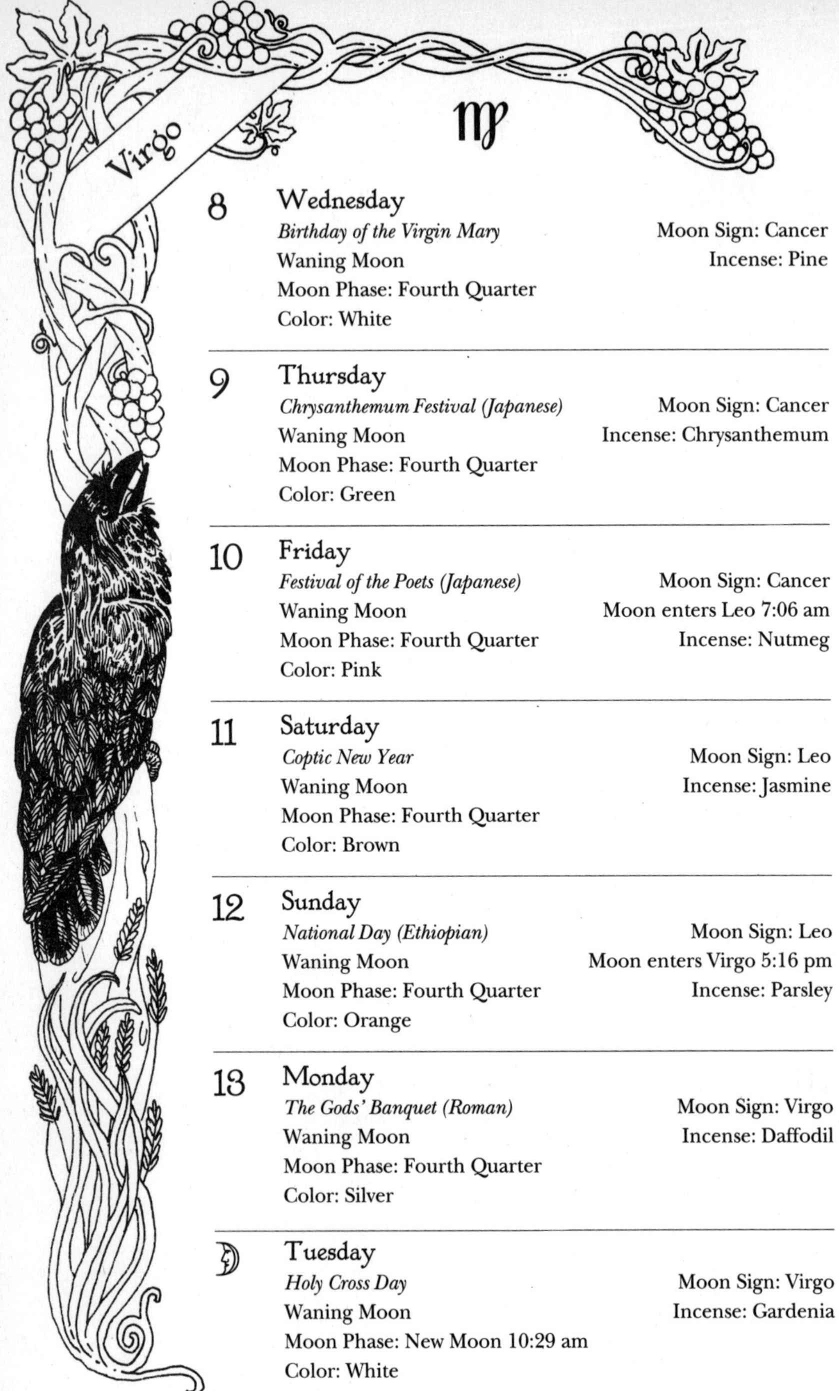

8 **Wednesday**
Birthday of the Virgin Mary
Waning Moon
Moon Phase: Fourth Quarter
Color: White

Moon Sign: Cancer
Incense: Pine

---

9 **Thursday**
Chrysanthemum Festival (Japanese)
Waning Moon
Moon Phase: Fourth Quarter
Color: Green

Moon Sign: Cancer
Incense: Chrysanthemum

---

10 **Friday**
Festival of the Poets (Japanese)
Waning Moon
Moon Phase: Fourth Quarter
Color: Pink

Moon Sign: Cancer
Moon enters Leo 7:06 am
Incense: Nutmeg

---

11 **Saturday**
Coptic New Year
Waning Moon
Moon Phase: Fourth Quarter
Color: Brown

Moon Sign: Leo
Incense: Jasmine

---

12 **Sunday**
National Day (Ethiopian)
Waning Moon
Moon Phase: Fourth Quarter
Color: Orange

Moon Sign: Leo
Moon enters Virgo 5:16 pm
Incense: Parsley

---

13 **Monday**
The Gods' Banquet (Roman)
Waning Moon
Moon Phase: Fourth Quarter
Color: Silver

Moon Sign: Virgo
Incense: Daffodil

☽ **Tuesday**
Holy Cross Day
Waning Moon
Moon Phase: New Moon 10:29 am
Color: White

Moon Sign: Virgo
Incense: Gardenia

15 Wednesday

Birthday of the Moon (Chinese) — Moon Sign: Virgo
Waxing Moon — Moon enters Libra 12:54 am
Moon Phase: First Quarter — Incense: Neroli
Color: Topaz

---

16 Thursday

Rosh Hashanah — Moon Sign: Libra
Waxing Moon — Incense: Evergreen
Moon Phase: First Quarter
Color: Turquoise

---

17 Friday

Von Steuben's Day — Moon Sign: Libra
Waxing Moon — Moon enters Scorpio 6:25 am
Moon Phase: First Quarter — Incense: Ginger
Color: Purple

---

18 Saturday

Dr. Johnson's Birthday — Moon Sign: Scorpio
Waxing Moon — Incense: Violet
Moon Phase: First Quarter
Color: Gray

---

19 Sunday

St. Januarius' Day (Italian) — Moon Sign: Scorpio
Waxing Moon — Moon enters Sagittarius 10:30 am
Moon Phase: First Quarter — Incense: Poplar
Color: Amber

---

20 Monday

St. Eustace's Day — Moon Sign: Sagittarius
Waxing Moon — Incense: Peony
Moon Phase: First Quarter
Color: Ivory

◐ Tuesday

Christ's Hospital Founder's Day (British) — Moon Sign: Sagittarius
Waxing Moon — Moon enters Capricorn 1:35 pm
Moon Phase: Second Quarter 11:54 am — Incense: Pine
Color: Black

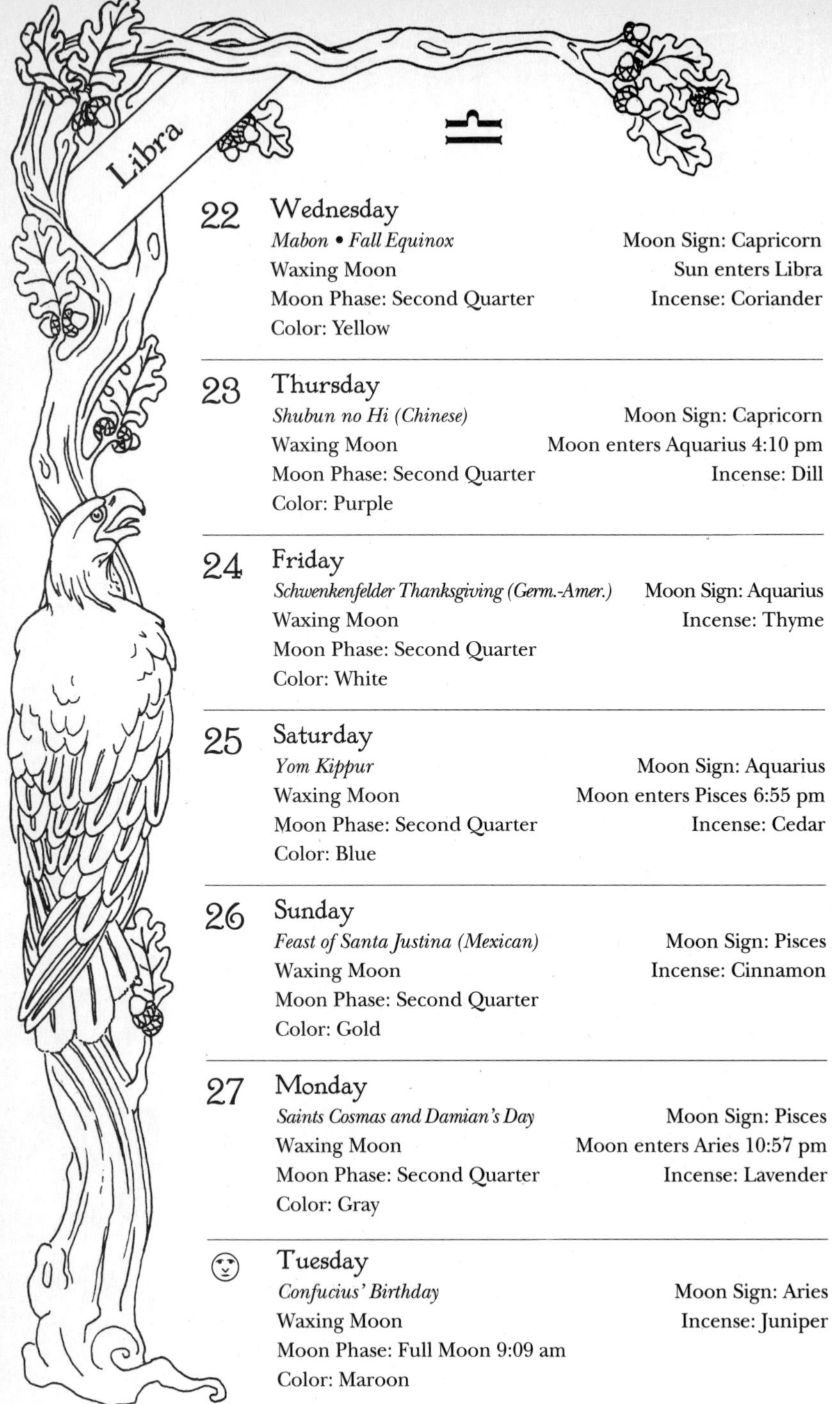

♎

22 **Wednesday**
Mabon • Fall Equinox
Waxing Moon
Moon Phase: Second Quarter
Color: Yellow

Moon Sign: Capricorn
Sun enters Libra
Incense: Coriander

---

23 **Thursday**
Shubun no Hi (Chinese)
Waxing Moon
Moon Phase: Second Quarter
Color: Purple

Moon Sign: Capricorn
Moon enters Aquarius 4:10 pm
Incense: Dill

---

24 **Friday**
Schwenkenfelder Thanksgiving (Germ.-Amer.)
Waxing Moon
Moon Phase: Second Quarter
Color: White

Moon Sign: Aquarius
Incense: Thyme

---

25 **Saturday**
Yom Kippur
Waxing Moon
Moon Phase: Second Quarter
Color: Blue

Moon Sign: Aquarius
Moon enters Pisces 6:55 pm
Incense: Cedar

---

26 **Sunday**
Feast of Santa Justina (Mexican)
Waxing Moon
Moon Phase: Second Quarter
Color: Gold

Moon Sign: Pisces
Incense: Cinnamon

---

27 **Monday**
Saints Cosmas and Damian's Day
Waxing Moon
Moon Phase: Second Quarter
Color: Gray

Moon Sign: Pisces
Moon enters Aries 10:57 pm
Incense: Lavender

Tuesday
Confucius' Birthday
Waxing Moon
Moon Phase: Full Moon 9:09 am
Color: Maroon

Moon Sign: Aries
Incense: Juniper

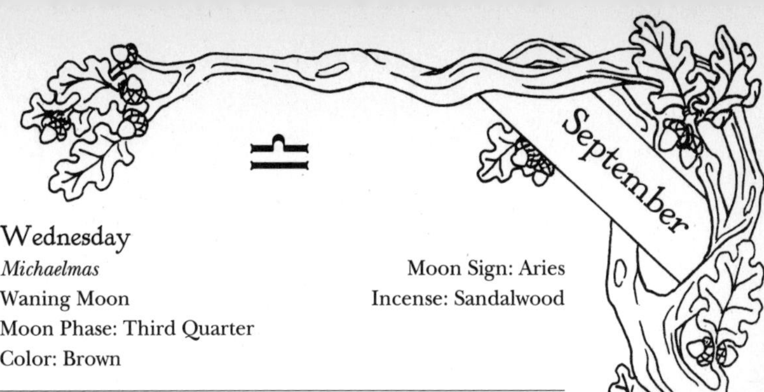

29 Wednesday

Michaelmas

Waning Moon

Moon Phase: Third Quarter

Color: Brown

Moon Sign: Aries

Incense: Sandalwood

---

30 Thursday

Sukkot begins

Waning Moon

Moon Phase: Third Quarter

Color: White

Moon Sign: Aries

Moon enters Taurus 5:24 am

Incense: Carnation

Autumn Weather Folklore

Here are some weather signs to watch for in autumn.

A long hot summer indicates a windy autumn.
A windy autumn precedes a mild winter.
The first frost in autumn will be exactly six months after the first thunderstorm of the spring.
It will be a long and hard winter if:
Woolly caterpillars are more black than brown.
Squirrels gather and bury their nuts early.
Trees produce an abundance of nuts.
The leaves fall late.
Apple skins are tough.
Cornhusks are thick.
Onion skins are thick.
Birds migrate early.
Fruit trees bloom in the fall.

—Kristin Madden

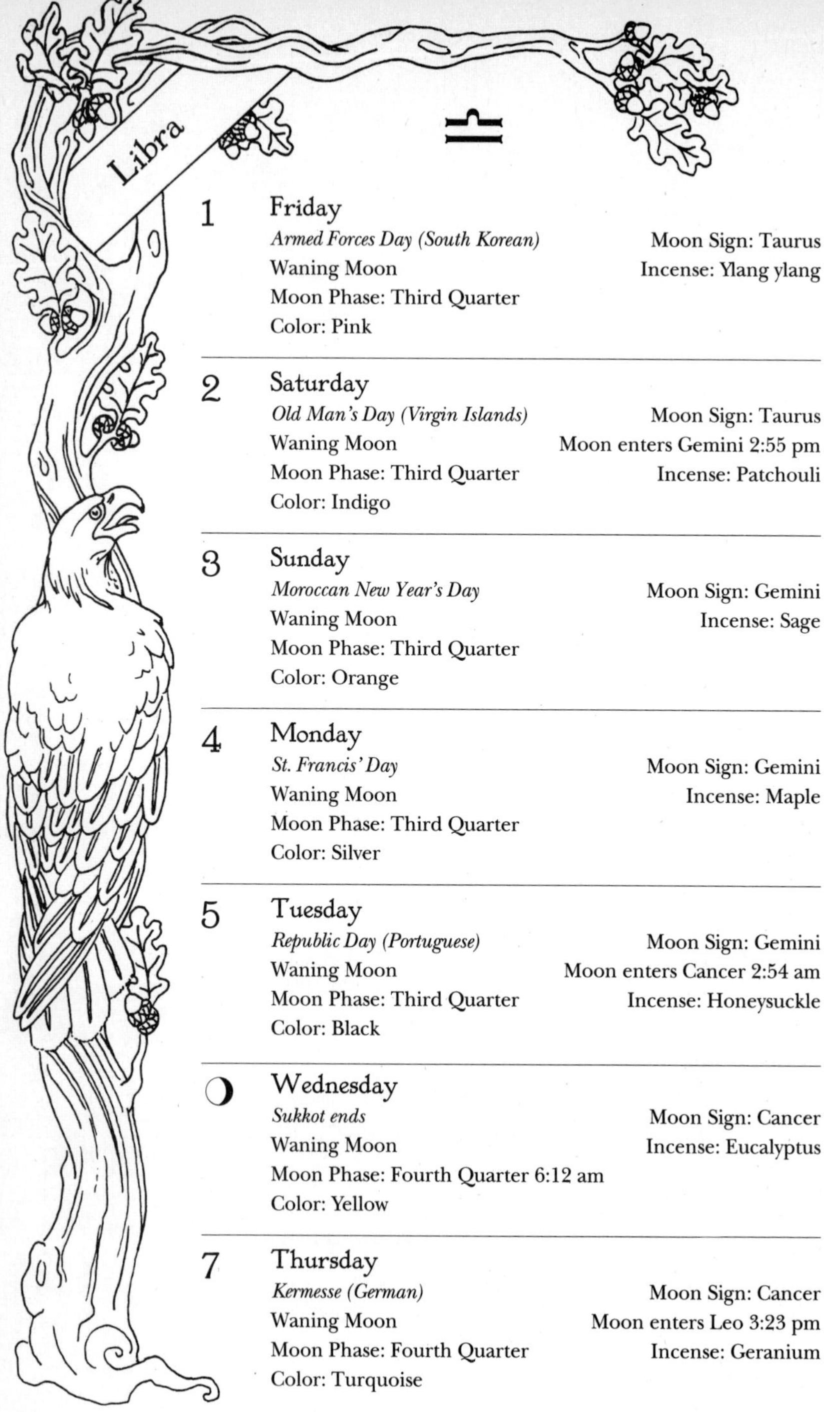

♎

1 Friday
Armed Forces Day (South Korean)
Waning Moon
Moon Phase: Third Quarter
Color: Pink
Moon Sign: Taurus
Incense: Ylang ylang

---

2 Saturday
Old Man's Day (Virgin Islands)
Waning Moon
Moon Phase: Third Quarter
Color: Indigo
Moon Sign: Taurus
Moon enters Gemini 2:55 pm
Incense: Patchouli

---

3 Sunday
Moroccan New Year's Day
Waning Moon
Moon Phase: Third Quarter
Color: Orange
Moon Sign: Gemini
Incense: Sage

---

4 Monday
St. Francis' Day
Waning Moon
Moon Phase: Third Quarter
Color: Silver
Moon Sign: Gemini
Incense: Maple

---

5 Tuesday
Republic Day (Portuguese)
Waning Moon
Moon Phase: Third Quarter
Color: Black
Moon Sign: Gemini
Moon enters Cancer 2:54 am
Incense: Honeysuckle

◑ Wednesday
Sukkot ends
Waning Moon
Moon Phase: Fourth Quarter 6:12 am
Color: Yellow
Moon Sign: Cancer
Incense: Eucalyptus

---

7 Thursday
Kermesse (German)
Waning Moon
Moon Phase: Fourth Quarter
Color: Turquoise
Moon Sign: Cancer
Moon enters Leo 3:23 pm
Incense: Geranium

8 Friday
Okunchi (Japanese)
Waning Moon
Moon Phase: Fourth Quarter
Color: Coral

Moon Sign: Leo
Incense: Almond

---

9 Saturday
Alphabet Day (South Korean)
Waning Moon
Moon Phase: Fourth Quarter
Color: Blue

Moon Sign: Leo
Incense: Lilac

---

10 Sunday
Health Day (Japanese)
Waning Moon
Moon Phase: Fourth Quarter
Color: Gold

Moon Sign: Leo
Moon enters Virgo 2:00 am
Incense: Clove

---

11 Monday
Columbus Day (observed)
Waning Moon
Moon Phase: Fourth Quarter
Color: Ivory

Moon Sign: Virgo
Incense: Chrysanthemum

---

12 Tuesday
National Day (Spanish)
Waning Moon
Moon Phase: Fourth Quarter
Color: Red

Moon Sign: Virgo
Moon enters Libra 9:32 am
Incense: Evergreen

---

13 Wednesday
Fontinalia (Roman)
Waning Moon
Moon Phase: New Moon 10:48 pm
Color: Brown

Moon Sign: Libra
Incense: Cedar

---

14 Thursday
Battle Festival (Japanese)
Waxing Moon
Moon Phase: First Quarter
Color: Purple

Moon Sign: Libra
Moon enters Scorpio 2:10 pm
Incense: Musk

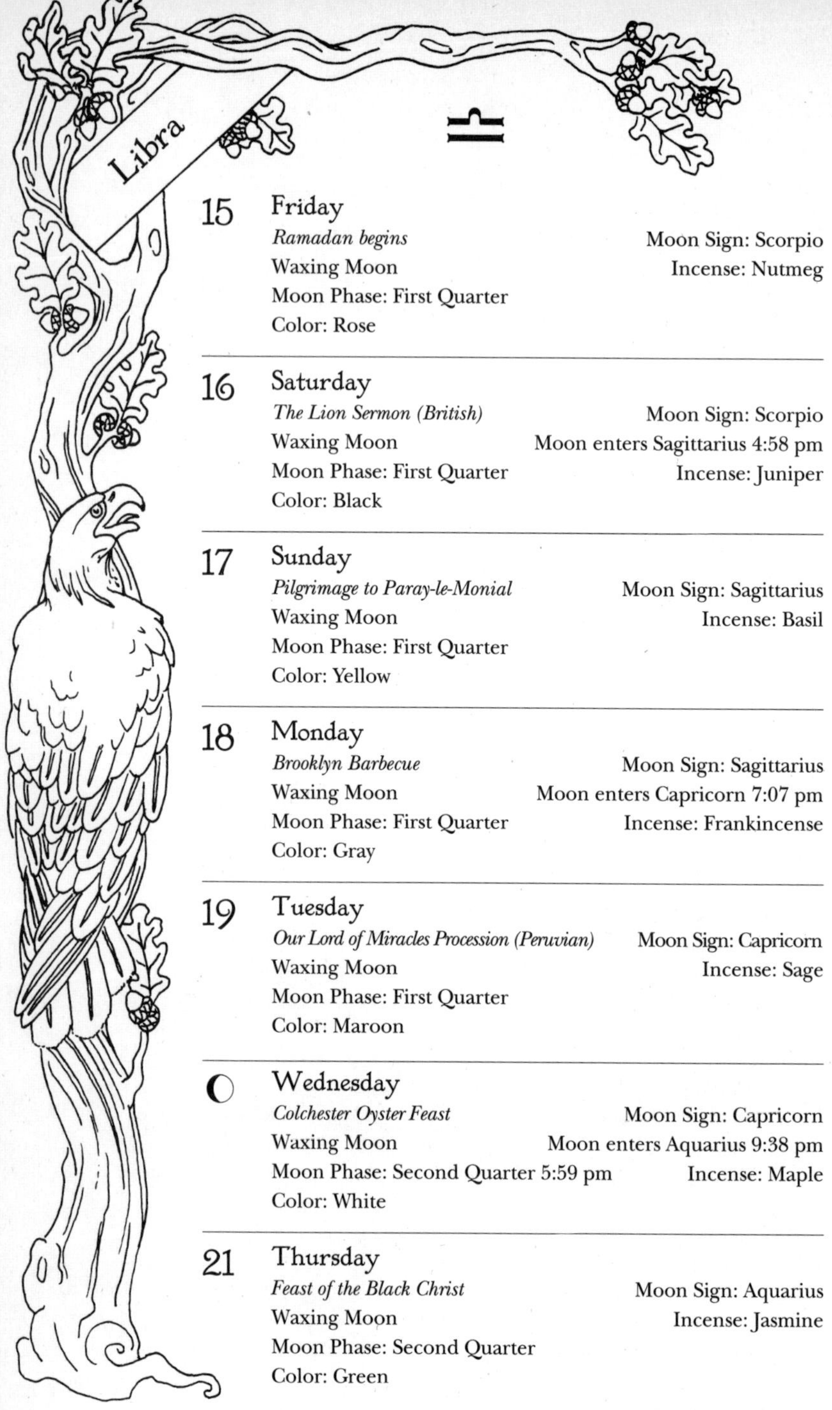

15 Friday
Ramadan begins
Waxing Moon
Moon Phase: First Quarter
Color: Rose
Moon Sign: Scorpio
Incense: Nutmeg

---

16 Saturday
The Lion Sermon (British)
Waxing Moon
Moon Phase: First Quarter
Color: Black
Moon Sign: Scorpio
Moon enters Sagittarius 4:58 pm
Incense: Juniper

---

17 Sunday
Pilgrimage to Paray-le-Monial
Waxing Moon
Moon Phase: First Quarter
Color: Yellow
Moon Sign: Sagittarius
Incense: Basil

---

18 Monday
Brooklyn Barbecue
Waxing Moon
Moon Phase: First Quarter
Color: Gray
Moon Sign: Sagittarius
Moon enters Capricorn 7:07 pm
Incense: Frankincense

---

19 Tuesday
Our Lord of Miracles Procession (Peruvian)
Waxing Moon
Moon Phase: First Quarter
Color: Maroon
Moon Sign: Capricorn
Incense: Sage

◐ Wednesday
Colchester Oyster Feast
Waxing Moon
Moon Phase: Second Quarter 5:59 pm
Color: White
Moon Sign: Capricorn
Moon enters Aquarius 9:38 pm
Incense: Maple

---

21 Thursday
Feast of the Black Christ
Waxing Moon
Moon Phase: Second Quarter
Color: Green
Moon Sign: Aquarius
Incense: Jasmine

22 Friday

Goddess of Mercy Day (Chinese)
Waxing Moon
Moon Phase: Second Quarter
Color: Purple

Moon Sign: Aquarius
Sun enters Scorpio 9:49 pm
Incense: Ginger

---

23 Saturday

Revolution Day (Hungarian)
Waxing Moon
Moon Phase: Second Quarter
Color: Brown

Moon Sign: Aquarius
Moon enters Pisces 1:13 am
Incense: Pine

---

24 Sunday

United Nations Day
Waxing Moon
Moon Phase: Second Quarter
Color: Amber

Moon Sign: Pisces
Incense: Coriander

---

25 Monday

St. Crispin's Day
Waxing Moon
Moon Phase: Second Quarter
Color: Lavender

Moon Sign: Pisces
Moon enters Aries 6:24 am
Incense: Myrrh

---

26 Tuesday

Quit Rent Ceremony (England)
Waxing Moon
Moon Phase: Second Quarter
Color: White

Moon Sign: Aries
Incense: Musk

Wednesday

Feast of the Holy Souls
Waxing Moon
Moon Phase: Full Moon 11:07 pm
Color: Topaz

Moon Sign: Aries
Moon enters Taurus 1:37 pm
Incense: Neroli

---

28 Thursday

Ochi Day (Greek)
Waning Moon
Moon Phase: Third Quarter
Color: Crimson

Moon Sign: Taurus
Incense: Vanilla

29 Friday
Iroquois Feast of the Dead — Moon Sign: Taurus
Waning Moon — Moon enters Gemini 11:11 pm
Moon Phase: Third Quarter — Incense: Parsley
Color: Pink

---

30 Saturday
Meiji Festival (Japanese) — Moon Sign: Gemini
Waning Moon — Incense: Lavender
Moon Phase: Third Quarter
Color: Gray

---

31 Sunday
Halloween • Samhain • Daylight Saving Time ends — Moon Sign: Gemini
Waning Moon — Incense: Poplar
Moon Phase: Third Quarter
Color: Gold

Roasted Pumpkin Seeds

It seems such a shame to waste all those seeds left over from baking or carving your pumpkins at this time of year. Pumpkin seeds are a delicious and healthy treat alone or added to salads. Once you have removed them from the pumpkin, rinse them well. Air-dry for at least three hours, then toast lightly spread on a baking sheet in the oven, or toss with a small amount of olive oil and bake for twenty minutes, until golden brown, at 350°F.

—Kristin Madden

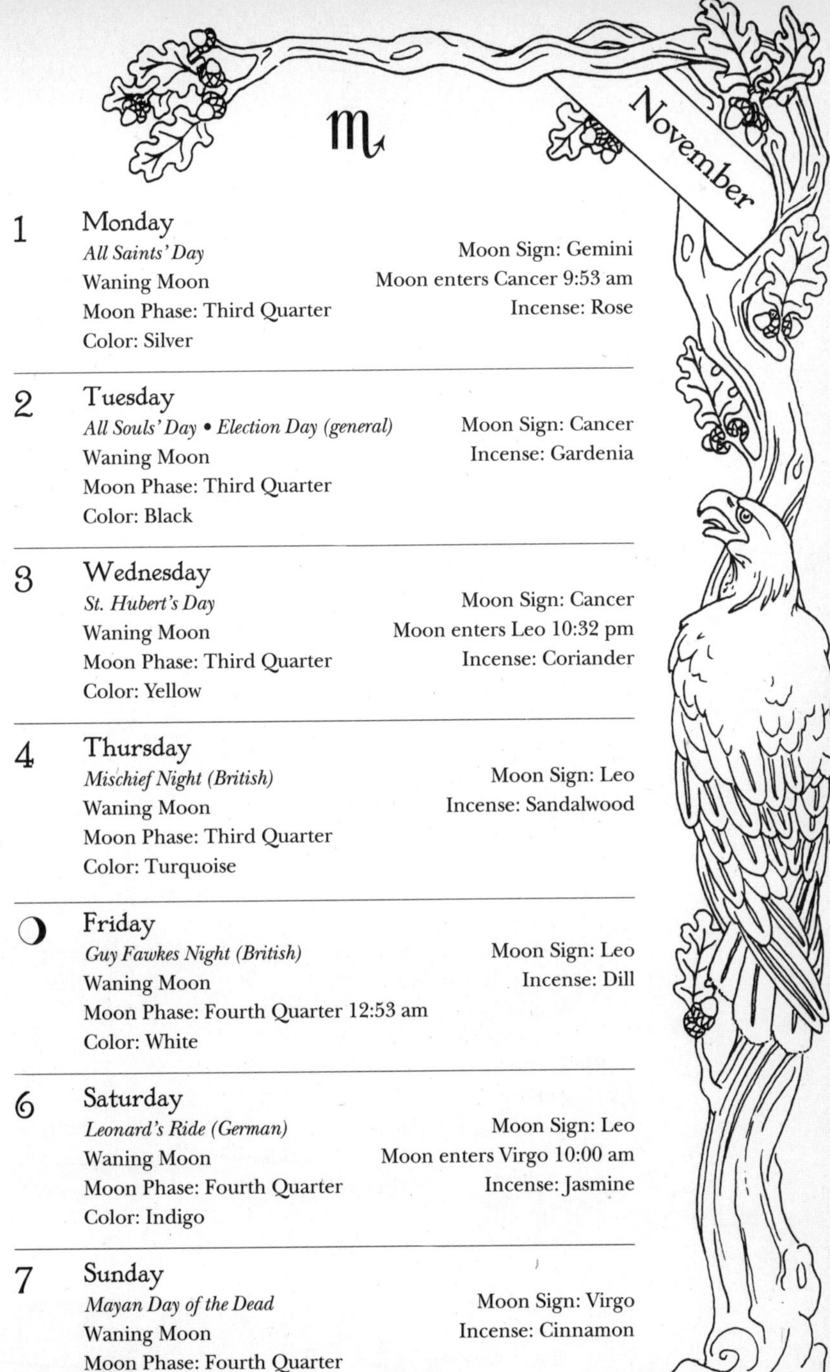

♏

1 Monday

All Saints' Day
Waning Moon
Moon Phase: Third Quarter
Color: Silver

Moon Sign: Gemini
Moon enters Cancer 9:53 am
Incense: Rose

---

2 Tuesday

All Souls' Day • Election Day (general)
Waning Moon
Moon Phase: Third Quarter
Color: Black

Moon Sign: Cancer
Incense: Gardenia

---

3 Wednesday

St. Hubert's Day
Waning Moon
Moon Phase: Third Quarter
Color: Yellow

Moon Sign: Cancer
Moon enters Leo 10:32 pm
Incense: Coriander

---

4 Thursday

Mischief Night (British)
Waning Moon
Moon Phase: Third Quarter
Color: Turquoise

Moon Sign: Leo
Incense: Sandalwood

◐ Friday

Guy Fawkes Night (British)
Waning Moon
Moon Phase: Fourth Quarter 12:53 am
Color: White

Moon Sign: Leo
Incense: Dill

---

6 Saturday

Leonard's Ride (German)
Waning Moon
Moon Phase: Fourth Quarter
Color: Indigo

Moon Sign: Leo
Moon enters Virgo 10:00 am
Incense: Jasmine

---

7 Sunday

Mayan Day of the Dead
Waning Moon
Moon Phase: Fourth Quarter
Color: Orange

Moon Sign: Virgo
Incense: Cinnamon

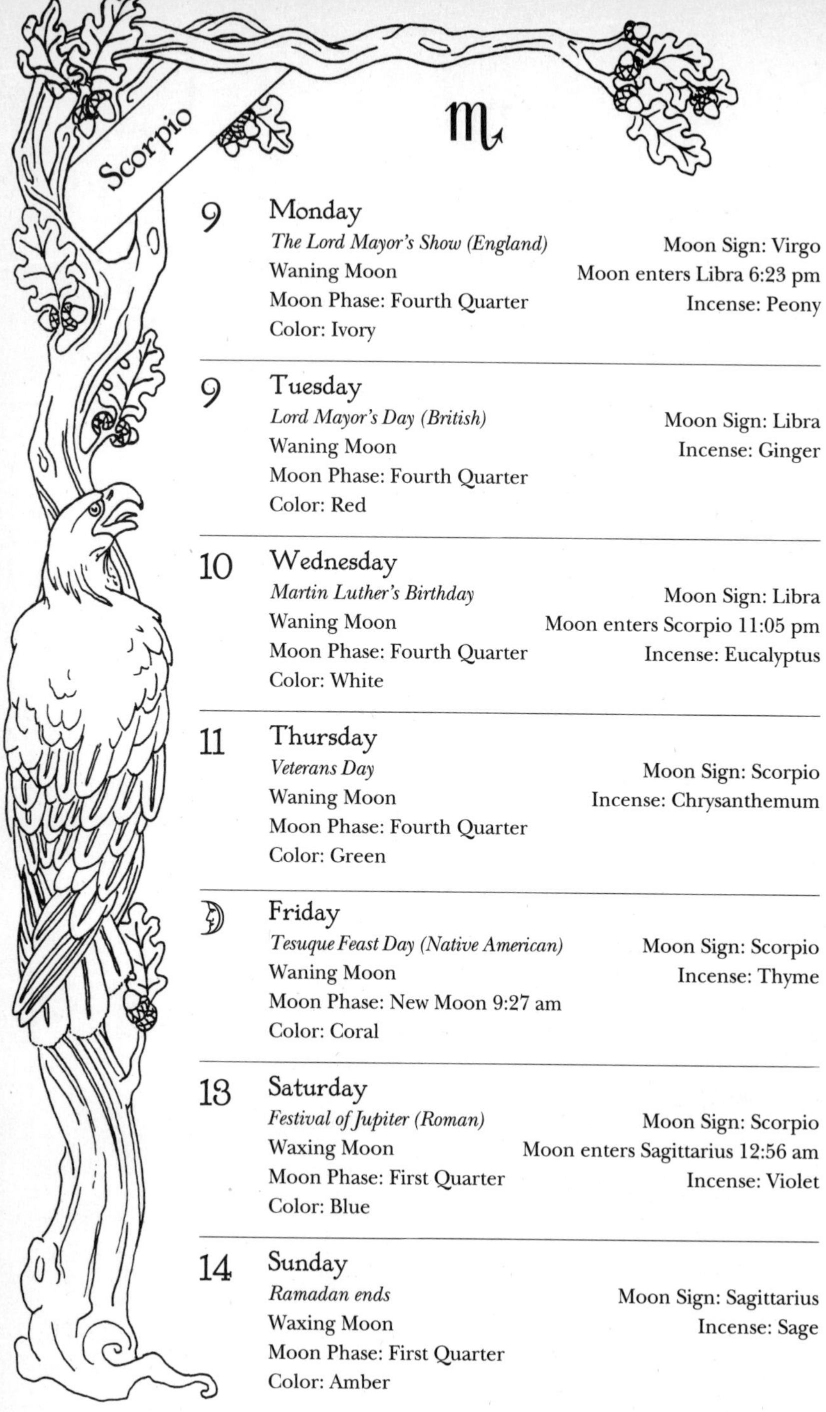

9 **Monday**
The Lord Mayor's Show (England)
Waning Moon
Moon Phase: Fourth Quarter
Color: Ivory

Moon Sign: Virgo
Moon enters Libra 6:23 pm
Incense: Peony

---

9 **Tuesday**
Lord Mayor's Day (British)
Waning Moon
Moon Phase: Fourth Quarter
Color: Red

Moon Sign: Libra
Incense: Ginger

---

10 **Wednesday**
Martin Luther's Birthday
Waning Moon
Moon Phase: Fourth Quarter
Color: White

Moon Sign: Libra
Moon enters Scorpio 11:05 pm
Incense: Eucalyptus

---

11 **Thursday**
Veterans Day
Waning Moon
Moon Phase: Fourth Quarter
Color: Green

Moon Sign: Scorpio
Incense: Chrysanthemum

☽ **Friday**
Tesuque Feast Day (Native American)
Waning Moon
Moon Phase: New Moon 9:27 am
Color: Coral

Moon Sign: Scorpio
Incense: Thyme

---

13 **Saturday**
Festival of Jupiter (Roman)
Waxing Moon
Moon Phase: First Quarter
Color: Blue

Moon Sign: Scorpio
Moon enters Sagittarius 12:56 am
Incense: Violet

---

14 **Sunday**
Ramadan ends
Waxing Moon
Moon Phase: First Quarter
Color: Amber

Moon Sign: Sagittarius
Incense: Sage

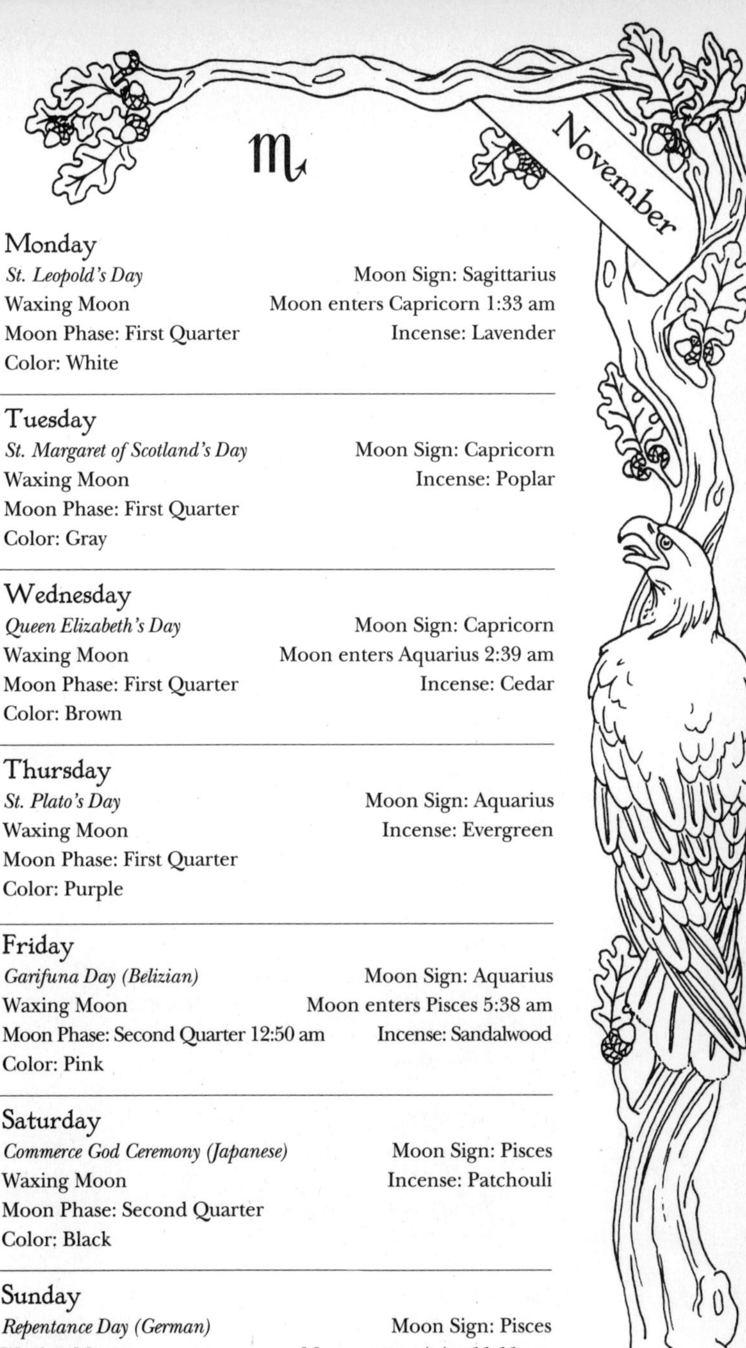

♏

15 **Monday**
St. Leopold's Day
Waxing Moon
Moon Phase: First Quarter
Color: White

Moon Sign: Sagittarius
Moon enters Capricorn 1:33 am
Incense: Lavender

---

16 **Tuesday**
St. Margaret of Scotland's Day
Waxing Moon
Moon Phase: First Quarter
Color: Gray

Moon Sign: Capricorn
Incense: Poplar

---

17 **Wednesday**
Queen Elizabeth's Day
Waxing Moon
Moon Phase: First Quarter
Color: Brown

Moon Sign: Capricorn
Moon enters Aquarius 2:39 am
Incense: Cedar

---

18 **Thursday**
St. Plato's Day
Waxing Moon
Moon Phase: First Quarter
Color: Purple

Moon Sign: Aquarius
Incense: Evergreen

◐ **Friday**
Garifuna Day (Belizian)
Waxing Moon
Moon Phase: Second Quarter 12:50 am
Color: Pink

Moon Sign: Aquarius
Moon enters Pisces 5:38 am
Incense: Sandalwood

---

20 **Saturday**
Commerce God Ceremony (Japanese)
Waxing Moon
Moon Phase: Second Quarter
Color: Black

Moon Sign: Pisces
Incense: Patchouli

---

21 **Sunday**
Repentance Day (German)
Waxing Moon
Moon Phase: Second Quarter
Color: Yellow

Moon Sign: Pisces
Moon enters Aries 11:11 am
Sun enters Sagittarius 6:22 pm
Incense: Clove

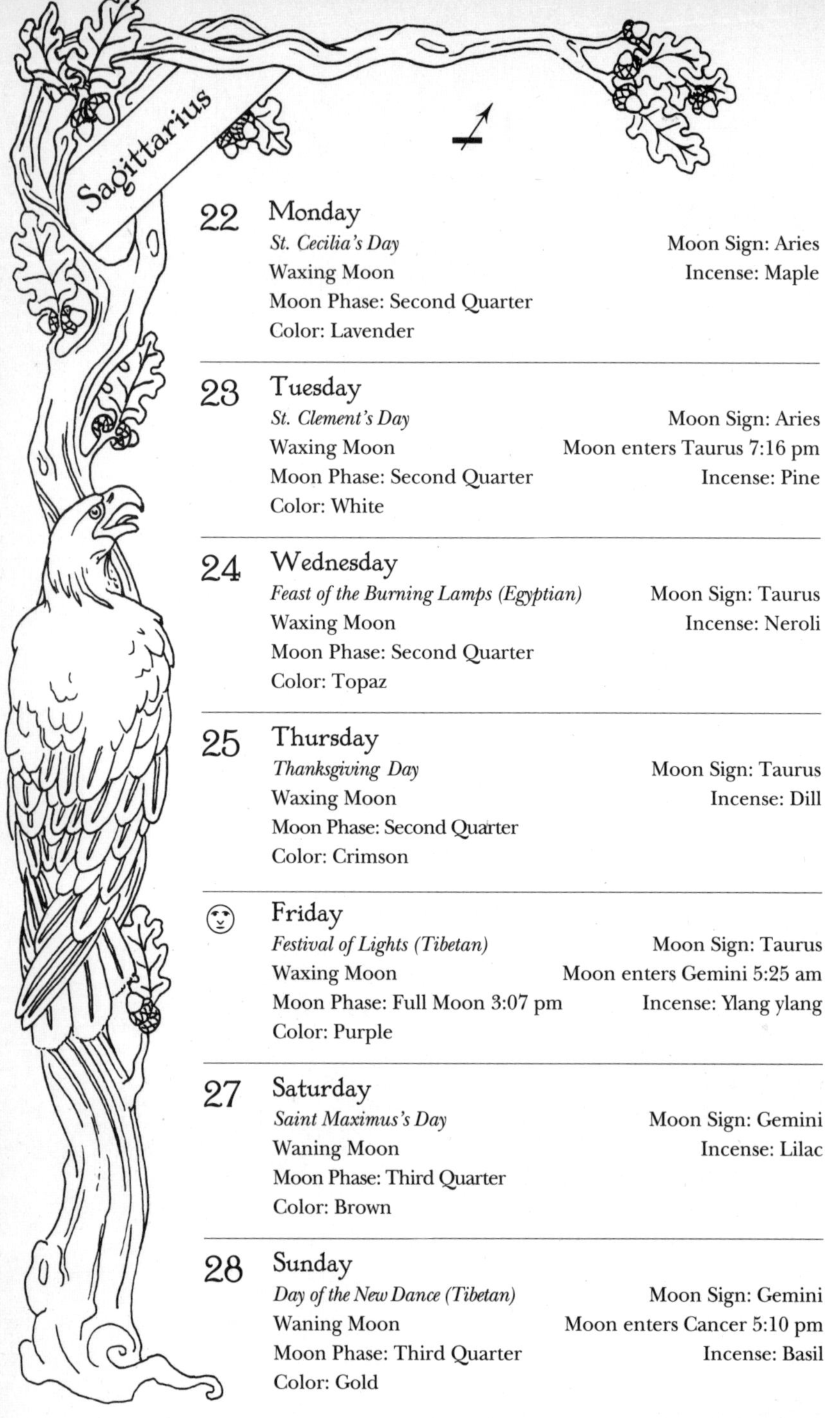

22 Monday
St. Cecilia's Day Moon Sign: Aries
Waxing Moon Incense: Maple
Moon Phase: Second Quarter
Color: Lavender

---

23 Tuesday
St. Clement's Day Moon Sign: Aries
Waxing Moon Moon enters Taurus 7:16 pm
Moon Phase: Second Quarter Incense: Pine
Color: White

---

24 Wednesday
Feast of the Burning Lamps (Egyptian) Moon Sign: Taurus
Waxing Moon Incense: Neroli
Moon Phase: Second Quarter
Color: Topaz

---

25 Thursday
Thanksgiving Day Moon Sign: Taurus
Waxing Moon Incense: Dill
Moon Phase: Second Quarter
Color: Crimson

Friday
Festival of Lights (Tibetan) Moon Sign: Taurus
Waxing Moon Moon enters Gemini 5:25 am
Moon Phase: Full Moon 3:07 pm Incense: Ylang ylang
Color: Purple

---

27 Saturday
Saint Maximus's Day Moon Sign: Gemini
Waning Moon Incense: Lilac
Moon Phase: Third Quarter
Color: Brown

---

28 Sunday
Day of the New Dance (Tibetan) Moon Sign: Gemini
Waning Moon Moon enters Cancer 5:10 pm
Moon Phase: Third Quarter Incense: Basil
Color: Gold

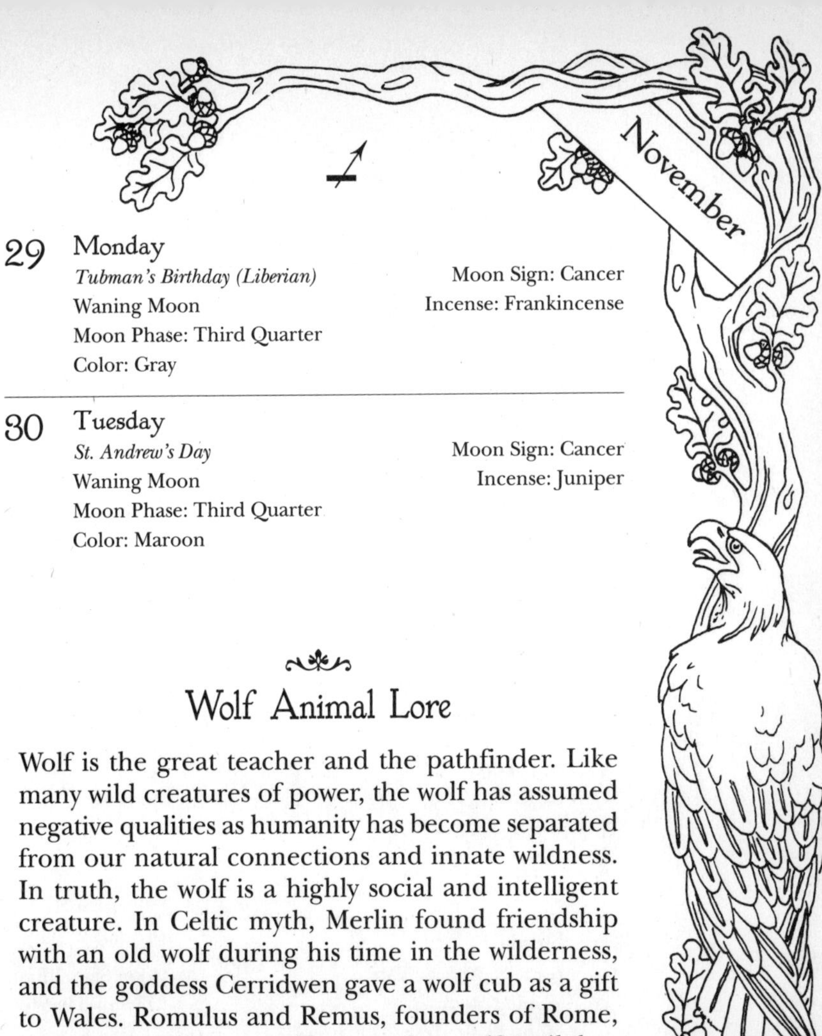

29 Monday
Tubman's Birthday (Liberian)
Waning Moon
Moon Phase: Third Quarter
Color: Gray

Moon Sign: Cancer
Incense: Frankincense

---

30 Tuesday
St. Andrew's Day
Waning Moon
Moon Phase: Third Quarter
Color: Maroon

Moon Sign: Cancer
Incense: Juniper

Wolf Animal Lore

Wolf is the great teacher and the pathfinder. Like many wild creatures of power, the wolf has assumed negative qualities as humanity has become separated from our natural connections and innate wildness. In truth, the wolf is a highly social and intelligent creature. In Celtic myth, Merlin found friendship with an old wolf during his time in the wilderness, and the goddess Cerridwen gave a wolf cub as a gift to Wales. Romulus and Remus, founders of Rome, were saved and nurtured by a mother wolf until they were taken in by a shepherd.

—Kristin Madden

1 Wednesday
Big Tea Party (Japanese)
Waning Moon
Moon Phase: Third Quarter
Color: Yellow

Moon Sign: Cancer
Moon enters Leo 5:50 am
Incense: Coriander

2 Thursday
Republic Day (Laotian)
Waning Moon
Moon Phase: Third Quarter
Color: Green

Moon Sign: Leo
Incense: Carnation

3 Friday
St. Francis Xavier's Day
Waning Moon
Moon Phase: Third Quarter
Color: Pink

Moon Sign: Leo
Moon enters Virgo 6:00 pm
Incense: Nutmeg

Saturday
St. Barbara's Day
Waning Moon
Moon Phase: Fourth Quarter 7:53 pm
Color: Blue

Moon Sign: Virgo
Incense: Pine

5 Sunday
Eve of St. Nicholas' Day
Waning Moon
Moon Phase: Fourth Quarter
Color: Orange

Moon Sign: Virgo
Incense: Parsley

6 Monday
St. Nicholas' Day
Waning Moon
Moon Phase: Fourth Quarter
Color: White

Moon Sign: Virgo
Moon enters Libra 3:46 am
Incense: Myrrh

7 Tuesday
Burning the Devil (Guatemalan)
Waning Moon
Moon Phase: Fourth Quarter
Color: Black

Moon Sign: Libra
Incense: Honeysuckle

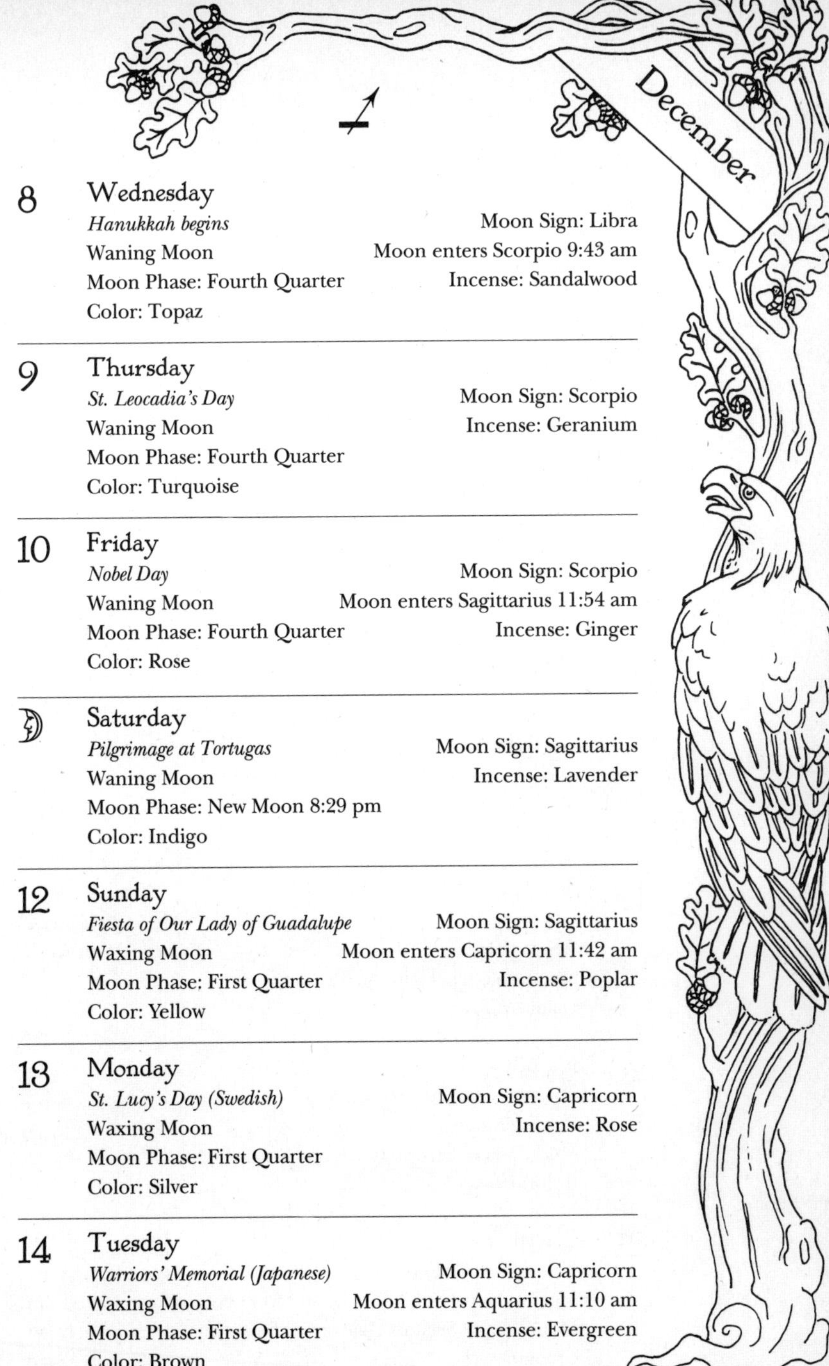

8 **Wednesday**

Hanukkah begins
Moon Sign: Libra
Waning Moon
Moon enters Scorpio 9:43 am
Moon Phase: Fourth Quarter
Incense: Sandalwood
Color: Topaz

---

9 **Thursday**

St. Leocadia's Day
Moon Sign: Scorpio
Waning Moon
Incense: Geranium
Moon Phase: Fourth Quarter
Color: Turquoise

---

10 **Friday**

Nobel Day
Moon Sign: Scorpio
Waning Moon
Moon enters Sagittarius 11:54 am
Moon Phase: Fourth Quarter
Incense: Ginger
Color: Rose

Saturday

Pilgrimage at Tortugas
Moon Sign: Sagittarius
Waning Moon
Incense: Lavender
Moon Phase: New Moon 8:29 pm
Color: Indigo

---

12 **Sunday**

Fiesta of Our Lady of Guadalupe
Moon Sign: Sagittarius
Waxing Moon
Moon enters Capricorn 11:42 am
Moon Phase: First Quarter
Incense: Poplar
Color: Yellow

---

13 **Monday**

St. Lucy's Day (Swedish)
Moon Sign: Capricorn
Waxing Moon
Incense: Rose
Moon Phase: First Quarter
Color: Silver

---

14 **Tuesday**

Warriors' Memorial (Japanese)
Moon Sign: Capricorn
Waxing Moon
Moon enters Aquarius 11:10 am
Moon Phase: First Quarter
Incense: Evergreen
Color: Brown

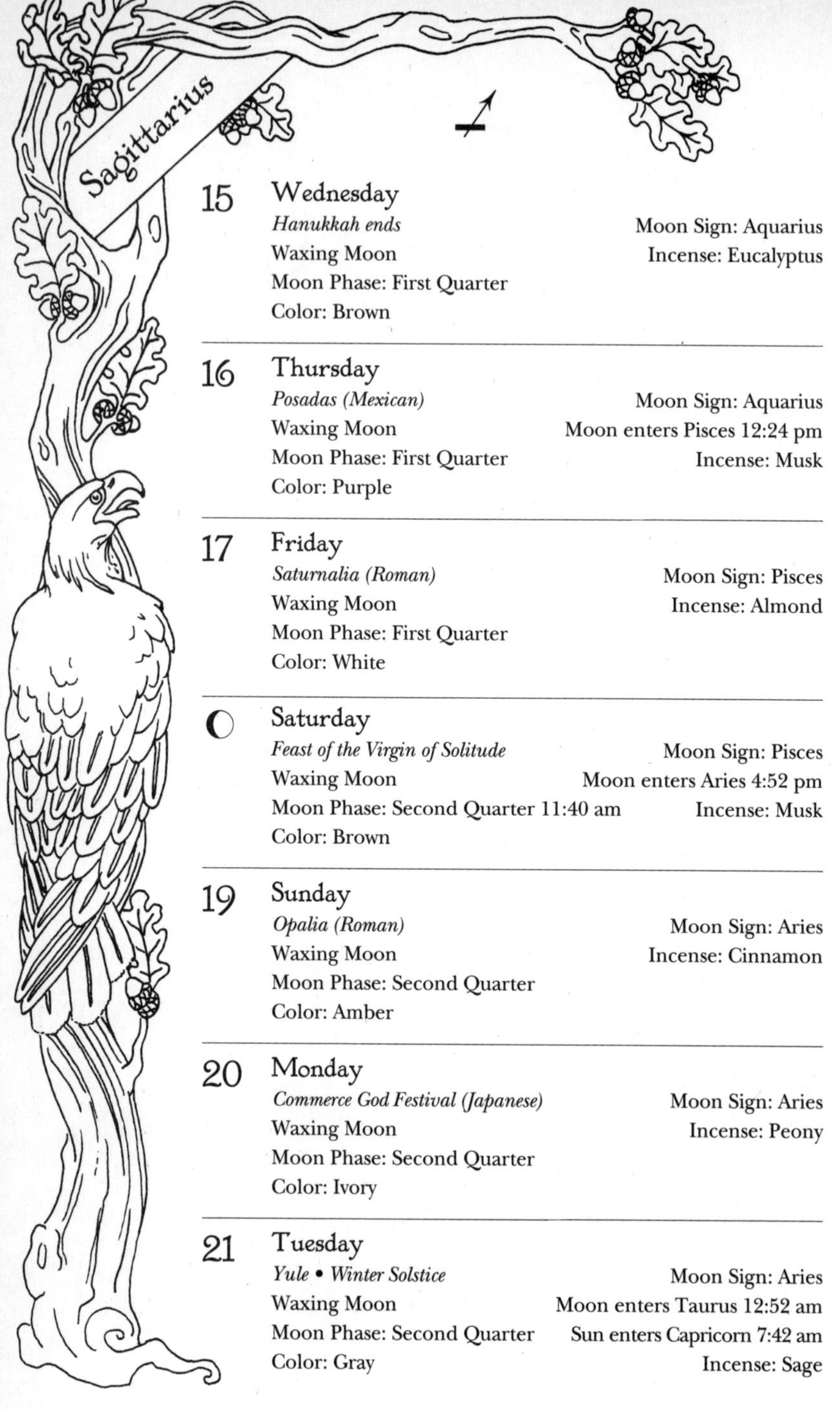

15 Wednesday
Hanukkah ends
Waxing Moon
Moon Phase: First Quarter
Color: Brown
Moon Sign: Aquarius
Incense: Eucalyptus

---

16 Thursday
Posadas (Mexican)
Waxing Moon
Moon Phase: First Quarter
Color: Purple
Moon Sign: Aquarius
Moon enters Pisces 12:24 pm
Incense: Musk

---

17 Friday
Saturnalia (Roman)
Waxing Moon
Moon Phase: First Quarter
Color: White
Moon Sign: Pisces
Incense: Almond

◐ Saturday
Feast of the Virgin of Solitude
Waxing Moon
Moon Phase: Second Quarter 11:40 am
Color: Brown
Moon Sign: Pisces
Moon enters Aries 4:52 pm
Incense: Musk

---

19 Sunday
Opalia (Roman)
Waxing Moon
Moon Phase: Second Quarter
Color: Amber
Moon Sign: Aries
Incense: Cinnamon

---

20 Monday
Commerce God Festival (Japanese)
Waxing Moon
Moon Phase: Second Quarter
Color: Ivory
Moon Sign: Aries
Incense: Peony

---

21 Tuesday
Yule • Winter Solstice
Waxing Moon
Moon Phase: Second Quarter
Color: Gray
Moon Sign: Aries
Moon enters Taurus 12:52 am
Sun enters Capricorn 7:42 am
Incense: Sage

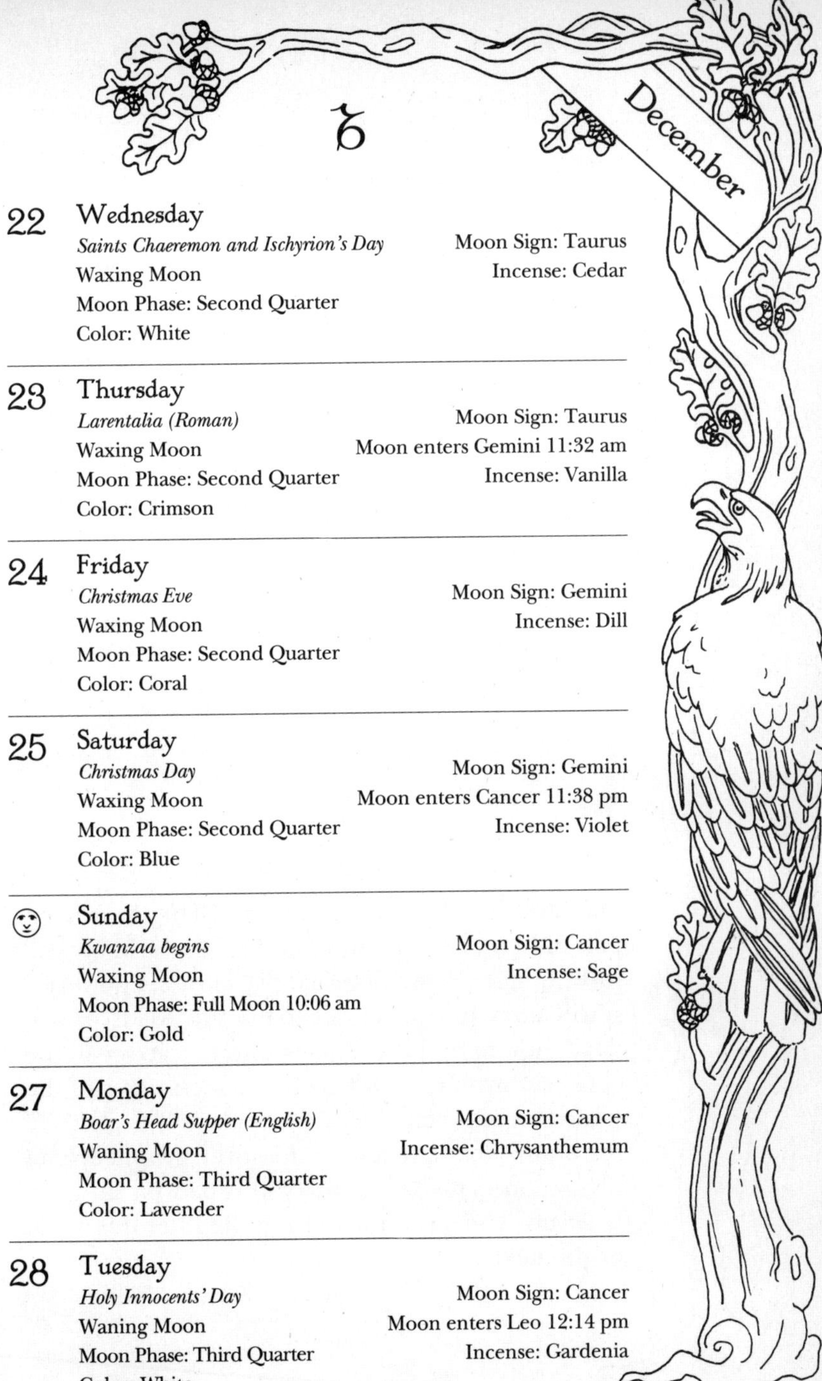

♑

22 Wednesday

Saints Chaeremon and Ischyrion's Day

Waxing Moon
Moon Phase: Second Quarter
Color: White

Moon Sign: Taurus
Incense: Cedar

23 Thursday

Larentalia (Roman)

Waxing Moon
Moon Phase: Second Quarter
Color: Crimson

Moon Sign: Taurus
Moon enters Gemini 11:32 am
Incense: Vanilla

24 Friday

Christmas Eve

Waxing Moon
Moon Phase: Second Quarter
Color: Coral

Moon Sign: Gemini
Incense: Dill

25 Saturday

Christmas Day

Waxing Moon
Moon Phase: Second Quarter
Color: Blue

Moon Sign: Gemini
Moon enters Cancer 11:38 pm
Incense: Violet

26 Sunday

Kwanzaa begins

Waxing Moon
Moon Phase: Full Moon 10:06 am
Color: Gold

Moon Sign: Cancer
Incense: Sage

27 Monday

Boar's Head Supper (English)

Waning Moon
Moon Phase: Third Quarter
Color: Lavender

Moon Sign: Cancer
Incense: Chrysanthemum

28 Tuesday

Holy Innocents' Day

Waning Moon
Moon Phase: Third Quarter
Color: White

Moon Sign: Cancer
Moon enters Leo 12:14 pm
Incense: Gardenia

♑

29 Wednesday
St. Thomas à Becket
Waning Moon
Moon Phase: Third Quarter
Color: Topaz

Moon Sign: Leo
Incense: Neroli

---

30 Thursday
Republic Day (Madagascar)
Waning Moon
Moon Phase: Third Quarter
Color: Green

Moon Sign: Leo
Incense: Evergreen

---

31 Friday
New Year's Eve
Waning Moon
Moon Phase: Third Quarter
Color: Purple

Moon Sign: Leo
Moon enters Virgo 12:33 am
Incense: Nutmeg

Owl Lore

Owls are silent hunters of the night. They have been part of human stories since earliest times. Many cultures honor these nocturnal predators as powerful spirit allies that teach shamans the roads of the dead, how to find lost objects, and how to see to the core of a problem. Owl is often a messenger of the transition between worlds, particularly the worlds of birth and death. They preside over prophecy and divination. This is a bird of the betwixt and the between. The owl is not entirely of either this world or the next.

—Kristin Madden

Articles for Summer

Magical Bali

by S Y Zenith

Bali, the most famous island of the Indonesian archipelago, is a comparatively small tract of forest-covered terrain around two thousand square miles. The Balinese peoples are descendants of the Malayo-Polynesians and an interesting mix of races from central and eastern Java, India, China, Polynesia, and Melanesia. Within the interiors are villages inhabited by descendants of the Bali-Aga, an aboriginal animistic people whose heritage may be traced back to ancient Mongoloid peoples.

Bali-Hindu Faith

Most Balinese natives practice the Agama Hindu religion, and believe in the Hindu trinity of Brahma, Vishnu, and Shiva. Being devoutly religious peoples, the Balinese have built tens of thousands of temples across the island and observe religious festivities. Since ancient times, Bali has also had gods of its own inherited from animistic ancestors. Today, the tenets of Hinduism are liberally interwoven with native animism and beliefs concerning gods, ghosts, and spirit healing.

Spiritual Practitioners

Traditional healers in Bali are generally known as *balian* and may be male or female. They perform simultaneous roles of masseur, priest, herbalist, and spiritual healer. The *balian urat* or *balian apun* are healers who specialize in massage. A *balian tulang* is dedicated to setting broken bones. Healers often combine therapy with mantras and offerings to gods and spirits. In performing massage, the healer clears blocked energy channels to stimulate and rejuvenate the body.

The *balian usada* possesses healing powers and arcane knowledge culled from traditional medicinal books and experience. These unique books were made from the leaves of a plant known as the lontar palm. They hold Balinese herbal pharmacopoeia, mantras, meditation practices, and other time-honored treatment systems. As such, the books are highly treasured sacred volumes, and they are handed down through the generations as receptacles of magical energy. This magical energy may be bestowed on a deserving individual through special prayers, offerings, and holy water.

Another category of healer are the *balian tenung,* who are specialists at discovering lost objects, revealing thieves, and performing shamanic rituals for controlling weather conditions (though they prefer never to predict future events). The trance medium is known as a *balian taksu.*

Those who visit a balian will find that the "waiting room" is often the family compound, and the "treatment room" is usually the floor of one of the pavilions. Patients are inclined to dress in ceremonial clothing as a mark of respect and bring offerings—such as water from healing springs or flowers. In preparing holy water, the balian recites mantras over the water to implant specific energies and enhance its potency. Most healers possess a wide range of skills and serve their communities by officiating during ceremonies and exorcising demons.

Tumbal Drawings

Art, medicine, and religion are entwined in Bali. A form of folk medicine for treating certain conditions requires the use of distinctive drawings known as *tumbal.* The conditions include infertility, weak metabolism and auras, family disharmony, and inability to meditate. Tumbal drawings are produced by the balian tenung or other artistically gifted spiritual healer. These drawings are displayed on a wall in the home—in the bedroom, living room, or wherever the patient spends a lot of time.

Spirits and Banten

To the Balinese, spirits are generally divided into two classes: the higher and the lower. Higher spirit groups are called *dewa, dewi, betara,* and *betari.* Lower entities are referred to by various names in different parts of the island but are most commonly called *butakala.* Higher spirits are not necessarily benevolent, and lower spirits may not be malevolent. Depending on how they are treated, spirits and entities of any sort can be both good or bad; they may help or hinder, bless or curse, or bring good or evil.

Banten means "offerings" in the local language. These are tangible means for the Balinese Hindus to placate or communicate with spirits. Some intangible means are prayer and mantra-repetition. The purpose of either is to accentuate the good and dispel the bad. Offerings are placed for higher spirits on high altars, while offerings to lower spirits are laid on the ground.

Higher Spirit Offerings

Offerings to higher spirits are given as thanks for favors bestowed on individuals, families, or communities. These contain food alongside flowers, fruit, leaves, and holy water, arranged with emphasis on color, beauty, and fragrance. In addition, arrays of rice cakes, nuts, fermented rice in banana leaves, sugar cane, and grated coconut or other delicacies may be presented. When offerings are completed and their essence believed to have been absorbed by gods and spirits, the food is taken home and eaten.

Lower Spirit Offerings

As the lower butakala spirits are collectively abundant at crossroads, front gates, wells, forests, and fields, offerings to them are regularly made at these locations. Some are proffered daily; others are offered only during auspicious or inauspicious days and when the Moon is full or new. A little rice wine is usually poured on the ground, and a stick of incense is used for transmitting the essence of offerings to spirit realms. Other common offerings consist of small triangular coconut-leaf containers that hold rice, onion, ginger, and a little salt.

Special offerings constitute a set of five containers holding rice of four colors: white, red, yellow, and black. Food dyes are used for making the colors. In accordance with color symbolism regarding the four directions, red rice is placed in the south, yellow in the west, black in the north, and white in the east. A container with rice of four colors is placed in the center.

Religion and Life

Despite decades of tourism and modernization, the Balinese remain faithful to their unique universe teeming with mysterious, divine, and diabolical beings. Their ceremonies involving dance and drama are fundamentals rituals that bind communities. With origins in religious rituals, Balinese dances are resplendent with masks and elaborate costumes. Accompanied by native musical instruments, the dances serve sacred purposes as well as communal entertainment.

As every phase of Balinese life is guided with religious rituals, there are ceremonies for just about every occasion or rite of passage, including betrothals, marriages, childbirth, the first birthday of an infant, and coming of age. As to this last ceremony, canines and incisors are ground to an even length so as to distinguish humans from fanged demons and animals. Finally, cremating the dead is taken as a sacred obligation to liberate the soul of the departed for future reincarnation.

From birth to death and into unseen ether realms beyond the funeral pyre, the Balinese are nurtured, guided, and reassured by the rites and celebrations of their faith.

The Titan Day Gods

by Elizabeth Hazel

The Titans were the early Greek pantheon that was eventually overthrown by the Hellenic Olympian gods. These beings were the gigantic children of Ouranos and Gaia (heaven and Earth), and were in turn the parents of the Olympians who conquered them.

The Titan day gods reveal the Indo-Aryan-Mesopotamian astronomical influence on Greek culture, as they may have been introduced by a colony of Canaanites and Hittites on the Isthmus of Corinth around 2000 BC. The day gods exist in male-female pairs, thus balancing the energies of each day. Because the Titans were a religious feature of preliterate Greece, the authors of the first millennium BC (Homer, Apollodorus,

Hesiod, Pausanias, and so on), provide scanty information about these early gods. As such, their names vary by region. As a result, each Titan has a number of alternate names.

The pre-Hellenic cult of central and southern Greece was the final bastion of Titan worship before the northern Greek tribes invaded and supplanted the Titans with the Olympian pantheon. The legend of the battle between the Titans and the Olympians is a reflection of this transitional period in the early Greek civilization.

The Titan day gods therefore represent a more primitive, but more balanced, view of day rulerships. The Titans were the chthonic gods embodying natural forces; they were less distinguished than their Olympian successors, but more identifiable than the primordial entities that they succeeded.

Sunday

Principle: Illumination

Theia (divine) and Hyperion (dweller on high). Theia and Hyperion ruled the powers of light, and are the parents of the Sun and Moon (Helius and Selene), and Eos, the triple aspect of daylight (dawn, midday, and dusk). Theia is also called Asterië, queen of the stars and planetary powers. Hyperion was a far-seeing god, as the ancient Greeks believed the gods could see all that is done by man. Sunday is a day for illumination, a day to let the gods see one at devotions or performing acts of reverence. The powers of the six remaining days are derived from the heavenly energy of Sunday.

Monday

Principle: Enchantment

Phoebe (bright Moon) and Atlas (he who endures). Phoebe is the Full Moon, the mother of Asteria, who in turn mothered an only daughter, Hecate. Thus the Moon, stars, and underworld are connected through matrilineal descent. Atlas was a strong and clever giant, and was the commander of the Titans in the battle against the Olympians. He was the father of the Hyades, Pleiades, Hesperides, and the nymph Maia—and thus the grandfather of Hermes. After the battle, Zeus sentenced Atlas to carry the weight of the heavens on his shoulders in order to keep the Earth and heavens separate. Atlas was the first astronomer and was consulted by the centaur Chiron about star lore. Monday is the day of enchantments, secrets, and waters—the magical laundry day. Its rulers represent the remote intelligence and influence of the Moon and stars on life on Earth, and the wisdom that may be gained by the study of the heavens.

Tuesday

Principle: Growth

Dione (divine queen) and Crius (shining one or golden ruler). Dione is a watery aspect of the Moon, also called Dia or Eurynassa. She was the original goddess of the oracle at Dodona, where priestesses read the movements of the doves at the sacred oak grove. Because of her affinity for doves, when Zeus usurped the oracle at Dodona, he made Dione the mother of Aphrodite. In some legends, she is the mother of Dionysus. Crius is a son of Heaven and Earth. Although no legends of Crius survive, his children allude to his powers as a fertility god. His son Astraeus, the dawn wind, is equated with morning sex (i.e., men awakening with an arousal). Thus Crius is the god of male sexual potency and the drive to produce offspring, both of the body and mind. Tuesday favors creative efforts, extension into new territories, and working to preserve progeny and original creations for posterity. One should forge ahead in opportunities and utilize intuition and forcefulness in achieving goals.

Wednesday

Principle: Wisdom

Metis (counsel) and Coeus (intelligence). Metis embodies wisdom and insight, and her legends are entwined with the ascending reign of Zeus. Zeus coveted her wisdom, and so swallowed her. As a result, Athena sprang from his head—a lesser goddess of wisdom subordinate to Zeus. Metis is related to Car, Carya, or Carmenta the Wise, goddess of almond or walnut trees and empowered in augury. Coeus was an ancient Titan, considered the greatest astronomer besides Atlas. He was an early Greek aspect of the Egyptian Thoth, the deity of wisdom and magic. Intelligent Coeus matched the wisdom of Metis and both possessed magical abilities. Wednesday is a thinking day, a day for exploring the mind, and for developing ideas and strategies. Inspiration, intuition, and messages from oracles, dreams, and omens should be contemplated; this wisdom applied to overcoming obstacles.

Thursday

Principle: Law

Themis (order) and Eurymedon (wide rule). Themis was Zeus's second wife and bore him the Horae (hours), Eunomia (order), Diké (justice), Eirene (peace), the Moirae (the fates), and the Seasons. She was a valuable advisor, and one of the few goddesses who mated with a mortal man. Themis ordered the calendar and changing seasons, and was, with Zeus, one of the prime divine influences in the Trojan War. She is depicted in the tarot card, Justice, blindfolded and holding the scales, granting impartial decisions to petitioners. Eurymedon, sometimes called Iapetus, was the father of Prometheus, Epimetheus, and Atlas. His legacy was wisdom and personal power, and he planted the seed that flowered when humans gained the gift of fire from Prometheus. Thursday is the day of order and law. This is a day to formalize arrangements and to examine policies and protocols. The consequences of decisions should be examined for their effect on the future.

Friday

Principle: Love

Tethys (disposer) and Oceanus (of the swift queen). Tethys and Oceanus gave birth to several rivers and to three thousand daughters that serve Earth and the ocean deep. Tethys is equated with Thetis or Eurynome, a watery version of the creatrix. She is featured in the legend of Deucalion's flood, the Greek equivalent of Noah's catastrophe, and to Tiamat and the Babylonian flood legend. Hers are the gushing waters of birth and destruction. Oceanus, also called Ogygia or Ogen, was the ruler of the seas before Poseidon. He was a primordial watery progenitor, ruling the mysteries of the deep sea. Both are connected with the human fluids of sexuality and reproduction. Friday is dedicated to love and to the flow of emotions between individuals. Tethys and Oceanus personify the power and diversity that the Greeks saw in the sea and its creatures, and their children expressed every mood and type of water. In this respect, Friday is the day most suited to love, physical bonding, sex, and fertility.

Saturday

Principle: Peace

Rhea (earth) and Cronos (crow). Saturday is ruled by the parents of Zeus and his siblings. Rhea is an aspect of the Great Earth Mother, and was responsible for determining Persephone's living arrangement after her abduction by Hades. She reconstituted Dionysus after his murder, and initiated him into her earth mysteries—much as her daughter Demeter initiated the mystery cult at Eleusis. Her sacred plants are ivy (the five-fingered leaf representing the creative hand of the earth goddess) and poppies (a red flower that represents blood, death, resurrection, and drugged sleep). Cronos was a crafty, sneaky competitor. He gained his sickle from his mother Gaia in order to castrate his father Ouranos. After the overthrow of the Titans, Cronos ruled the dark realm encircling the underworld, a place of eternal quiet and peace. Both Rhea and Cronos have prophetic qualities, representing the wisdom hidden in the depths of the earth. The seventh day is one of peace, a time for rest and reflection. Rhea and Cronos are archetypal grandparents, the culmination of human life in old age. Saturday returns to familial security and to an appreciation of future generations.

Planning a Pagan Handfast

by Dallas Jennifer Cobb

A handfast is the Pagan rite of marriage, by which a couple validates a relationship by joining hands in the presence of witnesses and publicly declaring their love. The handfasting pair faces one another and joins hands, thus forming the symbol of infinity through their linked arms. While this ritual has historically been used primarily for heterosexual couple, it is suitable for all couples. The circles of infinity can be applied to all.

The basic elements of a handfast are the joining of hands, the statement of vows, bestowing of blessings upon the union, the symbolic breaking apart of hands, and bestowing blessings upon each individual. Because of the ritual aspect, many people choose to cast a circle,

call in the elements or directions, and perform the handfast within sacred space. After the directions are released, and the circle is opened.

A handfast is a magical process arising from love in a relationship. It is also a tricky event to plan and coordinate. Whether you choose a simple ritual, or include feasting and celebration, you will need help. My experience below may help save you time, energy, and money, so you can focus on the love-sharing that occurs on this day.

My Handfast

On the Winter Equinox in 1999, my partner and I handfasted—exchanging vows and rings. We planned all aspects of the ritual, wrote vows, selected readings, and organized a celebration to which we invited two hundred people. The short ritual was followed by a feast, music, dancing, cake cutting, and lots of merrymaking.

We kept our costs low: ritual, feast, and celebration with a three-piece jazz ensemble for under $1,700. It was magical, memorable, and didn't empty our savings. We felt rich with blessings, and still financially solvent. My advice from this: Don't equate money with love. Conserve your money, and let love be the currency you spend with your handfast. Ask for a contribution from everyone.

All You Need to Handfast

Let planning be a love-filled activity shared with your partner. About three months before the event, take time to dream and plan: list who to invite, and how it will all look and feel. Talk about your love, and about this expression of it.

Make lists of what you need to cast the circle, to call in the directions (candles, readings, music, drums, sacred objects, prayers, blessings), and to prepare for the ritual (vows, a cord to bind the hands, rings, a cup to drink from, bread, fruit to eat). For the celebration to follow, consider the food, drink, music, locale, altar, and decorations.

With a loose plan for the celebration, turn it over to friends. Contact your closest friends, and share your excitement. Ask for their involvement in the ceremony and in the preparation. Tell them exactly what is needed (from your above lists). Listen to what is suggested, and accept what feels right for you.

You may be pleasantly surprised by the resources available through friends. Be receptive to gifts like flowers for the altar, musical entertainment, or the use of an ideal space to hold the event. If you are watching your budget, be open to the circular energy of generosity. We used the hall at a friend's yacht club. A coworker offered to cook and serve food. My best friend arranged for his jazz trio to play, and his partner decorated the hall with flowers. Most of the big pieces were taken care of for us, so we used our money to purchase the supplies for a lovely meal, the candles to use in the ceremony, and for drinks.

With friends organizing the event, you can devote energy to the ritual, weaving in readings and writing your vows. Two months before, confirm who will act as priest or priestess, who will be involved in the ritual, and what readings will be used. As location options and date are confirmed, do up your invitations and send them out.

Writing vows is a personal and private process. I was overwhelmed by the daunting task of expressing in words how I felt about my partner, and what I wanted to bring to the relationship and to our future together. It took me many weeks to complete my vows.

My advice: Take time alone. Look within. Reflect on how your partner has enriched your life, and what you dream for the future. Imagine rereading the vows years from now. Let your deepest long-term desires guide you.

For the call of the directions and for readings, each of you could choose your closest friends. Invite your family to help cast the circle and close it. Find some way to involve everyone in the ceremony through chants, blessings, or candle lighting.

In our ceremony, my mother sparked a match in a darkened room and lit my candle. I lit the candle of the person next to me. The flame spread around the entire circle, quietly illuminating us. My partner, on my right, was the final recipient. We walked together, with our candles in hand into the circle to stand with the priestess. The directions were called and readings done, then the priestess spoke: about the handfast, its origins, and its power. We declared our vows, exchanged rings, and had our hands fastened together. Linked, we received blessings from everyone present, shared drink and food, and then were symbolically separated. As the winds of heaven flowed between us, we were blessed again, in our solitude. We picked up our individual candles, lit a third candle together, and placed all three on the altar, where they burned throughout the night. We then walked the circle together, counterclockwise, thanking everyone who came and opening the circle with our gratitude.

Whatever your ceremonial choices, let this ritual reflect you, your love, and your riches. Whether it is wild and wonderful, quiet and soulful, or solemn and sensuous, keep the ritual short and sweet and hold on to good energy throughout. Afterward, let loose, dance a little, eat a lot, and feel love everywhere.

Celebrate your wealth, your partnership, your community, and the priceless individuality that you have brought as your most valuable asset to the relationship. May the grace of the Goddess go in your heart. Blessed be.

Atalanta, Goddess and Heroine

by Eileen Holland

Atalanta, the Impassable One, is a pre-Hellenic goddess from Arcadia, in northern Greece. Her name means "unswaying." She was the goddess of the inevitability of death, the great hunter whom no one can outrun. Earth is her element; lions are her sacred animals, and Virgo is her astrological house.

Atalanta was a goddess of the hunt, and she also had a mountain goddess aspect, but the Greeks wove a new legend for her after they invaded Arcadia. Under Greek rule, the goddess Atalanta devolved into a heroine, Atalanta the Virgin Huntress.

In Greek mythology it is said that Atalanta was a princess, the daughter of King Iasus and Queen Clymene of Arcadia. When Atalanta was born, her father exposed her on the Parthenian Hill because he had wanted a son. A she-bear, sent by the goddess Artemis, found and nursed the baby. A clan of hunters later found Atalanta and reared her. She grew into a beautiful and athletic young woman who was renowned as a swift runner. It is said that once, in Cyphanta, she was very thirsty but was unable to find water. Atalanta, invoking the aid of Artemis, struck a rock with the point of her spear, and water gushed forth. Atalanta was one of the Argonauts who accompanied Jason on his quest for the Golden Fleece. She was wounded in the battle that ensued after they took the fleece, but Medea healed her when they were all safely back aboard the *Argo.*

Atalanta is described as wearing a golden buckle at her waist, and using an ivory quiver to hold her arrows. She wore male attire, always went armed, and was such an excellent hunter that she took part in the legendary hunt for the Calydonian Boar. Artemis (or Diana) sent a mighty boar to ravage Calydon, because worship of her was being neglected there. Prince Meleager assembled all the bravest warriors in Greece to hunt down the animal. The hide and the or tusks of the boar were pro-mised to the warrior who killed the boar.

The large hunting party, which included Jason, Theseus, and Atalanta, went forth to challenge the giant boar. Some of the warriors had balked at hunting with a woman, but Meleager, a married man who was in love with Atalanta, had threatened to call off the hunt unless they accepted her. To their chagrin, Atalanta became the first hunter to wound the boar, even though she had been assigned to the end of the line of hunters. Meleager delivered the coup de grace to the boar with his spear, and he awarded the head and the hide of the beast to Atalanta as trophies, saying: "You drew first blood, and had we left the beast alone, it would soon have succumbed to your arrows."

Meleager's uncles, who had also been in the hunting party, were angered by this, and they took the trophies back from Atalanta. This insult to Atalanta so infuriated Meleager that he killed them. His own mother, Althaea, later caused his death to avenge her slain brothers.

After the boar-hunt, Atalanta's father welcomed her back to the palace, and decreed that it was time for her to marry. This was unacceptable to Atalanta, because the Oracle at Delphi had foretold that marriage would be her ruin. She had devoted herself to sports and hunting because of this. Iasus tried to impose his right, as her father, to choose a husband for her. Atalanta refused and set what she thought was an impossible condition for her suitors to meet. Atalanta said that she would only marry the man who could beat her in a foot race. The penalty for losing to her was death, but princes still wanted to win her hand. Hippomenes was appointed the judge of the contest, and he fell in love with Atalanta when he saw her run. She easily won the race and her suitors were all put to death, but Hippomenes resolved to win Atalanta for himself.

Hippomenes enlisted the aid of Aphrodite to win Atalanta, and the goddess of love gave him the golden apples of the Hesperides. He dropped them onto the track as he ran, and Atalanta stopped to look at the apples, thus losing the race.

Hippomenes and Atalanta were married, and she was very happy with her handsome young husband. They had a son named Parthenopaeus. Some myths have it that he was actually the son of Atalanta and Meleager, or that the god Ares was his father. Atalanta exposed her baby on the same hill where she had been left to die. Parthenopaeus means "son of a pierced maidenhead," so in the myths where her husband is not her child's father, it is said that Atalanta exposed him to conceal the fact that she was no longer a virgin. Parthenopaeus survived and grew to manhood.

There are several myths about what became of Atalanta and Hippomenes. In each myth, the couple somehow offends the gods and are punished for it. Some say that they forgot to offer sacrifices to Aphrodite as part of their wedding feast. Others say that they were out hunting, and stopped to make love unknowingly in the sacred grove of Zeus.

Whatever the case, the newlyweds were punished by being turned into lions. Greeks believed, at that time, that lions mated with leopards, not other lions, so this punishment was thought to prevent the couple from ever having sex together again.

Invoke Atalanta for speed, courage, achievement, hunting, archery, passion, self-control, independence, self-determination, women's rights, pushing the envelope, living a life of adventure, outlasting patriarchal rule, respecting oracles, making your own way in the world, surviving in the wilderness, overcoming a bad childhood, poor parenting, or other obstacles, owning your own sexuality, setting high standards for yourself, learning not to anger the gods, and competing successfully in athletic events.

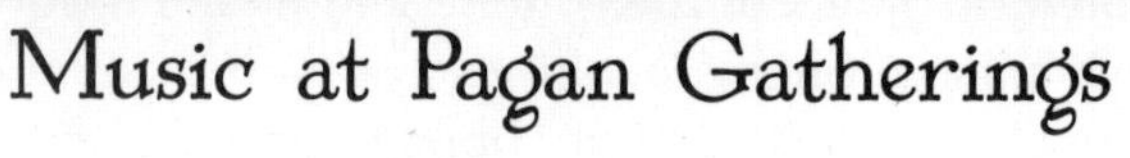

Music at Pagan Gatherings

by Peg Aloi

I started going to Pagan gatherings in 1991. At the time, there was enormous interest in African style drumming. One could purchase all varieties of drums from vendors, attend workshops on drumming technique and drumming "etiquette," and then drum and dance all night around a fire built for this purpose.

At the first gathering I attended, Rites of Spring, the all-night drum circle was in a clearing in the woods, shielded from sight and acoustically muffled by trees. The bonfire was of modest size, and the energy was fairly focused. The following year, the gathering's main ritual took place before hundreds of people in the main ritual field (where a huge maypole had been erected a few days earlier). One elder of the community took part in this mythically-charged performance, in which the history of the modern Pagan movement was explored through ritual theatre. He stood tall and told a tongue-in-cheek story of ancient times. "There were no drums . . . " he began, and this soon became a humorous mantra that punctuated his story. People gathered around fires and told stories and laughter, played guitars and other handheld instruments, and sang songs. But no drums!

Recently, I read an essay on the Witches' Voice website written by another elder in the community. She described what it was like before the overwhelming presence of drums at gatherings. She believes the reason we do not see many elders at gatherings anymore is because they can't handle the noise, especially when the drumming goes on all night. Several weeks later, I took part in

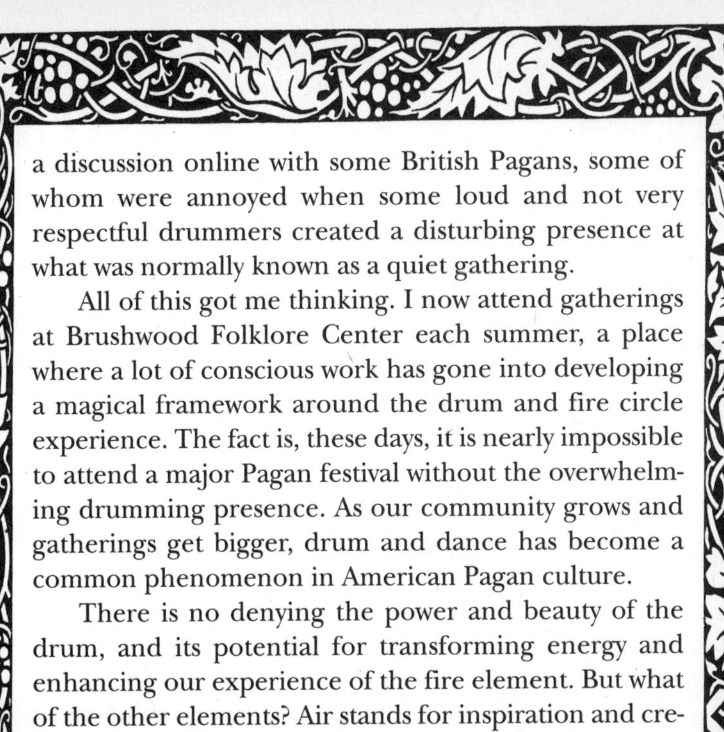

a discussion online with some British Pagans, some of whom were annoyed when some loud and not very respectful drummers created a disturbing presence at what was normally known as a quiet gathering.

All of this got me thinking. I now attend gatherings at Brushwood Folklore Center each summer, a place where a lot of conscious work has gone into developing a magical framework around the drum and fire circle experience. The fact is, these days, it is nearly impossible to attend a major Pagan festival without the overwhelming drumming presence. As our community grows and gatherings get bigger, drum and dance has become a common phenomenon in American Pagan culture.

There is no denying the power and beauty of the drum, and its potential for transforming energy and enhancing our experience of the fire element. But what of the other elements? Air stands for inspiration and creative expression, water represents the realm of emotion and deeper thought. And earth is the element of reception and healing. Aren't these applicable to performance as well? It seems to me that the nature of the drum's sound, and the attraction of the intense and often highly sexualized energy of the drum circles, relegates "old-fashioned" forms of musical expression to a back seat.

This is a shame. Our community is gifted with many wonderful performers, whose stories, songs, dances, and musical offerings are every bit as compelling and magical (and sexy) as a night of drumming and dancing. It all depends on what one is looking for.

Personally, I would like to see more of a mix of different kinds of performance around fires. At a gathering I attended in Canada (Wiccan-Fest), the bardic circle had a rather famous reputation. It always followed a particular structure based on the idea of a medieval or "mead-hall" atmosphere, where traveling minstrels performed for their hosts. The main rule was that whoever won the top prize the previous year was allowed to be the judge in the following year. And what an incredible night this was. Despite the customary heckling and laughter, there were also moments of profound stillness and rapt attention during songs and stories.

But this sort of performance focuses on an individual. Drumming is seen more as a group activity. At Pagan festival, singular performance is somewhat frowned upon. Oddly enough, however, one does see very ego-driven behavior at drum circles. Often, it is the beginner who buys the biggest, loudest drum they can find. After all, the bigger the drum, the more their individual sound will stand out in a group (a dear friend of mine calls these folks "djembe cowboys"). The result often is an unpleasant cacophony.

Not to say all drumming is bad. I have also been to gatherings where the drumming is quite contained and very impressive, often thanks to some skilled and well-respected drummers, who set the tone and guide the energy without being intrusive. Some drummers will "lead" the drumming in more ostentatious ways, but towards a similar end: making sure the rhythms stay together in some sort of shape and structure.

It sometimes seems there is a "male versus female" energy to all this, too. The drum is about fire and power and passion, and this energy is aggressive at times. The urge to drown out all other sounds comes across like a "power-over" spell-casting. For years, most of the fire tenders and builders were men, while most of the dancers around the fire were women, who, even if they were only dancing for themselves, could not escape being observed by others. Pagans of course are generally very comfortable with sexual energy and nudity, but there is no denying that this dynamic of the male drummer/female dancer does seem an outmoded gender-structure. Fortunately, this has started to shift in recent years, and many more women are active as drummers and fire tenders, and not just as dancers.

What does a Pagan do when seeking a quieter, less-intense night of music around a fire? I have seen some alternatives crop up over the years. Fire circles have been created specifically for those who want a drug- and alcohol-free space, just for women or children, and, more and more, for quieter modes of musical expression. At Brushwood, a "didge dome" was built by people who play the Australian didgeridoo, and the playing, drumming, and chanting that happened here had a much softer energy and focus. Bardic circles are also growing in popularity; we had one at Autumn Meet in Florida that was fantastic. One night, too, a fortunate few friends and I were invited to participate in a Native American tobacco ceremony—we gave thanks, and this eventually turned into a song circle. It is not unusual to be "making the rounds" some night at a gathering and find small pockets of high-quality musical entertainment, often attended by our well-loved elders.

Sometimes one has to go off the beaten path to find gentler moments of magic. I hope that the creative growth and transformation of drum circle energy will continue, but I hope that we will continue to honor the traditions of our elders of the previous generation, who sat around fires in quiet contemplation and fellowship, and who occasionally break out in lusty song.

Seashell Spells for Your Health

by Janina Renée

When concentrating on mental imagery for bodily healing, it is helpful to use visual and tactile objects that inspire the unconscious mind. Seashells can be used as symbolic objects to assist some visualizations. Certain shells have been likened to body parts, and their pleasing shapes and glossy surfaces also suggest lustrous health and beauty.

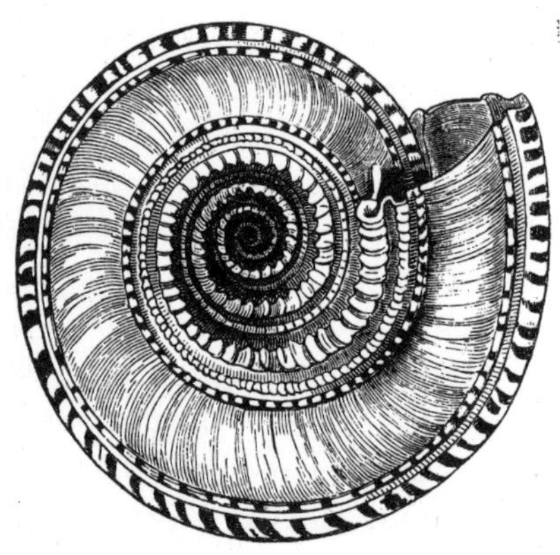

For dental care, smooth, glossy white shells suggest perfect teeth. For example, if cavities or sensitive teeth are a problem, place such a shell before you as you treat your teeth with a fluoride gel or rinse, or even while sipping milk or green tea (as green tea contains fluoride). Visualize the fluoride or calcium doing its work to help repair the enamel shell of your teeth. Visualize your enamel becoming thicker, stronger, and healthier.

If you have a shell that has both white and pink surfaces, use it to visualize healthy teeth and gums. As you brush, mentally recite the words "bright white teeth, perfect pink gums," glancing at the shell to reinforce your imagery.

For improved hearing, gather shells that are associated with hearing. Ears are sometimes described as shell-like; the cochlea, the part of the inner ear that is responsible for hearing, resembles a small shell. Some Moon snails and abalones are referred to as "ear shells." And, of course, we fancy that holding a shell to the ear allows us to hear the call of the ocean (though this is actually ambient noise trapped and bounced around inside the shell). For any sort of hearing problem, you should always seek proper medical care. However, for some minor problems, such as impaired hearing due to allergies or colds, low-level ear infections, mild intermittent cases of tinnitus or Meniere's disease, cysts and other obstructions in the ear, and normal diminution of hearing due to the aging process, you can complement your treatment with the following exercise.

Hold a shell up to your afflicted ear or ears, listening as best you can to the oceanlike roaring within. (Medium-sized conch shells may get the best results.) Visualize yourself by the side of the ocean, your attention fully attuned to the sound of rolling waves, and then recite to yourself: "In this vibration, the song of the ocean, a song of healing, restores my hearing." Imagine the sound waves transformed into waves of psychic energy, vibrating your inner ear in a way that restores its optimum functioning, setting everything right. If this exercise causes the slightest pain, desist at once and seek medical treatment. (Persons with mild cases of Meniere's and other balance problems should perform it sitting down.)

For reproductive well-being, cowries have been valued as amulets for good health throughout the world. Aside from their beauty, cowries bear resemblance to several body parts. Because their long ventrical slits suggest half-closed eyes, cowries are used as facial features in African and Middle Eastern masks and figurines. Their apertures also resemble mouths or vulvas, and the general shape of a cowrie is similar to a uterus. Thus, the Romans called them "little wombs," and in Japan, the cowrie is known as the "easy delivery shell." Women giving birth hold one in each hand to ensure a successful and healthy birth. Associations with fertility are also seen in their group name *Cypraediae* (in honor of Aphrodite, called the Cyprean because legend said she was born on the island of Cyprus). Cowries found in prehistoric graves may have been symbols of rebirth.

If you are a mother-to-be, try stroking a cowrie while saying affirmations such as "Smooth and easy; easy delivery." The white eggshell cowrie is ideal for this purpose. To promote general feminine health and pride in sexuality, any woman could caress a cowrie while beaming some loving energy to her reproductive organs.

In regard to bone health, the calcareous composition of the corals, as well as the stems and branches of certain species, call to mind a skeletal structure. In fact, some calcium supplements are derived from coral. If you are concerned about osteoporosis or healing a broken bone, you might enjoy contemplating a piece of coral while taking your daily calcium supplement and mentally reciting "Strong body, strong bones. Strong body, strong bones." In addition to stimulating the unconscious mind, handling a seashell engages the etheric "virtues" of the minerals in the shell.

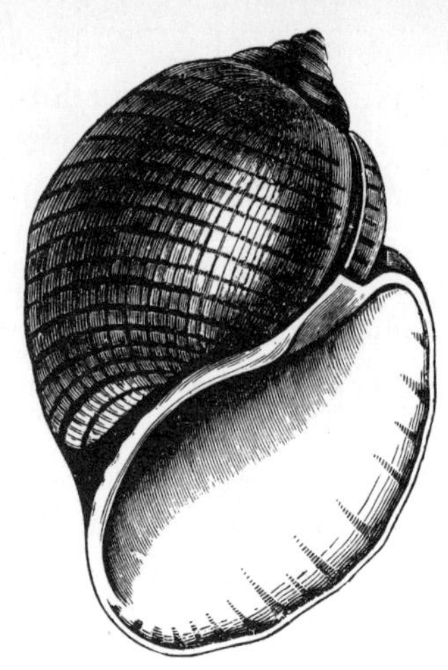

For mental power, consider brain coral. While investigating the magic of the Deep South during the Depression, Zora Neale Hurston studied under a man known as Father Watson, who was renowned for removing curses. Watson's wife believed that the source of his power was a large piece of brain coral that he kept on his altar. Brain coral (species of the genus *Meandrina)* have folds and ridges that resemble the convolutions of the human brain. A piece of brain coral can inspire students, creative people, and others whose work requires mental acuity.

To amplify your brain power, spend a few moments contemplating a piece of coral. Allow your gaze to follow its valleys and ridges. Trace them with your fingers. Relax your eyes as you take in its larger patterns. Feel that you are becoming calmer and calmer, yet also more alert, as you explore its convolutions. If there is a special question on your mind—perhaps you need the solution to some problem—state it aloud, and then continue to contemplate the coral. After a few moments, set it aside. If the answer has not already popped into your mind, have faith that unconscious forces have gone to work on it. For persons who suffer from certain minor forms of nervous or neurological problems (such as sensory processing disorders that affect learning abilities), regular contemplation of brain coral might help modulate mental energies.

If you enjoy the beauty of seashells, you will no doubt think of many additional ways to use them for healing magic.

Chanting in Spells and Ritual

by Steven Repko

Like candlelight and soft music, chanting can definitely set the mood in your rituals and spell casting. The first effective chant was the wolf's successful call to raise the Moon. As humans we elaborated with words and worship. The Buddhists include mantras with bells and gongs in their meditations. Almost every aboriginal culture at one time or another used drums and dancing with chanting to raise personal power.

The Bible literally blasts chanting in the book of Matthew: "And when you are praying, do not use meaningless repetition as the Gentiles do, for they suppose that they will be heard for their many words." Yet when you really need something accomplished, a series of prayers in repetition is the shortest distance between two points. Chanting is a major power generator.

What makes chanting effective is that it works on two levels: the internal and external. Internally our subconscious is stimulated by the patterns of rhythms, rhymes, and tones. This opens up direct access to our deepest emotions and beliefs. Content then fills this sensitive part of us with information. Even if we are too busy chanting, dancing, and banging to think, the words are readily absorbed into our psyche. This fills our subconscious with the belief that we are making changes, and that our intentions will be manifested.

Externally, we are also marking our patterns of rhythms and tones with our "intent" and escalating our resolve into the fabric of the universe. This creates a small universal "push" that brings energy from the cosmic to the physical or the spiritual.

One of the best ways to create a "common mind" in a ritual is through chanting. Pagans use chants to cast a circle, invoke the gods, and, of course, raise power. The best part of chanting in a group is that your participants can use more than one chant at a time to create some very impressive dynamics. Ritual chanting allows everyone participate equally within a structure.

During the past Lammas, we split the circle into two groups. The first group repeated the words "the wheel," while the other group repeated "the wheel that turns and turns and turns." Atop this droning chant, a caller recited: "We cast and protect this circle with the powers of the ages and the ties that bind the universe. As seeds that are sown then grown then blown we return and honor this circle within a circle." It was very powerful ritual.

One of the biggest reasons for "spell failure" is poor focus caused by "split intention." In spell casting, chanting maintains a specific pinpoint focus and greatly increases your success rate. You can only speak one chant at a time and therein lies the efficiency. By the same token, in the group setting chanting provides a unique opportunity to share communal energy for individual intentions or to orchestrate a single-minded focus. In this way, chanting makes everyone part of the group and ensures proper participation. I am a firm believer in the power of group magic, but I also realize how difficult it can be to bring a group together. Chanting allows a casual communion of practitioners to work in unison, yielding amazing results.

The Ending Spell

A perfect ritual for practicing the use of chant is an Ending Spell. In this spell, the chant is raised in a rhythm of threes. As such, it can be used for groups of any size. The Ending Spell is used to clean out your spiritual closet. It can be performed as needed or once every month during the dark Moon to keep your energies clear.

To start, place banishing or dark Moon incense placed on hot coals. Split into three "caller" groups. Each group repeats their chant thirteen times, then concludes with "All."

Part One

Caller one: *We stand at the crossroads.*
Caller two: *Ending what is old.*
Caller three: *A new beginning.*

All (once only): *So mote it be!*

Part Two

Caller one: *Ending illness.*
Caller two: *Ending negativity.*
Caller three: *Ending pain.*

All (once): *So mote it be!*

Part Three

Caller one (once): *As I will it!*
All (once): *So mote it be!*
Caller two (once): *As I will it!*
All (once): *So mote it be!*
Caller three (once): *As I will it!*
All (once): *So mote it be!*

The power of the spoken word is phenomenal. When you speak what is only a thought in your mind, it becomes real. When you "say it" over and over and over, it becomes a freight train of intent that will not be denied. Chanting simply is the most effective magical system anyone can use.

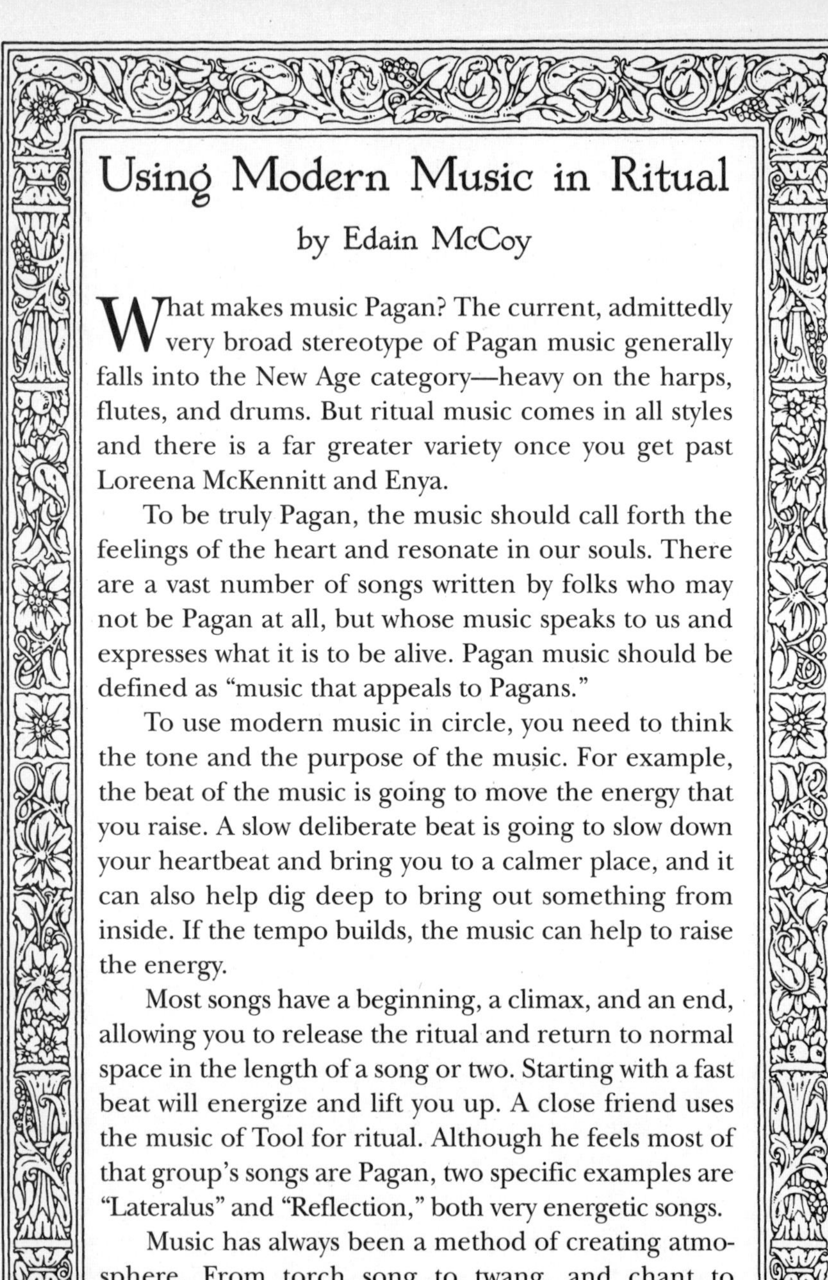

Using Modern Music in Ritual

by Edain McCoy

What makes music Pagan? The current, admittedly very broad stereotype of Pagan music generally falls into the New Age category—heavy on the harps, flutes, and drums. But ritual music comes in all styles and there is a far greater variety once you get past Loreena McKennitt and Enya.

To be truly Pagan, the music should call forth the feelings of the heart and resonate in our souls. There are a vast number of songs written by folks who may not be Pagan at all, but whose music speaks to us and expresses what it is to be alive. Pagan music should be defined as "music that appeals to Pagans."

To use modern music in circle, you need to think the tone and the purpose of the music. For example, the beat of the music is going to move the energy that you raise. A slow deliberate beat is going to slow down your heartbeat and bring you to a calmer place, and it can also help dig deep to bring out something from inside. If the tempo builds, the music can help to raise the energy.

Most songs have a beginning, a climax, and an end, allowing you to release the ritual and return to normal space in the length of a song or two. Starting with a fast beat will energize and lift you up. A close friend uses the music of Tool for ritual. Although he feels most of that group's songs are Pagan, two specific examples are "Lateralus" and "Reflection," both very energetic songs.

Music has always been a method of creating atmosphere. From torch song to twang, and chant to

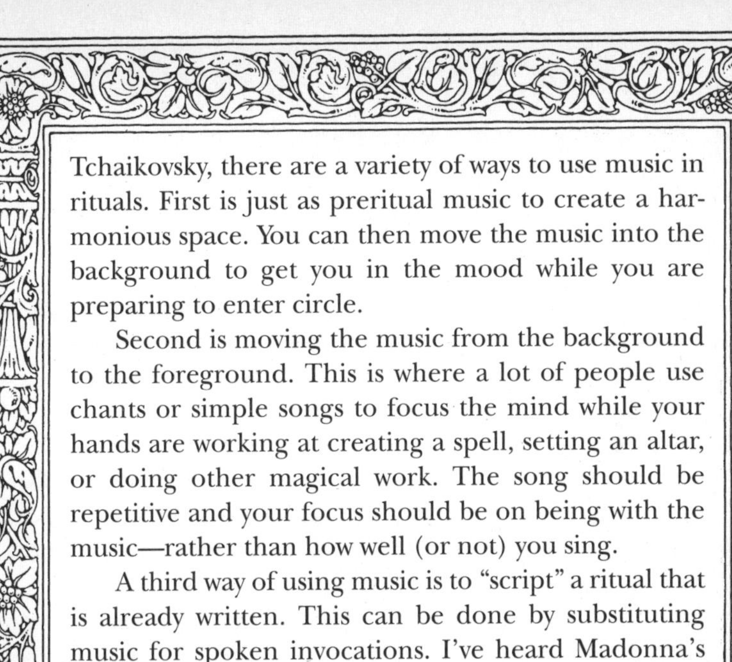

Tchaikovsky, there are a variety of ways to use music in rituals. First is just as preritual music to create a harmonious space. You can then move the music into the background to get you in the mood while you are preparing to enter circle.

Second is moving the music from the background to the foreground. This is where a lot of people use chants or simple songs to focus the mind while your hands are working at creating a spell, setting an altar, or doing other magical work. The song should be repetitive and your focus should be on being with the music—rather than how well (or not) you sing.

A third way of using music is to "script" a ritual that is already written. This can be done by substituting music for spoken invocations. I've heard Madonna's "Like a Virgin" used this way to call the Goddess.

Music can also be a blessing, prayer, or invocation to focus energy on your activity. This differs from foreground music in that the lyrics need to be about whatever you are doing. For example, a prosperity spell could be accompanied by Pink Floyd's "Money."

Finally, music can be used after the ritual, as a way to send the energy on its way. Lots of folks use drumming or heavy percussion tapes for this, since drum energy is very grounding. You want to avoid the fiery energy of strong guitar or bass lines here. This is about changing your perceptions from ritual space to normal space, so you need to focus on "real world" stuff here.

Different results will come with different songs. Some music simply isn't going to bring you into a spiritual space, and will more likely to chase you out of the circle. Use whatever makes you relax, even if it's flutes and harps . . . or Enya.

Inanna, Queen of Heaven

by Scott Paul

Her name was Inanna, and to the Sumerians she ruled all. Her followers called her the Queen of Heaven, and there is archeological evidence of a mass cult of her worship at a temple in Uruk (modern-day Iraq) that dates back nearly six thousand years. The Babylonians called her Ishtar (or Istar), the Hebrews called her the "great whore of Babylon." As civilizations rose and fell, through it all there was always Inanna.

Inanna was a goddess of many faces. She was the daughter of the Moon god Nanna, so the heavens were her domain. Known as the mother goddess of Sumer, she was also nurturing mother. She was goddess of the harvest, of the fruits of the vine, and of the apple tree. In her role as virgin goddess she was imagined as a young and beautiful girl. Young women went to her temple to

offer their own virginity to her. The priestesses were known as hierodules or servants of the holy. We know them as sacred prostitutes. This activity later shocked the early Hebrew prophets. But she was also goddess of war, a warrior riding a dragon into battle. As Ishtar of Assyria, she glorified war and promoted human sacrifice.

The hymns to Inanna are the oldest known written poetry in the world. They were written in cuneiform on clay tablets by a Sumerian priestess named Eheduanna. She was daughter of King Sargon I, who united the city-states of Sumer into a cohesive empire. His daughter played a decisive role in his empire by elevating the worship of Inanna above all other gods.

The myth of Inanna echoes across the ages. In the epic of Gilgamesh, Inanna was friend to the young king. It is from her that Gilgamesh received the powers of kingship and the right to rule, though later she became his enemy after he lost his power over men.

In another tale, Inanna, wanting more power, descended to the underworld to challenge her sister Ershkigal. In this yin/yang struggle, Inanna had to pass through seven gates to enter the world of the dead. At each gate she was forced to leave some of her raiment and jewelry behind, until she was naked before Ershkigal. As Ershkigal descended her throne, Inanna rushed over and assumed the empty seat. Shocked at her sister's attempt to seize power, Ershkigal turned Inanna into a corpse and hung her on a hook for three days. Emissaries of Enki the god of wisdom freed Inanna, but Ershkigal decreed that Inanna would have to leave a substitute behind. So Inanna went to her lover Dumuzi, who had shown no grief at her apparent death. She allowed the demons of the underworld to capture him.

As her high priestess wrote four thousand years ago, Inanna is the "Lady of all powers, in whom light appears. Radiant one, beloved of heaven and earth." The goddess of many names and places shall live in our hearts forever.

Sehkmet, Fierce Goddess of Summer

by Lily Gardner

Sehkmet, as she is represented in Egyptian temples, is a most intimidating goddess. The first Sehkmet I saw was carved from black stone, with the head of a lioness and the body of a woman. Seated on a throne, she stood twelve feet high, an image of power and might—fitting for a daughter of the sun god, Ra, whose name translates as "she who is powerful."

Lions have long been associated with the Sun. They symbolize sovereignty and effortless strength. Their golden color reminds us of sunlight, their manes remind us of rays of Sun. Sehkmet's crown is a solar disc encircled by a cobra that spits fire. Her breath is the hot desert wind. Her face glows red-orange like the Sun, and a fiery aura surrounds her body. She is the noon-day goddess and her realm is the fierce heat of summer.

Like many of her fellow gods and goddesses, Sehkmet represents our dual nature, both beautiful and terrible. She is the personification of the Sun, life renewing as well as destructive. The Sun is the source of fertility, but at the same time it can burn and kill. As the lion, Sehkmet is a powerful sovereign and capable of blind greed. Sehkment is a protector and a destroyer.

Sehkmet began her career as the goddess of rain. Ra, her father, gave birth to twins, Shu, the god of wind, and Tefnut, also known as the "spitter," the goddess of rain. Shu was depicted in human form supporting the sky from the Earth, in much the same way Atlas is depicted. Tefnut had the body of a woman and the head of a lion. She was called the eye of Ra. What angered her, no one can remember, but in time she left Egypt, taking all her moisture with her. The countryside grew parched and all the vegetation died, starving the people and animals. As people died, it was said that the lion-goddess was on a killing spree. Thoth was eventually able to persuade her to return in peace to her father, and with her return came the rains back to the land of Egypt. But from then on, Tefnut was associated with the hot Sun and drought. This aspect of Tefnut dominated Egyptian imagination, and Tefnut became Sehkmet, the Sun goddess.

The most famous account of Sehkment is in her role of Destructor. The human race grew too proud to worship Ra in the way he felt was his due. He sent Sehkmet to teach them a lesson. She went on a killing spree that threatened the extinction of the human race. The other gods pleaded with her to end her rampage but she was filled with blood lust. The gods tricked her by spilling seven thousand jars of beer, colored with pomegranate juice so that it resembled blood. Sehkment lapped up what she thought was blood until she was too drunk to continue her rampage. And so the human race was saved.

Because of her power, Sehkmet is often seen in her negative aspect. But she is also the goddess that all Egyptian physicians and healers invoke to guide them in their work. The cobra in her headdress is a symbol of healing. The caduceus—two serpents twined around a staff—is still used today as the emblem of the medical profession. She is also called on to protect people from pestilence.

In modern-day Paganism, Sehkment has dominion over the south, the element of fire, the season of summer, and the daylight hours—especially high noon. She rules all things solar. The light radiating from the Sun represents knowledge, and the Sun itself is cosmic knowledge. The Sun also represents resurrection. It is believed that the Sun descended into the underworld at sunset to be reborn each sunrise. Lions were said to hold the image of the setting Sun in their eyes at night, which allowed the Sun to resurrect each morning.

The Sun corresponds with fire. Like the Sun, fire is both life and death. The element of fire rules the imagination. The upward motion of flames represents the yearning for the heavens. Fire is linked with sexuality. We say animals are "in heat" when they are ready to mate. As fire represents both imagination and sexuality, it only follows that it also rules creativity.

Fire also corresponds with will. In our lives, many of us experience power through magic. To make magic requires four things: to know, to will, to dare, and to be silent. The knowing is the imagination to visualize what we wish to manifest for ourselves. The will begins with asking ourselves what we're willing to pay to achieve our desire. The will is the enthusiasm and persistence to carry forward our desire.

Doreen Valiente tells a story about a powerful shaman, Mehmet Karagoz, in her book, *Natural Magic.* When he was a young man, his father gave him this advice: "Believe in the possibility of what you intend to do, hold it strongly in your mind, and it will happen." These words transformed Mehmet's life and they have inspired mine. I am also inspired by these words from the papers of the Golden Dawn: "To practice magic, both imagination and will must be called into action. They are co-equal in the work."

Sehkment is a powerful ally for creativity, magic working, healing, protection, and for any endeavor that calls for strength. Any spell work using candle or fire magic would be appropriate for her. The duality of her solar nature reminds us that we have the power to both create and destroy ourselves.

When a Skunk Crosses Your Path

By Cerridwen Iris Shea

During the thirteen years I lived in Manhattan, my daily contact with animals was limited. There were my cats, of course, and pigeons. There was the occasional seagull and rat, and there were forays to the zoo, or to my friend's barn out on Long Island to visit her horses. But this was the extent of my interaction with "wildlife."

Now, I live in the suburbs. Out here, my animal encounters expand. It's part of my plan to wean myself from urban life and move even further out to the country eventually, so that I can have my own horses, and tend to whatever animals decide to stop by and stay awhile.

The cats are delighted that other birds—such as blue jays, wrens, sparrows, crows, grackles, Canada geese—exist in abundance. There is a particular squirrel who stands outside the window and teases them mercilessly, confident that he can't be reached. He stands there chattering at the cats while they chatter back—it doesn't sound threatening to me, but more like the type of conversation neighbors used to have over backyard fences.

Fat raccoons waddle across the courtyard. They stop and stare thoughtfully, wondering if I carry something they might like. When they decide that I useless, I am dismissed, and they continue to their den.

And the skunks. In my neighborhood, there are several skunks. They are bold little fellows, ambling around in the evening and late at night. I cried the other morning when I found out that one had been hit by a car during the night. The skunks sometimes spray the raccoons or wandering cats, so there is no doubt as to their presence. My cats are strictly indoor cats. I have no doubt that my tortoiseshell, who is not very bright (but is sweet) would come home every night smelling of skunk if I ever let her out.

I believe that animals cross your path at certain times for definite reasons, much the way people do. I looked up traditional meanings for these animals, and they did not make sense with the whats and whens of the creatures appearing to me. I took notes of what animals approached, what I felt at the time, and how the animal affected what happened next. And I came up with my own list, which I share with you below.

Ants: Teamwork
Bat: View things from a different angle; new vision
Bees: Hard work brings sweet rewards
Blue heron: Self-reflection
Blue jay: Assertiveness
Canada goose: Life cycles, protection (an acquaintance in another state took in a goose when it was injured; he litter-box trained it, and keeps it as a pet, and it behaves like a watch dog. Even the UPS man is terrified)
Cardinal: Self-esteem
Cat: Independence, grace, thoughtfulness, humor
Cow: Contentment
Crow: Magical messenger; you're not listening to some very important message
Deer: Awareness
Dog: Loyalty, unconditional love
Earthworm: Creativity; alternate pathways
Fox: Intelligence, creative thinking
Frog: Meditation, contemplation
Goldfinch: Family ties
Grackle: Persistence
Horse: Freedom, messenger; healthy eating habits, physical fitness
Mouse: Discovery, an eye for detail
Oriole: Lightheartedness; looseness and freedom-of-spirit
Owl: Intuition; vision
Raccoon: Adaptability, dexterity; using castoffs to create something useful
Robin: Joy
Seagull: Limitless opportunity; creating one's own luck
Skunk: Reputation, self-respect, confidence; tolerance, setting boundaries

Squirrel: Hearth and home; saving for a rainy day
Sparrow: Curiosity
Woodpecker: Tenacity
Wren: Diligence
Turtle: Relaxation; earth and water rhythms

Each of these associations is the result of nearly a year's worth of experiences and anecdotes. Through it all, skunk has had the most influence on me. As I spent the past year riding out extensive transitions in residence, job, and relationships, skunk always turned up when I felt insecure. I would drive home late at night, and slam on the brakes as I saw two yellow orbs glow. Skunk stood in the road, tail waving, staring down the car. I stopped at a respectful distance, and Skunk watched me thoughtfully. The whiskers twitched, and the head tilted first one way and then the other. The white stripe glowed against the dark, glossy fur.

Then, the animal lifted one paw in my direction, almost as a wave, and then ambled off to the bushes on the side of the road, tail waving like a flag. Skunk accepted me for who I am, and I accepted him for who he is. Had we not given each other mutual respect and tolerance, he would have sprayed me and continued on his way. It wouldn't matter to him. But I would have suffered.

Every time I experienced self-doubt in the past year, Skunk turned up for a similar encounter. Each time, I felt better and within twenty-four hours of the encounter, by maintaining my own combination of self-respect, tolerance, and boundaries, something positive came about. Skunk has become one of my totem animals.

I encourage each of you to keep track of the animals who cross your path, and how they affect your lives. You will find surprising totems, and you will find your own meanings for each of them. It doesn't matter what someone else says is the animal's meaning. What matters is your own experience, and building your own relationships with the inhabitants of the world around you. You will find surprises and joy.

Under a Balsam Moon

by Elizabeth Barrette

Most material about lunar mysteries focuses on the Full Moon or the waxing crescent, and maybe occasionally the dark Moon. But the waning crescent has a power all its own that we seldom acknowledge.

The Moon passes through eight phases: dark, crescent, first quarter, gibbous, full, disseminating, last quarter, and balsamic. We see the waxing crescent in the western sky in late afternoon; we see the Full Moon in the east at sunset. Few people see the balsamic Moon, because she appears just before dawn, very close to the Sun.

During the dark phase, we miss the Moon. We watch eagerly for her return and greet the crescent with much joy. We watch her grow. We celebrate the richness of the Full Moon, then the Moon slips away again, hiding in the shadows of the night. Her later phases get less attention. The balsamic Moon is like an old woman, working quietly late at night while the rest of the world sleeps. But that doesn't make her unimportant. As the crescent embodies the strongest energy for youth, exuberance, and growth, so the balsamic Moon embodies the strongest energy for age, wisdom, and release. When you work magic, don't forget this quiet phase. She is subtle yet powerful.

Goddesses of the Waning Moon

Most Moon goddesses relate to the waxing or full phases, but a few preside over the dark phase. A careful search turned up only one specializing solely in the waning Moon, but several goddesses do correspond to all phases.

Hecate, a Greek goddess, has three faces. One of the most famous "triple goddesses," she can see the past, present, and future at once. She also embodies the three ages of womanhood: maiden, mother, and crone. Her sacred animals include serpents, dogs, and horses. She represents the power of old women who have survived life's challenges to reach the age of wisdom. Hers is the third road, the road less traveled; her rites often take place at three-way crossroads. In ancient times, housewives hung her image over the doorway to protect their homes when they went out.

Ishtar, a Babylonian goddess, is related to the Sumerian goddess Inanna and shares similar myths. In one, Ishtar's lover Tammuz dies and she goes to seek him in the land of the dead. At each of seven gates, she faces a warden and must give up part of her regalia: crown, earrings, necklace, diadem, belt, and bracelets. As Ishtar descends into the underworld, the Moon wanes and the sky darkens. The seventh gate is that of the balsamic Moon, the final sliver of light before total darkness, where Ishtar gives up her garment and goes to stand naked before Eriskegal. The power of this goddess lies in her willingness to surrender and make herself vulnerable in order to achieve her desires. Her myth illustrates how the balsamic Moon is the phase right before attainment.

Muireartach, an Irish-Scottish goddess, is associated with the waning Moon. Her other areas of expertise include battle and the sea. Indeed, Scottish folklore gives her name to a race of marine fairies. Another Celtic goddess, the Morrigan, also relates to the waning and dark Moon. In her three faces—Badb, Macha, and Nemain—she rules over strife, death, and destruction. The balsamic Moon can be a time when things come apart, or the calm before the storm. Sometimes these moments are necessary.

Tlazoltéotl, an Aztec goddess, represents the fourfold Moon. Each of her aspects has a different name: Tiacapan, Teicu, Tlaco, and Xocutxin. She rules over a wide range of spheres, both positive and negative. Some of her associations include sexuality, licentiousness, gambling, temptation, black magic, and purification. She also presides over crossroads, physical four-way intersections, and important decisions in a person's life. The balsamic Moon, like the hours just before dawn and the end of one's lifespan, offers a perfect time to contemplate decisions and implications.

Balsamic Moon Spells and Rituals

The Moon conveniently provides us with a fluctuating base for magic, much like the tides in the ocean. During the waxing phase, the Moon's energy supports growth and expression; during the waning phase, it supports reduction and introspection. The full and new phases are times of stillness and achievement, manifestation and subtlety. So the balsamic Moon marks the time when the "outflow" of energy peaks.

The best-known spells for the waning Moon are banishing spells. This covers all manner of workings intended to repel, reduce, or remove something from your life. However, you can do many other kinds of magic at this time. Divination and meditation work well. If you garden, pay attention to compost during this phase—start a heap, turn an existing one, or spread finished compost on the ground. The balsamic Moon helps break down the materials, preparing the compost to support new life.

Look to the above goddesses for ideas, too. You could cast a protective charm for your house in Hecate's name. You might study animal magic relating to dogs or snakes. Another option would be to explore renunciation and vulnerability, as recounted in the myth of Ishtar. For Muireartach and the Morrigan, gird yourself for battle and face up to the confrontations you've been avoiding. Tlazoltéotl reminds us to think carefully before making decisions, and to make amends when things go wrong because of our actions. This is also a good time to consider your present life circumstances, to apologize if you've hurt someone, or to halt an unproductive course of action so that you can try something different.

Timing is important. The balsamic phase of the Moon lasts only a few days. You can find it in the calendar section of this almanac by locating the New Moon and counting back three to four days.

Although you can cast your spells any time during this phase, you'll often get the best results working in the predawn hours when the balsamic Moon actually appears in the sky. Also, holy days dedicated to the above or other lunar deities add extra emphasis, especially for honoring ceremonies. If you can't greet the balsamic Moon herself, set a stone or a bowl of water in a moonlit window to absorb the energy. You can then use this water in your rituals, or carry it with you through the next month.

In Conclusion

So much of modern culture centers around youth, action, and expansion. The natural world, however, is all about cycles. There is no such thing as limitless perpetual growth. Now more than ever we need time to rest, to relax, and to discard that which we find unhelpful. We must look inward and think about our choices. We need to honor our elders and the wisdom developing within each of us. The balsamic Moon gives us these opportunities. How you use them is up to you.

For Further Study

Budapest, Zsuzsanna Emese. *Grandmother Moon: Lunar Magic in our Lives; Spells, Rituals, Goddesses, Legends, and Emotions under the Moon.* San Francisco, Calif.: HarperSanFrancisco, 1991.

McCoy, Edain. *Lady of the Night: A Handbook of Moon Magick and Rituals.* St. Paul, Minn.: Llewellyn Publications, 1995.

Brueton, Diana. *Many Moons: The Myth and Magic, Fact and Fantasy of our Nearest Heavenly Body.* New York: Prentice Hall Press, 1991.

Elen Hawke. *Praise to the Moon: Magic and Myth of the Lunar Cycle.* St. Paul, Minn.: Llewellyn Publications, 2002.

The Witch's Wedding Bottle

by Olivia O'Meir

Two years ago now, I was invited to a friend's Pagan wedding. When it came time to purchase a present, I was at a loss. I had little money, but still I wanted to give her a meaningful, beautiful, and magical gift. For inspiration, I researched charms and talismans. And as I read about Witches' bottles, I decided this was the perfect idea. Then and there, I vowed to create one for my friend's wedding. In the end, the couple loved it—not only was the bottle gorgeous, but also special because it was created by the magical touch of the hand.

Witches' bottles were traditionally used for protection against witchcraft. They were filled with red wine, sharp objects, and herbs for protection. Traditionally, the bottles were hidden in the walls or buried in a corner of the yard.

Witches' bottles can be used for other purposes as well. For example, they can be used in money spells. To attract money, a Witch might add to her bottle magnets, coins, and herbs such as patchouli. For my wedding Witches' bottle, I added ingredients to manifest love, passion, union, and fertility for the couple.

How to Create a Wedding Witches' Bottle

Start by choosing a specific goal for the bottle. This will make the charm more powerful. A specific goal allows a witch to focus his or her energy more effectively.

Pick the bottle. You can choose any color, shape, or size. Mason jars are ideal because they have large mouths and can be tightly sealed.

Decide the herbs and items you want to add to symbolize your goal. Take into account not only symbolism, but also your available resources, money, and time. You may need to make substitutions. For example, I used wedding ring favors from a dollar store. If you need help, check out the list of ingredients and substitutions at the end of the article.

Choose a particular time to create the bottle. Friday is an ideal day because it is sacred to Venus and Aphrodite, two love goddesses. The waxing Moon is a great time to add ingredients to the bottle. A Moon in Taurus and Libra will also be a blessed time.

Add the ingredients to the bottle. There are two ways to do this. You can place the ingredients in the bottle directly. Or you can put your ingredients into a fabric square first. The square will be tied up and dropped into the bottle.

Put the ingredients in one at a time. Everytime you add an ingredient state its purpose aloud. For example, say "Some dragon's blood for passion" as you add the dragon's blood. Stating the purpose helps you to focus and magically charge the ingredients with your will and intent.

Seal the bottle securely. After closing the lid, you can use wax to permanently seal it. Red and pink are good colors, but white can be used too. To conceal the wax, cover the top with fabric, and tie ribbon around the neck.

Decorate the outside of the bottle. Fabric, lace, or felt can be used. Tie decorative wedding favors to the ribbon around the neck. How fancy you decorate the bottle is up to you. You can decorate the entire bottle if you choose.

Finish the bottle by typing up a small description of what a Witches' bottle is. The bottle's ingredients can be included as well. You can use fancy papers, fonts, and inks. The paper can be placed in a card or rolled into a scroll to accompany the bottle.

Ingredient Suggestions

For love and romance: Vanilla, jasmine, rose petals, rose quartz, heart figures, red wine

For fertility and sensuality: Dragon's Blood, patchouli, allspice, cinnamon, apple, garnet, cat figures

For union: Rings, interlocking rings, bride and groom figures, Adam and Eve root, lavender, braided ribbon, lodestones

For Further Study

Cunningham, Scott, and David Harrington. *Spell Crafts: Creating Magical Objects.* St. Paul, Minn.: Llewellyn Publications, 1993.

Farrar, Janet and Stewart. *A Witches' Bible.* Custer, Wash.: Phoenix Publishing Inc., 1981.

Morrison, Dorothy. *Everyday Magic: Spells and Rituals for Modern Living.* St. Paul, Minn.: Llewellyn Publications, 1998.

Telesco, Patricia. *Your Book of Shadows.* Secaucus, N.J.: Citadel Press, 1999.

Romance Body Powder

by Muse

Use this Romance Body Powder recipe to feel feminine and beautiful on those long, hot, sticky summer days when nothing else seems to cool you. You can use a mortar and pestle, or, for a more modern twist, a coffee grinder or blender.

The Powder Recipe

½ cup dried lavender flowers

½ cup dried rose petals

½ cup arrowroot powder

Add dried flowers to to your chosen grinding device, and grind them into a powder. Then add arrowroot powder (available at any supermarket in the spice isle), and grind this with the flowers. Dust the powder on your body for a baby-powder effect with a romantic scent.

Success Candle Anointing Oil

by Muse

Sometimes you need a little extra magic to help you find your way to the mysterious path of success (in career, in life, with a particular task). Use this oil to anoint candles during success spells and rituals.

Oil Recipe

8 ozs. carrier oil, such as grapeseed oil

2 drops cinnamon oil

2 drops patchouli oil

1 drop myrrh oil

1 drop frankincense oil

1 drop juniper oil

Add essential oils to your carrier oil in a jar while you focus your intent.

Simple Success Candle Ritual

Seven days before the Full Moon, anoint a purple candle with the success oil above. Chant the following over the candle, then light the candle and let it burn for seven minutes. Repeat this ritual every night until the Full Moon.

My path to success becomes ever clearer.
My desires are met, and success grows nearer.
The earth manifests, the air inspires,
The water gives heart, and power from fire.

Essential Oil Perfumes

by Muse

There are millions of magical oil recipes available today, but what do we do with the oil once it's made? Well, you can apply oils in the standard ways—on candles, ritual items, and the spellcasters themselves during ritual. But why not use these oils in a different, yet still potent, way? Why not use these oils as perfumes?

With the following blends, you can make some amazing concoctions that will get more reaction from the higher energies. and from people around you, than any in the Chanel line. Now, not all oils can be used safely on the skin, so all essential oils should be diluted in carrier oil such as grapeseed or jojoba. Test the completed oil concoction on a small area of your skin to be sure there is no reaction before use. If you choose to use synthetic oil rather than natural essential oil—which is sometimes a wise choice, as some pure oils are expensive—the scent will not last as long.

Love Oil Perfume

3 drops rose oil and vanilla oil

2 drops jasmine oil

Lust Oil Perfume

1 drop patchouli oil

3 drops rose oil and ylang ylang oil

Success Oil Perfume

1 drop cinnamon oil

2 drops frankincense, myrrh, and juniper oils

3 drops patchouli oil

Burmese Astrology

by Lynne Sturtevant

In Burma, people regularly consult astrologers about everything from whether to enter business deals to when to get haircuts. The walkways to Buddhist temples are lined with astrologers in lawn chairs and squatting on the ground. The magical formulas they use are old, but the advice they dispense helps people navigate the complexities of the complicated twenty-first century.

The Burmese astrological system is based on eight—the number that reflects the nature of the universe when all elements are in balance. There are eight astrological signs, eight cardinal directions, and eight sacred animals.

In addition to the seven planets recognized by other ancient cultures (Sun, Moon, Mercury, Venus, Mars, Jupiter, and Saturn), the Burmese include an eighth secret planet called Rahu. Rahu is the barely discernable celestial body that causes eclipses.

The month and date of a person's birth are not important. The day of the week on which a person is born determines his or her astrological sign. Wednesday is divided into morning and afternoon—changing the seven days of the week into a form that accommodates the mystical number eight.

Sunday belongs to Garuda, the mythical king of the birds. If you are Sunday-born, northeast is your lucky direction and the Sun is your ruling planet. The more difficult a task or subject, the more it interests you. You are energetic, focused, and very stubborn. You are also too generous and have a tendency to allow others to take advantage of you.

Monday is the day of the tiger. If you are Monday-born, east is your lucky direction and the Moon is your ruling planet. You are patient, steady, and reliable. Your ability to persevere against great odds is your finest trait. You are ambitious and like to succeed at everything you attempt.

Tuesday is the day of the lion. If you are Tuesday-born, southeast is your lucky direction, and Mars is your ruling planet. You are opinionated, idealistic, and you love a good challenge. People are attracted to your strong and honorable character. You respect dignity and prestige in others and are drawn to great causes.

The elephant rules Wednesday morning. If you are Wednesday-born, south is your lucky direction, and Mercury is your ruling planet. You are impulsive and quick-tempered. You are independent and like to be in charge, but you also frequently take on more than you can handle.

If you are born on Wednesday afternoon, you are called Rahu-born because the secret planet Rahu rules your sign. Your animal is the tuskless elephant, and northwest is your lucky direction. You have a wide circle of acquaintances but few close friends. You are a tireless self-promoter driven by the desire for success, though you will go to great lengths to protect your privacy.

Thursday is the day of the rat. If you are Thursday-born, west is your lucky direction, and Jupiter is your ruling planet. You are serious, intelligent, and quiet. Other people would be surprised to learn how ambitious you are and how highly you value professional success. In business, your singlemindedness can lead to great things. It can also evolve into ruthless, destructive behavior.

Friday is the day of the guinea pig. If you are Friday-born, north is your lucky direction, and Venus is your ruling planet. You are sensitive and emotional and you empathize with others. You are also restless and quickly tire of people, jobs, and places. You have a strong artistic streak, but tend to be a dabbler. If you can stick with art or music long enough to develop your talents, you are capable of creating great beauty.

Saturday is the day of the dragon. If you are Saturday-born, southwest is your lucky direction, and Saturn is your ruling planet. You are intelligent, witty, and industrious. You like working alone and controlling your own destiny. You find it tedious to be part of a group or team. However, if you can overcome your reluctance to delegate and can improve your interpersonal skills, you can become an outstanding leader.

When a person consults a Burmese astrologer, the astrologer uses ancient charts, magical symbols, and tables to devise a ritual to enhance good luck for the person. Through a series of complex calculations, the astrologer determines the day and time the ritual must be performed. The details of the ritual vary, but it always involves visiting one or more of the planetary posts located on the outdoor platforms surrounding Buddhist temples. Planetary posts are situated at the eight cardinal directions in relation to the temple's main entrance. Each post is a shrine representing a day of the week and its corresponding astrological sign. It includes a table for offerings and a stone statue of that day's sacred animal. Large bowls of clear water and lacquered cups sit in front of the animal statue.

An astrologer may send a person to the planetary post associated with his or her birthday or may recommend visits to several planetary posts. For example, a Thursday-born could be sent to the planetary posts for Saturday and Monday. The astrologer will instruct the questioner to place *yadaya,* which are offerings of fruit, flowers, incense, or paper umbrellas, at the appropriate shrine. The person will also be told to pour a specific number of cups of water on the sacred animal statue. Water is cool, and pouring it helps restore balance to the universe. Even during torrential rainstorms, the temple platforms are crowded with people pouring water on the statues. As they pour, they utter wishes and prayers. The Burmese know, as their ancestors did, that when the rituals are performed correctly, harmony and balance will be restored.

The Magic of Music, Words, and Sounds

by Ember

Ancient cultures have always believed in the power of sounds and the spoken word. And scientists have documented the effects sound vibrations have on the brain—such as causing people to reach altered states of consciousness and trance. You can use sound in spell and ritual to add power and joy to every act, and you will be rewarded with a wonderful, mystical experience.

Music is one of the simplest ways to add sound and words to rituals and spells. If you play an instrument, doing so during ritual is an ideal way to use your own personal power of sound. If not, you can improvise and create some pleasant melodies without knowing exactly how to play. You'll be surprised at the rhythms you can create with your own drum, or the lovely tones you can produce with simple wooden flute, even if you have never read or played music. And, of course, we have our voices. Raised in song or chant, our voices are a powerful mode of expression. Also, if you prefer, there are varieties of recorded sounds to suit any need—your favorite pop anthems from the radio, classical pieces performed by orchestra or choir, or the sounds of nature and animals.

We often feel a sense of peace and awe at the sound of birds and crickets, rain and thunderstorms, wind in the trees, wolves howling, or the mysterious sound of whales. Recordings of nature sounds add a nice effect on their own or when combined with music. Having appropriate sounds in the background sets the tone for all things magical. Ideally, we should all be outside listening nature's own music, but this isn't always possible. In choosing appropriate sounds for your specific need, consider the elements with which you are working.

Spells involving the element of water, for example, would be enhanced by the sound of ocean waves or a running stream—either real or recorded. Or you can use a corresponding sound to symbolize the particular season you are celebrating. Spring might call for the sound of rain, and who can imagine a summer ritual without hearing crickets in the night? Allow these sounds, whether naturally occurring or recorded, to penetrate the mood of your ritual. With an indoor fountain and recording of birds, you can close your eyes and your living room becomes a tranquil forest.

Words often cause anxiety in creating spells and rituals. Many people believe they must have elaborate rhythmic chants or poetry to be successful. But whatever words you speak, as long as they come from the heart they will be effective. Often, however, a simple rhyming chant is easier to remember if you're planning to use it again in the future.

When designing a spell or ritual simply think of your specific and sincere need. Imagine yourself speaking to a friend, and visualize your need clearly. You may whisper, speak normally, or shout—whatever you feel is right at the moment. Never be afraid to do what you feel. If you prefer, write down your feelings ahead of time as though you were writing in a journal. This may also reveal opportunities for rhyming or making other complimentary sounds. If you don't have an ear for rhyme, try alliteration—using words that begin with the same letter. This can evoke a very nice rhythmic feel as well. Also consider using a refrain, repeating the same words or lines at the end of a set

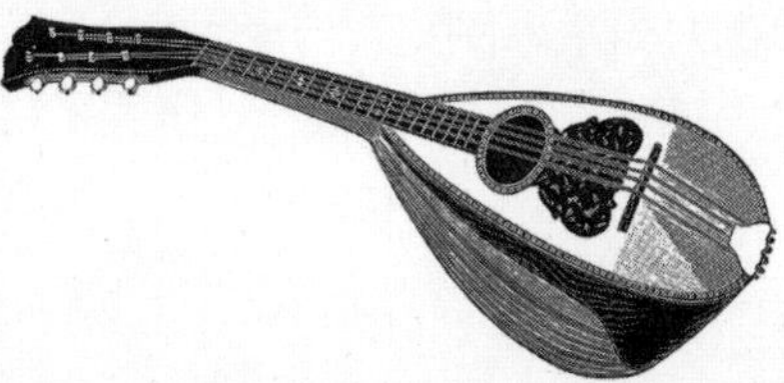

of lines. For example, in one of my Moon chants, I repeat "waxing, waning" after each of my four stanzas. Then, at the end of the verse, I chant "waxing, waning" slowly, over and over again until it becomes almost hypnotic.

Often this repetition can be sufficient for spell casting. When cleansing a room or an entire home, perhaps after some family member has been ill, you can walk with a smoldering sage wand and chant over and over again: "Banish illness, cleanse this space." Although this does not rhyme, it states the purpose simply and leaves your mind free to concentrate on the words and visualize their manifestation.

If you enjoy writing, let your imagination flow with ideas and images. If you need a chant for a Full Moon ritual, consider how you feel, how the Moon looks, how all the phases appear to you—and create simple rhyming lines. I have composed nonrhyming poetry that I thought would be useful in such times, only to find I couldn't remember the words. Rhyming allows us to focus on the key words and makes memorization easier. When you use the same chant or poem for each ritual, it will soon be easy to recite.

You may read your poetic lines if you like, but memorization frees your mind for easier visualization. Many times you can find existing words for a spell or ritual and adapt them for your own use. I believe changing them adds to their personal power and focuses their energy to your particular need.

Whichever method you choose, sound can add depth to any ritual or spell. How you use music, words, and sounds in your magic will make your experience more memorable—and uniquely your own.

Music in Ritual

By Reverend Gina Pace

Right from the start, I'd like to explain that while it is a valid topic in its own right, using recorded music as background material during a ritual is not my intended topic here. Many people like to play recorded music during a ritual, and I myself have done so on several occasions—with good results. However, what I'm discussing in this article is the use of music within the ritual structure itself.

Having been raised Catholic, song and music were always considered an integral part of my early religious upbringing. The priest would often sing various parts of the Mass, with the congregation singing in response to him. I can honestly say that I always felt that the Mass seemed a little more "special" or "sacred" when the parts were sung.

There are several intervals in which songs are also inserted. This is also true of other mainstream Christian services, as well as other religious services. I remember a music teacher of mine back in sixth grade who always used to say that singing was praying twice. I guess it's a belief that stuck.

There is no need to feel musically perfect or superior when offering one's ritual to the God and Goddess. I think it's safe to say, if they gave you a voice, they'd rather you lift it up in prayer to them than feel embarrassed that you can't carry a

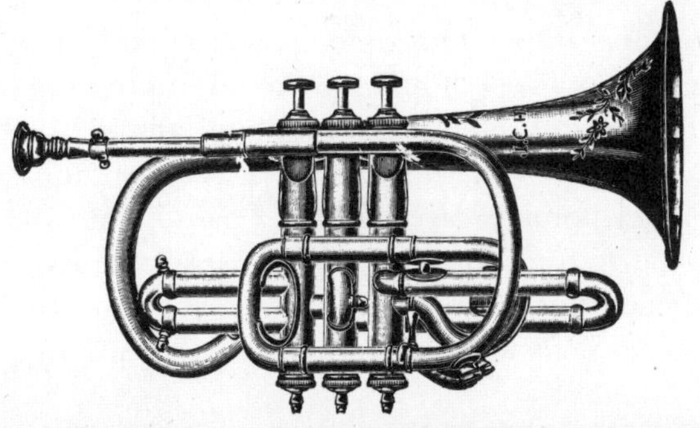

tune as well as you'd like. After all, freeform singing is not a precise talent. Priests in churches don't dwell on how they sound. Nor do you have to feel as though you are being judged. Lift your voice up and don't be afraid to use it.

Another way of using music in ritual is to use various instruments to symbolize, call upon, or simulate the different elements for the circle. When I am working a ritual circle, I always begin by calling the four elements to witness the ritual. This does not have to be a terribly formal event. In fact, you can do it without saying a word if you use musical instruments to bring in each element. Let's say, for example, you wish to open your circle by calling in the element of air. A woodwind instrument, such as a flute, can represent air. There are many types of indigenous native flutes available, pan flutes, zen flutes, and cedar flutes among these. I use a tin penny whistle, which is an old Irish favorite that I bought many years ago at a local music store for about five dollars. The memories alone make it a worthwhile addition to ritual. And its close affiliation with air make it a perfect instrument with which to summon the element to the circle.

I begin in the east corner, which belongs to air, and I move slowly about the ritual space in a clockwise, or sunwise, direction, playing my flute in a freeform manner. It tends to have an eerie kind of sound that adds to the ambience of the ritual. When I have completed the circle, I place the flute in the eastern corner, and move to the southern corner to call the next element, fire.

It is more difficult to come up with a good instrument for the element of fire. I thought of the various traits of fire—passion, excitement, energy, momentum, ambition, and joy—and I chose a pair of Mexican maracas that I found on eBay. They are elaborately carved out of a pair of gourds. Many different native traditions have similar instruments. Shaking a pair of maracas has a primitive feeling of passion and joy to it that fits perfectly with the fire element. I begin in the southern corner of the circle and again, moving clockwise through the circle, shake my maracas and welcome in the passion of fire. When I am back to the south again, I place them down and move to the west.

The west represents the element of water, which for me is a softer, emotionally nurturing element—so its instrument will have a softer, gentler sound. I have always associated the sound of bells and chimes with water, so I use a Tibetan singing bell, which is a handheld bronze bell that comes with a wooden wand (as opposed to a clapper). For those who have never seen a singing bell before, it works like a singing bowl, only you hold the bell and you rub the wand around the edge of it and the bell's song becomes louder and louder as you continue. Its song will eventually fill the room with a pure sound that is less jarring than if you rang the bell. I walk with the bell slowly as I make it sing along the entire circumference of the circle, and then place it back in the west when I am done. Finally, I move to the north.

The north corner is the home of the element of earth. This is also a nurturing energy, but in a grounding, growing sense. I like to use a drum for the earth that is made with a natural skin head and a carved wooden body. The style of drum you use is not important, but you should feel comfortable walking around with it. Mine is an African djembe that has a somewhat hourglass-shaped body. Any kind of drum works, as long as you feel a kinship with it. Again, beginning in the north corner, and moving clockwise, I drum the entire circle round, coming to a stop in the north again. There, I set the drum down. I am now ready to begin my ritual.

Many people like to use their instruments during the ritual itself. I find this a bit cumbersome unless you are doing a group ritual. In that case, you would have four people chosen to each represent an element, and each step described above would be carried out by its respective person in turn. During the ritual itself, each person may play their instrument when the element is evokes. Whenever my circle meets to do ritual, we have a period of time when we each reflect deeply on what we are grateful for in our lives, what we would like to ask for, and what we have seen come to pass that we had wished for previously. During these times, it is a wonderful thing to have the circlemates playing their instruments softly in support while you are talking about things that often become quite emotional.

After the prayers come the cakes and ale. I like to have everyone play their instruments again during this time, only this time we play more joyfully. One person will begin a rhythm, and each person will add to it until everyone is playing. This freeform music takes on a life of its own and helps to express great joy and happiness.

When I am doing my solitary ritual, I drum a single powerful rhythm at this point in the ritual, starting more slowly but gradually increasing in frequency till I feel I have released my energy properly. I always feel greatly satisfied after this.

If you have other instruments that you are interested in—a guitar, a tuba, you name it—feel free to incorporate them into your own ritual in similar fashion. Even a piano can be used creatively. I have a friend who moves her piano into the center of the circle as the altar table, and then pounds away on it brilliantly near the end of the rite.

As with any ritual circle, when you are ready to close, reverse all your directions to release the circle. Begin by releasing earth, which you called in last. Move counterclockwise, and drum the circle round till you come back to the north, thank the Earth for its energy, and release it.

Moving to the west, releasing water in a counterclockwise motion as well. Follow suit with each of the other elements until you have completed the circle.

The Meaning of Divination

by Robert Place

Most people today associate the tarot with divination. In the Renaissance, however, when the tarot was first created its primary use was for playing a game of cards. Still, there is evidence that it was used for divination from its beginning.

Often the word "divination" is equated with fortunetelling, which means to predict what Fortuna has in store for us. When someone goes to a fortuneteller they are hoping that they will receive good news about their future—so they can sit back and wait for it to happen. To relinquish the responsibility for ones future in this way is fatalistic, and the downside of leaving things to fate is that if the future is bad there is nothing that can be done but wait and dread the event.

However, the word "divination" literally means "to get in touch with the divine." It is derived from the Latin *divinus,* which derived from the word for "god." Its primary concern is not prediction, but conversation with the divine.

Divination was an integral part of classical religion. In the ancient world, it was generally believed that the gods desired to speak with people, and divination was how that communication happened. Techniques for divination included dream interpretation, interpretation of bird flight and other omens, the examination of animal entrails, the declarations of oracles, astrology, and throwing dice or lots. All of the most important decisions involved divination.

The most famous oracle was the one dedicated to Apollo at Delphi, but there were many others—Herodotus writes of six. At the oracle dedicated to

Asclepius, the god of health, the most common question asked was: "How can I cure this illness?" Often the querent was asked to sleep in the temple of the god in the hope that an answer would be delivered in a dream. At the oracle of Zeus in Dodona, archeologists have uncovered lead tablets on which the querents inscribed their questions for the god. The questions are predictable: "Will my wife conceive?" "Is my child legitimate?" "How can I win divine favor?" As you can see, most of these questions do not ask for a prediction of the future, they ask for the help of the god in making decisions.

In popular history, the Greeks are often characterized as fatalistic because of their reliance on the oracles. But the Greeks did not sit back and accept fate, they interacted with the gods in a creative way to change fate. This can be seen in the following famous example.

In 480 BC, the Persian king Xerxes amassed a huge army and invaded Greece. Xerxes's father, Darius, had suffered a humiliating defeat at the hands of the Athenians a few years before. Xerxes' wanted to avenge his father's defeat by destroying Athens, and as Xerxes army was the largest the Greeks had ever seen the Athenians were concerned for their fate. So they sent a messenger to consult the Oracle at Delphi. The Oracle sent back this answer: "Why sit, you doomed one? Fly to the ends of the earth. All is ruin for fire and headlong the god of war shall bring you low."

Such a prediction of doom would send a fatalistic person into despair, but the Athenians held a council to decide what to do. The general Themistocles was sure that there was a way to defeat the Persians, and convinced the Athenians to send a second messenger to Delphi. This time the question was specific: "What can we do to defeat the Persians?" The Oracle's answer was: "Though all else shall be taken, Zeus, the all seeing, grants that the wooden wall shall not fail." Themistocles, even though Persia's navy was larger, interpreted the "wooden wall" as his fleet of ships. Themistocles knew that his smaller, faster triremes were superior in capability. The general convinced the population of Athens to abandon the city to Xerxes' army, and he tricked the Persians into attacking the Athenian fleet in the narrow Strait of Salamis, where the Greek triremes were able to outmaneuver the larger Persian ships, ram them, and sink them. The result was one of the most famous victories in all of History, and the beginning of the Athens' dominant role in the Greek history.

From the classical times to the Renaissance, dice were the most popular tool for both gambling and divination. In the Renaissance, dice began to be replaced with cards, and gambling and divination techniques that were developed for dice became the models for gambling and divination with cards. There is a direct connection between the structure of the tarot deck and the numerical possibilities that emerge from the throws of dice. In games that use three dice, there are fifty-six possible combinations that can be thrown—this is the number of cards in the four minor suits of the tarot. Also in the tarot, the trumps bear numbers from one to twenty-one (the Fool is not a trump but an unnumbered wild card). When we throw two dice, there are twenty-one possible combinations, the same number as the trumps.

Evidence that cards were used for divination in the Renaissance can be found in the Mainz fortunetelling book published in 1487, and in Marcolino's *Le Sorti* published in Venice in 1540. In both of these books, the techniques described only use the cards of the minor suits. The best evidence for the use of the trumps in divination are the poems and accounts of games from the Renaissance that give allegorical meaning to the trumps.

Then, there is the *Triumpho di Fortuna* by the astrologer Fanti. This fortunetelling device was published in Venice in 1527 and is believed to have influenced *Le Sorti.* In Fanti's system, after the querent picks a question he or she is directed to a series of wheels, each with twenty-one divisions. One has the choice of using the hour in which the question was asked, or the throw of two dice, to find the correct answer on the appropriate wheel. The allegorical illustration on the title-page of Fanti's book is with the tarot trumps. Here, we see a large figure of Atlas supporting a globe on his back. Around the globe is a vertical band with the signs of the zodiac on it, and at the central point of the circle formed by this band there is an axle that pierces the globe and extends out to the left and right. On our left, there is an angel representing good fortune, and on our right, there is a devil representing bad fortune. This is one of numerous Renaissance illustrations that demonstrate that Fortuna's wheel was considered to be the wheel of the cosmos and time.

On either side of the wheel in Fanti's illustration sits one of two women, with their names written above their heads. On our left is Virtue and on our right, the same side as the devil, sits Sensuality. In the foreground there is an athletic male nude—possibly Hermes, who was a god of divination—holding a die, and an astrologer, holding calipers and an astronomical devise. In the landscape that dominates the lower portion of the scene there is a river with smaller figures rowing their boats on a journey that leads through an arched gate, past a large tower, and into a celestial city.

This is a similar allegory to the one presented in the tarot's fifth suit. The small figures in the boats are like the Fool in the tarot. They are the ones taking the Fool's journey through the trumps. This journey leads through the Tower card and to the final reward of the celestial city, which is illustrated on the earliest World cards. The first person that the Fool encounters on this journey is a man much like the Magician with his dice on his table. He also meets the astrologer who measures time and fate with the help of the Star, the Moon, and the Sun cards.

The success of this journey involves personal choice. The Fool has to deal with the central problem presented by the Wheel of Fortune. As a role model he can look to the Pope card, which is the highest of the four temporal rulers. The Pope is presented with this choice on the Lovers card. Will he choose the easy path of sensuality and fall to the Devil or choose the three virtues, Justice, Strength, and Temperance, and be able to proceed to the celestial city? His fate is in his hands and for help with his choice he can use divination.

Celtic Love Magic

by Sharynne NicMhacha

All around the world, rites and ceremonies associated with the New Year include the interpretation of omens and divination concerning prosperity in the coming year. This was certainly the case in Celtic countries, where many types of divination were performed at Samhain, the Celtic New Year. One of the most popular types of divination performed was connected with love and romance. Here are some examples of love magic and divination from Scottish, Irish, and Welsh folklore for you to explore and enjoy.

Scotland

Eating the apple at the glass. Just before midnight, cut an apple into nine pieces. Go alone into a room that contains a mirror. Stand with your back to the mirror, and eat eight of the apple slices. Throw the ninth slice over your left shoulder. As you turn your head over your left shoulder you will see the face of your future partner in the glass.

Burning the nuts. Take two hazelnuts and "name" one after yourself and the other after the object of your affection. Place them on a hot ember or log. If the match is ill advised, the nuts will sputter and smoke and one of them will jump away from the other. However, if you are meant to be true lovers, the nuts will burn steadily side by side.

Paring the apple. Pare an apple very carefully so that the skin comes off in one piece (in a long unbroken twisted ribbon). As the clock strikes midnight, swing the paring three times around your head without breaking it, and then fling it over your left shoulder. The shape that the paring creates on the floor may indicate the initial of your future partner. If it breaks, this signifies that you will not marry in the coming year.

The three luggies. Place three small bowls, or *luggies,* in a row on a table. Put clear water in one, dirty water in the second (sometimes soot is used), and leave the third bowl empty. Each person seeking divination is blindfolded and led to the table. Dip your left hand into any of the three dishes. If you choose the clear water, you will marry a "maiden" (or someone pure of heart or intention). The dirty or cloudy water signifies you will marry a widow(er) or unchaste or dishonest person, and the empty one means you will remain single in the upcoming year. The ceremony is repeated three times, rearranging the bowls before each attempt. The bowls may also be placed on the hearth, and the person's selection indicated with a stick or wand.

The salt herring. Just before bed, eat a salted herring in three bites. Afterward, you must not speak, nor drink water. Your future spouse will appear to you in your dreams and offer you water to quench your thirst.

Circling the rick. Walk nine times around a corn rick or haystack. You will be able to catch a glimpse of your future partner behind you.

Willow wand rite. Slip out of the house unobserved, taking with you a wand made of willow. Run three times around the house in a sunwise direction. Then, holding out the wand, say: "She (or he) that is to be my partner, come and grip the end of this wand." You may feel a tug on the end of the wand and see the likeness of your future love.

Knitting the knot. Take a piece of red thread or string, and tie three knots in it. As each knot is made, repeat this rhyme:

I knit this knot, this knot I knit,
to see the sight I ne'er saw yet
My true love in his (or her) best array,
or clad as he (she) is every day;
And if his (her) livery I'm to wear,

and if his (her) bairns I am to bear,
blithe and merry may we be,
And may his (her) face be turned to me.

Ireland

The couple made of holly. Twelve "couples" are created out of two holly twigs tied together with hempen thread. These are named after couples who are present for the divination. The couples are stuck into the ground, and arrayed in a circle. A live coal is placed in the center, and whichever couple catches fire first will be married.

The dream of the stocking. Fill your left sock or stocking with nine ivy leaves, and tie the end with your right sock or garter. Place this under your pillow, and say:

Nine ivy leaves I place under my head,
To dream of the living and not of the dead,
To dream of the one I am going to wed,
And see him (or her) tonight at the foot of my bed.

Clippings in the fire. Placing hair or nail clippings into the last embers of the fire is a powerful charm that will induce a dream of your future husband or wife.

Rite at the crossroads. Before midnight, make your way to a crossroads. Sprinkle flax seed on the pathway. At the stroke of midnight, your future partner will be seen stepping across them.

The name in the ash. Take some ashes from the fire and spread them evenly over the hearthstone. In the morning, footprints and symbolic shapes may be seen in the ashes. These may indicate the first initial of lover's name.

Initials in the water. Take scraps of paper, and mark them with the letters of the alphabet. Float them face downward in a vessel of water. In the morning, most will have sunk. Those pieces which have turned themselves over represent the initial or name of your future spouse.

Wales

Hazel, wheat, and ivy. In Wales, hazelnuts were used in divination rites much as they were in Scotland. Grains of wheat or ivy leaves, named after the parties involved, could be used in the same way as well. A brightly burning nut indicated that the person would be married in the next year. Nuts to be used in love divination were often sold at fairs.

The dream of sacred wood. Take pieces of nine different types of wood and place them in your left stocking. Tie the end with your right stocking, and place it under your pillow. During the night, you will dream of your true love.

The nine-fold cake. Nine women meet together to perform this rite. As a group they create a pancake (or other type of cake), which has nine ingredients in it. The cake is divided equally among the participants. During the night, each person will see their future partner in a dream. This ceremony was performed in Wales as late as 1895.

The glove rite. Leave the house and walk around it nine times. Holding a glove in your hand say: "Here's the glove, where is the hand?" You will then meet the spirit of your true love, who will stretch out their hand in response to your call. It was also sometimes possible to see the image of the person's face.

Mash of nine sorts. Prepare a dish made of these nine ingredients: mashed potatoes, carrots, turnips, peas, leeks, parsnips, pepper, salt, and new milk. Place a wedding ring into the dish. With a spoon, each person takes a bit of the mash. Whoever finds the ring will be the first one married.

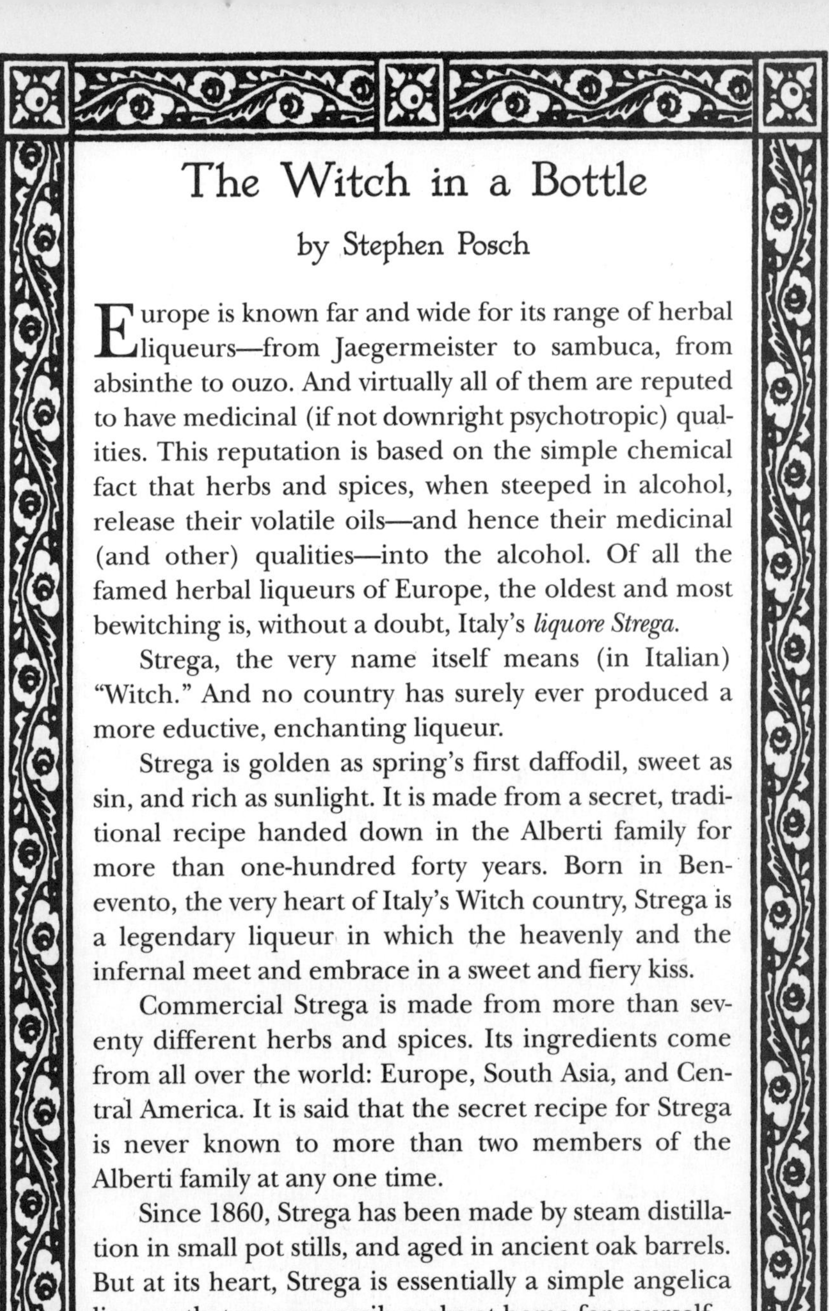

The Witch in a Bottle

by Stephen Posch

Europe is known far and wide for its range of herbal liqueurs—from Jaegermeister to sambuca, from absinthe to ouzo. And virtually all of them are reputed to have medicinal (if not downright psychotropic) qualities. This reputation is based on the simple chemical fact that herbs and spices, when steeped in alcohol, release their volatile oils—and hence their medicinal (and other) qualities—into the alcohol. Of all the famed herbal liqueurs of Europe, the oldest and most bewitching is, without a doubt, Italy's *liquore Strega.*

Strega, the very name itself means (in Italian) "Witch." And no country has surely ever produced a more eductive, enchanting liqueur.

Strega is golden as spring's first daffodil, sweet as sin, and rich as sunlight. It is made from a secret, traditional recipe handed down in the Alberti family for more than one-hundred forty years. Born in Benevento, the very heart of Italy's Witch country, Strega is a legendary liqueur in which the heavenly and the infernal meet and embrace in a sweet and fiery kiss.

Commercial Strega is made from more than seventy different herbs and spices. Its ingredients come from all over the world: Europe, South Asia, and Central America. It is said that the secret recipe for Strega is never known to more than two members of the Alberti family at any one time.

Since 1860, Strega has been made by steam distillation in small pot stills, and aged in ancient oak barrels. But at its heart, Strega is essentially a simple angelica liqueur that you can easily make at home for yourself.

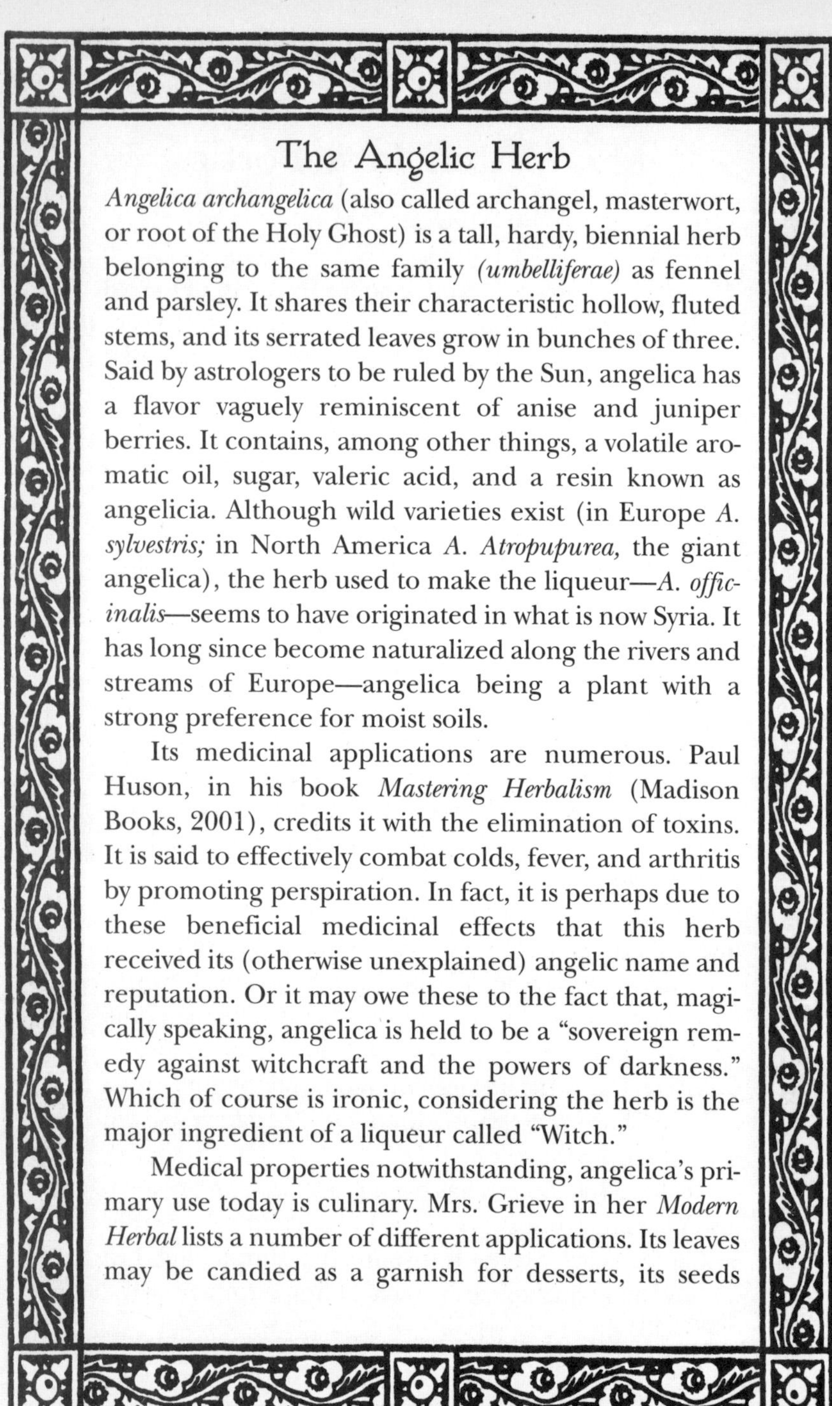

The Angelic Herb

Angelica archangelica (also called archangel, masterwort, or root of the Holy Ghost) is a tall, hardy, biennial herb belonging to the same family *(umbelliferae)* as fennel and parsley. It shares their characteristic hollow, fluted stems, and its serrated leaves grow in bunches of three. Said by astrologers to be ruled by the Sun, angelica has a flavor vaguely reminiscent of anise and juniper berries. It contains, among other things, a volatile aromatic oil, sugar, valeric acid, and a resin known as angelicia. Although wild varieties exist (in Europe *A. sylvestris;* in North America *A. Atropupurea,* the giant angelica), the herb used to make the liqueur—*A. officinalis*—seems to have originated in what is now Syria. It has long since become naturalized along the rivers and streams of Europe—angelica being a plant with a strong preference for moist soils.

Its medicinal applications are numerous. Paul Huson, in his book *Mastering Herbalism* (Madison Books, 2001), credits it with the elimination of toxins. It is said to effectively combat colds, fever, and arthritis by promoting perspiration. In fact, it is perhaps due to these beneficial medicinal effects that this herb received its (otherwise unexplained) angelic name and reputation. Or it may owe these to the fact that, magically speaking, angelica is held to be a "sovereign remedy against witchcraft and the powers of darkness." Which of course is ironic, considering the herb is the major ingredient of a liqueur called "Witch."

Medical properties notwithstanding, angelica's primary use today is culinary. Mrs. Grieve in her *Modern Herbal* lists a number of different applications. Its leaves may be candied as a garnish for desserts, its seeds

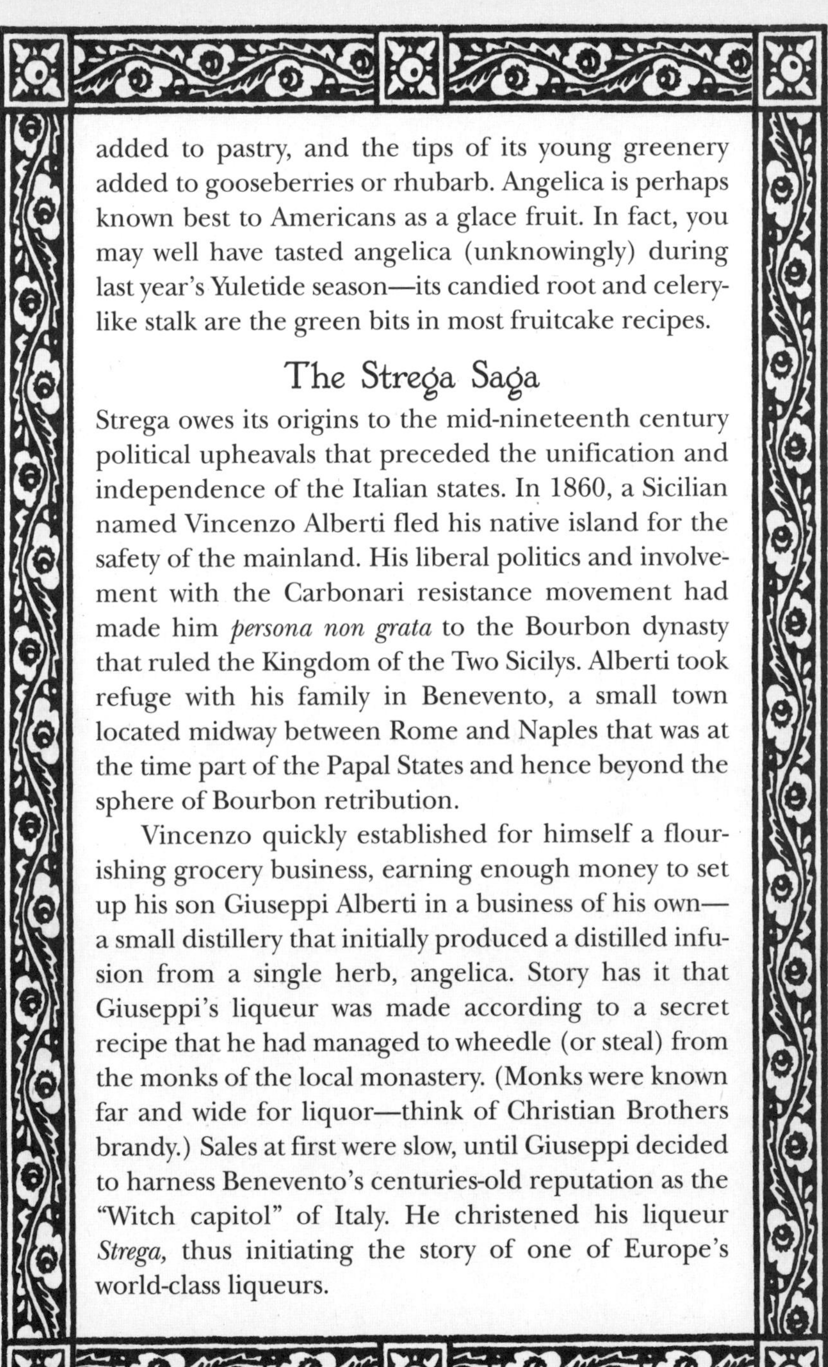

added to pastry, and the tips of its young greenery added to gooseberries or rhubarb. Angelica is perhaps known best to Americans as a glace fruit. In fact, you may well have tasted angelica (unknowingly) during last year's Yuletide season—its candied root and celery-like stalk are the green bits in most fruitcake recipes.

The Strega Saga

Strega owes its origins to the mid-nineteenth century political upheavals that preceded the unification and independence of the Italian states. In 1860, a Sicilian named Vincenzo Alberti fled his native island for the safety of the mainland. His liberal politics and involvement with the Carbonari resistance movement had made him *persona non grata* to the Bourbon dynasty that ruled the Kingdom of the Two Sicilys. Alberti took refuge with his family in Benevento, a small town located midway between Rome and Naples that was at the time part of the Papal States and hence beyond the sphere of Bourbon retribution.

Vincenzo quickly established for himself a flourishing grocery business, earning enough money to set up his son Giuseppi Alberti in a business of his own—a small distillery that initially produced a distilled infusion from a single herb, angelica. Story has it that Giuseppi's liqueur was made according to a secret recipe that he had managed to wheedle (or steal) from the monks of the local monastery. (Monks were known far and wide for liquor—think of Christian Brothers brandy.) Sales at first were slow, until Giuseppi decided to harness Benevento's centuries-old reputation as the "Witch capitol" of Italy. He christened his liqueur *Strega,* thus initiating the story of one of Europe's world-class liqueurs.

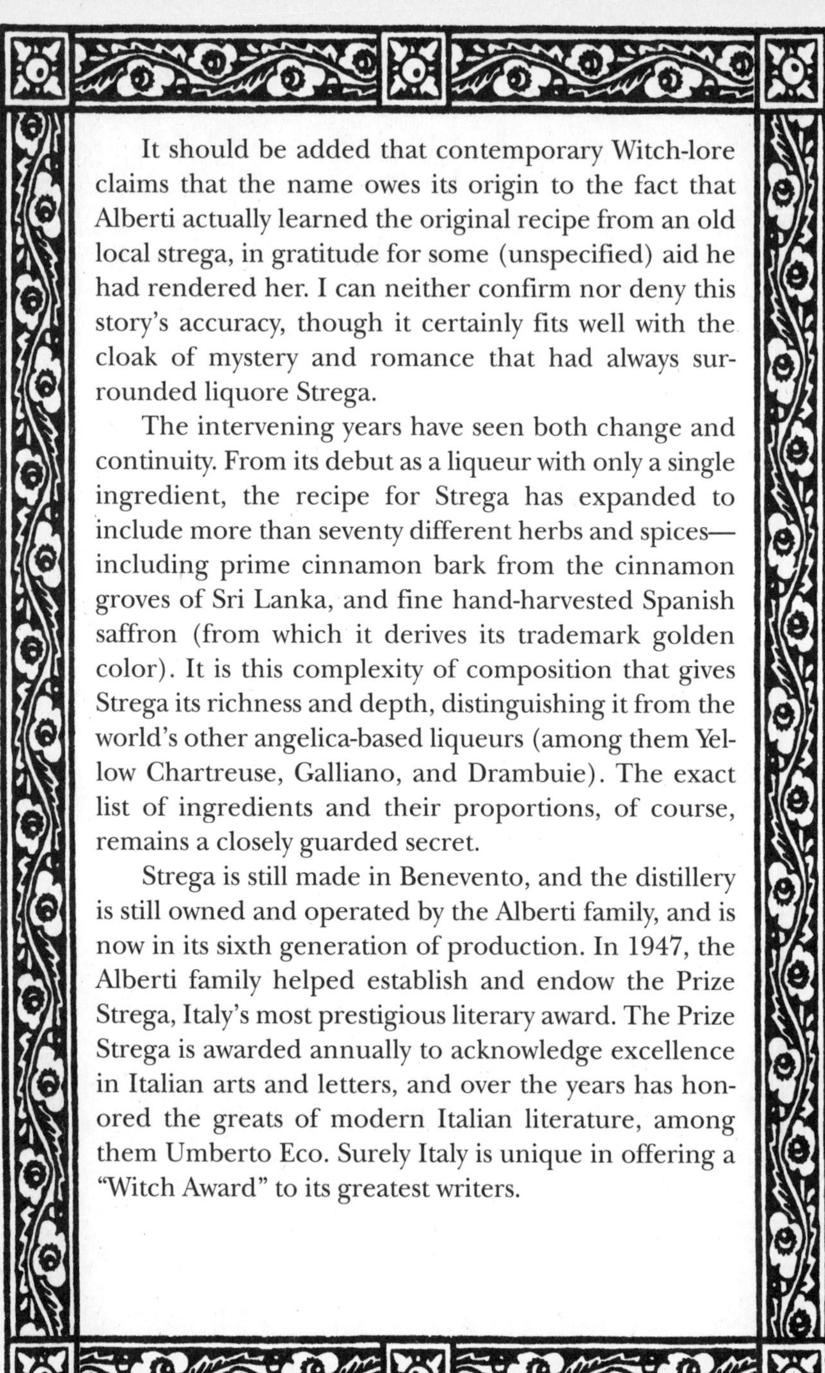

It should be added that contemporary Witch-lore claims that the name owes its origin to the fact that Alberti actually learned the original recipe from an old local strega, in gratitude for some (unspecified) aid he had rendered her. I can neither confirm nor deny this story's accuracy, though it certainly fits well with the cloak of mystery and romance that had always surrounded liquore Strega.

The intervening years have seen both change and continuity. From its debut as a liqueur with only a single ingredient, the recipe for Strega has expanded to include more than seventy different herbs and spices—including prime cinnamon bark from the cinnamon groves of Sri Lanka, and fine hand-harvested Spanish saffron (from which it derives its trademark golden color). It is this complexity of composition that gives Strega its richness and depth, distinguishing it from the world's other angelica-based liqueurs (among them Yellow Chartreuse, Galliano, and Drambuie). The exact list of ingredients and their proportions, of course, remains a closely guarded secret.

Strega is still made in Benevento, and the distillery is still owned and operated by the Alberti family, and is now in its sixth generation of production. In 1947, the Alberti family helped establish and endow the Prize Strega, Italy's most prestigious literary award. The Prize Strega is awarded annually to acknowledge excellence in Italian arts and letters, and over the years has honored the greats of modern Italian literature, among them Umberto Eco. Surely Italy is unique in offering a "Witch Award" to its greatest writers.

Articles for Fall

There'll Be No More Sorrow

by Stephanie Rose Bird

O freedom
O freedom over me
And before I'd be a slave
I'd be buried in my grave
And go home to my Lord
And be free.

–Traditional

To understand African-American attitudes towards grief, mourning, and burial, one must begin in West Africa on the Atlantic Coast. The vast area encompasses a wide variety of peoples—Bakongo, KiKongo, Fang, Djema, Bobangi, Luba, Kimbundu, Umbundu, Ibibio, Efik, Nupe, Beni, Igbo, Yoruba, Ewe, Fon, Popo, Ga, Akan, Ashanti, Fanti, and Bantu. While many of

these tribes are as different in appearance, language, and custom as, say, a Finnish person is to a Greek, many Africans do share a fundamental set of beliefs.

As we consider the striking qualities of African-American ways of dealing with loss and sorrow, it is important to keep in mind the impact that slavery had on Black culture. Africans who were transplanted in the Americas came from well-developed societies. Within this wide group of slavers there were craftsmen, metalsmiths, musicians, teachers, midwives, medicine women and men, warriors, and children of noble birth. For many of these people, being stripped of both their community and their role within society was a fate much worse than death. To the mind of a slave, surely death was better than a half-life as property in an alien culture.

Ibo warriors perhaps made the biggest statement regarding an unwillingness to accept what fate had imposed upon them. When a slave ship filled with Ibo arrived on the coast of Georgia, the entire human cargo, still in chains, walked into the Atlantic ocean and never were seen again. This mass suicide still survives in African-American lore—the warriors are believed to have walked through the waters back home to Mother Africa.

Folklore and songs became a rich source of hope as well as a reservoir for culture. In Negro spirituals, singers became masters of the double entendres. They sang of home—sometimes meaning Africa, but most often meaning the realm of the spirit.

I Want to Go Home

I want to go home,
Dere's no rain to wet you.
O, yes, I want to go home,
There'll be no more sorrow.
Dere's no sun to burn you.
Dere's no hard trials,
Dere's no whips a-crackin',
Dere's no stormy weather,
Dere's no tribulation.
No more slavery in de kingdom.
No evil-doers in the kingdom.
All is gladness in de kingdom.

Animism, the idea that nature is animated with spirits, is a unifying belief among various tribal groups transported to the Americas. In the animistic pantheon, human life in the spirit realm is as active as on Earth. In *The Healing Wisdom of Africa*, author Malidoma Patrice Some speaks about how he, as a Dagara, deals with grief and mourning. A *kontomble* (spirit messenger) that he calls the Green Lady, taught him how to recognize the presence of the ancestors as they exist in nature and in our community. He came to recognize the interdependence of the living on the dead.

The jazz funeral, popular in New Orleans,is a dramatic manifestation of the Dagara grieving concept. At the inception of the ceremony, solemn music sets the tone of the procession. The music encourages reflection, solemnity, and memories. Tears, the water element, run freely. But the ceremony ends on an upbeat note. Hand clapping, dancing, and sometimes singing lend an air of hope to a community united by a joyous, jubilant celebration.

Here is a ritual that marries the Dagara's principle of communal sharing and water with the spirit of a New Orleans jazz. Gather a circle of friends, associates, and family. Chant, clap, and act out the directions.

First half of the group: *Done laid your burden down*
Other half of the group: *Laid your burden down*
(Lay down an offering wrapped in cloth or paper: a photo, favorite food, letter, article of clothing or other memento.)
First half: *Now, go on to the next plane*
Other half: *Don't turn yourself around; don't turn yourself around*
(Grab hands as a group, slowly walk clockwise around the offerings; the leader sets the offerings on fire)
First half: *Light as a feather*
Other half: *That's how things gonna' be*
(Leader lights sage and lavender smudge stick and smudges members of the group)
First half: *Missin' you, lovin' you*
Other half: *So happy that you're free; happy that you're free!*
(Pour cool water, vodka, rum, or gin libation around perimeter of the fire, and then douse the fire with the libation; group leaders bury the remains; everyone leaves)

You may follow this ritual with a bath. Water is gentle, soothing, and cool. Malidoma Patrice Some describes the importance of water and water rituals as a crucial survival mechanism among his people. To begin, take a spirit-cleansing bath in cool water. Fresh or ocean water is best, but a cool indoor bath will work. Before the bath, place gardenia petals or a gardenia plant on a silver or white silk cloth on your bathroom window sill or table. Focus intently on conjuring healing power, and mix a healing soak.

- 2 cups Dead Sea salt
- 2 cups fine sea salt
- 2 cups Epsom salt
- ⅛ cup pulverized orange rinds
- ¼ cup crumbled peppermint
- 2 Tbls. myrrh, sweet orange, and sandalwood essential oils

Begin this magical work on a Friday waning Moon. Mix salts in a large nonreactive bowl, reciting: "Precious gift from the mothers of river and sea." Grind orange rinds in mortar and pestle, food processor, or clean coffee grinder, saying: "Uplift my spirits with your blessed fruit." Add this to the salts, and mix well. Stir in crumbled peppermint, saying: "In honor of Yemoya-Oshun, please hear my plea." In a small separate bowl blend the three essential oils, then pour them over the salt mixture. Mix well, and add to a screw top container. Shake all ingredients gently, to mix well, for three days. Scoop out two cups per bath.

Take the spiritual wash on a Friday waning moon evening. Burn soothing incense in a sea shell over a hot charcoal. Release your grief, sorrow, despair, or whatever you are feeling into the water and into the smoke. As you watch the tub drain when you are finished, visualize your anguish or sorrow leaving along with the water.

Money Magic

by Ellen Dugan

In truth, prosperity tries the souls even of the wise.
–Sallust 86–34 BC

What do you suppose are the most popular items at metaphysical and magic shops?

As I strolled through my friend's shop the other day, she and her husband were busily taking inventory. I picked up a few sticks of incense and then stopped to admire a brand new display of dried magical herbs. "I could use a fresher supply of vervain for my spells," I thought to myself, as I examined the packaged herbs.

While I made my selection, I could hear them talking about trouble they were having keeping certain items in stock. I tucked the vervain into my basket, alongside my favorite incense, and went to check out.

"So, what's the big seller?" I asked them at the register.

According to my buddy Mickie, it's actually the little green candles and money-drawing incense. "I can't keep them in stock." Mickie confided to me as she moved behind the counter to ring up my purchase.

"You're kidding. It sells that fast?" I asked her.

Her reply was somewhere between a sigh and a groan. She plopped down into a high-backed stool and pushed her dark curly hair out of her face. "Just shows you where most people's priorities lie."

Well, that comment sent the little wheels in my brain to spinning. She seemed to read my mind: "You should write an article about money magic."

I stood there and mulled it over for a moment. Then with a grin, I took my purchases and started for the door. "Yeah . . . I should."

Money magic or prosperity magic is among the more popular forms of spells and charms. There are books devoted to the subject of prosperity spells, and there are tons of magical candles, incense, and paraphernalia just begging to be purchased. However before you run out and snap up every huge, green jar-candle with "Prosperity" and "Money" plastered on it, consider a more practical and natural magic approach to working with money magic.

Natural Money Magic Items

Money magic or prosperity work aligns itself to the element of earth. Therefore, the color green, various crystals, and plants all are in sympathy with spells designed to draw money. And there are many common plants, herbs, and crystals that are harmonious to the prosperity energy that you are attempting to draw into your life. Some of these items you may have to purchase, but the others may well be in your kitchen cupboard or growing happily in the backyard.

For crystals, try using inexpensive tumbling stones. Here are a few easy to find crystals that are utilized in prosperity work: clear quartz, aventurine, tiger's-eye, malachite, and turquoise.

Work with these homegrown herbs and plants for prosperity: cinquefoil, mint of all varieties, bergamot, chamomile, dill, and fern varieties.

Checking your spice rack? Then look for these culinary herbs that double as magical money-drawing spices: basil, cloves, cinnamon, dill, ginger, and nutmeg.

If you do not grow your own herbs, then use the magical kitchen spices listed above, or work in a little dried vervain. The herb vervain is traditionally used in money-drawing and prosperity spells. It also helps to "speed the spell on its way," which is why I like to keep a fresh supply on hand.

Also, don't forget to check out the foliage of the trees and shrubs growing in your yard: cedar and pine needles, maple and oak leaves. Work with the blooms and foliage of the honeysuckle bush. Watch for acorns that have fallen to the ground. The acorn, a symbol of fertility, prosperity, and the God, is a great magical accessory to have on hand. Please remember that as you go to gather any foliage or blooms from a living tree, do so gently and take only one or two samples. Be sure and thank the tree when you are finished.

Money Magic 101

When it comes to casting your prosperity spells, intent is everything. However, if you want to hedge your bets, so to speak, then try working for prosperity during a waxing or Full Moon. The most popular day of the week for money spells is Thursday, a Jupiter day. This day has the correspondences of prosperity and wealth. You could also work for abundance and success on a Sunday, the Sun's day.

As for candle magic, you can either work with the affordable spell candles that most magic shops carry or pick up some inexpensive pine-scented, green votives next time you're out shopping. If you happen to like those big seven-day glass-jar candles, then by all means, knock yourself out. Go with what works for you.

If you would like to burn a money-drawing incense, and you discover that the "prosperity" incense is sold out, then either substitute with a pine or cinnamon incense. Both of these bewitching fragrances will encourage prosperity.

The colors to employ in your money spells are green, gold, and silver. These colors can be represented

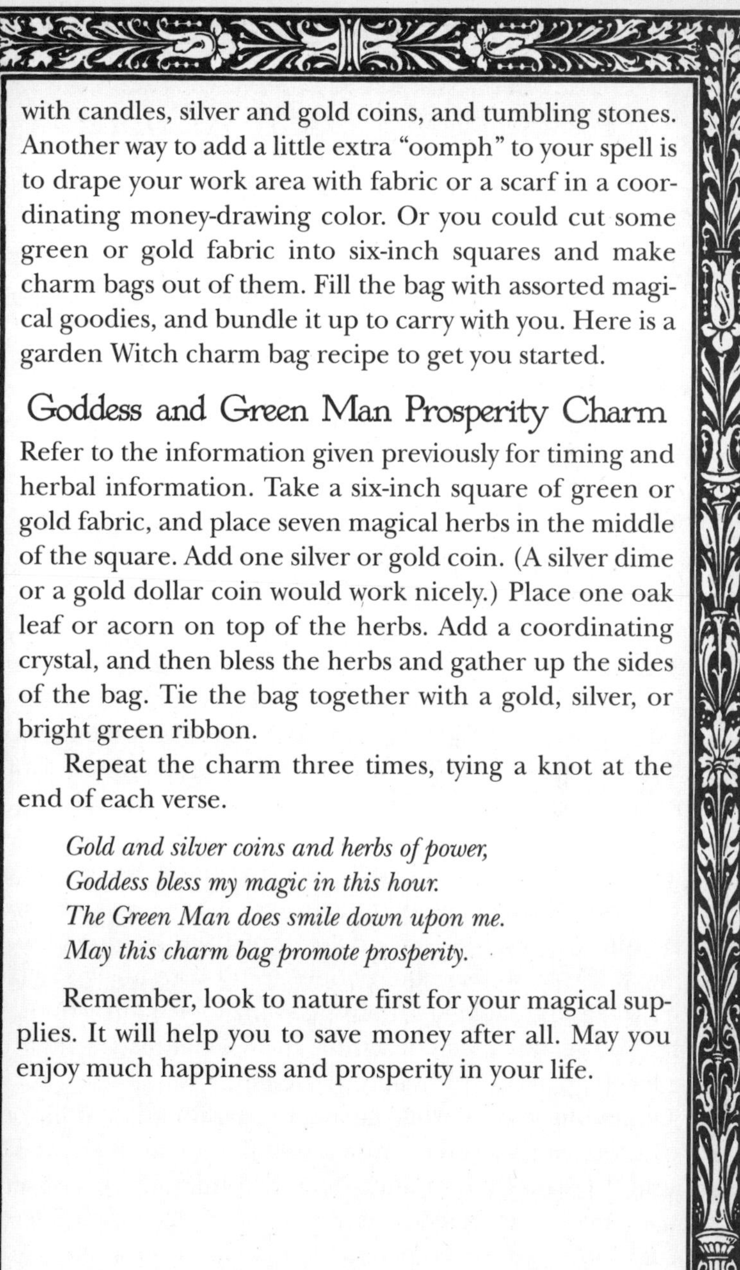

with candles, silver and gold coins, and tumbling stones. Another way to add a little extra "oomph" to your spell is to drape your work area with fabric or a scarf in a coordinating money-drawing color. Or you could cut some green or gold fabric into six-inch squares and make charm bags out of them. Fill the bag with assorted magical goodies, and bundle it up to carry with you. Here is a garden Witch charm bag recipe to get you started.

Goddess and Green Man Prosperity Charm

Refer to the information given previously for timing and herbal information. Take a six-inch square of green or gold fabric, and place seven magical herbs in the middle of the square. Add one silver or gold coin. (A silver dime or a gold dollar coin would work nicely.) Place one oak leaf or acorn on top of the herbs. Add a coordinating crystal, and then bless the herbs and gather up the sides of the bag. Tie the bag together with a gold, silver, or bright green ribbon.

Repeat the charm three times, tying a knot at the end of each verse.

Gold and silver coins and herbs of power,
Goddess bless my magic in this hour.
The Green Man does smile down upon me.
May this charm bag promote prosperity.

Remember, look to nature first for your magical supplies. It will help you to save money after all. May you enjoy much happiness and prosperity in your life.

Researching Local Folklore

by Breid Foxsong

Do you dream of Avalon or Tibet? Wish there was a circle of standing stones within driving range? Yearn for natural wonders that will resonate with your spirit and bring you closer to the Gods? And you can't afford the plane ticket to England, Mexico, or even Salem?

Well, try looking closer to home. There are thousands of sites that quietly murmur their faith all over the world. These are small sites, yes, but still powerful enough to resonate for many. And the chances are very good that one of them is near you.

How do you go about finding out if there is a sacred site near you? Obviously, the first place to check is the local library or historical society. See if there are any books out about the history of the town you live in, or about your region's folklore or a collection of ghost stories. Why ghost stories? Because often the energy of a site is manifested in ways that people don't understand. Most popular sacred sites are best known for the mystery that surrounds them. Such sites exhibit strong energy pools and weakened walls between the real and the unreal (or the mundane and the fairy, if you prefer), and people aren't sure how to react to these. You aren't looking for any gee-whiz tourist attractions, but rather you seek the quiet retreats, the special places, that long time locals go to for spiritual refreshment.

One thing to avoid while talking to your librarian or historian is the underlying reason for your quest. Keep your objective fairly general, lest you be misunderstood. You might be dismissed as strange, or else suspected of aiming to desecrate or commercialize such place. After all, people have defaced churches, tombstones and statues, and even the rocks of Stonehenge, the walls of the Grand Canyon, and the arch of the Rainbow Bridge. No one is likely to share a sacred spot with someone that will tear the veils of sanctity from it. Explain that you are looking for "hidden treasures of the local landscape," or places you can go "to escape the regular world."

You can also seek out regional sacred sites in the back files of the local newspaper. If you are blessed with computer access, try your town or county's name along with the terms "sacred," "ancient," "mysterious," or "spooky." Other key words you might add in a secondary search are: "hiking trail," "adventure," "experience," or "wonder." You will end up weeding through a lot of silly stories about Halloween costume parties and picnic sites, but even one reference can start you out on the right track toward your own local sites.

While you are researching the last fifty or sixty years of stories, you should also be looking at what was going on one-hundred or more years ago. That is, was there a local tribe of natives? Where did they live? Were they a fixed or transient tribe? It is very important to remember that people like the Navaho and the Sioux are worlds apart when it comes to styles and types of sacred practices. In European terms, it would be like comparing the Egyptians and the Norse. Knowing more about them will help you to understand what sorts of places they might have considered sacred in your region. Also look at some of the established religious sites in your area. Buddhist temples and other mainstream churches can be very peaceful and powerful. Of course, use courtesy when borrowing someone else's site.

You also need to look for information on the local terrain. Most sacred sites center around a mixture of two or more elements. For example, Stonehenge is in the middle of an open plain, and the site combines the elements of air and earth. The Grand Canyon and Niagara Falls, are earth and water sites. Sacred sites very often involve a spring. This makes sense logically, as water was a resource to be treasured and a spring that didn't dry up in the summer was a gift from the gods. One of my local sacred sites is a combination of three elements. A small natural gas vent sits behind a tiny waterfall. When lit, the flame behind the water is a wonderful and very natural miracle. I check it regularly, as do many others, to maintain that sacred flame. As part of that respect, I also make sure that I do not intrude on others who are visiting the site, no matter how secular their reasons (its a great picnic location as well).

If you don't find any information on sacred sites right away, keep looking. If you are really having trouble, you might try dowsing out a power spot. This can be done with a pendulum and a good map of the area. I find it easiest to use a topographical map, simply because I can eliminate the unworkable areas. It will do you no good to find a wonderful site if its in the parking lot of a local Walmart.

There are a number of books out on pendulums and how to use them. Once you have your pendulum, orient your map toward the north and cover it with a transparent sheet that you have divided into one-inch squares. (If the map is too large, fold it to fit—so that you are only working in a small area at a time). Hold a marker (to mark the pendulum's reactions) in one hand and the pendulum in the other. Start with the first column of squares. Keep your question firmly in mind. It should be as specific as possible, such as: "Is there a sacred site that I can easily and safely use in this column?" Start your pendulum moving from the twelve o'clock position to the six o'clock. Once the pendulum is moving, stop the force of movement and let the pendulum take over. If it slows to a stop, the answer is negative.

Move to the next column and repeat. If the pendulum changes direction, mark that column and move on. There may be more than one suitable site on your map. Once you have done all the vertical columns, turn the map sideways and repeat, going down the horizontal columns. The point where the two columns meet is where you will find your sacred spot. Continue until you have done the whole map of the area you are looking in. To pinpoint the area further, enlarge the section on a photocopier and repeat the procedure. Of course, the final test is to go out there in person and really feel the energy, but this will narrow down the number of places you have to visit to find the right one.

By combining all these techniques, you will find a sacred spot much closer to home.

The Epona Goddess Myth

by Kristin Madden

Worship of the horse goddess Epona extended from the British Isles through Europe and into Rome. Statues and inscriptions to the Great Mare have been found across this area. While she is most commonly regarded as a goddess of Gaul, carvings of a similar figure on Pictish stones lead some to believe that her worship predates the Celts in the British Isles.

In many of the portrayals, Epona is a woman sitting on or surrounded by horses. Her followers believed she would appear to them in the form of a beautiful white horse that was not of this world. Her legacy remains today—in our modern word "pony." The Great Mare was often seen as a Great Mother Goddess. As the Mother, she was depicted feeding foals from corn in her lap.

Sometimes she was shown with a sucking foal. As a mother goddess, she was also associated with fertility.

The Greek writer Agesilaos described Epona as the daughter of a man and a mare. She grew up to become the goddess of horses. Later, as goddess of the Gaulish Celts, the Roman cavalry adopted her as their patroness and carried her worship all the way to Rome. The Celts were quite skilled in horsemanship and actively recruited by the Romans. It is believed that they had a major role in spreading her worship. At one time, images of her were found in nearly all stables in the Roman empire. Niches containing small statues of Epona and decorated with roses were found in the walls of barns and stables. Her feast day among the Romans was celebrated on December 18. All horses, mules, and asses were allowed to rest on this day.

Epona's association with kingship was obvious in Rome, as she was invoked on behalf of the Emperor. In the Celtic lands, her connection to sovereignty was a more personal affair. Certain kingship rituals required the would-be king to mate with a mare, usually a white one. That mare would be sacrificed and the king either bathed in or drank a broth made from the mare's body.

Sovereignty equally applies to the individual. Just as the true king aligns himself with the land and its people through his symbolic marriage with the goddess, so do we align ourselves with our own truths and our world through establishing connections with the land and its spirits. Epona, as a goddess of the land, is called upon by many modern Pagans in their search for self-knowledge and integrity.

Epona was frequently portrayed carrying keys or one large key. Many believe this indicates her ability to open the gates to the otherworld where she guided the souls of the departed. Because hobbyhorses are also a folk custom at Samhain, this leads many to understand the Great Mare as a guide and guardian to the human soul. At Beltane, she brings fertility and guides the souls into this world. At Samhain, she gathers and leads them beyond this life into the afterlife.

Epona remains a popular goddess. Her name is invoked in Pagan rituals even today.

Wind Magic

by James Kambos

Long ago, before the footsteps of human or beast were heard on Earth, there was the wind. And it was magic. It whistled over the hills and sang as it soared above the mountain peaks. So great was its strength it even penetrated the dark virgin forests, whispering its secrets to the majestic trees.

When our earliest ancestors first encountered the wind, they were in awe of its great invisible power. After all, it had chiseled great masses of stone, creating canyons and other unique rock formations in all parts of the world. In the deserts, the winds created the eerie beauty of constantly shifting sand dunes. And in the snowy regions, wind pushed the snows into mounds of icy crystals.

Air and wind give our planet life. The ancients, thus drawn to the invisible energy of the wind, made it part of early folk magic. Sailors of the Aegean Sea believed the wind power could be captured by tying knots in their ship's sails. When a gust of wind was needed, the knot was untied, releasing a breeze, which allowed the ship to move on. Such early magical beliefs prefigured the use of wind magic in much folk magic tradition.

The Four Winds

Understanding the four winds lays the groundwork for performing wind magic. Each wind corresponds to each of the four directions, or quarters, or our Earth. These are, the north, south, east, and west winds. In different parts of the world, the wind patterns vary, so you must adjust this to your magical needs. The following list gives the attributes of each wind according to the weather conditions of North America and Europe. Remember also, when we speak of a prevailing wind, this means the direction from which the wind is coming. That is, the east wind is the wind blowing from the east, not toward it.

The North Wind

In magic, the north wind is the wind of the mysteries, for it comes from the darkness of the north. Use it in spells when you wish to banish a bad habit, destroy a disease, or rid your life of any negativity. It is a cold and barren wind. Its season is winter; its colors are black, or the deepest navy blue. Its element is earth, and its hour is midnight.

The South Wind

This is the hottest of the four winds. Use it in spells where you need a sudden burst of energy or change. But be careful, the south wind can bring you more than you've asked for. It is a hot, dry wind associated with summer. Its colors are brilliant white, yellow, and orange. Fire is its element, and noon is its time of day.

The East Wind

The East wind comes from the direction of the sunrise and moonrise. The east wind is the wind of renewal. Use the east wind in spells where you need a fresh start—a new job, career change, new home, and so on. It is a warm fresh wind; its season is spring. It belongs to the element air. Crimson and warm pinks are its colors, and dawn is its time of day.

The West Wind

Cool and moist best describes the west wind. It is the wind to use if you are casting a love or fertility spell. Its element is water, and its colors include green, blue, and misty gray. Autumn is its season. The west rules the hours of twilight, so it is a potent wind for spirit contact or seeing into the future.

Working Wind Magic

Before calling on the winds in your magical work, you must prepare yourself. Wind magic is simple, but most of us have

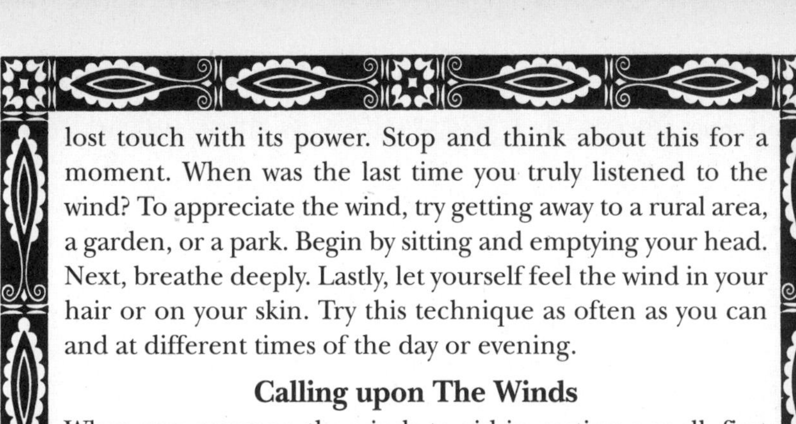

lost touch with its power. Stop and think about this for a moment. When was the last time you truly listened to the wind? To appreciate the wind, try getting away to a rural area, a garden, or a park. Begin by sitting and emptying your head. Next, breathe deeply. Lastly, let yourself feel the wind in your hair or on your skin. Try this technique as often as you can and at different times of the day or evening.

Calling upon The Winds

When you summon the winds to aid in casting a spell, first clear your mind. Focus on your one desire. Write this wish down on a piece of virgin white paper

Cast your circle, outdoors if possible, and begin by facing north. Ask the winds for their help, speaking words of power, such as:

North wind, wind of mystery, clear away any negativity that would prevent my desire from coming to me. Thank you.

Turn east and say:

East wind, the wind of renewal, bring this change into my life, with harm to none. Thank you.

Face south and say:

South wind, I ask you to melt away any obstacles that would hinder my desire, with harm to none. Thank you.

And last, facing west, saying:

West wind, the wind of emotions, fuel my desire. Bring my wish to me, here and now, with harm to none. It must be. Thank you.

Burn your wish paper, and sprinkle the ashes in a circle, starting at the north and moving clockwise. Thank the winds, and release your circle. Let the winds carry your wish to the divine. You can ask the winds to assist in almost any type of magic. Remember to ask politely when seeking the wind's help. Never be demanding. The four winds are ancient and powerful.

The Sacred Quest for Knowledge

by Raven Kaldera and Tannin Schwartzstein

The door of the underground tunnel looms dark and mysterious at the feet of the brave questers. They wonder if they will be up to the challenge, for in the labyrinth below lies a challenge that will tax their wit, their perseverance, and their mettle. They seek the Key of Knowledge, a talisman that will give them insight into their faith and unlock the door to their spiritual heritage. They remember the words of the old wizard who warned them about the dangers they might encounter . . .

The quester's tale has been told and retold many times over the ages. These days, the modern Neopagan pursuit of knowledge about the lost roots of their faith rivals that of mythical adventurers. It may seem more exciting and romantic to search for swords and magical items, but the modern research-adventurer's quest can be just as fulfilling.

The first question that most Pagans have, of course, is: Why should I bother? What's the point of doing all that historical research? After all, a Pagan's faith is found in the natural world—the earth, stones, wind, ocean, and the music of the body.

Yes. We fully agree that the deepest spiritual experiences are ones that happen without books or other lore. It is quite valid to build your religious faith and tradition on your own feelings and intuition—as long as you are clear and open about the fact that this is what you are doing. If you're basing your devotional work on your personal interpretation of a handful of historical images, however, you must be aware that you're not practicing the ancient religion of the Celts or the Norse or the Saxons. It may have some relationship to the ancient religion, but it does not match their actual practices.

We are of the opinion that this does not make any spiritual practice less valid. There are a lot of things that our ancestors did that aren't appropriate now. As twenty-first-century people, we should all be practicing twenty-first-century religion. Magic that you make up on the spot can work just as well as five-hundred-year-old spells. However, we as Pagans need to be clear about what we are doing. If we pretend that what we're doing looks like what our foremothers were doing, it is possible that anyone reasonably literate who can read and do research can find out otherwise. If this happens, we look deluded or dishonest in the end. It is in our best interest to be forthcoming, and to do this we have to agree that historicity does not legitimate spirituality.

The Priest and the Warrior

So why bother with the research? There are a variety of reasons. First, it is inspiring. You can find things in the ancient practices that can deepen your experience of spirituality and magic. Recreating ancient practices is a way to get in touch with humanity's ancestors; it's a way to time travel, and get just an inkling of how they might have thought and felt. This is a noble pursuit, but it takes a lot of work. It's awfully tempting to pick up one or two small practices from the past and then presume to know "what they were feeling." But this is arrogant folly. We can't absolutely know an ancient person's mindset—though we can make an educated guess.

That's the priest's reason for research. The warrior's reason is a little different. The warrior wants to be able to defend the faith against all enemies and detractors. However, a defender of their faith should not go into battle armed only with fallacies or assumptions. That is, always be armed with knowledge and truth.

And lastly, do it because you can. Most of your ancestors could not read, and had limited access to information. Our modern ability to acquire huge amounts of such is a privilege. We should do it, if only to do our ancestors proud.

Snares and Fiends

Of course, there are pitfalls on every quest. The earnest quester, if he or she is not careful and critical, can be duped.

The first trap is the snare of generalization. Be careful to avoid a conclusion based on one or two facts or ideas. For example, Vikings are often shown with horned helmets, even though all historical research has proved that their helmets were quite plain and round, and the horned helmets were used only for ceremonial occasions. Don't assume that one small discovery defines an entire idea or concept.

In general, don't be fooled, check multiple sources. There is no book in existence that will make your eyeballs melt if you read it, or that will change your opinions against your will. Some people become reluctant to read something that has opposing views to their own. While it is true that any book may turn out to waste your time, you may learn by reading opposing viewpoints. Similarly, avoid falling into the trap of assuming just because you do not like a person that his or her findings are invalid.

When your subject combines fields of research, go to the trouble of checking out each field separately. For instance, if you're examining feminist Celtic spirituality, also check out Celtic studies and women's studies as well. When an author refers to someone else's work, try to discern whether they are merely summarizing it, or giving their opinion on it.

Maps to the Mysteries

Now that you know how to proceed, where can you begin to seek out historical truths? A few suggestions follow.

Look at bibliographies in the back of books, and check those sources, and the sources' sources. Any work may have something interesting to say—and even may affect the context of the information.

Look at periodicals. Try the Wilson Index on the Humanities and other subject indexes to find relevant journal articles. Scholarly journals will give you detailed information on specific topics. Do be aware of the dates on the articles, though; old is not necessarily better in historical studies. Research from decades ago may be outdated or have archaic biases.

Many libraries provide electronic databases that allow one to search through decades of scholarly journals and reviews of out-of-print or rare books. These reviews can help give you an idea as to the credibility of a given book, although it must be admitted that academic writing is full of backbiting and competition.

Correspond with experts on your topic. Don't be afraid to ask scholars for their credentials, and also to ask others in the field about who is and isn't an expert. The more information you have, the better.

Talk to the research librarian in the closest large city library. They're skilled at mentoring people on information searches—it's their job, after all. They can often help you find the specifics that you want.

The Internet can be a good source of information, or it can be as inaccurate as a bathroom wall. It tends to be overflowing with both good and very error-ridden scholarship, often existing within inches of each other. Many personal websites, too, are cannibalized from other websites via cut-and-paste. That is, just because ten websites say the same thing doesn't make it valid.

When you're actually writing about your beliefs and you want to establish that a practice or piece of lore has historical content, do the documentation. If you're making a leap of speculation, go ahead and admit it. When appropriate, it's all right to say something like: "We don't know if this is anything like what people did back then, but it's what works for us now." You can also claim that your work is "inspired" by historical information, but does not attempt to reproduce it.

As the questers pursue their search down into the furthest reaches of the dungeon, they remember the words told to them by the wise wizard: "When you have found the key of knowledge, my children, your journey will just have begun!"

As they enter the hall, having braved the guards and escaped the traps set for them, a great dragon rears up before them. Acknowledging their victory, the dragon bows deeply before them, and drops at their feet the Key of Knowledge . . . a library card.

The Magical Lore of the Celtic Harp

by Roslyn Reid

Art was a big part of ancient Celtic society, and there are many legends about the enchantment of music. Druids used music to open the day, and to put it to bed, and bards kept "perpetual choirs of song" to pass along the oral histories of their clans. The ancient Celts made instruments from animal hide and bones (drums), wood (whistles), metal (bells), and anything else that could produce a sound pleasing to them and the gods.

Of all the instruments used by the ancient Celts, none seems to hold more fascination for us than the harp. Somewhere around the seventh century AD, triangular-framed harps began appearing in Scotland and Ireland. A hundred years later, Diodorus Siculus mentioned the Celtic harp when he wrote about the Druids: "They have poets who they call bards, who sing songs of eulogy and satire, accompanying themselves on an instrument very like the lyre." In fact, even King Arthur had a harp that was mentioned by Ross Nichols as one of the ancient Celts' "thirty-seven remarkable sights."

Why is this instrument so intriguing to so many people? Well, the instrument has long been loved for its beauty of form, as well as for its sound. In his song, "The Harp of Cnoc I Chosgair," written in 1385, the well-known Irish bard Gofraidh Fionn O'Dalaigh sang: "Excellent instrument with the smooth gentle curve, trilling under red fingers. Musician that has charmed us, red, lion-like, of full melody."

In old days, strings were typically made of animal gut. Instrument makers tended to use whatever was cheap or plentiful. Metal and nylon strings replaced gut as soon as they became viable alternatives. The type of wood used in a harp was important to how it sounded. Spruce was the standard for the soundboard of most stringed instruments. Preferably the wood for this component of the harp came from trees grown in the north country, because their grain was especially tight.

The most magical aspect of the harp was likely its decoration. The wood was customarily dyed with magical colors. Many Celtic harps had some kind of figurehead carved on to them. Birds were popular to help the harp "sing," but women's heads were another widely used motif. This tradition seems to have come down from the ancient Greeks, who carved their harps with the likenesses of the female death spirits known as harpies. The name translates to "pluckers," as in plucking souls from the earth like one would pluck harp strings.

Harps were found in Celtic legends. Dagda, the god who turned the wheel of the year, brought the change of the seasons by playing his harp. Celts were particularly fond of these in-between spaces, or "a time out of time, a world between the worlds." And Dagda and his harp were at home in every world.

In the end, rationality and construction may not have much to do with the mysterious magic of the harp. Most of the Celtic harp's magic seems to come from the performer. Still played today, the Celtic harp is one of the most popular components of Celtic Pagan music. If you are in search of authentic Celtic harp music, I suggest you look into the recordings produced by the record company Maggie's Music (you can find them on the web at www.maggiesmusic.com).

Several Celtic harpers record for this label, performing the works of early Celtic bards. Listen to this music and see what conclusion you come to about the roots of this fabulous instrument's magic.

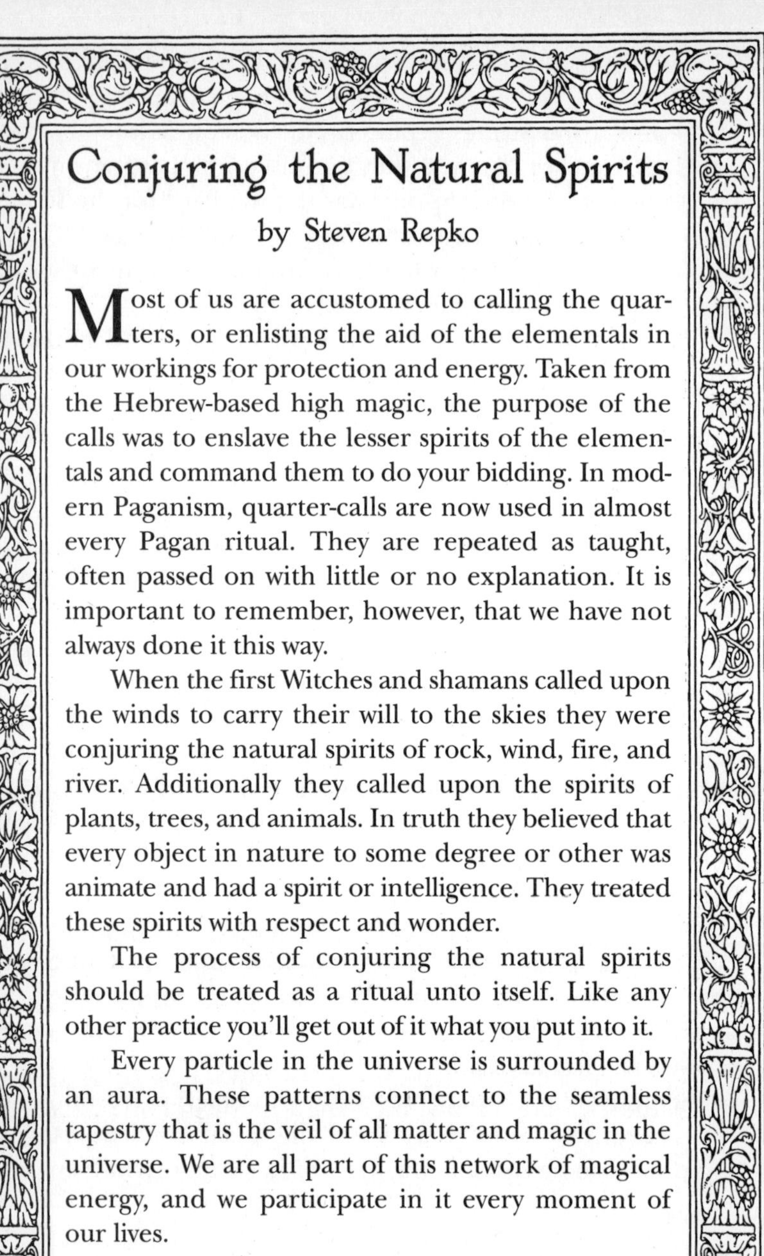

Conjuring the Natural Spirits

by Steven Repko

Most of us are accustomed to calling the quarters, or enlisting the aid of the elementals in our workings for protection and energy. Taken from the Hebrew-based high magic, the purpose of the calls was to enslave the lesser spirits of the elementals and command them to do your bidding. In modern Paganism, quarter-calls are now used in almost every Pagan ritual. They are repeated as taught, often passed on with little or no explanation. It is important to remember, however, that we have not always done it this way.

When the first Witches and shamans called upon the winds to carry their will to the skies they were conjuring the natural spirits of rock, wind, fire, and river. Additionally they called upon the spirits of plants, trees, and animals. In truth they believed that every object in nature to some degree or other was animate and had a spirit or intelligence. They treated these spirits with respect and wonder.

The process of conjuring the natural spirits should be treated as a ritual unto itself. Like any other practice you'll get out of it what you put into it.

Every particle in the universe is surrounded by an aura. These patterns connect to the seamless tapestry that is the veil of all matter and magic in the universe. We are all part of this network of magical energy, and we participate in it every moment of our lives.

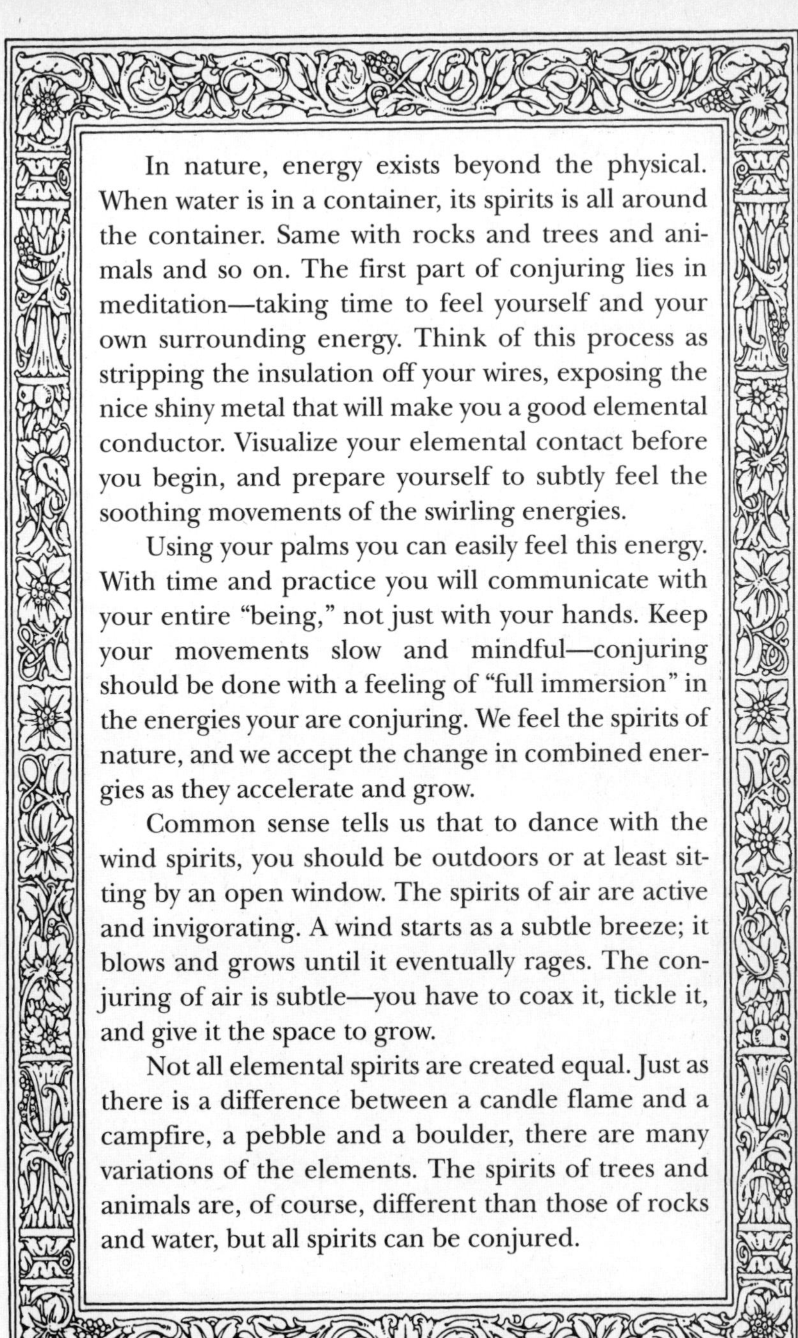

In nature, energy exists beyond the physical. When water is in a container, its spirits is all around the container. Same with rocks and trees and animals and so on. The first part of conjuring lies in meditation—taking time to feel yourself and your own surrounding energy. Think of this process as stripping the insulation off your wires, exposing the nice shiny metal that will make you a good elemental conductor. Visualize your elemental contact before you begin, and prepare yourself to subtly feel the soothing movements of the swirling energies.

Using your palms you can easily feel this energy. With time and practice you will communicate with your entire "being," not just with your hands. Keep your movements slow and mindful—conjuring should be done with a feeling of "full immersion" in the energies your are conjuring. We feel the spirits of nature, and we accept the change in combined energies as they accelerate and grow.

Common sense tells us that to dance with the wind spirits, you should be outdoors or at least sitting by an open window. The spirits of air are active and invigorating. A wind starts as a subtle breeze; it blows and grows until it eventually rages. The conjuring of air is subtle—you have to coax it, tickle it, and give it the space to grow.

Not all elemental spirits are created equal. Just as there is a difference between a candle flame and a campfire, a pebble and a boulder, there are many variations of the elements. The spirits of trees and animals are, of course, different than those of rocks and water, but all spirits can be conjured.

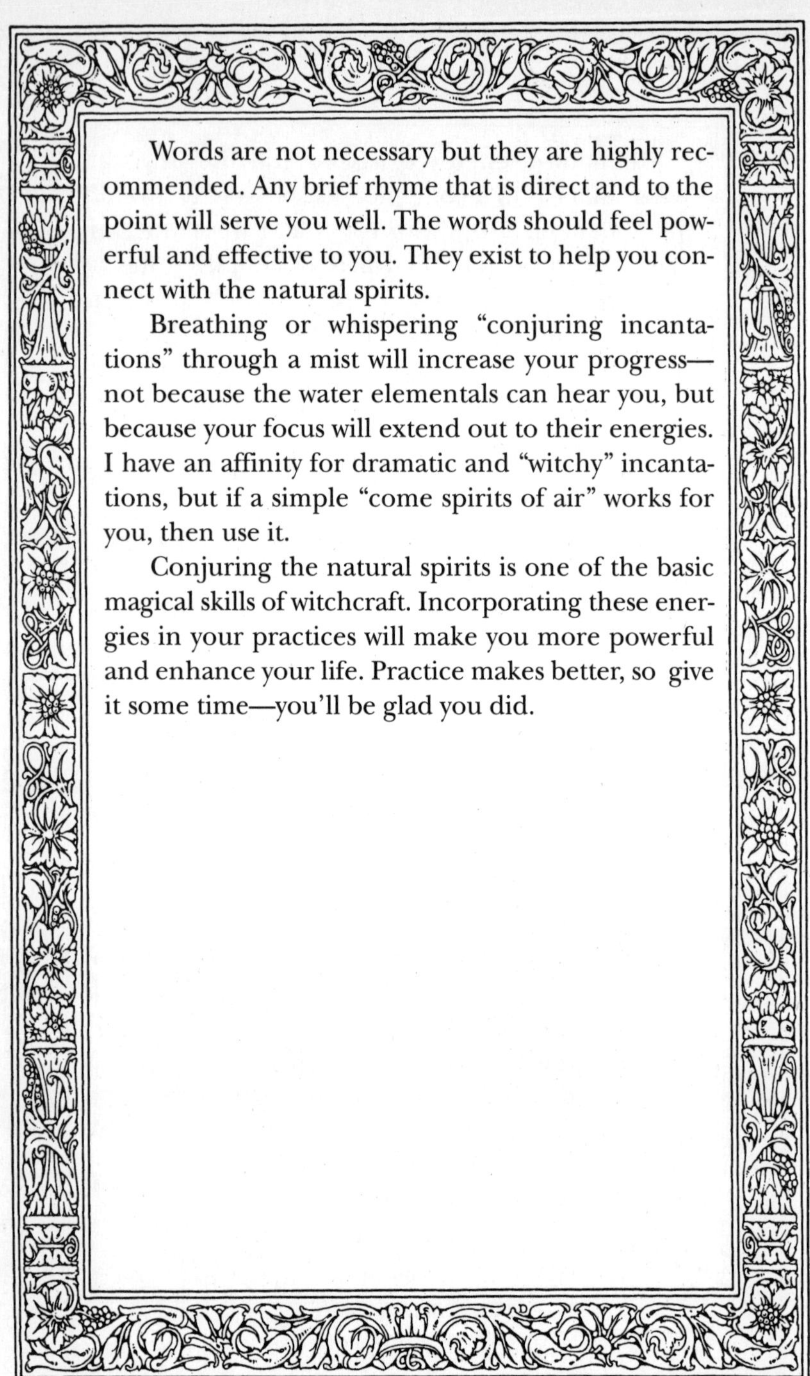

Words are not necessary but they are highly recommended. Any brief rhyme that is direct and to the point will serve you well. The words should feel powerful and effective to you. They exist to help you connect with the natural spirits.

Breathing or whispering "conjuring incantations" through a mist will increase your progress—not because the water elementals can hear you, but because your focus will extend out to their energies. I have an affinity for dramatic and "witchy" incantations, but if a simple "come spirits of air" works for you, then use it.

Conjuring the natural spirits is one of the basic magical skills of witchcraft. Incorporating these energies in your practices will make you more powerful and enhance your life. Practice makes better, so give it some time—you'll be glad you did.

Creating a Tarot Altar

by Reverend Gina Pace

As a Wiccan, I keep in my home an altar dedicated to the Goddess on which stand many small statues of her various faces—Bast, Kuan Yin, Mary the Blessed Mother, and so on. I keep a statue of Ganesha as well, to honor the God energy, and an always-burning devotional altar candle

One corner of my altar is always dedicated to the tarot—since I am a spiritual person, and the tarot is (for me) a spiritual tool. I display different tarot cards that I have accumulated over time that have special magical significance for me. I have several snail-shaped sterling-silver placecard holders that keep these cards upright on the altar.

In general, I like to draw a different tarot card every day to see what the "theme" is going to be for the day. The card often

points out some difficulty I will have to deal with. One day, for instance, I chose the Seven of Pentacles, and I kept finding myself in situations where I needed to step back and look at how various situations were unfolding in my life compared to my own preconceived expectations. The Seven of Pentacles is a card that indicates that the "watched pot doesn't boil." I certainly saw that lesson come through in a variety of ways.

Other days I will see a card that tends to have a more universal spiritual theme—and not just for that day, but for the larger picture of my life. Mostly this will occur with court cards and major arcana cards. I find that getting a card like the Magician, for example, usually signifies a life-lesson is due.

Whichever card I draw and focus on for the day I place in a prominent spot on my altar. I then spend some time meditating upon the greater meaning of the card before beginning my daily routines. In this context, one must look to the chosen card for the generalized and larger meaning in one's life (as opposed to how the card's meaning fits into a reading). A great example of this is the Star card. When this comes up in a reading, I usually focus on how it inspires and guides the querent, helping them "get the job done." However, in meditation, I am more likely to focus on the image itself—a young woman, whom I see as a metaphor for the divine energy of the universe, holding two jars of water. One jar is being poured onto the ground, which has grass and flowers on it; the other is being poured into a moonlit pool of water. I am reminded of the fact that the divine energy of the universe pours inspiration into all lives. Some of this inspiration falls on fertile ground and is cherished, and some is wasted and goes back into the source to be recycled and later poured out again.

A tarot altar is a great way to get in touch with your higher self. Remember to seek the divine through understanding and loving yourself, and cherish the lessons you are given. If you remember that the fertile ground of inspiration is ready to be watered, nothing sacred in your life will ever be wasted.

Temples of the Goddesses

by Emely Flak

Imagine a place where women are regarded as an embodiment of the Goddess, and sex is considered sacred. In fact, sex is so revered that an annual festival is dedicated to it. The women of the temple, as temple priestesses, serve the Goddess, and men come not to worship or supplicate to a divine force, but to honor the Great Goddess. This may sound too erotic to be true, but this was how sex and spirituality were celebrated in the ancient world.

Although it is difficult to pinpoint the origins of this practice, the most reliable accounts of temple priestesses are found in written records kept by the Sumerians. Here, fertility was revered through the worship of Baal, the male deity and god of war, and the female divine force and goddess of fertility, Ishtar. Ishtar was worshiped with offerings of money and local produce, along with the offering of sacred sex through the temple priestesses.

The celebration of fertility took place around the time of the Spring Equinox. This was a time of feasting and perfuming oneself with aromatic oils to create pleasure for the senses. A sacred and symbolic marriage took place between the king and a priestess in the temple. In their physical union, the king represented the Sun god, and the priestess was a manifestation of the goddess.

As providers of sacred sex, temple priestesses have been called "prostitutes," but in reality their duty was held in high regard as an honoring of the life force associated with sexual union. This respect for the priestesses demonstrates that women in these cultures enjoyed a strong and positive role. The temple priestess was also acknowledged for her healing gifts and powers. Ancient artifacts and paintings also suggest that these women performed the sensual belly dance to affirm their dedication to the fertility goddesses.

You might be thinking: If life was so good in this erotic utopia, what changed it? The fall of the goddess cultures goes hand in hand with the reduced status of women. In the new religions, it is implied that all sins of the flesh were attributed to feminine temptation. Eve was blamed for the downfall of man and his paradise. The Book of Exodus explains that all ill fate can be blamed on Pagan ways and worship of Pagan idols.

By around 2300 BC, Sumerian documents start to record the decline of women's status. It is no coincidence that this took place as the same time as a patriarchal religious structure asserted more authority in that part of the civilized world. Christianity validated the teachings of the Old Testament. Goddess qualities and feminine attributes of sensuality, fertility, and seduction were devalued. With this new order, carnal desire quickly became associated with guilt and sin.

We may be a long way away from seeing a civilization that once again honors a temple priestess. Earth-based religions like Paganism and Wicca hold great appeal for both men and women, because somewhere in our collective memories we know that both male and female deities are necessary for a balance.

The New Mythology

by Cerridwen Iris Shea

We all grew up on stories. Most of us were read bedtime stories by parents or babysitters. Hopefully, we grew up with a love of stories—a love that translated into a love of reading. We also read stories in school. And, we spend a lot of time as adults watching stories being told on TV (so it's good to know when they are being told badly, which is often enough on TV).

Whether we read stories in school, or come to them later in life as we explore the Pagan paths, stories teach us—and myths in particular teach us as Pagans. We connect to gods and goddesses and learn from the legends, especially as we marvel at how dysfunctional immortals manage to be.

As we build daily magical practice, it is sometimes difficult to relate Apollo with his Sun-chariot to our need for a parking space. How often have you leafed through book after book of

mythology, and still not found exactly the entity who covers the area in which you need help? In Terry Pratchett's delightful Discworld novels, he comments that gods and goddesses exist because of belief. If the entity no longer has anyone to believe in him or her, the entity ceases to exist. If a new belief arises, so does a new deity. We can use that theory to develop deities that help us through modern life.

Since magic is energy focused by need and will, you have to name the need. Once you do that, you have to decide on the characteristics of the energy you wish to access. Writers and actors will have a good time with this one, because it is the same exercise as creating a character.

For instance, two friends of mine traveled to Ireland together a few years ago, and wanted to create a goddess to take care of them on their voyage. They christened this goddess "Voyaga" and performed rituals in her honor throughout the trip. The next time I traveled, I invoked Voyaga. I also created a background for her: She is a distant cousin to Neptune (sea), Hestia (fire), Bleudowedd (air), and Demeter (earth). She travels on a winged horse. As we travel, I put fresh local flowers and a tiny, locally purchased token on her altar. She is partial to local wines and beers. And she punishes those who think it's funny to give out wrong directions.

I sometimes also work with Petula the parking elf who likes offerings of quarters, gingersnaps, and buttercups. There is also Cederic the sock gremlin who steals odd socks. Tracy the train fairy likes jingly, sparkly jewelry and regular offerings to her keep the trains running on time. Sally the shopping goddess leads me to the best bargains, and Rowena the research goddess leads me to the information I need for my writing—all she asks in return is that I donate books I am not using and return books to the library on time. And finally, Creatron and Destroyo are the twins of the computer. Creatron helps keep the computer in good order and works with me on deadlines. The mischievous Destroyo takes delight in eating, dumping, and generally trashing whatever he can when I am on a tight deadline. I haven't figured out how to keep them both happy, but I'm seriously considering investigating Shiriko, the goddess of the primal scream, to help me deal with the twins' antics.

These modern entities are not flippant and disrespectful to the archetypes of the past. Instead, they are an outgrowth of the universal energy into modern life. They all have a gentle, humorous component, but they also demand that I pay attention to the situation of the moment.

These days, as we are bombarded with constant electronic stimulation (from cell phones, television broadcast news and screen crawlers, radio traffic reports, the latest big Hollywood blockbuster, and the dog barking), multitasking takes us away from the sensual experience of life. More importantly, modern life distracts from the experience of each other. The more technology advances, the less we truly connect. The modern deities remind us that without connection to the planet, to what happens in the moment, and to each other, we are living only half a life.

Find some of your own deities to aid you in your daily life. Draw them, sketch them, paint them, and sew dolls to celebrate and represent them. Create backgrounds and stories for them. And share those stories with those around you.

Pop some popcorn, build a fire in the fireplace, and tell your new tales. Be your own bard. The deities may be modern, and the stories may be new, but the connection will reach back to our ancient archetypes, and the bond will strengthen. You will feel the tension ease, you will feel the sense of tradition and continuity, and you will experience the positive changes in your life.

Pardon me. I have to hop around the laundry room on one foot singing "I'm a Little Teapot." Maybe that will convince Cederic to return my socks. I'm out of matched pairs.

Native American Myths

by Julianna Yau

Native American myths are as plentiful as European myths, encompassing many different cultures. And like myths from most cultures, Native American myths explain a phenomenon or offer morality lessons.

As part of the very nature of cultures with a strong oral tradition, myths in Native American cultures have (until the relatively recent introduction of written language) been transmitted verbally. Because of this method of mythtelling, each myth-teller relates a story differently. Sometimes, a myth-teller provides one audience with a version of a myth that is an alternate version than what would be told to another audience. This kind of variety is created by the myth-teller because a certain message might be desired for a particular audience, or the audience may be familiar with a specific background information relating to the myth.

Although European myths usually include a mix of a pantheon of gods, demigods, and humans, Native American myths commonly include merely animals from a region. These animals appear either as a single animal from a species, or as animal-spirits. Native American myths also include some featuring merely persons or spirits, but they rarely ever include deities similar to the ones found in European mythology. Similar to Greek myths, however, is the presence of a strong connection with the earth and sky.

There is, for example, a myth of the fishermen of the Northwest American coast that tells of how the Moon was brought into existence. This myth features a raven (ravens and crows often appear in Native American myths)—referred to generally as Raven—a fisherman, and the fisherman's daughter. This myth tells of how the Moon came to be.

A Retelling of "Raven and the Moon"

Raven heard of a bright spherical light called the Moon, which was kept in a fisherman's home, and felt that he should obtain it. To obtain the Moon, Raven first provided himself with a way to enter the fisherman's home. Raven flew to a bush nearby to the home of the fisherman, and turned himself into a leaf. Afterwards, when the fisherman's daughter went to pick berries from the bush on which Raven had become a leaf, Raven-as-a-leaf fell from the bush on to the body of the fisherman's body.

After some time, the fisherman's daughter gave birth to a dark-skinned child. This child had a peculiar nose, not unlike a bird's beak. From a very young age, the child would cry to be given the Moon, and would knock at the box in which the Moon was kept. The fisherman and his daughter ignored the child's original cries, but the child became louder in his cries and knocked harder at the box. One day, the fisherman said to his daughter that perhaps they should allow the child to play with the ball of light.

The fisherman's daughter agreed, and opened the box. Inside of the box was another box, in which was another box containing more boxes within boxes, each slightly smaller than the previous. The boxes were elaborately crafted and painted. Inside the tenth box was a nestle of thread that the fisherman's daughter unraveled to reveal the innermost box.

The final box was opened to reveal the Moon—a bright ball of light. The fisherman's daughter tossed the ball to the child, who then played happily with the ball for a few days. But it was not long before the child began to cry again. Feeling sorry for the child, the fisherman asked his daughter what the child was trying to say. After listening intently to the child, she said that the child wanted to see the dark sky and shining stars but couldn't because the smoke-hole was covered by a board.

Sympathetic to the child's wishes, the fisherman told his daughter to remove the board that covered the smoke-hole. As soon as the smoke-hole was opened, the child turned himself back into Raven. With the Moon in his beak, Raven flew out through the smoke-hole. After a moment, Raven was at the top of a mountain and threw the Moon into the sky. To this day, the Moon remains in the sky where Raven threw it.

Stories such as this are quite predominant in North American mythology. The myths that do not feature an animal-spirit commonly tell of events in the more recent past.

Because there are many different tribes of Native Americans, each with their own culture, the collection of Native American myths is quite expansive. This is true even in light of the many myths that overlap, are similar to each other, or are shared among the tribes. Although there are a few tribes with which many of us are commonly familiar (such as the Navajo, Iroquois, Intuit, Mayans, and Cherokee), many tribes are less known to us that also have a rich accumulation of myths (for example, the Lakota, Oto, Chocktaw, Lenape, and Shawnee). Persons who are interested in myths, or simply enjoy a new myth, may find North American myths enrich their experience of mythology.

Bird Omens

by Elizabeth Hazel

Reading the movements of birds can be traced back to early civilizations. Perhaps the most famous practitioner of this divinatory art is Teiresias, the blind prophet of Thebes. Teiresias was led by a young boy, who described the flight patterns of birds to the prophet. He was then able to make accurate predictions from these movements—including the overthrow of Thebes and an exact description of his own death.

Birds are creatures of the air, and humans have long envied birds their capacity for flight. This is perhaps the reason for connecting birds with sacred oracles. Different birds were affiliated with different gods and goddesses, and there are myths describing why certain birds are black or white.

Bird omens are a special way of receiving the wisdom of nature. The diviner will need to examine avian activity for several criteria in order to determine the content of the omen. Every aspect of a bird or a flock of birds may be interpreted for meaning.

To start, the species of bird gives a good clue to the nature of omen. Predatory birds are the most powerful omens. Eagles are the bird of Zeus, considered significant in both ancient Greece and Rome as signaling the fortunes of kings and rulers. An eagle catching prey is an omen of a ruler conquering his opponents; an

eagle dying is an omen of a ruler dying. Eagles are the highest flying species, thus noted for their far-seeing capacities, and the sighting of an eagle should be considered a sign of important historic events in the future. For the individual, an eagle omen signals a personal turning point or a burst of illumination.

Members of the hawk family (including hawks, falcons, ospreys, and so on) are sacred to Isis. The flight of a hawk should be watched for its direction. If the hawk flies in a straight line, the qualities of the directions should be considered (see below). If a hawk flies in circles, an important message will arrive quickly, or the past should be reconsidered. A hawk perched on a utility pole or a tree is an omen that the big-picture viewpoint should be examined with care. The cry of a hawk is a warning of potential enemies or dangers.

Buzzards, vultures, and condors are primarily consumers of carrion. Circling buzzards are an ominous sign of death or serious illness. Yet sighting a buzzard should also be considered an omen to eliminate unnecessary emotional baggage.

Doves (and pigeons) were the oracle at the ancient oak grove at Dodona in northern Greece. Doves are connected with Aphrodite, the goddess of love. Doves bring messages of mating, pairing, bonding, and human sentiment. A dove alone represents an omen of loneliness, while a pair of doves cooing together is an omen of a happy relationship and increased sexuality.

Migrating birds form V-patterns during their journeys. Many of these species inhabit the space between land and water, and exhibit communal habits. A

V-shaped pattern of ducks or geese is notable when it is not flying south (in autumn) or north (in spring). This omen indicates a change of lifestyle of family members.

Herons, egrets, and cranes are large marsh-dwellers, and are very fortunate when seen in flight. The Chinese have a particular reverence for the white crane, considering it a sign of good fortune, longevity, and marital happiness. Since these birds avoid human developments, they are only rarely spotted in inhabited areas.

Smaller birds bring smaller oracles. The song of a wren signals welcome news soon to arrive. Attracting a wren to your yard is an omen of coming good luck for the household, a sign of domestic improvements and needed acquisitions for comfort. Still smaller is the hummingbird, a speed demon of tiny proportions. Because of their wee size, hummingbirds are a fairylike omen, a sign of special assistance from little earth spirits.

North American finches include cardinals and the plain sparrow. Finches chirp rather than sing and are sexually active and territorial. Male finches build nests to attract willing females in mid to late spring. A finch building a nest is a sign of impending success in a choice opportunity. If he attracts a mate, it is an omen of good luck in love. Finches enjoy gathering in groups, and are an omen of social gatherings and reunions.

Blue jays and magpies are noisy, raucous birds. They are an omen of bullies, overweening dominance, or abuse of power. Members of the pheasant family (pheasants, partridges, grouse, turkeys, and quail) are omens of family responsibilities, the need to nurture and protect, or the ability to blend in with the crowd. Some of these birds are known for their elaborate mating dances by the male of the species, and may be an omen of courtship rituals or of personal adornment.

Crows are a popular source of omens. A single crow, standing on the ground, is an omen of trouble—the closer the crow is to the viewer, the sooner the trouble will arrive. Two crows on the ground, conversely, are an omen of laughter and joy. Three crows represent celebrations—weddings, showers, birthday parties, and so on. Four crows indicate a birth—of a baby, of a new idea, or of new items for personal use. Watching crows can be tricky. Sometimes an extra crow is hidden nearby. These should be added to the total count.

Members of the owl family are mostly seen at dark when searching for prey. Due to their keen sight and hearing are considered birds of wisdom. An owl is a profound omen of totemic protection or divine wisdom. If you see an owl in the act of catching prey, you must determine if it is an omen of success or an omen of impending victimization.

Bird diviners should consider the direction a bird is moving. Movement to the north is a sign of financial and property matters. Movement toward the south signals inspiration, sexual attraction, and enthusiasm in ventures. The east signals important ideas are in the offing. The west signals matters of the heart and emotions.

If a bird circles west to east and back to the west, the omen concerns the family and touches upon emotional issues. If a bird flies from the south to the north, turning back to the south, the omen is one of inspiration in money matters, or encouragement to apply new ideas or gain new partners for business dealings.

Overall, small birds bring smaller omens, while the large and predatory birds offer much more critically important messages.

Keep watching the skies—the messengers of the gods have something to tell you.

The Magical Power of Gargoyles

by Lily Gardner

Dragons, lions, hydras, wyverns, and trolls—what are all these monsters doing on the rooftops of Europe? What do they have in common?

They all belong to the wonderous and frightening family of gargoyles. And of course, it gets even more confused when you look at it closely.

One type of gargoyle is the *grotesque,* a carved statue that stands sentry over doors and peers down from the eaves of libraries and the gables of churches. A grotesque, strictly speaking, is any figure that is exaggerated or is a hybrid of two or more creatures. The griffin with its eagle head and wings and lion body is one example of a grotesque.

At the same time, true gargoyles are decorated downspouts. They were added to buildings not just for their looks, but also to control the flow of water off of a building's roof. Rain water runs down the gutters of a building into a drain and out the gargoyle's mouth. Gargoyle, in fact, shares the root word for "gargle," an indication of its watery roots.

The mouth is a fitting symbol for the gargoyle, because this organ represents the dual nature of life—that is, it both devours and regurgitates. Gargoyles, with their curious power to both attract and repel are a wonderful symbol of life's polarities.

The French will tell you that gargoyles originated from the dragon La Gargouille who terrorized the Seine. He devoured ships, burned warehouses and wharves, and barbecued any pedestrians along the shoreline. The only way to appease him was to give him a human victim once a year. Legend has it that this went on for years until St. Romain made the sign of the cross over the dragon and was able to lead him back to town on a leash. Afterward, the townspeople burned the dragon at the stake. The body of La Gargouille burned down to ash, but his head and neck remained, and these were mounted on the town wall as a warning to any future dragons who might think of taking up residence in the neighborhood.

Even though the French would have us believe the gargoyle originated in France, evidence of gargoyles and grotesques goes back to the Bronze Age. The Egyptians placed the figures of lions, eagles, and odd hybrid creatures on their buildings. They served as talismans for luck and protection. As with many cultures, the Egyptians used animals to represent abstract concepts such as wisdom, creativity, fertility and strength. This pictorial symbolism was known and understood by both the literate and illiterate. At the same time, representations of various animals served as more than symbols. As talismans, Egyptians believed these carvings attracted divine forces for good and repelled forces for evil.

The Greeks used animal symbolism and also produced a whole cast of grotesques—centaurs, satyrs, harpies, griffins, gorgons, and many other creatures—that combined the traits of two or more animals. A carved griffin stood guard on the four corners of the roof of every Greek temple and treasury because it was common knowledge that griffins guarded gold. To represent strength and protection, lion gargoyles were carved over front doors or used on city gates.

Further west, the barbaric Celts believed that the head was the source of spiritual power for both human and beast. They used the heads of their enemies or the animals they hunted to protect their homes and villages.

Still, it was gothic Europe that put gargoyles on the map. There are many theories as to why gargoyles were so popular in the medieval imagination, but there is no hard evidence that tells us why the Green Man or mythical beasts adorned the rooflines of so many public buildings. We are nearly certain that Christian monks used faces of the Green Man, the Horned God, and the Sheila na Gig to attract rural Pagans to their church. Gargoyles may have represented demons stuck to the outside of the church—the flip side of the angels and saints who were gathered the church. It also seems likely that other grotesques were used to protect buildings from evil. The gargoyle's hideous body and leering face would scare off any evil spirits lurking around the streets or churchyard.

Many people believed the gargoyles came alive at night while their charges were asleep. They flew down from their rooftop perches and patrolled the streets, only returning to the rooftop at sunrise. The gargoyles of Notre Dame Cathedral were said to watch for drowning victims in the Seine.

Besides their role as sentries, gargoyles served as a medieval entertainment. We humans have always been intrigued by the monstrous. We love the combination of disgust and pleasure that the grotesque excites within us. We are, even today in the twenty-first century, still intrigued by the scowl of the gargoyle. Why is another question. Perhaps we love the gargoyle because it gives form to our dream images. That is, gargoyles are the shadow images that reveal our baser nature.

Whatever the reason, as creatures from our subconscious gargoyles are as relevant today as they were in medieval Europe. Pagans believe that wisdom can be attained through integrating our shadow nature with our reasoning nature. We can use gargoyles as symbols of our subconscious or as talismans for protection, luck, or creativity.

To use gargoyles as a magical tool in our lives we need to decide what kind of a talisman we are looking for. Once we've decided then we're ready to choose our gargoyle. Most modern gargoyles are grotesques, a combination of two or more animals. Choose your gargoyle by the feelings the gargoyle inspires in you or use the centuries-old symbolism of animal figures.

Lion and dog gargoyles make excellent protection talismans. Snakes symbolize both healing and resurrection. Dragons guard secret places. The toad is linked with the Moon and transformations. Turtles are guardians of women. Goats and rams are talismans for fertility—the ram representing the day, the goat representing the night. Horses are said to carry souls from life to death. Monkeys are talismans of intelligence and creativity. Cats represent love and playfulness. Pigs are symbols for fertility and resurrection.

What all gargoyles have in common is a gaping mouth. The mouth is the archetypal symbol of initiation, connected with the mysteries of life and death. As a channel for food, drink, breath, and speech the mouth symbolizes the creative force. But a mouth can debase and destroy as easily as it sings and communicates. The mouth symbolizes the source of opposites.

Gargoyles are a provocative symbol to use in our lives. Humankind has used monsters to symbolize human qualities since the first cave drawings. They keep us in touch with our dream world and with the mystery inherent in life.

The Power of Three: A Tarot Meditation

by Christine Jette

People tend to get tarot readings at times of indecision or personal crisis. They are vulnerable to suggestions and looking for advice.

As professional readers, we have the power to influence our clients because people in need tend to hang on every word we say. This is a scary proposition for a lot of us because it carries awesome responsibility. Two things can happen. We either charge headfirst into a situation we are not prepared for and it blows up in our face, or we doubt our own abilities and run away from the awesome responsibility of a professional reading.

What does it take then to become a successful professional tarot reader? The answer depends on your definition of success. I believe people who earn money reading the cards—and stay with it over the long haul—share three essential traits: belief in self, the willingness to work, and a desire to be of service to others.

To discover if you have these traits, try a meditative journaling exercise called "The Power of Three." To do this, pull the Queen of Wands, Queen of Pentacles, and Queen of Cups from your favorite tarot deck. Have them in sight as

you do this activity. You'll draw on the energy of the Queen of Swords to make the journal entry because she, above all, is queen of the written word.

Underneath the Queen of Wands write the words "Belief in Self." Below the Queen of Pentacles write "Willingness to Work." And below the Queen of Cups write "Desire to be of Service." Look at each card as you pen your personal response to each Queen, as directed below.

Belief in Self (Queen of Wands)

The category ask you to examine what you believe? One way to identify your beliefs is to ask yourself what might happen if you actually did manifest a successful tarot consultation service. Do you worry you may be asking too much, or do you feel unworthy to realize your dream? Does bringing change into your life make you nervous? Will success change your life?

The Queen of Wands is businesslike and exuberant about everything she does. She has reserves of energy and is pas-

sionate about things she believes in. She devours details and follows her hunches because she trusts her intuition. The Queen of Wands believes in herself. So the real question here is how good can you stand it? That's as good as it gets. Make an entry in your journal.

Willingness to Work (Queen of Pentacles)

How much elbow grease are you willing to apply to make your dream real? Willingness to work requires that you identify and eliminate everything that keeps you from focusing on your dream. It means finding the time and discipline to establish the order that a successful business must have to grow. Chaos, clutter, and unfinished business on any level are energy bandits. Every moment you spend looking for things, apologizing for being late, or mentally hiding out from unfinished business is time you have lost forever.

The Queen of Pentacles is infinitely practical and is comfortable in both the home and the office. She also listens to what her body is telling her. If she is hungry, she eats. When tired, she rests. She takes care of herself in every way. By replenishing her reserves, she makes room for new energy and the creative life force to flow.

Desire equals discipline and there is no such thing as a free lunch, but the Queen of Pentacles succeeds by balancing work and personal life. Her life does not appear more unstable than the lives of her clients. Instincts and logic work together and she empowers others by empowering herself first. Make an entry in your journal.

Desire to Be of Service (Queen of Cups)

How much are you willing to love? When you choose to bring love and enthusiasm into your tarot practice, the whole process takes on a magical and healing quality. You stop hitting a brick wall. When you introduce love and enthusiasm into your work, it will remove obstacles and help you find balance.

Bringing love into your choices as you work toward your goal of being a professional reader draws in the support of the universe. When you are enthusiastic and loving, divine support will join you. This is about power—not the kind of power that erupts out of the personal ego, but the kind that gracefully flows through you when you tap into the powerful, loving support of the universe.

The Queen of Cups is filled with compassion, and her nurturing extends to all who come into her realm. She excels in metaphysics, and she accepts her natural psychic abilities. The Queen of Cups' nature is spiritual and loving, and her work must be emotionally satisfying. She practices the spiritual law of "give and it shall be given to you." This Queen understands the law of cause and effect. She is generous in her kindness to others, because she knows that as she gives it will return to her a thousand-fold.

When you expand your heart and generous spirit, you expand your capacity to be happy and fulfilled, and to operate from a sense of abundance. Thoughts are real. Let your thoughts be of divine awareness—rightfully expecting and easily sharing all the gifts the universe has to offer you. Surround yourself with supportive and loving family and friends. As a professional tarot reader, you can help many people deepen their connection to the divine and gain clarity about their chosen paths. Be proud of what you do as you prepare for positive life changes—and make an entry in your journal.

The Truth about Advanced Witchcraft

by Edain McCoy

The craft has exploded beyond what anyone would have believed possible only a decade ago. It has now become the fastest growing spiritual movement in the land. There are more Witches, Wiccans, and Pagans than ever before, and more and more young people are being raised in craft homes.

So much has happened in the past thirty-odd years, that many of us now may rightfully call ourselves elders, crones, and sages. But what does that really mean for us and for those with whom we live and work?

Just What Is Advanced Witchcraft?

It is a common misconception to think of advanced as being synonymous with more complex. With witchcraft, in fact, the opposite is true.

True advanced Witchcraft has little to do with magic, but instead with the rudimentary task of living a magical life. Anyone with advanced capabilities in visualization and an intuitive understanding of symbolism can add more catalysts to a spell for stronger, more precise, magic, but not everyone can live their wishes and have them manifest.

Answer the following questions and assess for yourself where you feel you fall on the craft continuum.

Do you feel compelled to argue with others over minor details such as the magical powers of the color blue or the best use for a cinnamon stick?

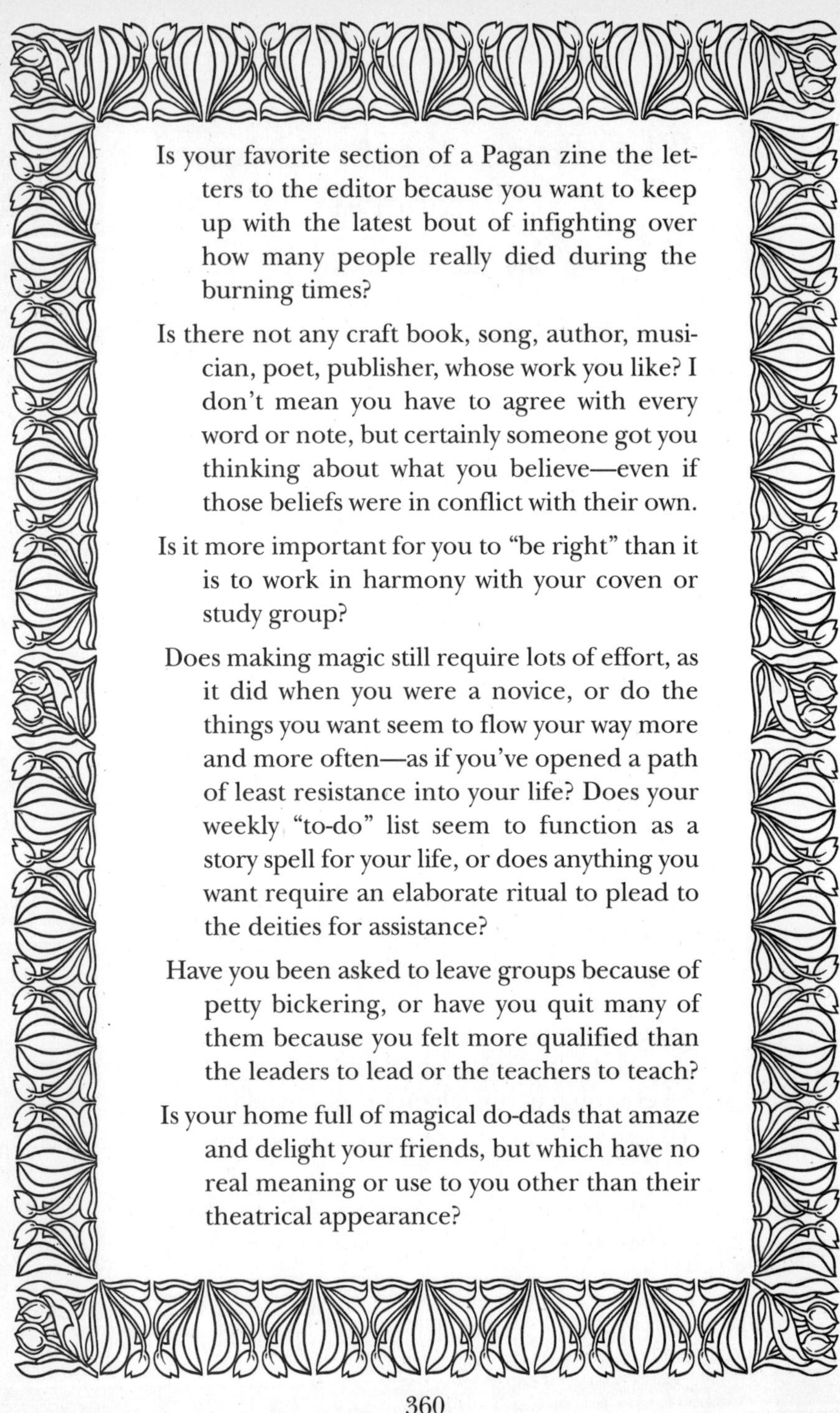

Is your favorite section of a Pagan zine the letters to the editor because you want to keep up with the latest bout of infighting over how many people really died during the burning times?

Is there not any craft book, song, author, musician, poet, publisher, whose work you like? I don't mean you have to agree with every word or note, but certainly someone got you thinking about what you believe—even if those beliefs were in conflict with their own.

Is it more important for you to "be right" than it is to work in harmony with your coven or study group?

Does making magic still require lots of effort, as it did when you were a novice, or do the things you want seem to flow your way more and more often—as if you've opened a path of least resistance into your life? Does your weekly "to-do" list seem to function as a story spell for your life, or does anything you want require an elaborate ritual to plead to the deities for assistance?

Have you been asked to leave groups because of petty bickering, or have you quit many of them because you felt more qualified than the leaders to lead or the teachers to teach?

Is your home full of magical do-dads that amaze and delight your friends, but which have no real meaning or use to you other than their theatrical appearance?

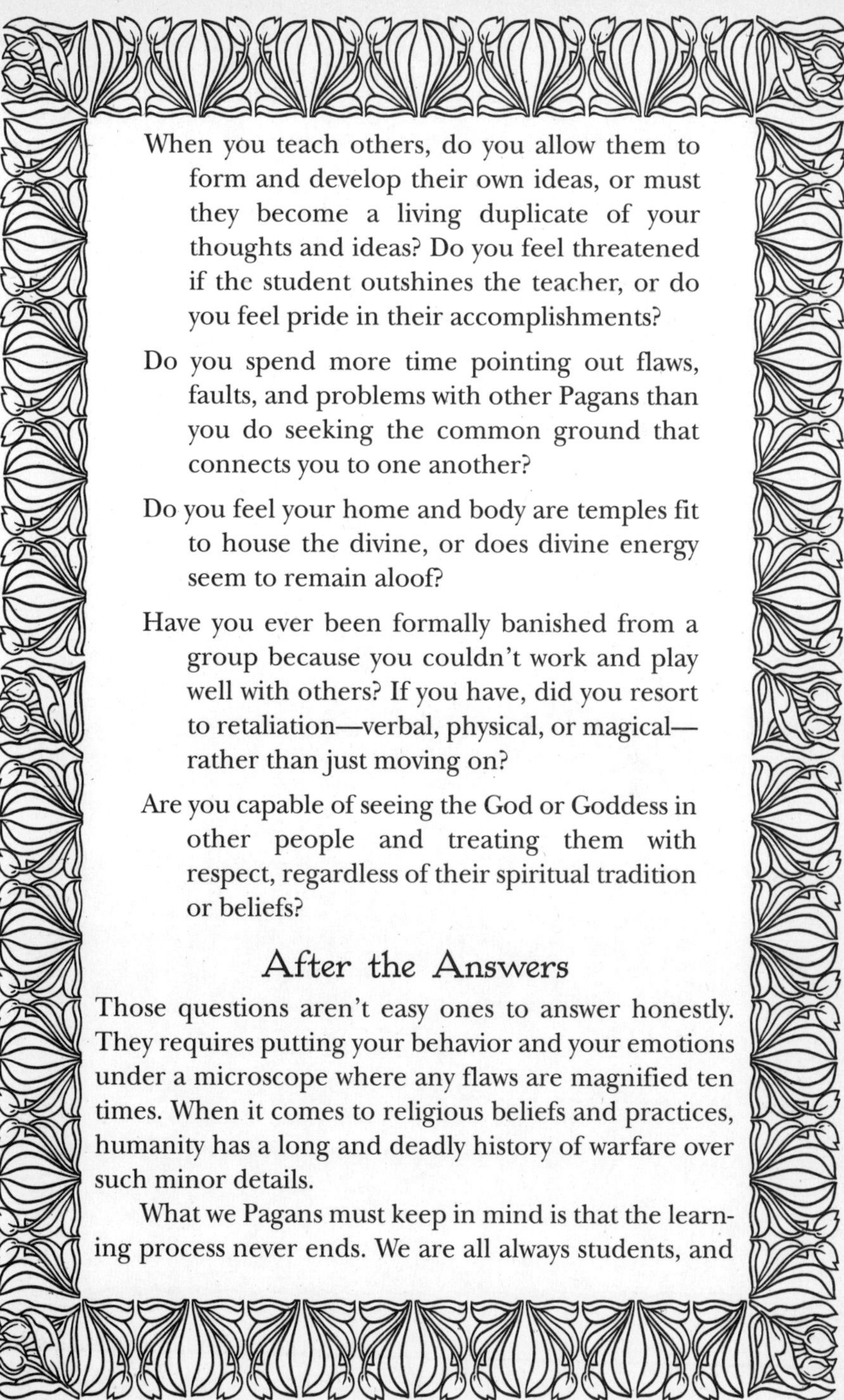

When you teach others, do you allow them to form and develop their own ideas, or must they become a living duplicate of your thoughts and ideas? Do you feel threatened if the student outshines the teacher, or do you feel pride in their accomplishments?

Do you spend more time pointing out flaws, faults, and problems with other Pagans than you do seeking the common ground that connects you to one another?

Do you feel your home and body are temples fit to house the divine, or does divine energy seem to remain aloof?

Have you ever been formally banished from a group because you couldn't work and play well with others? If you have, did you resort to retaliation—verbal, physical, or magical—rather than just moving on?

Are you capable of seeing the God or Goddess in other people and treating them with respect, regardless of their spiritual tradition or beliefs?

After the Answers

Those questions aren't easy ones to answer honestly. They requires putting your behavior and your emotions under a microscope where any flaws are magnified ten times. When it comes to religious beliefs and practices, humanity has a long and deadly history of warfare over such minor details.

What we Pagans must keep in mind is that the learning process never ends. We are all always students, and

we are all always teachers to one another. Our one shared goal is that we are all seeking the path to the divine. Some of us will take extended detours to both enjoy and learn, while some of us will climb straight up to the top, but then have lots of make-up work to do.

No way is wrong or right if it harms none.

Celtic Weather Divination

by Sharynne NicMhacha

People have long studied the natural world around them, seeking wisdom and guidance in the cycles of the seasons, the behavior of birds and animals, and the movements of the Sun, Moon, stars, wind, and sea. A great deal of weather lore that has been preserved in Celtic folk tradition can help us become more in tune with the energies, cycles, and wisdom of the earth and her elements.

At sea and on land, the clouds were studied in order to read the weather omens. This is an important skill for both the farmer and the fisherman. It is interesting to note that one of the forms of divination practiced in early Ireland by the Druids was known as *néladoireacht*—the reading of omens through the shape and movement of clouds.

The flight of birds was also studied by the Druids. The appearance or movement of birds was used to divine the weather in modern folklore as well. In Cornish folk tradition it was

believed that if crows built their nests high in the trees the weather would be fine. If they built them in the lower branches of trees, however, the weather would be rough.

A number of traditional weather rhymes come from Cornwall.

Mist on the moor, brings Sun to the door,
Mist on the hill, brings water to the mill.

If the ash is in leaf before the oak, then we will get a thorough soak.
If the oak is in leaf before the ash, then we only get a splash.

In Scotland, one traditional weather rhyme goes as follows:

Wild geese, wild geese, gangin' to the sea, bood weather it will be;
Wild geese, wild geese, gangin' to the hill, the weather it will spill.

In Cornwall, it was said that if the fire burned blue it was a sign of cold weather to come. If the smoke from the fire went straight up and out the chimney, fine weather was ahead. However, if the smoke went toward the ground, it was a sign of rain. Rain was also predicted if swallows flew low, rooks fell steeply in flight, cattle kept close together by a hedge, or the leaves of trees blew upward. Fine weather was coming if larks few high in the air, spiders were active, or cattle grazed on high ground.

The wind was very important to those who made their living at sea. In Scottish tradition, whistling on board a ship was believed to cause a storm. If the wind was too calm, gentle whistling was permitted to bring up a mild wind. A steel-bladed knife was sometimes stuck into the mast in the direction the wind was desired. A sealskin wrapped around the mast calmed the sea. Passing one's hand gently over the waves in the opposite direction from the swell of the wave was also calming.

There was traditional weather lore associated with the seasons and the holidays. In Scotland, it was considered a positive sign if the holly and the hazel tree "struck each other" on Hogmanay night, for a windy night was considered a good sign of the season. Another tradition states that when Candlemas was past, "the fox won't trust his tail to the ice." This means that while there may be hard frost at that time of year, the ice cannot be depended upon to support one's weight. Some traditions maintain that on Imbolc Bridget puts her hand into the sea. As a goddess associated with

fire, this is believed to warm the icy waters. In addition, the weather on Imbolc was said to determine the weather of the rest of the winter.

At Samhain many types of divination took place, including weather divination for the coming year. People read omens in the wind, sun, rain, snow, and floods and interpreted these to help guide them in months to come. In Scotland it was said that the prevailing wind for the coming winter was determined by the quarter the wind was in on November 1. In Wales, it was believed that each of the twelve days of Christmas corresponded with the twelve months of the coming year. The weather on each of those days was said to be a guide to the weather for each of the upcoming months.

In Scottish tradition, the weather between these Imbolc and Beltane, and years of observation, led to the creation of a system of weather lore that helped guide the people through this difficult season. Spring was divided into various periods of time. The longest was known as the Wolf Month, which corresponds roughly to our month of February. Sometime in this month three summer days were brought in as an exchange for three cold days in July. The Wolf Month was followed by a week known as the Plover, or the "whistle," referring to the piping or whistling winds that were commonly heard. Next came the Horse or Gelding, a period that differed in length in different regions, but most often ran from March 15 to April 11.

Next came the Cailleach, or "old woman," the week from April 12 to 18. The grass had begun to grow by this time, but the Cailleach tried to prevent the spring from coming by beating down the grass with her magic wand. The next three weeks (up to May 12, which is Beltane old style) were a foretaste of summer. Finally, the people were able to celebrate when they heard the song of the cuckoo on May Day.

Weather magic was also associated with Witches and wisewomen. In Scotland, fishermen took threads with them to sea that were tied with three knots by local wisewomen. If they needed a light breeze, the fishermen untied one knot. Two knots provided a strong breeze, but the third was not to be loosened or a storm would arise. Witches were believed to be able to conjure storms by chanting over a stone as they thrashed it with a knotted rag while repeating this rhyme:

I knot this ragg upon this stane,
to raise the wind in the Devill's name.
It sall not lye till I please agane.

Note that this rhyme has three lines (rather than four), which may indicate that it is quite old. The number three was sacred to the Celts, and magical words and actions were often repeated three times (or included three elements).

Modern Witches and Pagans, of course, do not worship the devil. They honor the Earth and its wisdom and seek to live and work in harmony with its cycles and energies. I leave it to those who honor these ways to restore this charm and use it for beneficial purposes, invoking the name of one of the old gods of the elements to shower blessings upon the earth.

A Simple Samhain Tarot Ritual

by Nina Lee Braden

Although each person celebrates the sabbats uniquely, Samhain is frequently a time to say farewell to those who have departed during the last year. Samhain rituals, therefore, tend to be darker and more intense than many other rituals. You may celebrate Samhain alone, or you may celebrate it with others—or you may even do both. No matter what your tradition, and no matter how you celebrate Samhain, you can use tarot cards to help you organize and celebrate your ritual.

For this Samhain tarot ritual, use two different decks. If possible, for the first deck, try to find one that shows a person walking away on the Eight of Cups (this is the most common image for the Eight of Cups, so it should not be difficult to find). For the other cards, no specific to images are needed.

From the first tarot deck, remove six cards: Death, Judgment, the Moon, the Eight of Cups, the Nine of Swords, and the Ten of Swords. When you decorate your sacred space, put the Nine of Swords in the east, the Ten of Swords in the south, the Death card in the west, Judgment in the north, and the Moon and the Eight of Cups in the center of your circle. As you cast your sacred space, say:

> *Let the spirits of the east come with us tonight to mourn and to grieve. We celebrate with you the message of the Nine of Swords. Let the spirits of the south come with us tonight to fall on the ground and surrender. We celebrate with you the message of the Ten of Swords. Let the spirits of the west come with us tonight to be transformed and*

reborn. We celebrate with you the message of the Death card. Let the spirits of the north come to us tonight to rise up in the darkness like a bright flame. We celebrate with you the message of Judgment. May the Lord and Lady join with us in this space, uniting this circle into a sphere, above, below, and in the center. Let all be contained in this sacred space in perfect love, peace, and trust. We celebrate with the messages of the Moon and the Eight of Cups.

Feel free to adapt these invocations to conform to any invocation that you are accustomed to using. After you have cast your sacred space, pull out your second deck of tarot cards. (If you do not have a second deck available, use the same deck.) Walk around your circle slowly clockwise, gently mixing your tarot cards as you go. As you walk, concentrate on each card as you pass it. What message does the Nine of Swords in the east seem to whisper to you? What message does the Ten of Swords in the south seem to flash? What message does the Death card in the west tell you? What message does Judgement in the north intone? Return to the center of your sacred space, and listen to messages from the Moon and Eight of Cups.

At this point, if you feel that you have received any messages from the spirits represented by the cards, speak them. Moving clockwise again, walk back to the east, asking: "Spirits of the east, show us a message for this Samhain ritual. Speak to us of how to interpret the Nine of Swords for the year to come." Then, facedown, choose a card from the deck. Let the spirits speak to you from this card. Place it over the Nine of Swords. Repeat this action, substituting the name of the card and the direction, for each of the other quarters. Then go to the center of your circle, saying:

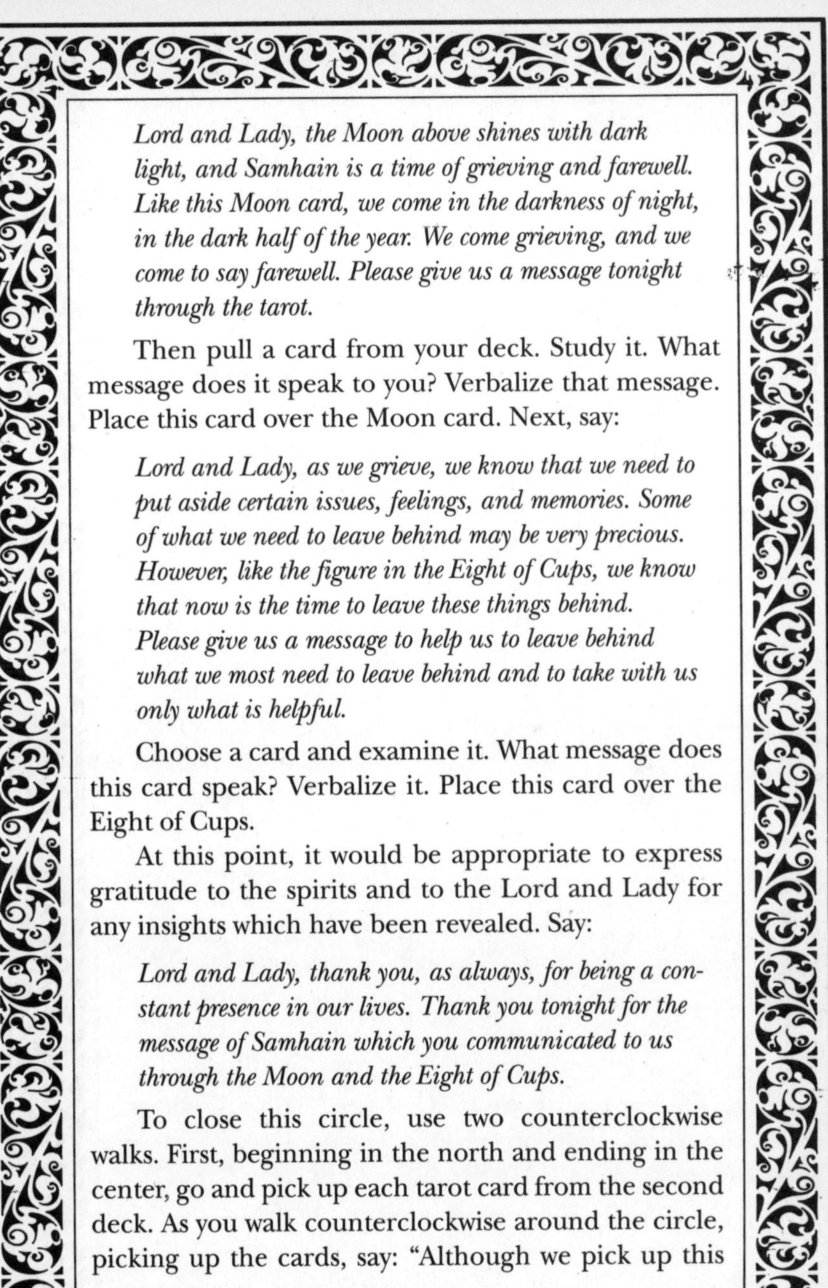

Lord and Lady, the Moon above shines with dark light, and Samhain is a time of grieving and farewell. Like this Moon card, we come in the darkness of night, in the dark half of the year. We come grieving, and we come to say farewell. Please give us a message tonight through the tarot.

Then pull a card from your deck. Study it. What message does it speak to you? Verbalize that message. Place this card over the Moon card. Next, say:

Lord and Lady, as we grieve, we know that we need to put aside certain issues, feelings, and memories. Some of what we need to leave behind may be very precious. However, like the figure in the Eight of Cups, we know that now is the time to leave these things behind. Please give us a message to help us to leave behind what we most need to leave behind and to take with us only what is helpful.

Choose a card and examine it. What message does this card speak? Verbalize it. Place this card over the Eight of Cups.

At this point, it would be appropriate to express gratitude to the spirits and to the Lord and Lady for any insights which have been revealed. Say:

Lord and Lady, thank you, as always, for being a constant presence in our lives. Thank you tonight for the message of Samhain which you communicated to us through the Moon and the Eight of Cups.

To close this circle, use two counterclockwise walks. First, beginning in the north and ending in the center, go and pick up each tarot card from the second deck. As you walk counterclockwise around the circle, picking up the cards, say: "Although we pick up this

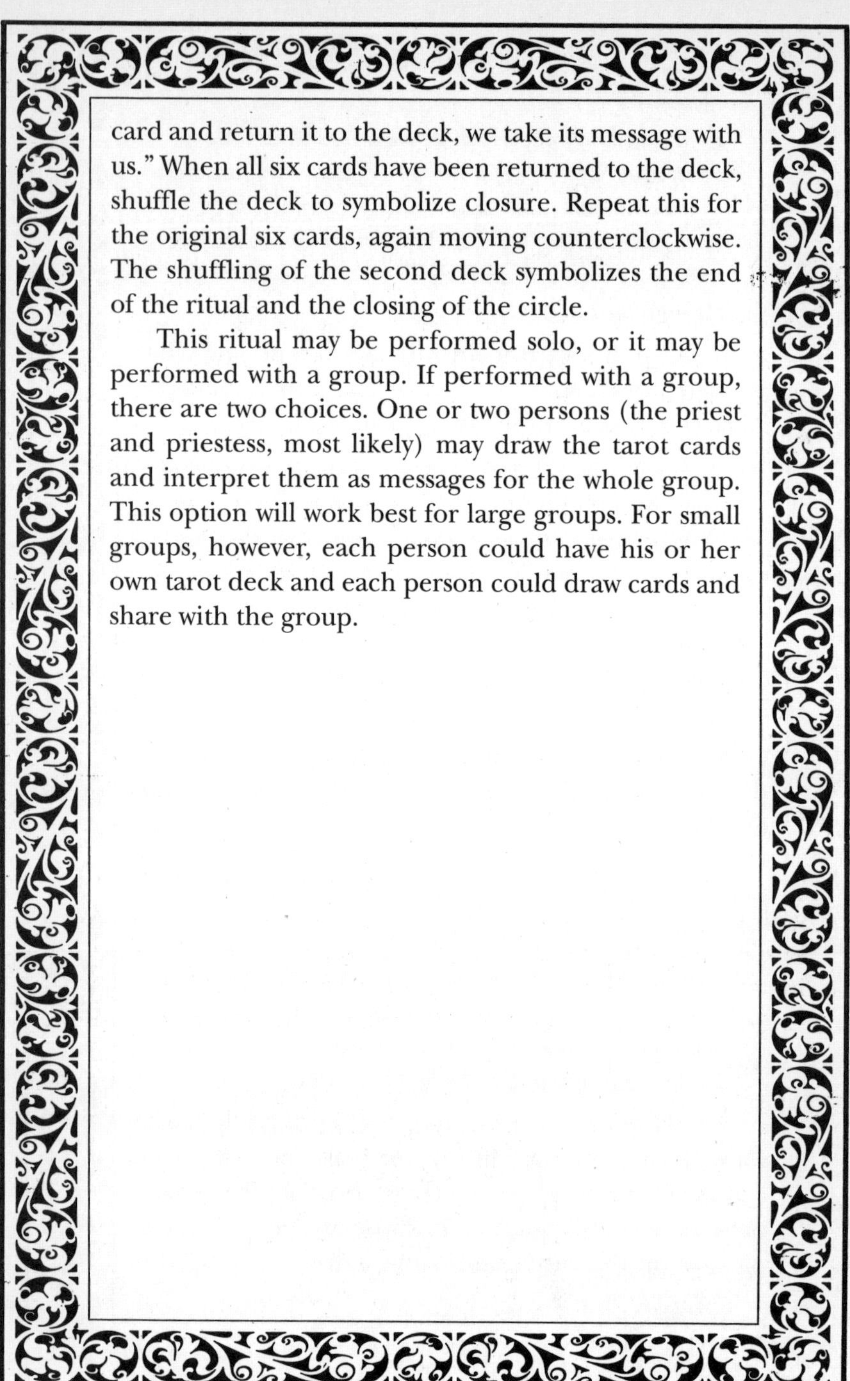

card and return it to the deck, we take its message with us." When all six cards have been returned to the deck, shuffle the deck to symbolize closure. Repeat this for the original six cards, again moving counterclockwise. The shuffling of the second deck symbolizes the end of the ritual and the closing of the circle.

This ritual may be performed solo, or it may be performed with a group. If performed with a group, there are two choices. One or two persons (the priest and priestess, most likely) may draw the tarot cards and interpret them as messages for the whole group. This option will work best for large groups. For small groups, however, each person could have his or her own tarot deck and each person could draw cards and share with the group.

The Cat Goddesses of Ancient Egypt

by Denise Dumars

When speaking of "cat goddesses," most of us think of Bast, the Egyptian goddess depicted as a woman with the head of a cat. Bast may currently be the most popular Egyptian cat goddess, but she is actually only one of many feline goddesses of ancient Egypt.

Bubastis was the city of Bast. Bast, also called Bastet, is a goddess of pleasure and joy, and when she is depicted with a basket of kittens, fertility. Cats earned their keep by reducing the rodent population, thereby safeguarding the precious Egyptian harvest. It was said that even the poorest person in Egypt could have a living votary of the goddess if he had a cat. Bast is also sometimes considered a daughter of Isis, and her name can be read as *Ba-Ast,* the soul *(ba)* of Isis *(Aset).*

The second most widely recognized cat goddess is Sehkmet, the fierce guardian depicted as a woman with a lioness head. Hundreds of black basalt statues of Sekhmet fronted major cities in Egypt as sentinels. The people of Egypt felt protected by Sekhmet, praying for her to defend them as zealously as a lioness protects her cubs.

The Egyptians regarded the cat family as feminine, and there were many cat goddesses. The earliest is Mut, the ancestral cat goddess who is also sometimes shown as a beautiful woman with a headdress suggesting a vulture. Mut was part of the Theban trinity, along with Amun-Ra and Mut as the divine parents and Khonsu, the Moon god, as their son. Mut therefore brings

together the sun god Ra with the Moon god Khonsu; and it is interesting to note that she was considered a solar deity as well. Mut's name can mean "mother," and she was also called "Mistress of Crowns." Mut was popular with women, and many women were named for her. For example, one Egyptian queen was named Mutnodjmet, which means "Mut is sweet."

Ra, the Egyptian creator deity, is also sometimes paired with a cocreator, the crone goddess Raet, who is depicted with the head of a lioness. Clearly this was a powerful symbol to the Egyptians, a symbolic "queen of the jungle." As anyone who knows anything about lions knows, it is the lioness who hunts and makes the kill.

All cat deities were seen as the children of Ra, probably through Mut or Raet. Other cat deities include Pakhet, a panther (black leopard) goddess, charmingly called "She Who Scratches," and Tefnut, daughter of Ra, a more ancient version of Sekhmet as the avenger, or "Lady of Terror."

Huge numbers of mummified cats were found in ancient Egyptian tombs. Sometimes these were family pets, prepared after death in order to rejoin the family in the afterlife. Others were mummified as offerings to the cat goddesses.

What was the appeal of the cat goddesses to ancient Egyptians? Well, as keepers of domestic cats they found the symbolism of the feline very attractive. The beauty, grace, sensuality, and fertility of these animals must have made their lives seem enviable. Their intelligence and fierceness were admired as well. Lions and leopards symbolized strength and regal bearing. Magic practitioners often wore the skins of leopards during their rituals, as did warriors.

Effigies of Bast and Sekhmet are found today in many museum and curio shops. Call upon Bast for fun and joy in your life, or if you wish to have a child. Call on Sekhmet when you need courage and strength to endure a stressful situation, such as a job evaluation or a court appearance. Either goddess can be invoked as a personal protector.

To invoke the cat goddesses, place one black and one gold candle on your altar, which should be facing east—as cat goddesses are solar deities. Offer a cup of milk and a dish of catnip. If invoking Sekhmet, add a glass of red ale. Place an image of

either goddess (or both) on your altar; or a photo of a black cat and of a lioness will do just fine. Smudge the area with an Egyptian incense blend such as kyphi. Frankincense and myrrh are also always appropriate. Invite your own cat into the room; it will stay if it wants to participate.

If you wish to write a petition to the goddess, do so with red ink. Place the petition under the appropriate candle—black for Bast, gold for Sekhmet—then light the candles. Now, facing east, draw an ankh in the air with your sistrum, wand, or your index finger. Sit down, close your eyes, and imagine the gates of the temple of cat goddesses opening to you. Visualize yourself walking toward the open gates to the temple. A priest and priestess greet you as you enter the temple. They squire you into the sacred chamber where a larger-than-life-size statue of the cat goddess awaits.

Visualize giving the goddess the offerings on your altar. Ask the goddess for her blessing, and for anything else you need. Listen for an answer. Stay with her for awhile. When you feel ready to leave, thank her, and see yourself leaving the temple, the priest and priestess closing the doors behind you.

Open your eyes. Thank the goddesses out loud, and once more make the sign of the ankh. Leave the candles burning as long as you are home. Extinguish them when you go out. Rest assured that the cat goddesses have heard your petition.